Shadows of a Princess

"Even if you have had it up to here with Diana books, THIS ONE IS SPECIAL AND IN A CLASS WAY ABOVE THE REST. WITTY, WELL-WRITTEN AND PACKED WITH REVELATIONS about ludicrous feuds and hysterical happenings behind the scenes in the offices at Kensington Palace, it made me laugh out loud a dozen times, and left me with the most indelible, authentic word–portrait ever painted of the People's Princess."

Daily Mail (London)

Shadows of a Princess

No one knows more about Diana's struggles than P. D. Jephson, her closest aide and adviser during her years of greatest public fame and deepest personal crisis. Based on eight years of firsthand experience, *Shadows of a Princess* is the most authoritative, balanced account ever published of the woman who became an icon yet still remains a contradictory enigma. This intimate behind–the–scenes portrait offers the Princess in all her disguises, as we've never seen her before.

Shadows of a Princess

SHADOWS OF A PRINCESS

DIANA, PRINCESS OF WALES

AN INTIMATE ACCOUNT BY HER PRIVATE SECRETARY

P. D. JEPHSON

HarperTorch
An Imprint of HarperCollins*Publishers*

HARPERTORCH

An Imprint of HarperCollins*Publishers*
10 East 53rd Street
New York, New York 10022-5299

Front cover photograph © by Rex Features
Back cover photograph of Princess Diana and P.D. Jephson courtesy of PA/Tim Ockenden

Photo insert illustration credits: Page 1: PA/John Stillwell. Page 2, top: PA/Martin Keene; bottom: PA/Barry Batchelor. Page 3: PA/Martin Keene. Page 4: Rex Features. Page 5: PA/John Stillwell. Page 6, top: PA/Michael Stephens; bottom: PA/Dave Cheskin. Page 7: Rex Features. Page 8: Rex Features/Tim Rooke.

First HarperTorch paperback printing: July 2001
First HarperCollins hardcover printing: October 2000

HarperCollins ®, HarperTorch™, and ❤ ™ are trademarks of Harper-Collins Publishers Inc.

Printed in the United States of America

Visit HarperTorch on the World Wide Web at www.harpercollins.com

10 9 8 7 6 5 4 3 2 1

Contents

❦

CONTENTS

Part II: *OUT*

Preface

❧

*F*or more than seven years, from 1988 to 1996, I shadowed the Princess of Wales. As her private secretary—her closest adviser—I was with her throughout the events leading up to her separation from Prince Charles. I helped her carve out a new life as an independent Princess on the world stage. I watched her struggle with enemies from outside as well as others, more murky, that threatened her from within.

As the darkness finally gathered around her, our paths parted. By then she was standing in her own light, obscuring the way ahead for herself and for many who would have acknowledged her as a global force for good.

Since her death in 1997 I have come to question the credentials of some of the self-appointed guardians of her thoughts, motives, and values. It seemed to me that history was recording an image that bore little resemblance to the Princess I knew better than most.

It is common sense, not treason, to believe that the truth will do her no harm now. Neglecting the truth will profit only those who seek to gain, personally, financially, or constitutionally, from letting the weeds of misrepresentation slowly overgrow her memory.

Of the many others who shared those years with me, I ask forbearance where their recollections differ from mine. Of the many more who did not, I ask nothing but an open mind. What follows, so far as it lies in my power, is the truth.

P. D. Jephson

PART I

IN

1

Over the Top

*T*he Princess of Wales was watching the man with un-usual intensity. She leaned forward in her chair, anxious not to miss any of the action she had just been promised. Her eyes widened with anticipation.

The man obviously did not know he was being watched, but he was ill at ease, definitely shifty. He seemed to be waiting for someone, and was losing patience. He took a few paces to the left, then a few to the right. He scratched his tangled, dirty hair and looked anxiously up and down the street. I did not like the look of him.

Then a second man appeared, dodging between a couple of pedestrians. If anything, the newcomer was even more nervous. He looked jumpy and his arms made strange twitching movements as he spoke rapidly into the other man's ear. They seemed to be making some kind of deal be-cause I saw money changing hands, but I could not hear what they said. Suddenly they were walking off together, slipping into a deserted alleyway next to the station. Still they did not know they were being watched.

What happened next made the Princess shriek with a

kind of thrilled horror. As we watched, with a final furtive look around, the first man loosened his jeans and crouched forward. There was a look of fixed concentration on his face. For five seconds he did not move. I had just realized he was defecating when his hand disappeared down the seat of his pants and emerged a few seconds later clutching a small package. Quickly he passed it to the other man, clearly his customer. Then, without a backward glance, the pusher adjusted his belt and returned to his position on the street.

The police officer stretched across the Princess and switched off the video with a click. Her hands were still clutched theatrically to her face, the shock of what she had seen still obvious in her eyes as she peeped from between her fingers. She caught my glance and giggled. Obscenity usually made her giggle.

"Ugh! Talk about a video nasty. I hope you arrested him."

"Oh, he's an old friend, Ma'am. And so are most of his customers. We keep them under surveillance with these TV cameras. Then we move in when we've got the evidence we need."

The inspector stood up and reached for his leather jacket. There was a whiff of aftershave. He looked every inch TV's idea of an undercover cop. I had noticed the Princess register his star quality as we arrived at his office half an hour earlier. That was good. An attractive male lead always brought out the best in our unpredictable royal performer. "If you're ready..." he said, heading for the door with an athlete's easy grace. His amused expression promised further treats in store.

The Princess followed him meekly. Her eyes were demurely lowered, as if to retain the image she had just seen. I knew she was enjoying herself—she was fascinated by the forbidden.

Two minutes later we were outside on the late rush-hour streets of King's Cross. Night had fallen. It started to rain. Out of the darkness a solitary flashbulb popped. I heard the Nikon's motor drive as my boss reacted with a loud sigh of exasperation. "Oh! Wretched press! They follow me *every-where*." The plaintive note was easy to hear. Too easy, I thought. You're overdoing it. But it earned her a sympathetic look from our handsome guide, so that was good too.

As we moved unnoticed into the hurrying crowds, I took up my familiar position slightly behind the tall figure with the expensively casual hairdo. Tonight she was in black jeans and a short, sexy jacket. This was our version of incognito. The Princess of Wales, icon of the oppressed and champion of the socially excluded, was beginning another "secret" fact-finding tour.

Tramping round King's Cross that night, I felt again the familiar wrench in my gut. It always came when I thought of where the Princess had been and where she was going. The sensation was becoming much more frequent. It was the same feeling you get on a roller coaster as it stops climbing and begins to dive toward the ground.

She had been so high: the future Queen. Now she was still high, at least with the people we were meeting on the street, and the papers said she was a phenomenon—the looks of a supermodel and the heart of a saint. But I knew the truth.

I had seen many saintly things done in her name, and even if she was not exactly saint material herself—as she would be quick, even too quick, to agree—she had certainly done a lot of suffering. Not all of it had been done in public either, as some would have you believe. Now, however, she was floundering. Where once she had been the ideal young wife and mother, now she was a self-proclaimed adulteress. Where once she had been worshipped by charities, now she was worshipped for her photo spreads. Where once she had summoned Air Force jets, now she bummed rides in planes smelling of rich men's cologne.

True, there were always going to be causes begging for this kind of celebrity patronage; and she had built up deep reserves of public sympathy. She still had that magical *forgivability*. But I knew these were the gifts more of others' mistakes than of her shining virtues. I knew she had begun to believe her own publicity, just as I was believing it less and less. I feared that others, like me, were every day seeing more of the steady fraying of her fragile mental stability, and I felt there was now no way back to the happy certainties of my early days at Kensington Palace.

How had it all changed? Eight years earlier it had all been so different—another world, almost another universe.

*A*utumn 1987. Somewhere on the long journey from Scotland I had lost my cuff links. Summoned from the frigate *Arethusa* while she was pausing in her patrol to refuel in a stormy west-coast sea loch, I had taken a boat, two buses, an airplane, and a taxi to reach the Kensington hotel that was my base for the coming ordeal. Along the way the cuff links, with their family crest and a wealth of sentimental value, had disappeared, never to return.

Some frantic improvisation was called for. Dejectedly I substituted collar studs, one of the archaic pieces of gear that gave the Navy its charm for me. It seemed a bad omen, not least because in those days any meeting with royalty was a signal for sartorial precision of the highest order. This was no ordinary meeting either: it was a job interview. By some quirk of fate, I had been chosen—along with five others— as a candidate to be the next equerry to the Princess of Wales.

I knew little about what an equerry actually did, but I did not greatly care. I already knew I wanted to do the job. Two years on loan to the royal household would surely be good for promotion, and even if it was not, it had to be better than slaving in the Ministry of Defence, which was the most likely alternative.

I wondered what it would be like to work in a palace. Through friends and relatives I had an idea it was not all red carpets and footmen. Running the royal family must involve a lot of hard work for somebody, I realized, but not, surely, for the type of tiny cog that was all I expected to be.

In the wardroom of the frigate, alongside in Loch Ewe, news of the signal summoning me to London for an interview had been greeted with predictable ribaldry and a swift expectation that I therefore owed everybody several free drinks.

Doug, our quiet American on loan from the US Navy, spoke for many. He observed me in skeptical silence for several minutes. Then he took a long pull at his beer, blew out his mustache, and said, "Let me get this straight. *You* are going to work for Princess Di?"

I had to admit it sounded improbable. Anyway, I had not even been selected yet. I did not honestly think I would be. "*Might* work for her, Doug. Only *might*. There're probably several smooth Army buggers ahead of me in the line. I'm just there to make it look democratic."

The First Lieutenant, thinking of duty rosters, was more practical. "Whatever about that, you've wangled a week ashore. Lucky bastard!" Everyone agreed with him, so I bought more drinks.

While these were being poured, my eye fell on the portraits hanging on the bulkhead. There were the regulation official photographs of the Queen and Prince Philip, and there, surprisingly, was a distinctly nonregulation picture of the Princess of Wales, cut from an old magazine and lovingly framed by an officer long since appointed elsewhere. The picture had been hung so that it lay between the formality of the official portraits and the misty eroticism of some art prints we had never quite got round to throwing away. The symbolic link did not require the services of one of the notoriously sex-obsessed naval psychologists for interpretation.

As she looked down at us in our off-duty moments the Princess represented youth, femininity, and a glamour beyond our gray steel world. She embodied the innocent vulnerability we were *in extremis* employed to defend. Also, being royal, she commanded the tribal loyalty our profession had valued above all else for more than a thousand years, since the days of King Alfred. In addition, as a matter of simple fact, this tasty-looking bird was our future Queen.

Later, when that day in Loch Ewe felt like a relic from another lifetime, I often marveled at the Princess's effect on military people. That unabashed loyalty symbolized by *Arethusa*'s portrait was typical of reactions in messhalls and barracks worldwide. Sometimes the men gave the impression that they would have died for her not because it was their duty, but because they *wanted* to. She really seemed worth it.

*S*o this is where she lives, I thought. I stood by the gates to Kensington Palace (or "KP" as I came to call it) and looked up the long drive to where another set of gates—the security barrier—guarded the entrance to what is in fact a kind of royal compound.

The usual picture the public sees of KP is only one short face of a rectangular complex of buildings. Behind this facade—the favored backdrop of TV reporters doing a Princess Di story—lies a warren of courtyards and gardens. Around these are an assortment of grand state apartments and smaller private apartments where the Waleses, Princess Margaret, and other royal people have their London homes.

I suppose if you have to live in a palace this is the one to choose, in London at least. It sits at one end of Hyde Park, and if you look out of a window facing north, east, or south the view is mostly of trees and grass. If you look west you can see the smart houses in "Millionaires' Row." Insulated from the noise of London's traffic, I discovered that it was a tranquil spot, especially in summer. On a fine day the only noise was of birds and crackling police radios—sometimes punctuated by the shouts of the Princes, William and Harry, riding their bikes, or by the penetrating laughter of the

Princess of Wales, as she stood at the front door telling a new joke to her PPO, her personal protection officer, before revving up her convertible and racing off.

I had imagined that the heir to the throne and his family would live somewhere elegant and spacious, in an atmosphere of restrained grandeur. I pictured French windows leading onto a lawn and perhaps a smaller version of the terrace I knew they had at Buckingham Palace. In fact, their apartment did not have much of a view at all. Tucked into the heart of the Palace complex, it was surprisingly dark. The Princess had a love-hate relationship with it. It was convenient for her public work and for shopping, and it was secure. But by 1987 it was the backdrop to a dying marriage and its walls had heard too many angry words.

Not only was the apartment dark and viewless, it was also surprisingly small. Everybody could hear everybody else. If you needed to get away from someone, there was just not enough space. The reception rooms were no bigger than you would expect in any smart town house and the private quarters were very unpalatial. Although I did not yet know it, the Prince had already moved out of the matrimonial bed and into his dressing room.

Most of the time the house was still. The Prince and Princess were usually out and the staff retreated to their places behind the scenes. Bursts of sudden activity broke the stillness, however. Every royal arrival or departure was marked by the slamming of doors, the bustle of domestic staff, and, as often as not, the anxious pacing of the private secretary. Meanwhile, in the sewing room, the pantry, the kitchen, and the nursery (not to mention the brushing room, the police room, and the cellar) a large staff unobtrusively maintained a style of life that had changed little in a hundred years. Yet if you sent the staff home, closed the curtains, and forgot to turn on *all* the lights, no amount of TV channels, loud music, or ringing telephones could keep the darkness at bay.

Of course the house had been made comfortable—espe-

cially if you like lime-green carpet—but unless you had all
the lights on, even in daytime it was gloomy. The Princess's
sitting room was the sunniest in the house. Its tall windows
looked down on a pretty walled garden where she sometimes relaxed on summer evenings (though her favorite
place for sunbathing was on the roof terrace). It also looked
down on the front door so she could see or hear everybody
approaching. She had *very* acute hearing. Inside, it was a
grown-up version of a teenager's room. There were two
pink sofas by the fire and a smart writing desk by the window, but there were also soft toys, cushions that said GOOD
GIRLS GO TO HEAVEN—BAD GIRLS GO EVERYWHERE, and
children's school paintings on the walls. Every flat surface
had photos, Halcyon Days enamel boxes or Herrend fig-
urines crammed onto it. It was cheerful, girlish, and very
cluttered. It smelled good too. There were always flowers—
lilies were a favorite—as well as potpourri and scented candles.

She must have been in her sitting room that day as I
made my cautious approach to the anonymous black door
that was to be my entrance to the world of the Waleses. I
tried to look calm on the outside, as if I turned up at palaces
every day, but inside I was quaking...and curious.

Before going back to the reality of my very different life
in the Navy, I decided to enjoy this unexpected opportunity
for as long as it lasted. I would use the chance to find out as
much as I could about this woman who fascinated millions
of people who had never met her and never would do so. I
was not fascinated myself; not really. I already knew that
would *not* be an advantage for anyone trying to work for
her. But if I was going to have to meet this beauty, about
whom I had unavoidably read and heard so much, I might
as well make the most of the experience.

Nervously I tried to check my reflection in the opaque
window of the front door. I had an idea that equerries to
Her Royal Highness the Princess of Wales were several
inches taller than me in their Gucci loafers and carried a re-

assuring air of Labradors and sports cars. They certainly did not lose their cuff links.

Summoning up all my stiffening thoughts, I pressed the bell. I could not hear if it had rung, so after several minutes I pressed it again, just as the door opened to reveal the Prince of Wales's butler. He was about my height and wore a dark blue jacket with the Prince of Wales's monogram on the lapels. He looked politely unimpressed. "Oh yes," he said. "Come in."

Later, I came to know Harold Brown well and grew to admire his professionalism. At home and abroad, he quietly bore the hundreds of little stresses that came with dealing with his royal employers at their less attractive moments. His gift as a mimic had me crying tears of laughter into my whiskey on many foreign tours. That afternoon, however, he was every inch the guardian of his master's privacy and impassively allowed me to follow him to the Equerries' Room where I was to await the royal summons.

Like so much of the apartment, although undeniably comfortable and well appointed, the Equerries' Room was dark. Clever effects had been achieved with concealed lighting, pastel colorings, and flowers, but the overriding impression was one of pervasive gloom.

Two people were already there—the Princess's lady-in-waiting, Anne Beckwith-Smith, and her current equerry, Richard Aylard. They were there to examine me as a possible recruit to their exclusive way of life. During the last few days they had been examining five others as well, of course, so they were understandably distant, if polite.

I was polite too—this was surely part of the selection process—and determined, like the butler, to look unimpressed. But I did need to go to the loo. Badly.

Groping in the semigloom of the cloakroom, I became the latest visitor to fumble for the trick light switch on a fiendish *trompe l'oeil* before finding the real switch on the wall behind me. The humor continued on the other walls, where original cartoons celebrated the Prince of Wales's talent for self-deprecation. Other pictures showed the Prince and Princess in mostly military group shots, and the image of country-house-style domestic harmony was completed with some equestrian prints. Looking more closely, however, I could not help noticing that even the most recent photograph must have been at least five years old and all the cartoons featured a distinctly bachelor Prince.

Of course I had read the tabloid rumors about the marriage—there had recently been a furor about a visit to a badly flooded area of Wales, when the couple's visible estrangement had been more of a story than the floods themselves. Like practically everyone else in the wardroom, I had also tittered over Sylvie Krin's imaginatively romanticized reports in the magazine *Private Eye*. But nobody really *knew* what was happening. Everybody just assumed that, whatever their private difficulties, the Prince and Princess would stoically maintain the outward unity that was expected of them.

Although schooled by my upbringing to view the monarchy with reverence—and still very much in awe of my surroundings—I already felt an inkling of critical detachment. Later, it was this ability to put some distance between myself and the job that helped keep me sane. Having no strong English "county" background made this easier, I thought. So did the years I had spent living in the Irish Republic. Nevertheless, I happily accepted that if I was to become even a temporary member of the courtiers' charmed circle I had to accept the fact that royal people by definition exercise a supreme authority. It was an article of faith.

This was obviously a historical anachronism, but I rather liked that. Anyway, I felt quite sure that somewhere wise heads must long ago have worked out the answer to a nagging question. How, I wondered, would I reconcile that historical anachronism with the harsh realities of a world that did not swallow articles of faith quite as readily as it had in more deferential times? Perhaps, from my seat on the sidelines, I would learn how it was done.

Without apparent warning we were on the move. Following the impassive butler up KP's broad staircase—a steep hill of lime green with pink fleurs-de-lis—our conversation seemed suddenly too loud. As we approached the summit our voices fell to the self-conscious level you might hear in a church or a ward for the gravely ill. We were led into the drawing room, blinking against the sudden bright sunshine. In the glare I registered the room only as an over-exposed negative. Impressions of family photographs, great art, and pastel fabrics swam at me against the light. Conversation dwindled to nothing as we stood and fidgeted.

Suddenly a door at the far end of the room opened and the Princess of Wales swept in. Squinting horribly against the sun, I prepared to make my bow while trying desperately to see if she was even looking in my direction.

She was. I had seen the blue-eyed gaze in photographs, of course, and it lost none of its unsettling power at close range. When I looked again, though, I saw the gaze was tempered by an undeniable friendliness mixed with frank appraisal. In my peripheral vision I noticed some incidental details. She was wearing a cream cotton suit that set off her tan nicely. A bit too many rays on the chest, I thought absently, noticing a rosy tint to the even golden appearance. No jewelry.

Her handshake was cool and firm, my bow instinctive. In the distance somebody was introducing me. "It's good of you to come all this way, Jeph," said the Princess. Even as I realized she had only misheard the introduction, I thought how nice it was that she used an old family nickname. As I was to learn, she seemed to have a knack for attracting such happy coincidences.

We went through to the dining room for lunch, and the same sun that had dazzled me in the drawing room bathed our small round table in a golden light. The Princess sat on my left, while Anne and Richard arranged themselves in the other seats. I took stock of my surroundings, trying not to goggle too obviously.

The KP dining room was tall and square, furnished with antiques and softened with pink and peach pastel fabrics. A complicated flower arrangement seemed to burst out of the middle of the table. Silver and crystal sparkled against the crisp whiteness of the napkins. Portraits from the Royal Collection looked down at the scene and I was just practicing meeting their regal gaze unblinkingly when a voice on my left diverted my attention to the real thing.

"I hope you like chicken," said the Princess. "I'm afraid we seem to have it all the time." This was true, I discovered later. At the time I was only aware that, for all I cared, I might have been eating the royal underpadding that no doubt lay beneath the deep-pile carpet. There were tiny potatoes and salad with the chicken, and white wine. I watched the Princess covertly for signs of an eating disorder, even though I had no idea what those signs might be. She seemed to eat like anybody else, and drank the wine too.

I now realized that the energetic flurry of our introduction was an affectation. As she probably intended, her breezy bonhomie blew away our nervousness. It also seemed to dispel an air of preoccupation that had hung about her as she entered the room. In later years I came to recognize the technique, which she often used to shrug off—however temporarily—the cares that beset her.

It was time to practice my small talk. "Are you looking forward to going to Germany, Ma'am?" I had done some research and knew that she and the Prince were due to go on a tour the following week.

She nodded, but without much enthusiasm. "It's an outing for my husband, really," she said. (It was strange to hear him described like that, as it was when I first heard her mention "my mother-in-law" or "Granny.") "He gets a chance to meet his old rellies. Half the royal family's German!" She giggled. Later, when she was in trouble for buying a German rather than a British sports car, she joked,

"Well, I've got a German husband, why can't I have a German car?"

For me this was daring stuff. "Better be careful," I said. "Don't mention the war."

She laughed again—not because she recognized my quote from *Fawlty Towers* but because she recognized that I had been trying to tell a joke. She laughed as a reflex, whether she understood it or not. Later I learned that she would laugh at anything. Sometimes I thought you could read her the phone book in a funny voice, then look at her expectantly, and she would laugh. She was that desperate to be happy. Happy people laugh a lot, so she would laugh whenever she could—and often when she should not.

This made her a quick pupil for anyone who had the nerve to tell her something really filthy or offensive. That was a double thrill for her—she could be shocked and amused at the same time. Smut was a surefire way of getting her to laugh. It would not be a natural, convivial sound, however, but a great, honking, nasal guffaw. The more offensive the joke, the more unattractive would be her reaction. She also enjoyed the shock she could achieve by repeating the worst from her collection. Needless to say, we did not plumb quite those depths on the first day. It took a week at least.

If I had expected a lively, informed debate about the function and purpose of a modern constitutional monarchy, I was wrong. This was a relief, although as a politics graduate I was keen to study the reality at close quarters. I felt like a medical student with a theoretical understanding of anatomy who is suddenly confronted by a real patient. Only in this case, I suspected that the patient was free to prescribe her own treatment.

Our conversation cantered along at a surprisingly easy pace. I gleaned little about my prospective duties, except that one of them at least was to fill a lunchtime with polite chat. Nor was I asked to reveal much about my own background. I assumed this was because she was already well briefed on my personal details, but later I realized she was not really very interested in where I came from, only in whether I would be bearable to have around for a year or so.

Like many of the family into which she had married, she only reluctantly acknowledged that her staff had a life either before or beyond their contact with her. Employees came and went with such rapidity that this was possibly an understandable reaction. Sometimes she certainly did make a conspicuous and generous effort to be a concerned employer—more so, in fact, than most other royal people—but it did not come naturally. In any case, nothing enforces the concept of royalty being different more effectively than a bit of healthy indifference toward the underlings.

The underlings, therefore, had to look after themselves. It did not take me long to realize that, whenever I was uncertain what to do next in any royal situation, usually the best option was to do nothing and enjoy whatever pleasurable compensations were to hand. A sense of humor was essential survival equipment in the palace jungle—but nothing too clever. So was an ability to enjoy food and drink.

To these I secretly added an ability to enjoy plane-spotting. It turned out to be quite useful. Many of my tensest moments were experienced in royal airplanes, but surprisingly often I could deflect the Princess's fiercest rocket with a calculated display of nerdish interest in what I could see out of the window.

As it happened, I was able to indulge this lonely vice almost immediately as I caught the bus back to Heathrow. Farewells at KP were polite but perfunctory, and Richard and Anne gave no hint as to the outcome of my interview. Richard ventured the comment that I had given "a remarkable performance," but this only added to the general air of theatrical unreality. I was pretty sure I had eaten my first and last royal Jersey Royal potato.

Back in Scotland, my despondency deepened as I inhaled

the pungent aroma of my allocated bedroom in the Faslane transit mess. It was not fair, I moaned to myself, to expose someone as sensitive as me to lunch with the most beautiful woman in the world and then consign him to dinner with the duty engineer at the Clyde Submarine Base. And how could I ever face the future when every time the Princess appeared in the papers I would say to myself—or, far worse, to anyone in earshot—"Oh yes, I've met her. Had lunch with her in fact. Absolutely charming. Laughed at all my jokes..."

Now thoroughly depressed, I was preparing for a miserable night's sleep when I was interrupted by the wardroom night porter. He wore a belligerent expression so convincing that it was clearly the result of long practice. No doubt drawing on years of observing submarine officers at play, he clearly suspected he was being made the victim of a distinctly unamusing practical joke. In asthmatic Glaswegian he accused me of being wanted on the phone "frae Bucknum Paluss."

I rushed to the phone booth, suddenly wide-awake. The Palace operator connected me to Anne Beckwith-Smith. "*There* you are!" she said in her special lady-in-waiting voice. "We've been looking for you everywhere. *Would you like the job?*"

2

In the Pink

*S*ome events can be seen as milestones only in retrospect, while at the time they pass almost unnoticed. This was not such an event. The court circular for January 28, 1988, spelled it out in black and white: Jephson was going to the Palace and an insistent inner voice told me his life would never be the same again.

Reaction among my friends and relations was mixed. The American, Doug, thought it was a quaint English fairy tale. My father thought it inevitably meant promotion (he was wrong). My stepmother thought it was nice (she was mostly right). My brother thought it would make me an unbearably smug nuisance (no change).

Although I would never have admitted it, *I* thought I must be pretty clever, and I apologize belatedly to everyone who had to witness it. That was lesson one: breathing royal air can seriously damage your ability to laugh at yourself. It is sometimes called "red-carpet fever" and usually only lasts a few months, but severe cases never recover and spend the rest of their lives believing in their own acquired importance.

I reported to the offices of the Prince and Princess at the end of April. In those halcyon days their staff occupied a joint office in St. James's Palace. The couple shared a private secretary, a comptroller, a press secretary, and numerous administrative officials who helped run an organization some hundred strong. They themselves lived at KP and made the journey to "SJP" when required.

In the Prince's case this was frequently and—unlike his wife—he kept an office at St. James's for the purpose. Given the clutter of books and papers with which he usually surrounds himself, this elegant room—all lime-wash paneling and thick carpet—seemed strangely anonymous, its few personal touches almost an afterthought. The cleverly concealed lighting and carefully selected antiques seemed to have taken priority. Its enormous desk was naked but for a photo of William and Harry, while from the mantelpiece an unusual triple-portrait photo of his mother, aunt, and grandmother looked down on the inmate with matronly appraisal. The place smelled of polish and expensive fabrics and in every way satisfied what I suppose are masculine preferences in orderliness and understated good taste. It was a constant reminder—along with its equivalent in cars, clothes, and other accoutrements—that the heir's cares were shouldered in at least tolerable comfort.

The penalty of operating out of two palaces was the amount of time—and often anxiety—expended on getting from one to the other. My tendency to plan journeys to coincide with the sedate passage of the Household Cavalry always raised my blood pressure. I almost came to believe that the Mounted Division only ventured out in splendor to block Constitution Hill when they had word that the Princess had summoned me to an urgent meeting in KP.

There were benefits too. Even the most conscientious private secretary could sometimes be grateful that his boss kept at a distance from the office. Moreover, when peace and quiet and decent coffee were elusive at SJP, I often took refuge in the tranquillity of the KP Equerries' Room. The house staff always kept a warm welcome and would let you raid the pantry. Also, more often than I cared to admit, it was useful to be "unobtainable" while stuck in traffic somewhere on Kensington Gore, although the fitting of mobile phones to office cars made this an increasingly dodgy excuse.

The Wales household occupied offices in St. James's that had previously been used by the Lord Chamberlain's Department. The previous occupants' more sedate tastes were apparent in the dense brown carpet and heavy furniture. Against the sober backdrop of high ceilings, ornate plasterwork, and yellowing net curtains the youthful Wales staff sometimes seemed like children who had set up their office camp in an abandoned gentlemen's club. The average age could not have been more than twenty-two, and the secretaries were almost without exception from backgrounds where young women were expected to be seen *and* heard and enjoyed being both.

At that time the office worked as one unit with Their Royal Highnesses' private secretary—the genial Sir John Riddell—presiding over a team which, on the surface at least, owed equal loyalty to both. I soon discovered, however, that the Princess's small component was still regarded as a minor addition to what was essentially an enlarged bachelor establishment. This was especially evident in the planning of joint programs, when, as if part of the natural order, the Princess's requirements took second place—and sometimes not even that, unless the Prince's staff were gently reminded of her involvement. Despite this, thanks to a lot of goodwill, it was an addition that was loftily tolerated, despite its perceived irrelevance to the main work of the organization.

The private secretary's room lay at one end of a string of smaller offices on the first floor of York House. At the other end a swing door separated us from the decidedly grown-up world of the Central Chancery of the Orders of Chivalry. Between the two I found offices for the deputy private secretary, the comptroller, and the lady-in-waiting, interspersed with larger shared offices for lowlier forms of life such as equerries and secretaries.

My predecessor Commander Richard Aylard and his opposite number, the Prince's equerry Major Christopher Lavender, shared an office that seemed to be the size of a small ballroom, inelegantly partitioned to make a small adjoining space for three secretaries (or "lady clerks" in Palace-speak). I was planted behind a small table in a corner, from which I could observe the veterans at work. Now, I thought, I'll find out what an equerry actually *does*.

Many people then—and since—made dismissive comments about equerries being needed only to hand round gin and tonic or carry flowers for the lady-in-waiting, both tasks being about on the limit of my perceived ability. I performed these tasks on numerous occasions, but even at the outset I knew there must be rather more to a job that provoked such envy and contempt. I had an idea—reinforced by a helpful introductory letter from Richard—that I was expected to help implement the Princess's program and generally act as a kind of glorified aide-de-camp.

Listening to the confident instructions being rapped out by Richard and Christopher in a series of seemingly incessant phone calls, I was gripped by panic. How would I ever know what to do? How would I ever develop the easy blend of nonchalant authority and patient good humor that seemed to be the better courtier's stock-in-trade? Especially when all the time my novice high-wire act would be under unblinking scrutiny from royal employers, skeptical colleagues, and—worst of all—the royal press pack.

My panic deepened as I contemplated my first task. Thinking he was easing me in gently, Richard had thoughtfully given me the job of writing a memorandum to the Princess outlining program options for a forthcoming visit to the West Country. I stared transfixed at the notepad in front of me, my mind as blank as the paper. The letterhead grandly announced the writer as EQUERRY TO HRH THE

PRINCESS OF WALES and I dumbly wondered if I would ever have the temerity to sign anything that followed.

Eventually a lucky inspiration came to me. On the pretext of familiarizing myself with the office filing system (a feat still incomplete seven years later), I sauntered into the secretaries' room. The girl-talk came to a temporary halt as three laughing pairs of eyes appraised me.

"We've decided to call you PJ," the senior secretary said. "We can't possibly call you Pat in the office and there's already a Patrick in Buckingham Palace." Thinking of other things I could—and no doubt would—be called, I decided to accept this tag without protest. The secretaries' nicknames were acutely observed and tended to become universally accepted. Compared to some, I was fortunate.

"Can I help you, PJ?" asked the girl with the eyes that laughed the most. Jo had already been introduced as my secretary and was thus a crucial partner in the adventure that was about to begin. I explained my predicament and she rummaged in a filing cabinet that I could not help noticing seemed to act as an overflow for her handbag as well as secure storage for sensitive papers.

"We've got some examples here somewhere which you could copy..." With a triumphant toss of chestnut hair and a jangle of bracelets, she handed me some files in the distinctive dark red of the Wales office. "When you've drafted it, I'll type it for you. But we'd better get a move on. The Bag closes in half an hour."

This was obviously an important piece of information. I checked the instinct to rush back to my desk and instead asked what the "Bag" was. The women looked at each other significantly. "*That* is the Bag." A manicured nail indicated a red plastic pouch the size of a small pillowcase. It sat in isolation on one of the less cluttered shelves next to a basket of papers on which I could glimpse Anne's distinctive writing.

The Bag came to rule my life. It was the main means of written communication with KP and so carried the whole catalog of information, advice, pleading, cajoling, and obfuscation that seemed to compose our output. It also carried our letters of petition, contrition, and—occasionally—resignation. These were mixed with bills, pills, fan mail, hate mail, and any private mail that had not already gone directly to the KP breakfast tray. Those envelopes had to be delivered unopened on pain of death, but it was by no means obvious which were entreaties from ardent suitors and which were complaints about office incompetence from loyal subjects. A secretary who could sniff the difference (sometimes literally) was worth her weight in gold.

In return the Bag welcomed us each morning with the overnight products of the royal pen. Schoolday comparisons with waiting for homework to be marked were inescapable, especially when alternative programs such as the one I was struggling to draw up for the day in the West Country had been submitted for consideration.

The art, I discovered, was to submit the options in a way that led the Princess imperceptibly to the desired choice. The quickest way to learn that art was to watch what happened at the receiving end. Often, when I had been out with her all day, the Princess would find the Bag waiting in the car that came to collect us. It could be a tense moment. If we had enjoyed a good day, a bad Bag could take the shine off it in a second; and it took a very good Bag indeed to restore shine to a day that had been lousy.

She would snap the little plastic seal, pull back the heavy zip, and delve inside. Balancing the inner cardboard file on her lap, she quickly sorted the papers into piles. Fashion catalogues or designers' bills were dealt with first; then press cuttings; then loose minutes from the secretaries about things like therapists' appointments or school events for the boys; then personal mail—some of it saved for private reading later; then real work—memos from me that required a decision, outline programs, draft speeches, invitations, suggested letters... the list was endless.

She would hold out her hand for my pen, then go to

work. She was quick and decisive—and expected me to be the same. This was at least partly to draw a distinction between herself and the Prince, whose capacity to sit on paperwork was legendary.

What worked best was to reduce a complicated question to a few important points—the bits she really had to know—and then offer two alternative answers. It was pretty basic staffwork, but quite intellectually satisfying. Soon I could anticipate fairly accurately her reaction to most questions. If I expected her to go for option A ("Yes, please") but for reasons too complicated to explain I wanted her instead to pick option B ("No, thanks"), all I had to do was explain that A, while superficially attractive, risked controversy/conflict with another member of the royal family/bad press. "We don't want to do that, do we, Patrick?" she would say and I would look judicious, as if weighing up the pros and cons, and then agree with her. The pen would mark a big tick next to option B and everybody would be happy.

Mind you, she would not have been the Princess of Wales if there had not also been times when she would do the exact opposite out of spite. It seldom had anything to do with the pros and cons then. Eventually, however, I could sometimes predict these moods too. Then the procedure was reversed: all I had to do was extol the virtues of option A and she would automatically tick option B. It was a great game.

Much later, the game became less fun. The Princess bought a shredder and would unblushingly destroy papers that displeased her, then accuse me of not showing them to her in the first place. This enabled her to claim that she was not being supported, that her office (me) was incompetent, etc., etc. After a few such happy experiences, I learned to keep duplicates of anything that might end up in her shredder. I would then produce them when the original mysteriously "disappeared." She hated that.

On my first day, of course, I knew none of this. Back at

my temporary desk, I perused the files Jo had given me. One, labeled simply with MERSEYSIDE and a date, was thick with papers and looked as if it had already made several arduous journeys to Liverpool in the rain. The other was pristine, contained two small sheets of pink paper and was labeled SAVOY LUNCH.

"Merseyside" looked more promising, so, ignoring the background sounds of efficient equerries at work, I delved into its dog-eared contents. These read rather like a story whose plot assembles only gradually. Some characters—such as the Prince and Princess—we already know from previous novels in the series. Others we know by title if not yet as distinct personalities—the Lord Lieutenant, the Chief Constable, the local director of the Central Office of Information. Others again are complete newcomers whose place in the coming narrative is tantalizingly obscure. Will the leader of the Acorns Playgroup outbid the chairperson of the Drug Awareness workshop in the competition for the selector's eye? Are the patronages they represent in or out of favor and will this affect their chances? Or will all be bulldozed aside by the requirement to attend the opening of a semiconductor factory?

Such musings crowded into my mind as I composed my first memo for the Bag. What style would be best? I had already seen a document addressed to the Queen in which, as precedent demands, the writer opened with the sonorous "Madam, With my humble duty..." and, although I relished such verbal quaintness, it did not seem right for the lively Princess who had given me lunch. The examples I found in the "Merseyside" file were more reassuring, opening with a simple "Sir" or "Ma'am" and proceeding to describe complex choices in simple, straightforward English. The only peculiarities I noticed were neat abbreviations for unwieldy royal titles ("YRHes" for "Your Royal Highnesses") and a brisk respectfulness ("As YRH will recall...").

Eventually Jo forced me to hand over my meager draft. Once printed on thick office stationery, its tentative phrases

took on an air of authority that quite had me fooled until I
saw my signature at the bottom. Early days, I thought to
myself, as I saw it committed to the Bag, which was then
promptly sealed. "I'm going to the High Street during
lunch so I can drop the Bag at KP nice and early. You never
know, we might get it back this afternoon," said Jo, making
for the door.

I returned to my corner and sought comfort in thoughts
of lunch. Suddenly the phone on my desk rang. I went into
shock. It had not rung before. What should I do now? The
others were already talking on their own phones, so this one
was down to me.

It rang again, sounding louder. In my nervous, beginner's
state it even *sounded* royal...I picked up the receiver.
"Hello?" I said, clearing my throat. That didn't sound very
confident, I thought.

"Hello?" said a man's voice. It was crackly and faint, but
vaguely familiar. "Who's that?" The voice sounded rather
tetchy.

"Who's calling?" I asked, trying to sound as if I were
getting a grip.

"It's the Prince of Wales speaking," said the voice. Definitely tetchy. Panic.

"Oh...sorry, Sir. Um..."

Richard had finished his call and, from the far side of the
room, his antennae had already picked up my plight. Dab-
bing a key on his fiercely complicated-looking phone, he
cut in smoothly. "It's Richard here, Sir..."

I imagined I could hear the relief in His Master's Voice.
What a *great* start, I thought.

*T*he phone came to rule my life just as much as the Bag
and, by its nature, it proved a shrill and insistent mistress. I
admit now that I was too often ready to allow my patient
secretaries to screen calls, so I was left at the end of the day

with a callback list that reproachfully cataloged awkward conversations shirked and good news still untold.

My excuse—and it seemed a good one—was that I was fully occupied with priority calls, mostly from the Princess. She was a virtuoso with the instrument and I quickly came to measure the mood of the day by the first syllable of her morning greeting. It might have been telepathy, but I sometimes felt as if I knew just from the sound of the ringing tone that it was her. Taking a deep breath, I would pick up the receiver. Sometimes she would come straight through, calling from the car or her mobile. At other times she would be connected by the Palace switchboard.

The familiar voices of the imperturbable operators could spark a reply in neat adrenaline. I became quite good at interpreting the subtle nuances of *their* voices too. Some are indelibly linked in my mind to traumatic events of which they were the first harbingers. Invariably kind, often humorous, sometimes wonderfully motherly, they must have assisted unwittingly at many executions. On a shamefully rare visit to their subterranean den, I was not surprised to see knitting in progress.

The background noises could be a clue to how much you were going to enjoy the call that followed. Silence meant she was at her desk, probably perusing the Bag and about to ask an awkward question. If she was in the car and it was early morning, she was most likely on her way back from her morning swim and anxious to resolve a nagging problem that had surfaced during her fifty lengths.

Later in the day it probably meant she was shopping, so expect to be quizzed on men's taste in cashmere sweaters. The sound of a Harrier jet in the background meant she was under the hairdryer, so expect either the hairdresser's latest filthy joke or a piece of gossip that the Princess had picked up earlier in the day ("Did you know the Duchess of Blank's aromatherapist was having a raging affair with your neighbor?"). The sound of running bathwater meant we were in for a playful ten minutes during which I was supposed to imagine the saintly form up to its neck in bubbles. The distinctive sound of a dress being unzipped meant she was having a fitting with her current designer... or something.

That first syllable was crucial. It could be warm and conspiratorial: "*Patrick!* Have you seen the papers?" This induced a cautious relief at being singled out for speculation about the morning's unfortunate tabloid target, usually another member of the royal family.

Or it could be flat and accusatory: "Patrick... *have* you seen the papers?" (The "yet" was silent.) This produced a state of high alert. Good preparation was vital—I always tried to have an answer ready for every current subject of her potential displeasure. She was often working from a different list, however.

Or it could be light and carefree: "Patrick, have you *seen* the papers?" This might be an invitation to share joy at a prominent story showing her in a good light. Anything that described her as "serious," "independent," or "caring" would have this effect. Descriptions of her beauty or fashion genius got a similar but less fulsome reaction. A critical story, however—especially if she had predicted it—meant trouble. The lighthearted tone was designed to lower your guard, the better to deliver either a stinging rebuke or an invitation to join in the persecution of the perceived offender.

It was easy to be fooled, though. I quickly learned how misleading such judgments could be as I witnessed dramatically different moods being signaled to different listeners all in the space of one car journey. It was pointless to question such inconsistency. What mattered was the mood allocated to *you* and, until it changed, life was at least straightforward, if at times uncomfortable.

No less impressive was her use of the phone as scalpel and feather duster. Under the latter, the most recalcitrant member of the "old guard" would wag his tail with pleasure, but under the former, discarded favorites dumbly suffered their excommunication. In severe cases, any subsequent wailing or gnashing of teeth could be neatly avoided simply with a change of number. The magic digits—the coveted code to personal access—would abruptly fail to connect.

The common denominator was her absolute command of the conversation. This she achieved with artfully presented moods and a surprising fluency that served as a reminder of her mental sharpness. Her sense of timing was sometimes uncanny. In my case she would usually ring when I was late coming back from lunch.

Ultimately, of course, there was the royal hang-up, which could lend unprecedented significance to a simple click. On the other hand, a good call could put a smile on your face for the rest of the day.

I had hardly finished congratulating myself on completing my first piece of written work in my new job when I noticed a lull in the hitherto ceaseless activity at the equerries' desks. In unison, Richard and Christopher stretched and looked at their watches. It was 1:15, which my internal clock had already informed me was well past its customary lunch call.

"Good heavens, look at the time, better go to lunch!" said Richard.

"Come on!" said Christopher in a voice that would have galvanized his beloved Ghurkas, and I fell in behind the two veterans as we marched speedily down the stairs, across Ambassador's Court, and out into the sunshine of Green Park.

Approaching Buckingham Palace from St. James's, the great building seems less intimidating than when seen from the grand processional route of the Mall. Visiting heads of state, arriving by the more impressive route, can look up with relief from their open carriage as the Palace fills the horizon, knowing their horse-drawn ordeal is nearly over, while heedless tourists reverse suicidally into the traffic as they struggle to squeeze the whole building into their viewfinders. From Green Park the view is oblique, framed by leafy branches and altogether more human in scale.

The short walk between the palaces became a well-worn route for me as I shuttled to and from the senior household offices with their Olympian denizens. Sometimes the journey was an opportunity for self-congratulatory reflection or garden-party preening. At other times it was a true *via dolorosa* as the cares of the whole monarchy seemed to reach out at me from a hundred faceless windows on the monolithic facade.

When great events were in the offing, the international TV networks set up their outside broadcast studios among the trees, creating a media gypsy camp under a forest of aerial masts. From this cover, preoccupied courtiers could be ambushed as they hurried by, later to discover that they had become unwitting walk-on extras in the main feature. As additional entertainment, Lancaster House would occasionally lay on a G7 or NATO summit, allowing us the chance to peer at the visiting Presidents and Prime Ministers as they were conveyed past in their limousines.

Safely across the pedestrian crossing at the foot of Constitution Hill, our small detachment marched through the gates into the forecourt of Buckingham Palace, the focus of a hundred pairs of jaded tourist eyes. Were these men in the Simpson's off-the-peg suits important? They did not look royal, that was certain (especially the one at the back who was explaining to the police that he had not yet got his security pass). But just in case, we had better take a photograph anyway—through the railings as if they were animals in a zoo; or inmates, I sometimes thought, at a secure institution.

Buckingham Palace has two main working entrances— one round the side near the kitchens and one at the front on the right as you look at it. Like everything else, use of each entrance is determined by your place in the hierarchy. Being "household," we strode proprietorially up the steps to the Privy Purse Door, thus being spared the indignity of lining up with the deliverymen at the side gate.

A liveried doorman spared us the further indignity of having to open the door ourselves and, I noticed, greeted Richard and Christopher as if he really recognized them. This is the life, I thought, as my nostrils had their first sniff of the unique Palace smell: a mixture of polish and hot lightbulbs with just a hint of mothballs. My feet at last felt qualified to pad across the red carpet as I followed my hungry guides into the bowels of the building.

It was as well that I stayed close to them, because the route from the door to the dining room was labyrinthine to the uninitiated. The entrance gave onto a stairwell, which gave onto a corridor, which jinked, climbed, narrowed, and divided before at last turning into the great entrance hall from which the dining room debouched. Even after several months' practice the journey could seem hazardous, though whether this was from fear of getting lost or getting found I was never quite sure. The latter was a real anxiety at moments of internal tension, as my route even to the nearest exit offered ample opportunity for unexpected encounters with the Palace's most senior inhabitants.

Running this gauntlet was made slightly more pleasurable by detouring into the Queen's Equerry's Room for a preprandial drink. Every day without fail, it was full of courtiers intent on gin and gossip. While exploring the drinks tray on that first day I learned another lesson, which time was to reinforce. In a way reminiscent of the tolerance extended by the Prince's organization to his wife's, the senior household played forbearant host to its subordinate satellites. Among these the Waleses' organization constituted the most important—and certainly the largest—planet, but all down to the merest Pluto of royalty theoretically shared equal status as members of household. This entitled them to walk on red carpet, cruise the Royal Enclosure at Ascot, and enjoy a number of other perks, one of whose daily rituals I was now experiencing.

The atmosphere reminded me of one of those better military messes where the members had not forgotten some basic rules of communal living, principally the endangered art of making polite conversation. This was not surprising given the preponderance of ex-military personnel, but the similarity began to fray when I listened to the shoptalk that, inevitably, dominated the conversation. Beneath the surface conviviality I slowly detected a lack of the kind of common purpose to be expected even in the most incohesive wardroom.

This was obviously a valuable clearinghouse for the various informal royal intelligence services. The principal members of the royal family were represented by their private staffs and the heads of the Palace's great departments represented the behind-the-scenes support structure. This mixture of disparate interests genteelly fenced and bartered in a way that cannot have changed much, I supposed, since Victorian times. Then as now, representatives of lesser households might have felt themselves mere cousins admitted to the ancestral seat where the inner family carried on with its laundry, hiding its resentment that the visitors had the intrusiveness of kin without the discretion of polite guests. The soothing properties of civilized conversation were thus much needed—and were generously employed, not least in greeting the new boy, for which I was duly grateful.

The room quickly emptied in a general move toward lunch. I joined the throng feeling I was among friendly people whose friendship would nevertheless have carefully controlled limits. I would be accepted subject to certain constraints, most of which appeared reasonable to me. These would be imposed by my comparative youth, junior position, temporary appointment, and membership of a subordinate organization, tenants of a property outside the pale. In short, we were tolerated. Politely, entertainingly, and often warmly, but still only tolerated.

As senior staff, our "canteen" was the Buckingham Palace Household Dining Room. In its scale, decor, portraiture, and appointments it encouraged us to feel reassuringly exclusive. We helped ourselves from a sideboard and sat where we thought the best conversation could be found— or avoided.

On that first day I was surprised by the variety of my fellow lunchers. There were the Queen's ladies-in-waiting— treated with universal respect—and the Queen's private secretaries—also treated with respect, at least by me. But there were others further down the hierarchy who hinted at the bewildering diversity of the royal household. There was the captain of the Queen's Flight looking smooth. There was the keeper of the Royal Collection, looking not at all like Anthony Blunt (the former keeper of the Collection exposed as a Russian spy). There was the press secretary, wearing his poker-player's face. And there was the senior policeman, looking surprised to find himself there at all.

I am sure I did too. My morale was soon boosted when, in a ceremony that beat all the majestic pomp and circumstance of the British Crown, the duty footman Dymo-taped my name onto a napkin ring. I may only have been temporary, and I would often lunch somewhere else, but now I was a member of the club.

That first afternoon I strolled back across the park to St. James's feeling pretty pleased with myself. It was a sensation that soon became unfamiliar. The job often made me feel so anxious that the outward perks—even my own napkin ring—seemed like a bad joke. On some days I would have swapped them all for a friendly face somewhere, anywhere, else. As I returned to my new office that day, however, I was beginning to believe that I could act my part. From my temporary perch I felt the first stirrings of confidence as I measured Richard's desk with my eye and contemplated a suitable fate for his Australian beer mat if he was careless enough to leave it behind when he moved along the corridor to his new post as comptroller.

The afternoon's program was intended to begin my education in Palace life. I was to meet two of the more significant Palace officeholders for "a chat," and in their own way they neatly illustrated the latent tensions that I had detected at lunch. There was an old guard, almost literally. They were mostly ex-Guards Regiment, not very qualified in anything very much, but at least superficially friendly, if tending to be dogmatic about How Things Should Be Done. Then there was a younger guard, less overtly military, less dogmatic, no less friendly, and arguably better qualified. As members of the heir's office, we were usually grouped with this second category, not least by temperament.

The royal household is sometimes still caricatured as being made up of faceless courtiers drawn from public schools and the Army. During my time there, it was still quite true that both types were in the majority. Even those from a City or diplomatic background had mostly worn a uniform at some stage, but despite a predictably establishment outlook—which I shared—most also had a very realistic attitude to the institution they served. They had inherited a hidebound, antique machine. To make it work they had to be highly effective in the real world of power and personalities that ran national life—but they also had to be sensitive to the hothouse family politics of the royal world. It was sometimes an impossible job. Failure was always headline news and any success had to be passed modestly upward.

In a minority of cases, however, it was painfully apparent that the only journey some had taken to be reborn as courtiers was the short march from Wellington Barracks to Buckingham Palace. Their tone and style of working were therefore vaguely familiar to anyone who had ever humored an unstable commanding officer or in turn meted out patronizing encouragement to a subordinate. My first "chat" was with a prime specimen of this type. Order, precedent, and self-preservation were everything to him, which left little room, I observed, for intellect. It became apparent quite early in our conversation that it also left little room for humor, insight, empathy, or outside interests of any kind. These were optional in his post and, I suspected, in his world.

He clearly had a dilemma. His self-appointed task was to brief junior new arrivals such as myself about aspects of life at court. Under this heading he included the history of the British monarchy (a bizarre account of his own making), its relevance to modern Britain (akin to his own), and how an insect such as I should hold his knife and fork (an exaggeration, but only just). This performance may have been for our benefit but it was undoubtedly also for his own, since it gave us newcomers a wonderful opportunity to marvel at his mastery of arcane and irrelevant information. However, he plainly suffered doubts as to whether we were suitable receptacles for such priceless wisdom. I fear I did little to set his mind at rest, either then or in our subsequent uneasy encounters.

"Above all," he said, leaning forward for emphasis and fixing me with a watery glare, "we don't want any *nonsenses*! Nonsenses always lead to *nausea*!" He sat back, obviously feeling that no further explanation was required. There was a pause, presumably to allow me to dwell on my capacity for nonsenses. It seemed infinite to both of us.

"Thank you," I said, already aware that hollow pleasantries would be a necessity of life in this place. Then, seeing an opportunity, I added, "I really should be getting back..."

He took this news quite well, despite the fact that he had barely warmed to his theme. He left me feeling that I was but a passing aberration on the seamless splendor of royal existence. That may have been quite true, but it did not stop me outlasting him by many years.

My next encounter was with a representative of the newer generation. Back at St. James's, I had time for a chipped mug of weak tea before the next stage of my indoctrination. I knew instinctively that I was about to learn matters of real relevance from an instructor who would closely monitor my performance, or lack of it. She would become one of the two most important women in my working life: the lady-in-waiting and assistant private secre-

tary to Her Royal Highness the Princess of Wales, Miss
Anne Beckwith-Smith.

Anne had been with the Princess from the start. In a
world built on precedent, she had created most of the procedures and conventions by which even our little office
needed to function. She set an example of dignity and common sense that belied our subordinate status. Later I discovered that she was also a lot of fun. But on day one I
recognized her as a formidable ambassador for her mistress,
unlikely to be tolerant of any backsliding on my part.

Her office was the most attractive in St. James's. For-
merly a royal dressing room (when our quarters had been a
royal residence), it retained an air of domesticity enhanced
by Anne's tasteful choice of decor. A wide bay window
looked down into Ambassador's Court, offering an ideal
vantage point from which to observe the daily traffic of the
Palace's visitors and occupants. To me it seemed like a
boudoir crossed with a throne room, an impression reinforced as I approached the desk behind which Anne
presided with a magisterial presence.

She was just one of many courtiers who had a difficult
decision to make when faced with a new recruit such as
myself: *How much do we tell him?* For the next half hour I listened attentively to Anne's introduction to the workings of
the Princess's office, and although this was accurate and informative, it left me still largely ignorant about the most important factor of all, namely what went on in the mind of
the Princess. By what Anne left out on this subject I drew a
generally accurate conclusion about Palace life—admit
nothing to anyone, especially if they are new. Let them find
out for themselves, the hard way.

In obedience to this principle Anne stuck to what I
naively thought were trivia. She explained my responsibility
to look after the ladies-in-waiting who would accompany
the Princess on all her official engagements. "You must
make sure they have their program and briefing notes at
least a week before each engagement," she told me, rather

optimistically as it turned out. "And you must help them out whenever they need helping out."

Out of what? I wondered. Cars? Elevators? In fact it was both, among many other things, including that state of Siberian ostracism to which our mistress occasionally committed all who served her closely. Anne, of course, knew that such unwelcome experiences of "helping out" would come my way soon enough. How I dealt with them would be an interesting test for me that I could be sure would be closely monitored.

Anne had been in the Wales business quite long enough to know that the marriage was now largely a sham. Thanks to tabloid coverage of separate sleeping arrangements on the recent German tour, almost anyone else could now come to the same conclusion. She knew also that this created powerful forces that could blow apart the image of normality that we existed to protect. There would be untold consequences, not least for the constitution, and never far from her thoughts was the potential effect on Princes William and Harry. Nothing was said about any of this in that first meeting.

In the Navy I had been used to living by the "need to know" principle. It was elementary security practice to restrict sensitive information just to those personnel who needed it to carry out their tasks. A rather haphazard version of this operated at the Palace. Those who knew the fractured state of the Waleses' marriage were like members of a secret society, bound by loyalty to their employers. Membership was not lightly to be granted to the new temporary equerry. For one thing, he may be out on his ear next week if he fouls up, and for another, the more people we tell, the more difficult it is to pretend that things might yet get better.

So I had to find out for myself, which I did, but only detail by painful detail over a long period of time. By then I had some sympathy for the hidebound old guard. How much more reassuring simply to lecture the new boys on regimental history and rules of the mess.

In a conscious effort to break this understandable but counterproductive culture of secrecy, I tried to be more open when it was my turn to break the bad news to new staff. Apart from courtesy, there was a more practical reason: such coyness bred an atmosphere of unreality and suspicion that did nothing for efficiency or morale.

In its more absurd forms it saw courtiers at lunch disdainful of discussing royal revelations already splashed on the morning's front pages. Sometimes I knew these revelations had been planted by royal leak; in fact, by my revered and respected boss, as when—some years later—she was notoriously photographed making a secret rendezvous with the *Daily Mail*'s court correspondent Richard Kay. Then it felt as if the world had turned upside down.

When I first realized that such things were possible, initially I felt as though I had entered a devastated landscape from which all signposts and familiar paths had been obliterated. Somewhere I knew civilization continued, the familiar routines of Palace life carried on regardless. Footmen brought tea to comfortable offices in which comfortable officials happily scanned guest lists for garden parties; in the mews contented horses were eating hay; in the Throne Room a smiling Queen received Ambassadors. Yet the whole facade of traditional royal management could be overturned by one phone call to a journalist from a young woman who happened to be married to the Prince of Wales. It made a mockery of the established order under which, if such dirty work needed doing, then a host of officials or "friends" would jump to the task. It was shocking to the royal establishment (but curiously refreshing too) that the Princess was prepared to commit such sins unblushingly and by herself.

I left Anne's office deep in thought. I was happy to leave premonitions to my more spiritually inquisitive employer, but the sense that events were not entirely under control was real enough. Nothing specific had been said, but it did not need to be. The instinctive reluctance to talk even dis-

creetly about calamitous stories blaring daily from the headlines told its own story: we would bury our heads in the
sand and hope for the best.

Much of the lunchtime euphoria had left me and I was
again conscious of the mountain I had to climb if I was
going to fit into my new world, let alone be a success in it.
My gloom deepened as I returned to the alien bustle of the
equerries' office. On my learner's desk I could see the note
I had sent to KP in the Bag that morning, promptly returned as Jo had predicted.

Despite my best efforts, the paper trembled slightly in my
fingers as I searched for the teacher's comments on my first
piece of prep. The sprawling, girlish script that I came to
know well spelled out just one word—"Perfect." There was
an exclamation mark too. I breathed again.

"Beginner's luck," said Jo's voice behind me.

I was half expecting the Princess to turn up at St. James's,
but she did not. Nor did she phone me. I was not sure
whether to be disappointed or relieved. I knew my Palace
life would not really have begun until I spoke to her in my
own right, rather than just as a jobhunter.

I went home late that night. As I passed KP I looked up
the long drive and wondered what was going on behind the
lighted windows. It looked cozy enough, but I remembered
the Princess's forced laughter and her clumsy jokes about
her in-laws. It did not take a psychologist to see there was a
great tension just below the surface.

Her popularity clearly gave her enormous power—I had
felt it very strongly when I met her. But, like a toppled
pyramid, it seemed an immense weight to rest on just her
slim shoulders. Were others helping her carry that weight?
Would I?

I already knew the answer to the second question. Even
at this early stage I felt a loyalty to the Princess. For all her

professional competence and innate nobility, there was an indefinable vulnerability about her that drew from me an unprompted wish to protect her. This developed into a complex mixture of duty and devotion that sometimes took more and sometimes less than strict professional loyalty required, but which has never entirely disappeared.

As for the first question, I already had the glimmerings of an answer to that too. My observations at lunch in Buckingham Palace had given me a clue. If I felt that I, a junior minion in a junior household, was just tolerated by the old guard, how much more was that true of my boss. If I looked up from my own small patch of red carpet, I could see my experience reflected in that of the Princess. Inside the organization of which she was a senior, popular, and accomplished partner, she was just tolerated.

Being tolerated was fine, I supposed, but I had expected a degree of supervision, if not actual direction. At times I came to feel that even a measure of *interest* would have been welcome. Raised in disciplined organizations, I was surprised to discover the extent of the autonomy given to the junior households. Some form of structured, central coordination was the Philosopher's Stone of royal strategic management and endless attempts were—and are—made to discover it. But even the sharpest sorcerer on the PR market is unlikely to work the magic for long. The base material of his potion is a thousand years of royal durability. It is hard, dull, and unyielding, not readily open to transformation. It is strong too—but its strength is not the kind you would want to cuddle up to. The best he can hope to create is media gold—a fool's delight.

Later, as events in the Waleses' marriage moved from concern to crisis, tolerance became pained aloofness in some cases and outright distaste in others. In the end, however, it was the indifference that caused such harm. Opportunities to alter the downward spiral of events were squandered. Those who could have helped preferred too often to look away or distract themselves with the accustomed routines that had proved an effective bulwark against intrusive reality in the past. I knew and understood why. The need to confront unfamiliar and painfully intimate issues was deeply unwelcome to us courtiers as a class. What I resentfully saw as indifference I eventually realized often masked a genuine concern—and an equally genuine sense of complete impotence in the face of events that constantly defied the rules of familiar experience.

Part of what drove the Princess on to endure and exploit her public duties was her wish to earn the active recognition and approval of the family into which she had married. Sometimes with bitterness, but increasingly with a resigned acceptance, she complained to me that nobody ever told her she was doing a good job.

Oh, the papers praised her to the heavens, but they could knock her down again the next day. The public adored her, but theirs—she thought—was a fickle love, lavished on her hairdo as much as on her soul. In any case, she left it behind with the slam of her car door. Her staff could try to redress the balance, but the line between true praise and toadying was always perilously fine.

It was a cruel irony that the better she did her job, the more she felt resented by some of her in-laws, unable to stomach the idea that she was a channel for emotions they struggled to feel, let alone express. Very well: if she could not please them, she would please herself. Little wonder, then, that she grew to prefer working for her own benefit and, as she saw them, the emotional needs of humanity at large. It might be selfish and it lacked intellectual discipline. It could—and did—expose her to criticism from agents of an older royal order, fearful of the public sentiment (or sentimentality, in their eyes) that she increasingly stirred up. But better that, she thought—even unconsciously—than deny her need for a recognition that accepted her *as she really was*.

The liberal, compassionate, and educated people who are the emerging face of royal authority might at this point feel entitled to a flicker of exasperation. "We did everything we could, but she was *impossible*!"

I can only reply, "Yes, you did. And yes, she was." But too many people who could have put things right did too little for too long. I will always believe it to be true: the Princess of Wales did not set out to rebel. What in the end was seen as her disaffection was what she did to compensate for a chronic feeling of rejection. Time and again, a small handful of sugar cubes would have been enough to lead this nervous thoroughbred back into the safety of the show ring. When none could be found for her, she set off into the crowd.

The organization I joined in 1988 nonetheless seemed, at least on the surface, to be united in its common aim of serving the Prince and Princess, both of whom for their part seemed equally united in keeping away from public gaze whatever private difficulties their marriage might have been experiencing. Even those well acquainted with the rumors, such as Georgina Howell, writing in the London *Sunday Times* on September 18, 1988, could still reassure themselves that "Diana [has decided] as royal women so often have . . . to make the best of a cool marriage instead of fighting it." Ominously she added, ". . . but she lacks romance. The danger is that she may find it." Given what was later disclosed to Andrew Morton about the Princess's love life at the time, this understatement is touching in its innocence. Captain Hewitt had already been on the scene for some time, carrying his own supply of romantic sugar cubes—and self-denial was never her strong point.

That first night, as I inched past the gates of KP in the London traffic, such thoughts were the merest inkling, easily pushed to the back of my mind. In the years that followed, however, they grew from idle speculation to grim reality.

Had I known it, the signs were all there from the beginning.

3

Under the Thumb

*T*he Princess's footsteps sounded hurried. I had been listening to them for about five minutes now, standing in the semigloom of the KP hallway. Upstairs, she was preparing for a day of engagements out of London—what we called an "awayday." Her high heels struck a distinctive note as she marched back and forth from her bedroom to the sitting room with, it seemed, several rapid diversions en route. To my nervous ears she was beginning to sound impatient. There was something increasingly agitated about her pacing.

Suddenly I heard a phone ring and there were a few minutes of silence, broken only by the low murmur of her voice. Then the footsteps started again, back to the bedroom, only this time more urgently, as I imagined her checking the time remaining before we were due to leave. She was fanatically punctual.

It was my first "real" day at work—the first day on which I was going out with the Princess. This was my chance to begin to see the world through her eyes, to experience what it was like to be royal, only slightly secondhand.

In a pattern that was repeated a thousand times over the next seven years, I waited in the darkness at the foot of the stairs and listened to her flitting from room to room on the floor above; trying to guess what mood she was in and what sort of day lay ahead of us. The phone call could have been from anybody. The tone of her voice was neutral and I could not catch the words. I hoped whoever it was would not keep her talking—I had already learned enough to know she would be irritated if we started late. Best of all, whoever it was might make her laugh and send us smiling all the way to the helicopter.

A door opened and closed. At the top of the stairs she paused, straightening her skirt. Her blue Catherine Walker suit and executive blow-dry told you that here was a woman who was ready to take a grip on the day. The phone call must have been OK, because she cantered down the stairs, spotted the new boy, and smiled, holding out her hand to me. It was to be seven years and a million royal hand-shakes later before we shook hands again. Then it was to say goodbye.

"Hello again, Patrick. We didn't scare you off then!"

I bowed and mumbled something.

"This is a crazy place to work," she continued, heading rapidly for the front door, "but on this team we all started as outsiders, so we know how strange it feels to begin with."

The lady-in-waiting and I followed her outside. After the darkness of the house the sun seemed dazzling. A car took us the short distance to Perk's Field—a green offshoot of Hyde Park—where a shiny red helicopter was waiting. "Yuck!" said the Princess through smiling teeth. "The flying tumble dryer. I just hope it won't be bumpy. I *hate* bumps." Later I came to hate bumps too; not because they made me airsick, but because bumps, like rain or hail or the temperature of her tea, could quickly become the excuse for a mood. Moods were what we all dreaded.

As we clattered eastward over London's rooftops, the Princess ignored the view and concentrated on her copy of

Vogue. The Queen's Flight always kept a well-stocked magazine rack. After *Vogue* she might reach for a tabloid newspaper—usually the *Daily Mail*—and furrow her brow over Nigel Dempster's column. Often there was a royal story. That was a good way of starting a mood too.

Luckily it was noisy on our thirty-minute flight, so there was no need to try to talk. On the occasions when I really *had* to communicate, shouting into her ear at close range made me paranoid about my breath. She had the same fear and regularly squirted Gold Spot into her famously perfect mouth.

Five minutes before landing the crewman signaled that we were nearly there. The Princess began rapid, expert work with the compact and lip gloss. With something of a shock, I realized the perfect complexion was not completely perfect close up. When I discovered her fluctuating intake of chocolate and sweets I could understand why—and sympathize too, as I contemplated the visible effects of a courtier's diet on my own appearance.

A generous blast of hair spray always followed. Months later, when she was sharing the helicopter with her husband, she made (almost) all of us laugh by theatrically overdoing this emission of ozone-hostile gases.

As our destination—an Essex seaside town—hove into sight, she pulled out her briefing notes and gave them a cursory final glance. She was pretty good at her homework and usually crammed up the main points of the program before she left the Palace. If her staff had done their planning properly, the day would run pretty much automatically. If she did not feel inspired to do more, all she really had to do was smile, shake hands, and drop the occasional well-worn royal platitude. Except, of course, she usually was inspired to do more. Once on duty she hardly ever coasted. She took a professional pride in giving her public full value, which was one reason why they were ready to wait in vast numbers in any weather for even a fleeting glimpse of her.

As the helicopter's rotor blades wound slowly to a stop,

she undid her seat belt and stooped by the door, waiting for it to be slid open, poised like an athlete before the starting gun. She gave a final tug to her jacket, smoothed her skirt, and caught my eye. "Another episode in the everyday story of royal folk!" she laughed, putting the newcomer at ease. (The sensation lasted for about two seconds.) Look, she was saying, I'm human, friendly, approachable. You're really lucky to be working for me...

As I watched her step nimbly out of the helicopter into the excited noise and good-natured bustle of a busy day of good works, I had no trouble agreeing. Disenchantment—hers and mine—came only slowly. That day, the picture was brand-new, glossy, and colorful. As she visited a factory, a hospital, and an old folks' home I saw the royal celebrity at work: professional to her fingertips but still a flirt; ready to laugh with those who laughed—and ready to *make* them laugh when nerves got the better of them; ready to comfort those who were weeping.

Halfway through the day we stopped for lunch. Lunches on an engagement were usually planned as buffets so that she could circulate among as many guests as possible. But circulating and eating do not mix—you risk spraying sausage roll over people when you speak—so the Princess would "retire" to a private room for a toilet break and a quick bite before joining the throng.

These short breaks were a great relaxation for her in the middle of a tiring day. "Have a drink, boys!" she would say to me and the policeman if a bottle of wine had been left for us. She would usually restrict herself to fizzy water and nibble a sandwich, but if she was tense she might do real justice to the caterer's pride and joy and eat forkfuls of salad and cold meat followed by pudding—or sometimes the other way round.

Without warning, she could be ravenous for sweet things. The wise lady-in-waiting carried gumdrops in her handbag and the chauffeur kept a stock of emergency chocolate in the car. I frequently watched her eat a whole bar of fruit-and-nut between engagements. Suddenly aware of her behavior, she would insist on everyone else eating sweets too. No wonder I spent much of the time feeling queasy.

It was not until later that I recognized these minibinges as comfort eating, vain attempts to console herself for her emotional hunger. The roots undoubtedly lay in childhood unhappiness. The broken home of her early years has been well documented and she spoke to me often of tensions with her father. "Once when he took me to school," she said, "I stood on the steps and screamed, 'If you leave me here you don't love me!'"

I did not probe into the Princess's childhood, but in a way I had no need to. Photographs of the teenage Diana Spencer show her at a glance to be knowing, dull-eyed, and self-conscious. Throughout my time with the Princess there were occasional signs of the scars of earlier traumas: insecurity in her attractiveness, a passionate need for unconditional love, an obsession with establishing emotional control, and a sabotaging approach to relationships. The distrust of men and the chronically poor image she had of herself told their own story.

The Princess was bulimic for most of the time I knew her. Despite a continuous battle with the condition, which she was popularly supposed to have won, she often suffered recurrent attacks. These were most frequent when the strains in her marriage were simultaneously driving her to comfort eating while fueling her innate self-doubt.

Once—on a hungry day—she took a big bite at a prawn sandwich. A solitary prawn escaped and fell with deadly accuracy down her front, disappearing into her cleavage. She squeaked with surprise and looked inside her jacket. I waited for the prawn to reappear, but it failed to do so.

"Bloody thing's stuck!" she said through a mouthful of sandwich.

"Poor prawn," I said lamely.

"Bloody lucky prawn!" she corrected me, turning away to deal with the intruder. I took the hint. Modesty was for her to indulge in when she wanted to. It was not for me to question her absolute desirability, even in fun, even by a syllable.

Perhaps surprisingly, there was never a ban on food jokes. Maybe it was her way of dealing with the potential embarrassment of the whole subject. I was later struck by the courage—or foolhardiness—of her self-mocking reference to constantly "sticking my head down the loo."

Later that day we flew back to London. As the helicopter lifted from the town park, so the tensions of the day lifted from her shoulders. It was instant party time. Now came the jokes and the gossip. Nobody cared about shouting. My newcomer's ears struggled to believe what they heard. Was this the same Princess who an hour ago had been the saintly hospital visitor?

"What d'you get if you cross a nun with an apple?" she yelled above the engine noise.

"I don't know, Ma'am. What *do* you get if you cross a nun with an apple?" I replied, looking dumbly at the lady-in-waiting to see if this was normal behavior. Her determined smile indicated that it was.

"A computer that won't go down on you!" shrieked the Princess, doubling up with mirth.

Even as I obediently joined in the laughter, I noted the sadness behind my new boss's taste in humor. She would not know how to switch a computer on, let alone use it for long enough to see it crash; and as for the oral sex...as a joke, it was reassuringly remote. The daring and crudity gave her the necessary thrill. Even if she did not fully understand what she was saying, she knew it would shock and that was what she wanted. It was the safest of safe sex.

The theme of sex was a standard feature of her joke repertoire. She seemed immune to the embarrassment it might cause others. Careful never to exceed the bounds of good taste while in the public eye, her reticence was thrown to the winds as soon as she felt she was in relatively safe surroundings. Even then her judgment was erratic. Many times I cringed as her crude jokes and braying laughter scandalized the delicate ears of outsiders such as Queen's

Flight crews, diplomats, and charity officials. The desire to shock outweighed any possible pleasure she might have gained from the humor of what she said.

The same desire was apparent in her infantile mockery of other members of the royal family—though only behind their backs. Thus her husband was referred to as "the Boy Wonder" or "the Great White Hope," while her father-in-law was labeled "Stavros" and her in-laws generally as "the Germans."

All this I could laugh off, however uneasily, as her way of coping with stress. However, the looks of worried disbelief on strangers' faces—and those of junior staff too, worst of all—made me realize that other people's feelings were less important to her than her desire for gratification.

By the time we were back at the Palace front door the Princess was cool and controlled again. We stood awkwardly, waiting to be dismissed. Each in turn, she held our eyes and inclined her head. We bowed.

This, I learned, was when she looked back over the day and judged our loyalty. If she failed to make eye contact— "blanked" you, in the jargon—you had been weighed in the balance and found wanting. Suddenly the jokes in the helicopter seemed a long time ago. I tried to guess if I had laughed enough.

"Thank you all very much," she said, her voice now carefully neutral. But I got the message. Yes, I can be fun, but I can also choose to be an imperious madame—and now I own you.

She disappeared back up the stairs. In the silence I heard her footsteps once again, heading toward her bedroom. The door slammed. Slowly I let out my breath. This job was going to be interesting.

I drove home slowly, my mind filled with images of the day. Most vivid, of course, were those of the Princess. I had to admit, I was surprised. From that first lunch and, I suppose, from the gossipy things I had read about her, I had expected a well-meaning but essentially shallow person, perhaps in need of my manly support and worldly wisdom—a sort of royal Super Sloane Ranger. Instead, what I had seen was a polished and confident performance from a professional celebrity. Every gesture, every glance, and every word—at least in public—had been consciously planned. Sometimes the planning had taken only a split second, but that simply showed how quickly she thought and how sharp were her public-pleasing instincts.

There was no doubt about it. Behind the good looks and the expensive grooming there was much more than the bimbo caricature to which her critics—even then—would have liked to limit her. That first day I saw, from her effect on the people she met, that she had a powerful, even hypnotic, charisma. Later I learned that it had the ability to conceal many flaws, or at least compensate for them.

Of all the day's new impressions, it was perhaps the Princess's fondness for crude humor that sat least comfortably with the public image that until now had been my only guide to her personality. When she was relaxed, the Princess's vocabulary and verbal mannerisms were pure Sloane. Consonants were an optional extra, so words often emerged in a lazy drawl. This suited the subject matter, which in private was not always very elevated. The cruder the humor, the more her verbal discipline deserted her, as if it shared our wish suddenly to be far away, preferably with someone not expected to ascend the throne.

When she was serious, however, she commanded phrases and delivery that could make her a witty and clever conversationalist. Her speaking style was that of the verbal sprinter not the marathon runner. I doubt if anybody ever suffered a Princess of Wales monologue, but many will remember—most with pleasure—being on the receiving end of one of her quicksilver one-liners.

These deserve special mention because they played a key

part in shaping the impression she left. On public occasions, amplified by the hushed, deferential expectation that is the royal visitor's usual reception, her spontaneity cut through the self-conscious small talk that thrives on British social nervousness. She reacted instinctively against pomposity—and just think how much of that she had to endure. Her favored weapon was the verbal pinprick that released the speaker and the audience from the tension that paralyzes truthful communication.

She might sit with an audience of drug addicts (or mental patients or battered wives) listening to a turgid briefing on their problems from an overly earnest therapist before leaning forward with a smile and perfect timing to whisper loudly, "Does he always go on like this?" In the laughter that she knew would follow, pent-up emotion was suddenly released and contact made between Princess and pariah. As an added test—or entertainment—the turgid speaker could pretend to laugh too.

This technique, honed in a hundred hospitals, drop-in centers, outreach projects, and community facilities, gave her public that feeling of intimate knowledge that is the secret ingredient of devotion. Also, like all really effective spontaneity, it knew its own boundaries. Even her wittiest remark contained a nugget of sympathy, understanding, or concern. She may have been short of O levels, but she never made a public faux pas, never mocked disability or disfiguration.

Except in the car going home, of course. Then the stress of so much emotional giving could be relieved with some pretty unedifying outbursts. By then, however, she had done her duty, left hope with the hopeless and smiles on stricken faces. We told her so, since nobody else was going to, swallowing our scruples to join in the desperate humor that she often called on in place of joy.

It was a very different world from the one I was used to. I was already beginning to learn that early impressions—whether of my new boss or my new surroundings—must never be taken at face value. I also knew that I was not there as a reward. I was there to work. Thus I quickly began to comprehend that being in royal service might provide a rather luxurious working environment, but only at my peril would I ever feel in any way entitled to it. The order of things had been made clear in the Princess's glance as we waited to be dismissed at the end of the day: she owned us, not the other way around.

In the years that followed there were times when the grandeur and privilege of my surroundings seemed to mock my efforts at running the newest royal household. I realized, though, that it was a healthy sign sometimes to be at odds with those surroundings. In fact, I came to view with suspicion anyone who seemed to take to them too easily. I already had an idea that our royal employers could be jealous of their inheritance and suffered our intrusion only as long as we were useful—or amusing. I resolved to be both to the Princess of Wales, given the chance.

During that first day out with her, I had been surprised by her conflicting displays of compassion and indifference. I had been shocked by her crude humor when out of the public eye, some of it at the expense of those she was visiting, but I had also recognized its value as a safety valve for the stresses of spending so much time being sympathetic to those in desperate suffering or need. Even so, it would have been hard to serve someone who was so ready to find humor in such tragic situations. Luckily for my own peace of mind, I quickly learned that much of the Princess's compassion was very definitely the genuine article.

As I watched her at a dying child's bedside, holding the girl's newly cold hand and comforting the stricken parents, she seemed to share their grief. Not self-consciously like a stranger, not distantly like a counselor, not even through any special experience or deep insight. Instead it just seemed that a tranquillity gathered around her. Into this stillness the weeping mother and heartbroken father poured their sorrow and there, somehow, it was safe. The young woman with the smart suit and soulful eyes had no answers for them, but they felt that somewhere inside she knew at least a part of what they were feeling. That was all the moment needed.

The Princess did have some experience of what they were feeling, and she usually managed to let it appear rather more, but the suffering she felt had none of the merciful clarity of bereavement. As I slowly discovered, it was dark and complex and grew from years of stunted emotional growth. The compassion she showed others was not drawn from some deep supply within her. Rather, it was a reflection of the attention she herself craved. Once we had returned her to the lonely privacy of her palace, I sensed she had little left over for herself.

Instead, she increasingly settled for the illusion of compassion. Reading about herself as "the caring Princess," she felt a soothing glow of achievement, but the reality was that her compassion came to be reserved largely for the cameras. It was not exclusively so, because along with a cynical use of her saintly reputation there was an erratic but genuine kindness. Even this struggled to remain anonymous, however. The surprised recipients of flowers or sympathetic messages after some well-publicized tragedy might justifiably have suspected that their good fortune—artlessly shared with a local newspaper—just added to the overall illusion.

As for the cumulative, corrosive effect of this on her own sense of self-worth, I was to discover that it could be severe. Even at the outset I could see that receiving credit for virtues she did not possess could not satisfy the hunger for recognition that burned within the Princess of Wales.

Gradually I slipped into my new routine, wearing the same few suits, parking under the same tree in the Mall, giving the same cheery greeting to Gladys the St. James's housekeeper, and offering up the same daily prayer for continued survival. Richard took his beer mat to his new office, the Princess began to ask for me instead of him, and I began to look forward to opening the return Bag with something less than panic.

After my first day out with her, my urgent priority was to gain confidence in planning the Princess's public appearances. An early milestone came with my first solo reconnaissance. The engagement was to be quite a routine London affair—the official opening of an office and resource center for a small children's charity, followed by a reception to meet the usual mixture of fund-raisers, charity workers, and local officials.

In later years the reconnaissance, or recce, might have taken me three-quarters of an hour—fifteen minutes for the recce and thirty minutes to chat up and generally get the measure of the hosts. As the rawest apprentice, however, I must have spent nearly two hours pacing out every inch of the route, nominating press positions, and marking places for individual presentations.

Then I changed everything and started again. I failed to get the measure of the hosts as well, but I think it can be safely concluded that they were very patient people.

From this I learned the importance of not hesitating to change my mind if I thought it necessary. However tempting it was to cultivate an air of infallibility, complacency was a risky companion when planning a royal visit and often led me into embarrassing U-turns. Such was my spurious authority—and their customary good manners—that few hosts objected and some, I think, even enjoyed the chance to prolong the royal experience. Generally, though, changing my mind—like confessing to my mistakes—was a pleasure to be indulged in sparingly.

Again and again I felt my lack of experience, but surprisingly quickly the time I spent on recces began to shrink. Even fifteen minutes eventually became too much for some engagements. By then I *knew* what would work and what would not. The extra time was needed only to reassure myself that my distilled experience as passed on to the hosts would be treated like the politely phrased commandments I felt them to be.

I knew, for example, that the Princess refused to be rushed when meeting people. If time was limited the only option was to reduce the number of people she met—not, as some hosts seemed determined to try, merely to persuade her to hurry up. Nothing was more calculated to make her slow down even more.

I had seen that she liked to be punctual and well briefed, preferably in humorous, bite-sized chunks. "YRH will remember Mr. X. Last time you visited he forgot to bow; he curtsied instead!"

She also liked plenty of elbow room when she was in the public eye. Apart from a protection officer, she preferred the gaggle of officials and dignitaries who inevitably accompanied her to keep well out of her way. I sometimes thought the equerry and lady-in-waiting were mainly there to conduct a type of genteel crowd control. With sharp elbows and distracting small talk, we became expert in buying our boss the uncrowded stage she needed to perform at her best.

I knew where the arrival lineup should be positioned, where the girl with the posy should stand, where the ribbon should be cut, and where the press pen should be sited. The Princess liked short line-ups, preferably with spouses excluded. The girl with the posy should be at the end of the line, well positioned for the cameras because there was always a moment of amused miscommunication—small fingers reluctant to let go at the crucial moment—as the flowers were handed over. If not, she would laughingly contrive it. The flowers should be in neutral colors, in theory to avoid clashing with the royal outfit, and unwired.

She liked the ribbon (or the plaque or the sapling or the pharmaceutical research laboratory) to provide a backdrop that identified the cause being supported and, ideally, someone very young or very old on hand to "assist" photogenically with the cutting, unveiling, or digging. She preferred the press to be well penned, unobtrusively positioned, and silent but for the whirr of their motor drives. Muffled yelps of delight were permitted and not infrequent, but groans and calls of "Just one more!" usually met the same contrary response as requests to hurry up.

She did not like the press party—unkindly termed the "rat pack"—to get too close. Cameras, flash guns, and the dreaded boom microphone could all ruin the carefully arranged spontaneity that we tried to make her trademark. But nor did she like the pack too far away. She traded skillfully on the knowledge that they needed her just as much as she needed them, so she theatrically "endured" their presence and could be sharp with her staff if any cameraman got too far out of line. All the players in this game knew it was a mutually advantageous conspiracy, however, and played by the rules accordingly. She gave them the shots both they and she needed, and they responded with enduring devotion.

I learned the crucial importance of seeing all planning decisions through royal rather than mortal eyes. In my ignorance I had imagined that, as with some naval chores, royalty regarded public duties as just that: duties that had to be performed as a matter of necessity, to be enjoyed if possible, to be endured if not, and all to be accomplished with a noble appreciation of the greater good being served—or at least with the satisfaction of a job well done. Now it slowly dawned on me that the process was more complex and allowed the intrusion of other personal considerations. While some might see only the outward appearance of royal concern—in, say, a children's hospice—the equerry has to allow for the emotional toll exacted by ninety minutes' close involvement in a dozen harrowing accounts of family distress.

The engagements that required the greatest display of outward compassion (hospices were a case in point) were often those that drew deepest on the Princess's reserves of inner goodwill and determination. I came to understand

that, while showing sympathy with those in distress sometimes rewarded her with a virtuous glow, it also emphasized
the loneliness with which her personal unhappiness had to
be faced.

Surprisingly often, even the most efficient and well-run
organization seemed unable to understand the simple practicalities of designing a visit program. Often it was the humblest charity that had the clearest idea of how long could be
spent talking to a certain number of patients and how welcome would be the obligatory shaking of influential but
otherwise ungripping hands.

Watching it wrestle with such small considerations frequently seemed a measure of how well a management knew
its own people. I quickly learned that the priority was not
just to allocate the required number of minutes to a particular event. Frequently it was more important to practice
ego-management, as a touchy official or departmental head
hotly insisted on more time as if it were a measure of his
importance or even—in extreme cases—his virility. Always
to be pitied were those who would bear disappointing news
home to their wives about the limit on lineup numbers, to
the equal dismay of local hat sellers.

Best of all were the organizations that simply explained
what they hoped would happen during their royal visit and
then left the rest to us, the assumed experts. Less welcome
were those that had considered every detail and were then
unwilling, understandably, to accommodate changes made
for reasons that I could not tell them, such as the fact that
the Princess would probably prefer to climb straight on the
plane home rather than sit next to an old bore like you during lunch. Least welcome were those who introduced their
plan with the words, "Now, you won't have to help *us* with
any of this. We know the ropes. We had the Duchess of
Blank here in 1971 and it was a *huge* success..."

A lexicon of soothing phrases, excuses, and explanations
quickly became part of my visit-planning tool kit as ministers, matrons, and monks were lulled into complying with a

program whose constraints they might often have found eccentric, trivial, or even offensive. Over time, however, the necessary mannerisms of speech accumulated into an oleaginous patina that proved hard to shake off when talking to people outside my narrow field of work. Thus can courtly talk slip into insincerity.

The final step in the planning process was to walk the course. An obvious precaution, you might think, but with surprising regularity it was possible to encounter host organizations that had overlooked elementary considerations such as the time actually spent walking from one part of a building to another.

To be fair, this was partly because their minds were quite properly concentrated on the people at the expense of less exciting aspects such as timing or camera angles. Also, until you had experienced it, it was difficult to estimate accurately just how quickly a twenty-six-year-old Princess with the ground-covering abilities of a mustang could move between the car and the briefing room, the lab and the packing center, the dayroom and the chapel, the royal box and the sidelines, the presidential jet and the guard of honor, and so on. It did sometimes seem, however, that concerned hosts were expecting a visitor with the frailty of the Queen Mother rather than a young woman whose athleticism was becoming legendary.

4

⚛

Double Up

*O*nce I had achieved a shaky confidence in organizing the Princess's UK engagements, I could look forward to the challenge of planning her overseas visits. I remembered pictures I had seen of the Princess looking cool and compassionate in a dozen exotic foreign locations. This, I thought, would be where my new job started to become a bit more glamorous. The reality, of course, was that it took a lot of very unglamorous hard work to reach the media-friendly results that she—and her public—expected.

I have always taken undue pleasure even from aimless travel, and to be offered transport and accommodation on such a royal scale *and* be paid to indulge my puerile desire seemed the best part of the job description. During my early days at St. James's I heard an endless travelogue of tour stories, some of dizzying tallness. As I was to learn, even in exaggerated form these tales struggled to convey the reality of transporting our royal circus to foreign countries. Not to be outdone, over the years I developed my own improbable repertoire of traveler's yarns from which, if nothing else, my audiences learned that the overseas tour encapsulated in concentrated form all the best and worst aspects of life with the Waleses.

Tours were a big challenge for our royal employers too. The task of representing the country overseas as a kind of superambassador makes great demands on their reserves of diplomacy, tact, confidence, and patience—not to mention the royal sense of humor, digestion, and general physical and mental constitution. There are therefore big demands for both external comforts and internal strength. These must somehow be supplied from the foreign surroundings in which duty has deposited the royal traveler and from internal resources, reinforced by years of heredity and training. However gilded the cage, though, no guest palace provides the familiar, reassuring touches of home.

To help achieve the external comforts, the Waleses usually traveled with a surprisingly large entourage. On one of my first tours the party totaled twenty-six. As well as more senior officials such as private secretaries and press secretaries, the cast included a doctor, four policemen, three secretaries, a butler, a valet, an assistant valet, a dresser, an assistant dresser, two chefs, and a hairdresser.

Not surprisingly, we also needed a baggage master to look after the small mountain of luggage. In order to achieve the desired result of making the Prince and Princess feel that their temporary accommodation was a real "home from home," an extraordinary amount of personal gear had to be carried with us. Everything from music equipment to favorite organic foods had their special containers—and came high on the list of priorities.

In-flight meals were seldom straightforward either. In later years when traveling on solo tours, the Princess was happy enough to choose from standard airline menus. This also applied to journeys with the Queen's Flight, who usually found reliable airline caterers whatever the exotic destination. Before the separation, however, the Princess took a leaf out of her husband's rather more fastidious book, and while their accompanying staff demolished the output of the British Airways first-class flight kitchen, our employers would pick at homegrown organic concoctions in Tupperware boxes like pensioners on an outing. They were a lot slimmer and fitter than most of us, of course, but it still looked like a pretty joyless experience.

Meanwhile, host government officials, Embassy staff, and senior members of the Wales household (the collective term for private secretaries and other top management) labored to produce a program befitting the stature of the visitors. The planes, boats, trains, and cars—as well as the cameras, crowds, guards of honor, and banquets—combined to create the overall theatrical effect without which no royal visit can be really royal. Adjusted for scale, the same principles apply equally to a visit to a crèche as much as to a continent. Add the scrutiny of the press and the unpredictability of foreign hosts' resources, and it is little wonder that touring is seen as one of the greatest tests royal service can provide. Little wonder either that it demands the full set of royal stage props to achieve its full effect.

Every month or so a list of forthcoming engagements was circulated in the office. For many excellent reasons it was treated as a confidential document, though whether to thwart terrorists or merely to baffle the Queen's Flight was never fully explained. Its colloquial name was *Mole News*, since it was assumed that its list of dates and places would form the leaker's basic fare. By the time of my arrival, however, the leaking was beginning to emanate from more exalted sources such as royal "friends" and other thinly disguised mouthpieces for the Prince and Princess themselves. Eventually *Mole News* practically lost its original innocent purpose as a simple planning aid and became instead just another piece on the board game of misinformation in the intelligence war between them. As they drew up their calendars with more and more of an eye to the media impact of their activities, information on each other's future movements became vital in the popularity contest that they were both beginning to wage.

Soon after my arrival I had scanned this program eagerly, looking for my first chance of an overseas trip. Disappointingly it seemed that I would have to wait almost a year before I could join the veterans whose briefcases sported the tour labels that I so coveted. I was scheduled to accompany Their Royal Highnesses on a tour of the Gulf States in March 1989. At least, I thought, it was a part of the world I knew slightly and liked a lot. Also it would be hot and I would at last have an excuse to wear that expensive tropical uniform—the preferred choice of most officers who had seen *Top Gun*.

In *Mole News* joint engagements were indicated with an asterisk. What had not yet been widely noticed, however, was that asterisks were becoming a rarity. In fact, by the late eighties joint appearances at home were already mostly confined to set-piece events such as the Queen's Birthday Parade, the Garter Ceremony, Ascot, and the staff Christmas lunch. The same trend of disappearing asterisks was visible in the overseas program. Solo expeditions had always been a feature of royal overseas work, but the Waleses were noticeably beginning to make more and more of their overseas trips alone. This was bad for publicity—it just fueled rumors about the state of the marriage—but for staff in the firing line it was also a bit of a relief. The *coup de grâce* was finally administered to joint tours by the Korea trip of November 1992, but the signs of a terminal divergence of interest were already perceptible in January 1989 when I joined the Gulf recce party at Heathrow.

Just as joint engagements gave the Prince and Princess the chance to work together (however reluctantly), so they drew their respective staffs into cautious cooperation. When they were in good form, we saw our employers put on a double act that carried the world before it. For our part, we enjoyed the opportunity to put aside the growing estrangements of the office and reclassify our differences as merely interesting variations of technique.

The Prince's team provided the lead. Under the direction of the private secretary or his deputy, His Royal Highness's press secretary and senior personal protection officer (PPO) were joined by either his own or his wife's equerry, depending on whose turn it was to swap the pressures of the St. James's office for the pressures of its temporary foreign equivalent. On the tour itself this would mean that I would primarily be in attendance on the Prince, particularly if any of the engagements called for military uniform to be worn. The Princess would take a lady-in-waiting and forgo the services of her equerry unless he could negotiate his absence from the Prince's entourage, a loss which His Royal Highness bore with increasing fortitude as time passed.

The gloss on my picture of royal tours soon began to look pretty patchy. I would be junior boy on the recce team—the private secretary's scribe, memory, and general bag-carrier. On the tour I would also be responsible for transport, accommodation, the traveling office, and a million undefined administrative details. The horrifying truth slowly dawned that I would take the rap for the great majority of potential blunders, and so it proved.

I found myself treading on eggshells even before I had left the UK. Taking leave of the Princess was never easy, even when going abroad "on duty" as I would be for this recce. Arrivals and departures were important to her. They were landmarks in an otherwise monotonous landscape of public and private routine. They presented opportunities for her to make a point. The simple exchanges involved often gained an extra theatrical value as she expressed delight with a greeting or wistful regret at a parting. Her natural ability to influence moods was at its strongest when first and last impressions could be created. This was a characteristic ideally suited to the life of transitory encounters that she led in public.

Also, I found that I missed her. This was partly sentiment—employed to serve and, metaphorically, to defend her, I sometimes felt a vague sense of negligence if separated from her for long. As I grew less impressionable, this was supplemented by a healthy suspicion of what she might be doing or saying in my absence.

In her moments of greatest doubt, any absence for any reason could be exploited to support a passing prejudice. Thus going away on holiday could provoke an envy bordering on resentment, apparently impervious to her own frequent absences on ski slopes or beaches. She paid lip service to the need for staff "R and R," but seldom missed a chance to make you feel just a little bit guilty for taking it. Going away on recces was scarcely less suspect. Even when I knew I was heading for a tough recce far from home in an inhospitable land, she somehow managed to make me feel like a truant, if not an actual deserter.

She would look up wearily from a desk that had suddenly become conspicuously crowded and give me a well-practiced, reproachful look. "It doesn't seem fair on you"—by which she meant her—"to be sending you away. We're *so busy* at the moment." (We were always "*so busy*.")

"Well, Ma'am, you know I can't get out of it—I'm duty for this tour. And everything's up to date here..." She looked meaningfully at the papers on her desk. "...and I won't be away for long. I'll phone."

"That would be nice."

"And take pictures. Then you can see what I'm letting you in for!"

"Hmm."

That was obviously an idea too far. I had failed to lighten the atmosphere and it took the application of several airline gin and tonics to ease the feeling that I was abandoning her.

That feeling never entirely left me and, if anything, it got worse as the years passed and her position in the hierarchy began to be threatened. She once memorably had me paged at Heathrow as I was about to leave for a decidedly non-recreational recce of Japan. Expecting some nameless catastrophe, I took her call with a heavy heart. She knew exactly where I was and that I was about to miss my plane, yet she spent ten minutes cross-examining me on a minor engagement diary item months in the future. Of course I had none of the paperwork with me and my memory refused to come to my rescue in the crisis. From her voice, the Princess's loneliness was transparently obvious, even when expressed in the reassuringly familiar format of chiding her scatterbrained private secretary. A call that began with contrived recrimination ended with genuine good wishes for my success and a quick return. No wonder I felt a heel.

Especially when feeling beleaguered—not uncommon—she would sometimes wonder aloud whether a protection officer could not achieve just as much as the private secretary now shuffling in front of her, visibly champing for his club-class dinner. In some households it was true that an experienced PPO could more than adequately organize security, logistics, and even domestic arrangements, but the requirements of the Waleses and their entourage demanded attention to a range and depth of subjects that were beyond the reasonable capacities of any single person.

Local British Embassies could also not be expected to shoulder more than the already considerable extra workload our visits entailed. A sensible rule was therefore followed by all with responsibility for royal programs: "Never recce anything you're not going to visit, but never visit anything you haven't recced." There was nothing more unsettling than arriving blind at an unknown destination for a high-profile engagement.

The other golden rule—"Avoid surprises"—was one you broke at your peril. Whatever the hardships (or compensations), everything that could be recced was recced, regardless of raised eyebrows from envious officebound colleagues or royal employers suspecting a shirker. The office folklore of recce excesses provided rich pickings for anyone wishing to believe that these foreign planning trips were not all work and no play. In due course I could add to them myself, albeit discreetly.

It was perfectly true that recceing gave you the chance to experience many royal delights twice over—and without the attentions of the press pack. Had I not flown all over the bush in Zimbabwe in search of the right refugee camp? Or lunched alone with six Indonesian princesses anxious to practice their royal conversational skills? Or even risen at dawn to see the sunrise from a frontier fort in the Khyber Pass? Too much of this kind of reminiscence could produce jaundice in the most tolerant listener, and the Princess seldom fell into that category except when on duty. I sometimes unfairly felt that there was nothing like another's good fortune to cloud her sunny outlook. Nor was there anything more guaranteed to stir up royal displeasure than the thought that those traveling on their coattails were enjoying the ride.

So if the Princess asked, apparently kindly, if your room in the guest palace was comfortable, it was wise not to make too much of its huge TV set, bottomless minibar, or big fluffy towels. She was not really that interested, except to find reasons for feeling resentful or exploited.

It could have gone either way, therefore, but when I said goodbye to her on the eve of my departure for the Kuwait recce she was touchingly solicitous, concerned for the hard work I faced, and anxious to let me know that I would be missed. This reflected her good nature. It also reflected her tendency to see duty on her husband's behalf—which this would largely be—as an unenviable hardship. I later concluded that it was also evidence of her foresight in realizing that this was not going to be one of those recces that anyone would sensibly envy.

*T*wenty-four hours later I lay in the darkness and shivered. I had not expected to feel cold in the Persian Gulf and this dusty chill had a penetrating quality. I was dog-tired, but sleep was impossible. The Embassy residence was quite small and, as a junior visitor, I had been given a room that could have been used in the fight against government cuts as convincing proof that there was no featherbedding in this corner of the Diplomatic Service. I soon started rummaging in my suitcase for extra clothes that I had not packed.

My thoughts turned enviously to my companions who, because of the lack of official accommodation, had been exiled to the nearest five-star American hotel.

The shivering was not just caused by the cold. The Ambassador's anecdotes, though intended to amuse and inform, had also contained warnings about the pitfalls awaiting us in the protocol departments of our later destinations in Bahrain, Abu Dhabi, Dubai, and Saudi Arabia.

I felt oppressed by our responsibilities, especially my own. I was scared stiff, in fact. I have never needed much excuse to indulge in a good bout of worrying and it often has the beneficial side effect of displacing my habitual lethargy. This time, however, I realized I had better reason than usual to feel apprehensive. A tour could be judged as successful against a host of different criteria—there were as many opinions as there were observers and any credit could therefore be widely distributed. No such latitude applied to the unsuccessful tour. I knew that if the verdict on our Gulf expedition was unfavorable, in the scramble to avoid the ensuing derision I would be at a disadvantage. Royal displeasure is an unstable pyrotechnic, but I had already observed that it favored soft targets—and I was pretty sure that they came no softer than the apprentice equerry.

Even more worrying was the discovery that this regal wrath could be directed almost at will by those whose domestic responsibilities kept them closest to the royal person at its less royal moments. It may be true that no man is a hero to his valet, but it was a law of Palace survival that only a hero (and a foolhardy one at that) would disoblige a royal valet and expect to escape the inevitable explosion. I now had almost unlimited power to disoblige valets and their ilk. One poisoned word from them would drop me deep in the mire. Two poisoned words, and I might as well run away to sea, assuming the Navy would have me back.

The reason we gave to skeptical hosts when they politely queried our extensive and precise domestic requirements was that to give of their best our employers had to feel that a little piece of KP was awaiting them at the end of an arduous day's hot and dusty engagements. In this need for domestic predictability they perhaps echoed the travel-weary businessman's preference for hotels whose location in the world is easily guessed from the name given to the bar, or the bartender.

Both being rather exacting in their personal requirements, the Prince and Princess induced an understandable nervousness in the valet and dresser, who would bear the brunt of any shortcomings. They in turn developed powers of critical invective that would be the envy of Michelin inspectors. Their judgment in such matters was absolute and would be shared sooner or later by the Prince and Princess. It was thus the equerry's overriding task on the recce to ensure that they never had cause to exercise their awesome power to turn cold toast (or a sticking window, or a hard mattress) into a tour-wrecking catastrophe.

As I dozed fitfully on my own lumpy Embassy mattress, I scared myself into a cold sweat with visions of royal domestic disaster. Missing baggage, inadequate transport, unpopular room allocations, unacceptable food...the list was endless. It was so unfair. Luck seemed to play such a huge part in deciding my success or failure. Every time—as the dream descended into nightmare—the vision ended with a posse of iron-wielding valets pursuing me, mouthing damning judgment on the arcane arrangements over which I had sweated blood.

I greeted my traveling companions blearily at breakfast. Their tasks all seemed so straightforward by comparison. No wonder they had all slept so well. Then I noticed John Riddell's expression. The normal half-amused, donnish detachment was missing, replaced by a look of unusual preoccupation. It might have been the Kuwaiti version of an English breakfast staring back at him from his plate, but I preferred to believe, with relief, that he shared some of my anxiety.

In the exotic surroundings of the desert state—and with

the excuse of jet lag and general mental disorientation—it was a struggle to remember that the basic rules of recceing were basically unchanged from those I was learning to apply in more mundane surroundings in Britain. To counteract this, I acquired the knack of dismissing my surroundings, however diverting, in order to concentrate on the simple staples of timing, route, press, protocol, and security.

Begun as an act of self-preservation, it became a habit that eventually passed for professionalism. Sadly, it also meant that I was often oblivious to which great event or personality I was trying to organize, save for the need to contrive my courtier's patter into a form I judged least provocative to the local culture. It is only now, years afterward and without the benefit of even the sketchiest diary, that this lid of detachment has been edged aside by memories that have stood the test of time. Having remained so vivid, they are probably the only ones worth having—a thought that somewhat justifies my slothful scorn of the assiduous diarist.

Assiduous was not a description I felt I could apply to my performance on the Kuwait recce, except perhaps in comparison with our delegation as a whole. I was probably applying attitudes still shaped by the demands of the Navy, however, and had yet to realize fully the deceptive way in which the courtier's imperturbable outer calm could be mistaken for ennui.

Against this background, you can perhaps imagine the trepidation with which I set off after breakfast to recce the Salaam guest palace. In an ominous development, none of my colleagues felt able to tear themselves away from their own duties in order to accompany me. The message was clear: this was definitely the equerry's job and I was welcome to it.

Salaam means "welcome" and nobody could doubt the sincerity of the Kuwaitis' hospitality. Nonetheless, as I stood in the grandiose marble hallway of the Salaam palace my senses slowly alerted me to the fact that however grand the title, and however warm the welcome, our temporary home was going to give the entourage plenty on which to sharpen their critical faculties.

The livid green carpet emitted an unidentifiable musky odor, which was taken up and queasily repeated in the chemical whiff I caught from voluminous drapes and curtains that billowed in the air conditioning. Insecticide, I thought. Drains, I thought, as I checked the bathrooms. What's *that*? I thought, as I peered into the subterranean kitchens.

Circular in design and labyrinthine in its floor plans, the guest palace offered a bewildering range of permutations when it came to allocating rooms to the tour party. There was, of course, a formula to guide ignorant equerries in this exacting science. Distance from the royal bedroom was not arbitrarily assigned and paid no regard at all to what an outsider might think the appropriate order by seniority. It was your job not your apparent status that determined your room.

Some, such as PPOs and valets, had to be close by. Most of the rest could be parked in an outer zone from which a short sprint could bring them to the door of the royal apartments, where they could cool their heels awaiting the summons. Others still were banished to the Intercontinental hotel down the road. These were the true fortunates, unless you counted royal proximity above reliable plumbing, crisp sheets, a minibar, and direct-dial phone. Few did.

The days of the recce passed in a flurry of planning visits to clinics, palaces, museums, crèches, schools, and even a camel racetrack. Everything had to be planned in minute detail—the protocol, the press, the security, and the transport. Everything became blurred by fatigue and desert sand; and by the aftereffects of an intensive round of expatriate entertainment. Down the Gulf the pattern was repeated, in Bahrain, Abu Dhabi, Dubai, and Saudi Arabia.

Punch-drunk with planning and giddy with jet lag, I returned to London and managed to sell the draft program successfully to the Princess, even though at times it threatened to remain just a confusing, technicolor jumble of memories.

*I*t was six weeks before I returned to the Middle East. This time I was in charge of the small advance party that flew out ahead of the Prince and Princess to check on last-minute arrangements. To my dismay, instead of a few minor adjustments, I discovered that the program needed quite major surgery. Since the recce, our hosts had made various "improvements" that, though undoubtedly well intended, nevertheless posed a serious threat to the delicate structure of compromises that made up the final version approved by the Prince and Princess.

The Ambassador and his staff worked heroically to explain this and placate our puzzled hosts. At last a compromise was reached which left our original program broadly recognizable, but I was still apprehensive as I prepared my uniform for the royal arrival next day. As if sensing my mood, several buttons chose that moment to come loose on my jacket. I clumsily set to work with the hotel repair kit, assailed by visions of bursting undone at a bad moment.

Later, I gave up the unequal struggle with my needle and thread and tackled the last of my chores for the evening. I phoned the Princess, as we had agreed I would. I imagined her at KP making her own last-minute preparations for departure in the morning. It seemed harder to imagine her waiting expectantly for me to phone.

This would not be an easy call, I thought, as I dialed the familiar number. The agreement was that I would tell her how I was getting on in general and, in particular, what she could expect to find when she finally stepped off the plane in Kuwait. She knew the program was liable to change at short notice and, like any element of uncertainty in her public life, she found that very unsettling.

Should I tell her the changes I had been forced to agree

to on my own initiative? Pretour morale—hers and mine—was fragile and I had no wish to incur her severe displeasure at this late stage. If I just presented her with a *fait accompli* when she arrived, however, I might face accusations of keeping her in the dark—a cardinal sin, if sometimes a necessary one. Perhaps I could fudge it...

"Patrick!" came a breathy voice. "I thought you must have fallen down an oil well. Where have you *been*?" She giggled expectantly.

This was terrible. Often it was worse if she was nice. Goodwill expenditure was carefully noted in the royal ledger and there was usually a price to be paid sooner or later. Still, it might be worth testing. Should I tell her that new joke about the camel who applied for a sex change? Or would any sign of levity be seen as damning proof that I had been living the life of Riley in the sunshine?

"Did you hear the one about the camel who—"

"Patrick! I haven't time for your smutty jokes now. Have you managed to sort the program out? Assuming you haven't been sitting by the pool all day."

"Well, there are a few small changes..." I explained them briefly. The silence on the other end of the line was heavy with disapproval. When I had finished my excuses her voice acquired an ominous tone of reproach.

"Patrick! All that extra work, and after such a long flight. We'll be on our *knees*." It always switched to "we" when she was trying to imply that I—or life in general—was being unfair.

"Yes, Ma'am, but it's serious stuff—it's not just something to keep you occupied while the Prince does the grown-up bits—and it'll give the press something to write about apart from what you're wearing."

There was a pause, and then a sigh. "So what you're telling me, Patrick, is 'Shut up, Diana, and do your job.' "

"Well, I wouldn't put it quite like that..."

"Ha! I know *you* wouldn't. All right, Patrick—I'll do what my male nanny tells me."

"Thank you, Ma'am." Hmm. Male nanny. It could be worse. It was certainly worth a facetious parting shot. "Have a *nice flight.*"

The reply was a violent raspberry.

In the event, of course, everything *did* work—at least as far as most people could see. The royal VC-10 whistled to an earsplitting halt precisely on time, raising the curtain on a show essentially as old as diplomacy itself. The stars smiled for the cameras, spoke their lines, and performed their routines with the charm and ease the world had come to expect. The machinery we had labored to set up whirred into action and carried us all along on a conveyor belt of engagements, each a one-act play before an audience as faithful to the script as we were.

Nobody saw the little dramas behind the scenes. Nothing stirred a ripple on the smooth public surface of the tour. There were no cameras to snap the Princess testing her mattress by bouncing on it. Nobody recorded the staff's impromptu late-night revue, complete with the butler's impersonation routine that had us crying tears of laughter into our whiskey. No outsiders, fortunately, witnessed the other tears and tantrums that inevitably erupted from time to time in our highly strung party far from its home base.

In fact, memorably, it was an outsider—a hysterical military attaché—who caused one of the greatest dramas by threatening a soldier in our team with court-martial for insubordination. The poor, choleric colonel did not realize that the offender was a vital part of the royal support system and hence beyond the reach of normal military censure. Later, he recovered sufficiently to try to wheedle an official portrait photo of the Prince and Princess out of me. These trinkets had a remarkable attraction for some people and I could see the attaché's mantelpiece was not going to be complete without this happy snap. There were real tears in his eyes as I explained that he was not on his Ambassador's list of those deemed worthy of such recognition.

Disaster always seemed a hair's-breadth away. Usually the

crises were self-inflicted, as with our departure from Bahrain. Until that point the whistle-stop visit for lunch with the ruler had lived up to its expectations as a stress-free interlude between the exertions of Kuwait and the Emirates. Everything had gone smoothly and we returned to the airport to resume our journey in a state approaching euphoria. The accompanying party were already installed back on the VC-10 and I could see their faces pressed against the portholes as they looked down at the departure ceremony at the foot of the aircraft steps.

With a final wave to their host, the Prince and Princess started to climb the steps to the forward door of the aircraft. The remaining members of the party, me included, hurried up our own set of stairs to the doorway farther aft (a sensible piece of aeronautical class distinction for which the venerable VC-10 might have been specifically designed). Speed took precedence over dignity, because we knew that slick RAF practice demanded that the engines should be started as soon as the senior VIP passengers were aboard. Any underlings following in their wake had therefore better look sharp or be left behind.

Sure enough, as we clattered up the last few steps I heard the first of the four Conway jets start to whine into life. Suddenly there was an urgent call from below. "Patrick!" I turned around. At the bottom of the steps one of the local Embassy staff was holding out a suitcase. Had I forgotten something? I racked my brains, ready to blush at the thought of some duty not done.

Then it hit me. The watches! This was the almost mythical bonus that awaited members of royal tour parties visiting certain countries where ancient customs of hospitality had survived into a more material age. The suitcase was filled with gold, cunningly disguised as wristwatches, and each member of the accompanying party, down to the most humble secretary, expected his or her share of the windfall. No wonder their noses had been pressed to the windows as my car drew up. I had almost forgotten the most important piece of luggage of them all!

Quickly I turned and ran back down the steps to the ground. Fervently thanking my guardian angel, I started the return climb to the beckoning doorway, swag secure in my clammy hand. Imagine going down in history as the Equerry Who Forgot the Rolexes!

Out of the corner of my eye I could see that the forward door was now firmly closed and a party of soldiers was hurriedly rolling the red carpet back toward the ceremonial dais from which our hosts were waving a final farewell. In my ears the Conways were rising to a crescendo. I did not have a second to spare.

With a final heave, I reached the platform at the top of the steps and thrust the suitcase at a large RAF figure who was blocking the doorway. "Quick, take this!" The figure did not move. What was the matter with the idiot? "Hurry up! They're waiting for us to go!" I shouted above the steady roar of the jets. I could sense a dozen sets of eyes burning resentfully into my back. This stupid naval officer was delaying everything and spoiling the perfection of their departure ceremony. And what is the problem with our suitcase? Are our gifts unworthy?

The RAF figure was quite oblivious. "Has this item been security cleared?" it asked impassively.

Still standing exposed on the platform, I felt a sudden rush of exasperated anger. "Of course it bloody well hasn't! It's a gift from the Emir and he's watching us right now wondering what the f——'s the matter with it!"

"I don't care who it's from," said the figure, still blocking the doorway. "It's not coming on this aircraft until it's been searched. It might be a bomb for all I know."

"All right then! *You* search it!" I shouted, dropping the case at his feet and pushing past him into the cabin.

To his credit and my shame, he squatted on the platform under the baleful gaze of the Bahraini ruling family and the jubilant scrutiny of the British press corps and searched the suitcase from top to bottom, very thoroughly.

*A*s we made our progress down the Gulf, schizophrenia seemed inevitable. One moment I was standing at the royal elbow, trying to wear an expression appropriate to the business in hand, be it the Emir's banquet, the center for children with disabilities, or the display of folk dancing. The next moment I was scurrying around in the false sanctuary of one of our guest palaces, humoring the hairdresser, placating the baggage master, or fighting with the unfamiliar shower controls as I hurried to change for the Embassy reception.

With astonishing speed, the engagements painstakingly researched, recced, and re-recced came and went. The closely typed pages of outline programs, detailed programs, administrative instructions, and security orders had their brief moment of frenzied importance and then were forgotten, turned to paper vermicelli in our mobile shredder.

The leading lady did not even appear in the final scenes. She made a suitably stylish departure from Dubai in a borrowed jumbo jet, lent by a solicitous Sheikh. Never one to disappoint a damsel in need, when he heard that her scheduled return flight was delayed, he sent for his pilots three and dispatched her toward London in nothing less than a flying palace.

It was not clear who felt most upset: the Queen's Flight at not being properly consulted about the use of an unfamiliar aircraft, or me at having to watch the Princess and her homebound team fly away in an airplane I would have liked to bore my grandchildren about.

The baggage master and I rattled back to our hotel in the elderly Embassy Land Rover and tortured ourselves with thoughts of the luxuries now being enjoyed by the lucky passengers. We had no trouble agreeing we were *much* more deserving. This was probably debatable. She had earned her seven hours of airborne fun.

With the departure of the Princess, her lady-in-waiting, dresser, assistant dresser, hairdresser, and detective—and practically all the press—something approaching a holiday mood settled over the remaining party. The last leg of the journey was a private visit by the Prince to another desert kingdom, a male sanctuary where the exclusive club rules of worldwide royalty offered an understanding welcome for a fellow member. Compared to the tensions of the preceding week, even someone feeling as neurotic as I was could afford to relax.

"Here's the medicine you ordered," said the man from the Embassy as we settled into the last of a series of guest palaces. He handed me a suspiciously heavy dispatch case.

"I didn't order any medicine," I replied, mystified. Then I heard a muffled chink from inside the box. "Ah . . . yes, of course. Medicine. Thank you!"

Our accompanying doctor was unimpressed. "What you lot don't need is more whiskey," he grumbled, handing out supplies of pills to help us either sleep or stay awake.

Now alone among the Prince's staff, I could not escape the feeling that the Princess's mark was metaphorically stamped on my forehead. Although encouraged to feel part of the team, I was still a guest among guests. Nonetheless, I enjoyed the unbuttoned atmosphere of the male court, where discussion of real political and philosophical issues was possible in an atmosphere reminiscent of the wardrooms I had left behind. I noticed the same cautious deference to the senior officer's opinion and marveled again at the intricacies of his domestic arrangements, which could suddenly override almost all other priorities.

In addition, the experience of working briefly in what was later to become a hostile camp was invaluable. In later years, when events suggested that this camp was capable of conspiracy against the Princess, I could reassure myself—and her—that its capacity for blundering was even greater.

The passage of time and further rotations of advisers has not greatly altered that early impression.

The Prince's office had acquired a rather patchy reputation, not because of incompetence or lack of effort, but because a support organization constantly on the verge of meltdown seemed to be an essential accompaniment to the Prince's sense of being unfairly burdened. In a revelation gleefully reported by the press, he even once disclosed that he was forced to spend time correcting elementary errors in correspondence originating from his own office. His obvious regret at such a slip was not quite in time to prevent an understandable dent in fragile secretarial morale.

At last we reached the end of the tour. The euphoria was almost tangible as we clambered out of the final motorcade, made our last farewells, and headed for the elegant white and blue VC-10 that was waiting to take us home. With a reassuring nod from the top of the steps, the baggage master signaled that all the other passengers and our mountain of luggage were safely aboard.

Taking a deep breath of scented Arabian air, I turned to follow my companions up the ladder. Out of the corner of my eye I saw the Prince give his final wave and disappear inside. As expected, the first of the four jets immediately began to whine into life. Remembering Bahrain, I smiled to myself. That fuss with the suitcase seemed a long time ago. I had come a long way since then.

I turned for a last look and saw something fluttering on the bonnet of the Prince's car. "Christ! The Standard!"

I ran back down the stairs and sprinted toward the car. It was my most elementary duty to ensure that we always carried with us the little flag that flew from the royal limousine. To leave it behind was a guarantee of ridicule, or worse. The royal Standard was a coveted object, laden even now with a mystical significance. Thank God I had spotted it.

Seeing me approach, the driver leapt out of the car and started to unscrew the flag from its special attachment. How helpful, I thought. Behind me I could hear the VC-10 getting up steam. Panting, I reached out to take the scrap of multicolored cloth, a grateful *"Shucran"* already on my lips. Suddenly it was snatched away. "No!" said the driver, his dark eyes flashing. "I keep! Always I keep VIP flag!"

I grabbed a handful of flag and started to pull. "Let go!" I shouted. "You can't keep this one!"

For a ludicrous few moments we tussled over the flag. I had a hysterical vision of it tearing down the middle as the VC-10 taxied away, leaving us to squabble in the gathering dusk. With a final, frantic tug it was mine. I ran back to the aircraft, cursing all collectors. The idling jets shrieked with laughter. It must have made a great cabaret for the invisible audience behind the row of lighted portholes.

Arriving gasping in the cabin, I was met by the chief steward. He was holding a tray on which a large gin and tonic clinked musically. "I expect you could do with this, sir," he said.

*M*y first overseas tour had given me a rare opportunity to work directly for the Prince. Although nominally in attendance as his equerry for the entire tour, in fact I had spent most of the time accompanying the Princess on her program. John Riddell had accompanied the Prince, who had been quite content for me to concentrate on looking after his wife in the same way as if we were in England. On this particular occasion, however, he had agreed to visit the British frigate *Hermione* currently taking a break from patrolling the Persian Gulf, and it made sense that he should be accompanied that day by an aide in uniform rather than the (very) civilian John.

This engagement had already caused me some amusement. Taking my seat at one of many *mahjlis* in the Emirates, I found myself next to the Prince's then polo manager, Ronnie Ferguson. I knew he had flown out to

Dubai some days earlier and I was anxious to confirm that the frigate had also arrived safely. "Is *Hermione* here yet?" I asked in a low whisper, conscious of the royal pleasantries being exchanged close by.

Ronnie started out of his reverie, looking at me with sudden new interest. "I say, you're a quick worker!"

"What *do* you mean, Ronnie?"

"Hermione. You've already got some bird lined up here! *Very* quick work!"

Under bushy brows, his eyes twinkled with admiration. It was painful to have to explain the identity of the distinctly unsexy Hermione with whom I had planned this tryst. The twinkle slowly died and Ronnie lapsed once more into thoughts of polo.

Although the Prince was undoubtedly the senior figure in my royal world, I approached my day with him with few qualms. In all my brief encounters with him since starting the job, he had been friendly but reassuringly distant. Unlike his more volatile wife—who could switch from warm intimacy to frozen exclusion in an instant—he had the air of a man who did not care very much who or what you were so long as you did your job. In this he resembled a certain type of senior naval officer, a species very familiar to me. The Captain's uniform he wore for the occasion reinforced this comforting impression.

As I sat with him in the back of the car I felt a distinct relief. The essentially female world I inhabited most of the time had its undoubted attractions, but it was a welcome break to be contemplating a day in uncomplicated masculine company in familiar surroundings. I felt as if I had been let out to play.

Hermione and the Prince both did themselves proud, I thought. The elderly ship looked brand new in the morning sun and her welcome was warm, enthusiastic, and self-assured. The Prince was in his element, adapting his script instinctively to suit his varied audience of sailors, senior ratings, and officers.

His visit was to end with a medal presentation in front of the entire ship's company and I knew he would be expected to make a short speech. In the car I had felt an attack of panic as I realized I had not drafted anything for him to say. The Princess would have needed a script cleared well in advance, and coaching too.

"I'm afraid I haven't drafted anything for you, Sir," I said in some trepidation.

The Prince examined the backs of his hands. It was impossible to know what was coming next. "Oh, that's all right," he said. "I'll think of something." And he did, completely unrehearsed and much to the delight of the assembled sailors.

A few days later I saw a different side of him.

The halfway point in the tour came and went, and I had my first experience of the phenomenon known as "midtrip dip." Even the best tour could suffer from an attack of midterm blues. The initial adrenaline surge wears off; the trip home lies on the other side of a mountain range of difficult engagements. An enervating climate and unsuitable food, bad sleep, and bad hangovers combine to dull the reflexes, stunt new thought, and confuse the body's systems.

As our fatigue accumulated, so too did our immunity to anxieties that had seemed overwhelming on day one. Who really cared where we sat on the airplane—a matter of supreme importance in some households—so long as everyone was actually on board? And did it really matter that I had run out of a certain type of key ring that the Prince gave as a farewell gift to local staff?

Late one night in Dubai I discovered that it *did* matter, very much indeed. I had arranged our dozen farewell gifts on a sideboard in the Prince's quarters, ready for him to hand them to the twelve—theoretically—most deserving officials who had helped with that leg of the tour. (This was the beauty parade for which the tearful Colonel had failed to qualify.)

My job was to adjudicate on the list submitted by the

Embassy, assemble the recipients, and make sure they appeared smartly when I announced them. The size and combination of gifts—mostly signed photos, but also a few small items such as cuff links or purses—had to correspond to the perceived importance of the recipient. A short briefing was required on each so that the appropriate royal platitude could be murmured while the lucky winner bowed and grinned expectantly.

It was without doubt the worst part of any tour. The list of things that could go wrong was endless. Even if the Embassy could produce their proposals on time—and it was required at a stage in the proceedings when they were already under enormous pressure—its composition was fraught with protocol poison as jealous officials vied to be included. We were strict to the point of meanness about the number of recipients allowed and I often felt there was scant justice in the compromises that resulted.

Even if we had remembered to bring the right number of gifts from London—and for a long tour like the Gulf it could take several large cases to carry them and all their likely permutations—the Waleses were always liable to impose last-minute changes to the choice of photograph, the design of cuff link, or the style of purse. In its most virulent form, this wish to control unimportant minutiae could grow to exclude all other considerations. It was as if this were the only part of our employers' lives that they could directly tinker with, and goodness, how they relished it.

The result was a tension bordering on suppressed hysteria as prizegiving time approached. It was always shoehorned into a passage of frenetic activity in the program—shortly before departure—and the logistic planning required to ensure the appearance of effortless efficiency was more appropriate, I felt, for the Nobel Prize itself. The tension was shared in full by our royal employers, who were sometimes unable to resist the temptation to be sharply pernickety with those responsible for any shortcoming. That night in Dubai, the responsible person was undoubtedly *me*.

The Prince had recently chosen a new style of key ring to give to drivers. Only a limited number had been available before we left, but enough, we thought, to cope with the expected demand. Just to be on the safe side we had brought a number of the old pattern as well. Fate—or the Prince's enthusiasm for his new design—now caused us to break into our reserve stock of the older version.

I was congratulating myself on my foresight in bringing this spare supply as I completed my preparations for the imminent ceremony. It was perhaps unrealistic of me to expect royal recognition for my prudent planning. In fact, self-congratulation was usually followed very quickly by nemesis, but I had not expected it to arrive quite so quickly.

My ears rang to the sound of princely disappointment. *Why* was he not being allowed to give out the new key ring he had chosen? The rebuke was addressed to an unfair world, but all available eyes turned inexorably in my direction. Disaster—never banished, only postponed—stared me in the face with a look that had been vaporizing erring equerries for a thousand years.

In my pristine white buckskin shoes, my toes wriggled in embarrassment. I squirmed. But I managed to stare back. Beneath my shame a vague sense of injustice stirred as I mentally scanned my endless list of responsibilities. All this fuss because of a key ring? Calling on distant naval experience, I fixed an expression of vague contrition on my face and simultaneously raised a quizzical eyebrow. Insolence, like beauty, is firmly in the eye of the beholder and I held my breath, awaiting the final thunderbolt, the prelude to dismissal, disgrace, and—probably—public execution.

It never came. The storm passed as suddenly as it had blown up. With a smile the Prince redirected the reproach to himself. I was preserved to sin again in the future. Relief washed over me, but not before I had registered two important points: (1) always bring lots of spare gifts (or "gizzits" in the jargon) to cater for sudden outbreaks of royal largesse; and (2) remember Princes get tired as well.

Like insolence and beauty, humor is also in the eye or ear of the beholder. Recovering from my experience with the gifts, I was tempted to try to be funny with the Prince on our return to England. The results were not encouraging, as I shall describe. This taught me another lesson: the Prince's ability—which he undoubtedly has—to enjoy certain types of joke is not to be taken as an encouragement to display your own scintillating wit. That was my experience, anyway.

That aside, I had liked my first experience of working with him. It was not just the reassuring familiarity of having a male boss again: there was a humor and a warmth behind the acquired remoteness that I felt was waiting to be released, if only I had the time and guts—not to mention the presumption—to try to unlock it.

It was true, I had also detected an occasional brooding menace. Like his famous charm, it was only revealed fleetingly to me, an outsider. It jostled in his face with self-pity and other, more uplifting emotions, but it was there nevertheless, in a vengeful look or anger explosively expressed.

I learned that, among other feelings he stirred in her, many of them still warm and affectionate, the Princess also felt fear. Except when she was roused with her own formidable brand of indignation, she would go to great lengths to avoid needlessly provoking the Prince. When she felt herself to be on the receiving end of his anger, before her characteristic defiance set in I often saw a look of trepidation cross her face, as if she were once again a small girl in trouble with the grown-ups. Though not his fault, I believe it joined with other fears deep within her to produce much of the temperamental instability that increasingly became his experience of her and from which, eventually, he would do anything to escape.

*S*peculating about the innermost secrets of the Waleses' marriage has often been a national pastime, at least according to the media. There is a horrifying fascination about watching other people's relationships disintegrating. The tour I had just finished had theoretically given me the chance to indulge such voyeuristic fascination at close range, but this was not an appropriate pastime for a member of staff.

The Prince and Princess were considerate enough with their staff and with each other to avoid all but a few public displays of their private problems. Whatever we staff saw or heard—including an obvious aversion for each other's company in private—we played along with the image, to outsiders, subordinates, and anyone else who might ask us for royal gossip. In fact, especially during the public acrimony of the separation a few years later, I often wondered if mine was the only dinner table in the country where the subject was banned.

By the time I awoke from an exhausted sleep on our homeward flight we were already over Italy. Far below, tiny lights reminded me of the existence of another world beyond the darkened aircraft and its dozing royal cargo. Outside this warm cocoon, like the chill air of the stratosphere, the real world waited. In time it would claim me back from princesses, palaces, caviar, and good whiskey.

That's OK, I thought. I'm only here till my time's up. Then the real world can have me back. But until then I'll enjoy the ride. I settled lower into the broad, comfortable seat. Idly I noticed the embroidered logo. How thrifty of the RAF to acquire seats from the defunct British Caledonian Airways. I dozed again, joined in my dreams by uninvited air stewardesses in tartan uniforms.

Some part of my brain, however, continued obstinately to play and replay scenes from the tour. The images and the restless thoughts that accompanied them would not switch off. It was the start of a mental treadmill, conscious and subconscious, that still turns ten years later.

This may have been because the people and issues involved demanded a huge commitment from anyone engaged in running the Wales production. For me, given my background and idealistic personality, that commitment became total. Unfortunately, the problems we were beginning to encounter in sustaining the marriage and the public image were to prove insoluble. Soon, the knowledge that we were fighting a losing battle in an atmosphere that could not countenance failure sometimes became very bad for morale. My sense of total commitment then became focused on one person—the Princess—and that put too great a burden of expectation on us both.

Back in my snug seat on the VC-10, unhappy thoughts and dim glimpses of the future chased each other round my head. Some things stood out clearly, even if their accuracy and full significance would only emerge later.

When they were working together, the Prince and Princess created a dynamism that was phenomenal. I had seen examples of it during the tour, especially during formal ceremonial moments. The effect of their arrival at something as staid as a diplomatic banquet left me in no doubt about their power. The world's most glamorous couple, the perfect mixture of regal gravitas and youthful beauty, could provoke a reaction among even the most jaded guests, inured to real emotion by years of protocol. I sat next to enough of these government hospitality veterans to observe the look of surprised, almost embarrassed awe—quickly suppressed—that this embodiment of living royalty inspired as it shone its two famous faces upon them.

Unfortunately, the stresses it laid on the owners of these public faces created powerful polarizing forces. These two egos were a match for any number of awestruck looks, and sharing the spotlight did not bring out the best in either of them. A reluctance to work as a team would inexorably drive them apart—he to resume a long-accustomed pattern of solo engagements, she to seek an undefined, independent new role.

It would be nice, but sadly false, to claim an inspired prescience about the events that were to follow. Based on my observations during the tour, however, added to what I had learned in a year at St. James's, even I could see that my employers seldom worked as a team anymore. If the stars were uncomfortable sharing top billing, then it was logical to think that they might be happier not sharing the same spotlight.

Two contrasting images stayed in my mind. The first was a glimpse of intimacy that I had never seen before, and that I was never to see again. The VC-10 had landed at one of our many ports of call—I think it was Abu Dhabi. As the plane taxied sedately toward the waiting red carpet, band, guard of honor, and ruling family, the usual controlled bedlam broke out inside. There was not the remotest chance that we would "remain seated until the captain has switched off the FASTEN SEATBELTS sign," or heed similar airline-style safety sense. Half the cabin was on its feet before we had even turned off the runway.

Valet and dresser headed forward to the royal compartment to tend to their charges. The private secretary, waking violently from a well-deserved doze, began urgently reading his program. The police were squinting through the portholes as if to satisfy themselves that no suicide bombers were lying obviously in wait, while anxiously trying to get their handheld radios to talk sense. The press secretary was at another porthole, awkwardly trying to glimpse the position of the rat pack. It seemed that only the secretaries were calmly staying put, looking out at the latest stretch of baking tarmac and methodically gathering their cabin baggage.

Supercharged with energy, I was hunting in the back of the capacious traveling wardrobe—one of our more essential "extras" that the RAF helpfully fitted into the aircraft to accommodate the yards of hanging luggage. It lay immediately aft of the royal compartment and through the partly open door the Prince and Princess could be seen conducting their more elegant version of the scenes in the main cabin. Scrabbling between the gently swaying, beautifully wrapped dresses and coats, I eventually found my ceremonial sword and stood up to buckle it on.

I was still tugging my tunic into place and trying to calm my accelerating pulse when, unseen by anyone else, I noticed the Prince lightly place a hand on the Princess's hip. It was the kind of small, encouraging gesture that might pass between any happily married couple about to face a common ordeal.

I felt an unexpected glow that such things were still possible between them. This was only slightly diminished by the further observation that the touch lasted for only a moment, and was not reciprocated. Also, there was something about the angle of the hip—which was all I could see of her—that made me think the Princess did not welcome it.

The second image came from an incident, probably related, that occurred soon afterward. As soon as the doors opened, the activity that had been fermenting in the confines of the aircraft's fuselage burst out into the glaring sunshine, as the supporting cast hurried down the aft gangway in time to see the Prince and Princess regally descending the front steps. I paused by the cargo hold long enough to ensure that actual violence did not erupt between our forthright baggage master and those less Welsh sent to help him, before joining the rest of the entourage in the blessed cool of the royal terminal.

It was the usual procedure. In a symbolic act of welcoming courtesy, the royal host offered his guests coffee as they sat on ornate armchairs while, at right angles, the gaggle of accompanying officials from both sides sat opposite each other on long sofas. Into the space in the middle were shepherded the press corps, who had half a minute to take the sort of staged pictures that are the staple diet of mainstream reports on all such airport encounters. After the press were shooed out, a further awkward five minutes had to be filled with small talk while energetic old men in beards refueled our coffee cups.

The royal host and his senior guest were sticking manfully to their scripts, while the rest of us thought it polite to pretend not to be able to hear the stilted pleasantries.

Plainly uncomfortable, the Princess was not joining in either, nor was she being invited to by the Prince or her host.

She seemed to have created an invisible barrier around herself, as if to say that she was apart from the polite charade going on around her. To me she looked excluded and vulnerable. To the host as well, presumably, because eventually he leaned across the Prince to ask her politely what she was hoping to do during her visit. Under the unexpected attention she visibly brightened, perhaps thinking—as I was—of the serious program we had arranged: visits to a day center for mentally handicapped children, a clinic for immigrant women, and a girls' business studies class.

The Prince also turned toward her, looking as if he were seeing her for the first time, ruefully indulgent, patronizing. There was an expectant hush. Before she could reply, he said with studied innocence, "Shopping, isn't it, darling?"

The words dropped into the marble stillness like bricks into plate glass. The Princess colored, mumbled something inaudible, and lapsed into silence. There was an awkward pause, broken by the Prince pointedly resuming his conversation with a host whose aquiline features now registered a politer version of the disbelief I felt.

When we were outside again I cornered John Riddell. "Did I see what I thought I saw in there?" I asked him.

He looked at me pityingly. "Oh yes, Patrick. Indeed you did. That is the world we have to live in."

*A*pproaching Lyneham at the end of our flight home, I perched in the spacious cockpit of the VC-10 and watched the lights of Wiltshire villages slip under the plane's nose. The Captain, a giant of a man, blocked much of the view as he sat hunched over the instrument panel. The controls seemed like toys in his huge hands as he gently followed directions from a radar controller on the ground.

The Navigator was timing our arrival to the second, giv-

90   P.D. JEPHSON

ing a running countdown to the magical "Doors open"
order that I had heard repeated half a dozen times in the
Gulf. I was always impressed by the RAF's mastery of such
precision. This time it was different, though. The doors
would open not onto blazing tarmac and a red carpet but
onto a patch of drizzly British concrete. There would be no
Sheikhs in flowing robes and no guard of honor. Instead
there would be an anxious-looking RAF duty officer and
the familiar Jaguar for the short drive to Highgrove. The
contrast amused me. I wondered if it would amuse the
Prince.

We landed exactly on time. Leaving the cockpit, I felt a
sudden blast of damp English air as I passed the crewmen
opening the door. After nearly two weeks of air conditioning and hot desert dust, it smelled delicious. As I entered the
royal compartment the Prince was peering out of the porthole. He looked up and I fell into the familiar routine for
arrival at a tour destination.

"This is Lyneham, Sir, in England. The outside temperature is 5. The ruler is not waiting at the foot of the steps.
There is no guard of honor to inspect and the band will not
play the anthems. There is no press position on either the
left or the right of the red carpet. In fact, there is no carpet.
But there is your car, Sir, and it will take you home."

The Prince's mouth twitched in what I hoped was fulsome approval of my uproarious joke. Well, it had been
worth a try. With a brief word of thanks he headed for the
door. The ever-present valet held out an overcoat and I
silently saluted the planning that had brought it magically to
hand after ten days in the desert. Then he was gone into the
night. Gone to Highgrove and the familiarity of house and
garden, of dogs and books and pictures, and a welcome we
all knew would not be his wife's.

5

❦

Double Take

I returned home exhausted and several pounds lighter, not least thanks to an energetic desert stomach bug. The Princess welcomed me back like a wandering stray and wrote me a typically generous note of appreciation. For a day or two I recuperated in the knowledge that I had survived my first tour, which had been generally recognized as a pretty challenging initiation.

Media coverage of the tour had been extensive. Still a novice, I took an immature pride in the glossy magazine stories and the TV special that followed in the days after our return. Somehow, I felt, it would not have been possible without me—which may have been true, but only to a very limited extent.

Not featured in the glossies but of growing interest to tabloid commentators was the state of The Marriage. I had seen some of its internal stresses while on tour—however careful the Prince and Princess were to keep their troubles to themselves, being "on the road" always accentuated differences that could be smoothed over more easily at home—and already the media sharks had scented blood in the water. They would not remain hungry for long.

To compensate for the lack of united leadership at the top, the Wales support organization had for some time been making its own arrangements to adapt to the unpalatable truth. Huge amounts of energy were diverted into concealing the real state of the marriage, and still more were expended on structuring our bosses' public lives to minimize friction between them. It is a tempting but pointless exercise to imagine what more could have been achieved if this energy had been available to support the global influence of a Prince and Princess who were able to work as a team.

My introduction to these realities had occurred during a visit by the Prince and Princess to the Glasgow Garden Festival in my early days in office in May 1988. Not unusually, Their Royal Highnesses had been apart in the days preceding the engagement but obviously had to appear as a couple, if not happily, then at least willingly united when they arrived at the Festival. They therefore made their ways in separate aircraft to what, fortunately, turned out to be a simultaneous rendezvous at Glasgow airport. Logistically this was no mean feat, but as I came to realize, the Queen's Flight, the police, and the respective staffs were not short of practice in this maneuver.

On the flight to Scotland I had been conscious of a heightened tension, but in my happy lack of awareness had ascribed it only to the prospect of an exciting day in the sunshine in front of what were sure to be huge crowds. Later, I came to recognize the nervous giggles interspersed with brooding introversion as characteristic of the Princess's agitation at the prospect of working with her husband. Also, it was only later that I realized the significance of her frequent trips to the royal loo. "Bulimia" was a word I did not even know how to spell in 1988.

John Riddell was in charge of the engagement. As ever, his charm and studied absentmindedness produced the intended mood of amused tolerance in the Princess as we arrived in Glasgow. Inside, he must have felt he was defusing a ticking time bomb. In this he was like many senior courtiers who lacked the benefit of regular contact with her—their understandable inclination was to treat her like a beautifully wrapped parcel of unstable explosive. His only acknowledgment of the unspoken matrimonial drama that waited on the tarmac was to smile reassuringly at her as we left the plane and say, "Let's hope we all reach the end of the day in the same happy mood we started it in!"

In bright sunshine the Prince and Princess met by their aircraft, brushed cheeks for a fraction of a second, and climbed into their car. The day *was* a success. The beautiful weather, happy crowds, and grand scale of the event perfectly set off their own professionalism.

They were an unbeatable double act who could anticipate each other's moves, instinctively work a crowd, and betray by neither a word nor a gesture the fact that they would jump back in their separate planes as soon as duty released them. In the brief moments of semiprivacy, however, away from all but the familiar company of their staffs, they might have been on separate engagements. Not a word or a glance passed between them.

Only the atmosphere of relief on the homeward journey, and the veiled references to disaster averted, alerted my novice's consciousness to the fact that we were playing a game. There was only one rule: nothing must be said to disturb the myth of permanence that was now the marriage's only certainty.

Competition between the stars of our show was never far below the surface, and set-piece joint events usually brought it into the open. A garden party at Buckingham Palace was the perfect opportunity for some rather pointed sparring. For those of us who saw beyond the myth this was entertaining too, in a painful way.

It was the sort of obligatory event that went into the Princess's diary automatically, at least twice every year. However much she denied it, I think she secretly rather looked forward to these occasions. The reason was not hard

to find. It came to me at the start of one afternoon's proceedings, as I paraded in my top hat and tails at the edge of
the Buckingham Palace lawn along with other members of
the Prince and Princess's senior household. At our backs a
lawn the size of a soccer field was crowded with a multicolored mob of deserving guests from all walks of life throughout the Commonwealth.

Three approximately equal gangways had been carved
through this crowd by Beefeaters in full ceremonial dress.
The idea was that three royal couples would descend the
steps from the Buckingham Palace Bow Room door onto
the lawn and split up, one couple per lane. They would then
proceed through the crowd at a slow pace toward their reward: tea in a special marquee at the other end of the lawn
with members of the diplomatic community.

In effect, it was a time-honored and rather formal version
of the walkabout that I had come to know so well on the
streets of provincial Britain. This time, however, the sun was
shining, the crowds were all in their Sunday best, if not better,
and the Princess was dressed in clothes she might happily
have appeared in on Ladies' Day at Ascot. In other words, despite the formal royal setting and order of events and ceremonies that had changed little since Victoria's time, here was
a chance for the Princess to do what she did best, in front of
an audience drawn from those she sometimes saw as her
greatest critics, namely other members of the royal family.

Apart from the Queen, who was naturally the symbolic
focus of all attention, with her Palace as a backdrop and her
Guards band playing her anthem, no one outshone the
Princess. She stood statuesquely, slightly to one side, eyes
demurely downcast, an object of wonder and curiosity,
holding the gaze of several thousand eyes.

She and the Prince decorously descended the steps onto
the lawn and the show began. The private secretary bowed,
I bowed, we all bowed. The Prince looked grumpy, the
Princess looked radiant. Then I detected a wicked edge to
the radiance. It came, I was sure, from the certain knowl-

edge that she was about to outshine her husband in public and intended to derive no little amusement from the task.

She winked at me and I fell into step slightly behind her. She took the right-hand side of the lane and the Prince took the left. The Prince's equerry and I then spent the next forty-five minutes striding up and down ahead of our royal charges, ensuring that some thirty or so preselected guests were hauled to the front of the crowd and made to stand prominently so that they could receive the handshake they had been promised.

We sometimes darted farther ahead to where the Queen's comptroller stood at the confluence of the three lanes, marching up and down and looking important— something he did very well, except that he glanced at his watch rather too often. He had the tricky task of trying to arrange for the occupants of all three lanes to arrive simultaneously at the door of the tea tent. It was a practically impossible task, because each of the six royal runners had their own technique for working the crowd and their rate of advance was anything but uniform. Nevertheless, he had to try and we had to try to help him.

After a few years of garden parties it dawned on me that there was only one game for the Princess more amusing than putting her husband in the shade for the afternoon, and that was frustrating her equerry's artful attempts to make her hurry up or slow down in order to fall in with the comptroller's master plan.

It was hard enough trying to make the Waleses coordinate speeds even in their own lane. One year the couple were particularly at odds and their progress had been anything but coordinated. With something approaching panic, I watched the Queen finish her lane and start to make her way toward the tea tent. We were going to be very late.

"You're going to be very late!" the comptroller snapped at me and I returned fretfully to my lane, trying to look blasé on the outside while feeling like an incompetent sheepdog on the inside.

I went to explain the problem to the Prince's equerry. Once again demonstrating that alarming ability that all royal people seemed to possess, the Prince overheard our muttered conversation, taking place some twenty feet behind him. "I didn't know it was a *race*." The words were flung peevishly over his shoulder.

Immediately I relaxed, reminding myself once again of that saying attributed to Balfour: "Nothing matters very much, and very few things matter at all." It was a piece of wisdom I sometimes wished had been carved in illuminated letters ten feet high across the whole facade of Buckingham Palace. It was a valuable lesson, and one that the Prince had evidently learned many years before, at least in relation to garden parties. I duly received a black look from the comptroller for spoiling the perfection of his arrangements, but he recognized the notorious independent-mindedness of the Waleses and was in any case already thinking about tea; and so, soon afterward, was I.

Hot on the heels of the garden party came another setpiece event at which the aim of portraying our household as one big happy family came rather closer to success. This was the annual Highgrove staff barbecue. Awnings were pitched on the Highgrove lawn, external caterers were brought in with superior sausages and steaks, and the Prince and Princess vied with each other to play gracious and relaxed host to their hundred or so staff and their guests.

The Princess was in her element. In a casual outfit that looked as though it had come straight from the set of a jeans ad, she worked the crowd as if this were a superior sort of walkabout. Most of the faces were familiar to her, of course. I watched as she adjusted her demeanor according to whether she pigeonholed the person she was speaking to as (1) friendly and therefore deserving proprietorial in-humor, or (2) potentially hostile and therefore marked down for commiserating good humor, on this occasion anyway, or (3) neutral between the two camps. For those in the last category she reserved her most winning smile of all.

Everyone seemed to be hyped up—the employees because their pleasure at feeling they were getting something from the management for free was moderated by the knowledge that they were still under royal surveillance, as they consumed as much food and drink as they decently could. They were also, in many cases, showing off for the benefit of their guests, who were either partners or family. For their part, most of the guests were overawed by being welcomed to Highgrove, which they knew was first and foremost a private residence. The Princess was vigorously marshaling her support and I, for one, was keeping a watchful eye on the progress of her own version of an internal opinion poll. The only person who seemed truly relaxed was the Prince, not least because the event gave him another opportunity to take small groups of reverential employees on guided tours of the gardens that were his consuming interest.

Visiting the house itself on barbecue days was not encouraged, but I had been there often enough before. Engagements that fell on Mondays or Fridays usually began or ended at Highgrove, with an associated trek, inevitably at the worst time of day, along the M4.

It has been said that the Princess disliked Highgrove and my own observations would confirm this, particularly toward the end of the marriage. As has also been said, it was in most ways a typical, comfortable country house with cartoons in the loo, boots in the porch, and Jack Russells, it seemed, almost everywhere. It was distinctly more homey than Kensington Palace and certainly, so far as the Princess was concerned, there was no distinction between family and staff areas of the house. When I arrived I might expect to find her perched on the kitchen table, swinging her legs and sharing gossip with the chef, or in the staff hall, listening to the housekeeper's latest personal crisis.

When the Waleses separated in 1992, the Princess collected all her belongings from the house and quit without much evident regret. No sooner had she gone than comprehensive redecoration took place, together with large-scale purging of the domestic staff. Highgrove then formally became what it had always seemed to be: the Prince's personal sanctuary and main domestic base. For the Princess's staff, it became foreign territory overnight. She never returned.

*A*s allegiances in the office and in the country hardened, I found myself firmly in the Princess's camp. This was not because she was blameless—she could not and did not claim this for herself, as I knew better than most. In fact, she was refreshingly honest about her capacity to run amok in the royal china shop, without ever surrendering her right to do so. "Everything's got to change, Patrick!" she would say, and I spent a few years trying to translate this aspiration into a reality that was acceptable to the institution and still recognizable to her.

I suppose I supported her because, in the end, she was younger and more naive than her husband was, and ultimately he bore responsibility for what happened in his family. In an organization that had such a highly developed sense of duty, this seemed logical, but I had not even begun to grasp the agony the Prince must have suffered trying to reconcile duty with the demands of the heart. Only now can I hope to have a better understanding of his dilemma.

From this comfortably conceited moral high ground, I felt able in the years that followed to criticize the Prince—if only privately—for failing to break the deadlock with his wife, a move that I knew she would welcome and the country would applaud. As the menace I had seen in him grew in my own mind into a force to be opposed on principle, I believed with righteous zeal that he represented the greater of two pretty unattractive wrongs.

If forced, I would still stand by that assessment, but it is an assessment now tempered by my own experience. All the while I was ministering to the needs of the royal family, I was neglecting those of my own. Ironically, I eventually found myself facing the same doubts about my personal morality for which I had so unhesitatingly condemned the Prince. In my small way, I also faced the opprobrium of observers snug in a moral certainty I could only envy. As my own marriage began to feel the consequences of my strange occupation, I blushed to remember my outrage on behalf of the wronged wife.

Even in what I thought to be the line of duty to the Princess, I cast more than my share of stones at the man I felt was the greater sinner. You may feel, as I do, that it says something about him that he declined to throw them back. Less charitably, you may also feel he had no need, there being plenty of volunteers to undertake such dirty work unbidden on his behalf. Yet in the end it is naive—however superficially justified—to criticize royal people for misdeeds carried out in their name. Being different, if not strictly better than the rest of us, is their *raison d'être*. Questions of blame also seem to become irrelevant when royalty is concerned for its own survival. All's fair in love, war, and royal service. Many people are attracted to it for that very reason.

As had been proved both at home and in the Gulf, our daily working lives were adapting to the Waleses' growing estrangement as a matter of professional routine. However, this uncritical acceptance of the facts of life ran into trouble when we had to explain them to others. It was uncomfortable to have to provide for the stark domestic reality behind the public illusion.

One very practical problem arose whenever we were making arrangements for accommodation on overseas tours. We now needed two royal bedrooms. Few hosts were so indelicate as to query this, although raised Embassy eyebrows sometimes had to be stared down. A line suggested for use in these circumstances went something like this: "The Prince and Princess often work to different programs on tour and it makes sense that they—and their immediate personal staff—don't get in each other's way when quick turnarounds are required between engagements. This sort of arrangement was perfectly normal for royal people historically and for much the same good reasons. To this day, many couples in the aristocracy organize their sleeping arrangements in the same way. It doesn't mean they don't have—and take—the chance to meet intimately when time and inclination coincide." In other words, mind your own business—which I, for one, was happy to do. It proved impossible at times.

Apart from the considerable duplication of effort this system dictated, not to mention the restrictions it sometimes placed on the types of accommodation we deemed acceptable, it struck an unwelcome, discordant note among our hosts and anybody else who was taking an interest. I sometimes felt we were arriving with our dirty laundry already on display.

In the mornings they would emerge from separate quarters like boxers from opposing corners of the ring, except that, unlike boxers governed by the bell, they could stage their entrances for effect. Sometimes she would keep him waiting, sometimes vice versa. Tension that might have been safely—if uncomfortably—vented behind closed doors was carried instead into the day's work, where it could fester.

It was like a secret deformity that our hosts never saw, but that restricted our freedom to program joint activities while doubling much of the administrative effort. Even something as simple as getting the end-of-tour presentation photographs signed by them both could call upon all Harold Brown's skills as the behind-the-scenes coordinator. Never were his talents as butler/diplomat in greater demand than when he had to preside over divided domestic quarters in an unfamiliar house.

There were benefits as well. One of the unresolved questions in the wake of their divorce was whether the Prince and Princess should have tried harder to "make a go of it." Looking at the situation from a different aspect, the question could be rephrased, "How long should you force people to stay together if they want to be apart?"

As I greeted the Princess in the mornings or took my leave at night, I knew the answer in practical if not in philosophical terms. There was absolutely no doubt that, however sadly solitary, her room was a haven of privacy between bouts of exhausting public exposure. Had she been forced to swap the media spotlight by day for a marital battleground by night, I doubt she would have performed her royal duties at all. Since I observed similar feelings in the Prince, it is safe to conclude that, this close to the end of their marriage, the royal double act was a performance best reserved for barely consenting adults in public only.

Other benefits looked attractive at first sight, especially to me as the inexperienced new equerry. On closer inspection, however, they stirred my early suspicion that my boss was anything but a guileless pretty face. These dubious benefits centered on the Princess's wish to be seen as more popular, approachable, flexible, and generally "normal" than her husband. When they were on tour together he was conveniently close by to act as a foil for this desire, much to the uncomfortable advantage of "her team."

As if to underline the contrast with the Prince's habitually more preoccupied appearance, she would burst from her quarters in the morning radiating popularity, approachability, and flexibility to the assembled entourages as we waited to depart for the day's program. Usually she would time it so that we had several minutes to bask in the effect and pick up the nonverbal signals with which she indicated who was in favor and who was to be conspicuously ignored.

Her husband's staff were a favorite target. It was seldom a hardship, however. Her desire to create an impression that contrasted with her husband's usually made her a welcome

visitor to the temporary office. There she might find two of
his secretaries wrestling with our primitive portable com-
puters and last-minute amendments to the Prince's next
speech.

"What is it today—global warming or Shakespeare?" she
would ask with a laugh, perching elegantly on a desk. Then
there would be girl-talk about clothes, or the heat, or the
hysterically ornate splendor of her quarters. There would
always be concerned inquiries about the staff's accommodation or general morale. Needless to say, I listened to the
answers with my heart in my mouth. Any complaint would
earn me a raised royal eyebrow. It all helped to prove her
point: I care about the workers, even if certain other people
are too busy.

She also managed to create the impression that her husband was unpunctual and lacked her enthusiasm for the
day's events. When he emerged and took in the scene, she
would chide him with a thin affability. In full view of an
audience she had already warmed up, he could do little to
express any irritation her teasing provoked.

This often left me feeling queasy. Public point-scoring
was one of the most unsettling aspects of the marital deterioration we had to witness, even if I was occasionally a temporary beneficiary. If I was obviously in favor, the resultant
inner glow was tempered by the thought that she was just as
likely to be trying to make someone else feel bad as she was
trying to make me feel good. In turn this produced an un-
healthy climate in which her praise could not be taken at
face value. It also sharpened the sting of her criticism,
which was seldom related to the actual gravity of the offense. Praise and criticism of her staff were both ploys she
used in the mental game of musical chairs with which she
played out her own emotional confusion.

Small wonder, then, that she and the Prince grew to prefer touring separately. The morning nonverbal signals indicating who was in and who was out never entirely vanished,
but at least the audience was smaller. Without the need to

strike a contrasting attitude to the Prince, the Princess's actions became a more honest reflection of her own feelings—and she enjoyed herself more, which was good for everyone.

My first royal tour marked the end of my apprenticeship. There were still mountains of experience to climb. If I served her for a hundred years, I would still have much to learn about the Princess of Wales, and even more about the reactions she sparked in others. At last, however, I had the tour labels on my briefcase; I could swap tall stories with the best of them. Even more important, I had shared with the Princess the pressures and prolonged proximity that only foreign tours provide, especially difficult ones, which this definitely had been.

I had passed through a barrier of acceptability—one of many on the twisting and ultimately futile path to royal intimacy. From now on our relationship would be slightly different. She began to see through my mask of deference and I began to see through her saintly image.

The most significant change was the one least discussed. To travel with the Prince and Princess at that time was to learn, inescapably, the truth of their growing estrangement. In the office it had been almost possible to pretend that all was well. On the road in Britain I had been supporting only one half of what was still seen as a formidable double act. There was nothing to stop me arguing—as I did—that press speculation about problems in the marriage was offensive and inaccurate. The whole issue could be ignored in the comforting round of day-to-day business.

This was true no longer. I had arranged the separate accommodation and sweated to ensure the hermetic separation of his and her programs, required for all but a few joint appearances. In Dubai I had been summoned into the cabin of the Princess's departing jet to be given a farewell that was effusive and undeniably a pact of loyalty as I stayed behind with the Prince. I had witnessed with naive alarm the small, telltale signs of mutual antipathy that were soon to become public knowledge—averted eyes, defiantly uncoordinated walkabouts, competitive glad-handing.

Eventually, when she was traveling on solo tours, there was a welcome outbreak of informality in the Princess's attitude toward me. Instead of the large numbers of their joint household who had previously paraded to greet her in the morning, she would find only me waiting at her door. I would be invited in, to steal extra breakfast, hear gossip from her phone calls, answer questions on the day's business and compliment—or assist with—the choice of outfit. She might try three different outfits before setting off for the day and would ask my opinion on each.

"Patrick, what d'you think of this hat?"

"Um...very royal, Ma'am."

"Thanks. I'll change it!"

The same process would operate in reverse in the evening, when she might ask me to pour a glass of champagne and join her in an irreverent postmortem on the people and issues that had made the most impression on her over the course of the day.

This was quite nice, as far as it went. I defy anyone employed by royalty not to feel even a fleeting glow of illicit pleasure at being invited to share such intimacies. As I was to discover to my cost, however, centuries of deference had not been built up just to make the important people feel more important. Deference protected the small people too, from royal favor too lightly granted and too quickly withdrawn. So I was wary, even as I joined in what was, after all, just her way of dealing with the demands her job placed on her.

When she had chopped up and disposed of the day's new players she often returned to a favorite subject: her husband. I once read extracts to her from Philip Ziegler's biography of Edward VIII, in which the Prince of Wales (as he then was) was described by a contemporary as "part child, part genius." She leapt at the comparison, as she did at many descriptions of her husband in which he appeared as naive, self-indulgent, or emotionally immature.

In fairness, these were adjectives she was quite quick to direct at almost any member of the male species, and she was not blind to the Prince's many virtues, among which she always included a touching vulnerability. When she spoke of him fondly—which admittedly was rare—it was with regret that he allowed his good intentions and good ideas (she stopped short of genius) to be hijacked by unscrupulous hangers-on. It was no surprise that many of her fiercest critics were drawn from these sycophantic ranks.

Even in the terminal stages of the marriage, when she was ready one minute to regard him as a wayward son and the next as her cold-blooded persecutor, I never knew her criticism of him to carry lasting malice. Nor do I doubt that she would have responded with pleasure and secret relief to marital peace overtures. For reasons that became clearer as my knowledge of them grew, however, the Waleses sadly found that they had less to contribute to their marriage than its survival demanded.

Meanwhile romance, in any of its forms, was what the Princess quite reasonably craved. She felt that it was withheld by her husband—deliberately or through incapacity— and therefore she sought and found it elsewhere.

Sometimes she found it in flirtatiousness at work, where her feminine charm was employed with precision and deadly effect. I was not immune to extravagant remarks such as "Oh Patrick, you're the moon and stars to me!"—even if the sentiment they implied did not seem to last very long.

Sometimes she found it in the supportive but necessarily circumscribed proximity of her personal staff. Any form of physical contact was, of course, unthinkable, but she would sometimes allow us all a playful *frisson* as we were invited to help her tie her army boots or check an evening gown's tricky zipper.

With rare but spectacular exceptions, she was very cautious about expressing the aridity of her love life. Sometimes, though, the banter with which the painful subject was made bearable would slip, and in a voice suddenly sad and reflective, she would say, "Sex is OK, but sex with love is the best, isn't it?" *That* was quite a tough one to answer.

Although these sources of consolation were safe, they were no real substitute for the pleasures and hazards of a passionate relationship. Instead she developed an ability to experience emotions vicariously, drawing on her existing skills as a shrewd people-watcher and a natural talent to be sympathetic. St. Paul's injunction to laugh with those who laugh and mourn with those who mourn might have been written for her. Sadly, joy is not an easy emotion to experience at second hand and after an initial expression of pleasure at another's good fortune, she often found that it left her feeling envious and dissatisfied. This always seemed to be most pronounced in maternity wards. It did not take a genius to work out why.

In addition, she did find some consolation in well-documented liaisons with other men, most notably with James Hewitt, who already rode high in her affections when I joined her staff. He was a regular but discreet visitor to KP, although our paths seldom crossed. Sometimes when I was leaving the red-haired Captain would be arriving, emitting a palpable sense of unease and a nervous but winning smile.

Later, the Princess closely involved me in her attempts—by then—to distance herself from him. I even carried discouraging messages to him at his barracks when he was planning a newspaper revelation about their relationship "to put the record straight" (something, incidentally, that I have never thought possible on practically any subject). In 1989, however, the affair was just one more thing to be ignored, another sign of our unhappy times.

Had I wanted to, I could have found out more and sometimes did, especially over a beer with a detective. I knew, however, that it was more important to be able to deny convincingly knowledge of anything that my boss might later wish she had not done. Being a royal conscience might be a wonderfully self-justifying job, but it would be a short one.

She was *paranoid* that her affair would be discovered—but only because it would weaken her moral superiority over her husband. She only admitted the affair with Hewitt after it had become public knowledge. After his return from the Gulf War in 1991, the Princess often visited Hewitt at his family home in Devon. She was terrified of being found out and I even warned the police that they might have to lie to cover up for her. I was shocked to hear myself say it, but they just smiled indulgently.

She wistfully imagined a house in the country—an idyllic domestic life for them both, full of children, dogs, and horses—but when he became too besotted, she was embarrassed and realized he was a liability in the battle against her husband for public sympathy.

Although I chose to be ignorant at the time, and naive too, it was sadly obvious even to me that these desperate, ill-starred affairs shared Jane Austen's description of adultery as merely consuming the participants with "universal longing." As I watched her struggle with this longing, but also with conscience, duty, and an enduring loyalty to her husband, I sometimes found it hard not to recognize some truth in her generally low opinion of men.

More than once I heard her reproduce a favorite and very secondhand phrase, picked up from TV I guessed, but no less sincere for that: "All men are bastards!" Sometimes, catching a flicker of reaction on my face, she might add, "Sorry, Patrick."

I began to watch closely how the Princess coped with the strains of her predicament. She was not good at relaxing, although she devoted increasing amounts of time and energy to finding the "peace of mind" she often told me she was searching for. Her luggage was always well stocked with the latest in a seemingly endless catalog of remedies—for stress, sleeplessness, and various unspecified deficiencies, aches, and pains. There were numerous varieties of homeopathic pills, tinctures, and oils, all accompanied by scrappy instructions that she would sometimes read aloud to me in search of guidance I could not give.

Aromatherapy was a continuing fascination, which was not surprising given her love of perfumes, flowers, and scented candles. Keen to share her belief in its revitalizing qualities, she once gave me some expensively prepared bath oil. It was a kind gesture, even if it did make the bath—and me—smell of Harpic to my uneducated nose.

An army of practitioners went in and out of favor. Among the masseurs, Stephen Twigg was a favorite. She believed that his trademark deep-tissue technique helped to relieve her of conveniently unspecific aches and pains caused by stress.

Colonic irrigation was another popular discovery, thanks to the Duchess of York. The semimedical procedures and professional intimacy were highly attractive. So too was the skill and sympathy of the eminent Chrissie Fitzgerald, who so dexterously wielded the various tubes and solutions. The attraction, which survived for several years, waned abruptly as Chrissie's treatment started to be accompanied by doses of robust common sense. Her crime, it appeared, was to be insufficiently sympathetic to the injustices of her royal client's existence—perhaps because she had witnessed darker shades of the same misfortune farther down the social scale. She also did not take kindly to the press attention that the Princess seemed powerless to stop bringing, literally, to her door. Chrissie was dropped abruptly, even brutally, soon afterward. Others found it easier to keep to their script.

Fitness trainers such as Carolan Brown remained in favor until the Princess's death, as did relays of astrologers. Some, however, such as psychotherapist Susie Orbach or self-improvement guru Anthony Robbins, found their work less conducive to the quick fix that she craved.

Sympathy and attention rather than reality were what the Princess sought. She paid no more than lip service to the alternative lifestyles on offer and did not embrace the complementary medicine philosophy in the way that her husband did. Nonetheless, if her exploration of her own health needs lacked conviction or direction, her attitude to her therapists did not. Their greatest value was in the attention they lavished on her.

Some became highly influential and colored her thinking, with unpredictable results. Called upon to speak publicly on health or social issues, she would sometimes show an alarming tendency to recycle advice she had imperfectly understood from one of these unofficial sources. Following the thoughts of a current favorite, she once spoke convincingly of children's status as "miniature adults"—to the consternation of the patronage involved, which preferred to think of them as anything but.

Quite apart from the frustration it caused her official advisers, this hunger for guidance from dubious sources had a destructive effect on the Princess's own judgment, a quality she did not lack when she applied herself. She sowed gossip and traded rumor with them and they in turn encouraged a sense of infallibility that undermined her innate sense of self-preservation. A blind belief in her own intuition increasingly became a substitute for balanced analysis, or even plain common sense.

It also undermined her sense of the ridiculous. "Do you know," she said to me one day in June 1992, "my astrologer says my husband will never be king!" That may have been exactly what she wanted to hear at the time, but it did not appear to alter her husband's daily routine one jot. Yet she continued to heed her astrologers' predictions, the more dire the better, particularly where the Prince was concerned. Sure enough, she was rewarded with regular forecasts of helicopter crashes, skiing accidents, and other calamities that obstinately refused to befall him—much to her relief, I have no doubt.

Ultimately she lost touch with reality in her restless desire for reassurance. In the last year of her life she was quoted in *Le Monde* as saying, "I don't need to take advice from anyone. I trust my own instincts."

The truth was, she consumed advice insatiably and, depending on her mood, she would take it from anyone. Her credulity seemed directly proportional to the thrill factor of whatever prediction she was being invited to believe— which made her pretty much like the rest of us, I reluctantly concluded.

Even so, I thought it important to affect a cheerful cynicism about every latest fad. My lighthearted attitude was intended to acknowledge the need for attention without conceding that she was anything other than physically fit as a fiddle. I never knew her to be genuinely ill for a single day. She kept her side of the pact by allowing—and maybe even welcoming—my theatrical disapproval as she swallowed the latest offerings from her army of alternative practitioners. As a reassuring contrast, I extolled the more traditional merits of hot whiskey and a good book as aids to happy slumber. Perhaps sensibly, however, she avoided alcohol.

The real problem was that she had no safe substitute for the wise, supportive, and *unpaid* company that, in the end, was the only medicine she really needed. Underneath the lightheartedness I was worried about her growing tendency to find pseudomedical excuses for attracting attention and sympathy. She became increasingly indiscriminate in her search for physical remedies for emotional disorders. Complementary cures were freely interspersed with more conventional sleeping pills and stimulants.

The effect of these combinations was anybody's guess, since no single doctor knew what she was dosing herself with, let alone controlled her intake. Deep-tissue massage and painful vitamin injections also became regular features of pretour preparations. Once, in a fit of hypochondria, she wangled an urgent MRI scan. Unsurprisingly, the scan confirmed my own less penetrating diagnosis: she *was* as fit as a fiddle.

Reassurances and remedies were all to little effect in lonely hotels and guest residences, however. All the pills in the world did not seem able to help then, and she fell back into less esoteric habits. Too often, time spent in her room supposedly relaxing was spent in obsessive phone calls— gossip with girlfriends; gossip and flirting with admirers; gossip and intrigue with palace staff back home; and, on the plus side, laughter and light relief with her children, whom she missed acutely whenever she was abroad without them.

*N*othing she took seemed to dull her quick-wittedness, or her quick tongue. Depending on her mood, I found that she could be perceptive and thoughtful with her praise and encouragement, if a little inconsistent. Getting a pat on the back one day did not protect you from being kicked the day after for doing the same thing.

When she was unhappy, her natural suspicion and deviousness took control. Then her verbal skills were employed to hurt and confuse. When roused, she used words like tomahawks and her aim seldom failed. She would know, with a cat's cunning, when to let you feel the claw in her velvet paw. Like the predator she sometimes was, she would stalk her victim, waiting for his or her attention to be distracted before striking.

Typically, we might be on a train about to arrive at our destination and my mind would be preoccupied with the practical demands of the next few minutes, when she would see her opportunity. Her voice would take on that tone of guileless inconsequentiality that always made the hairs stand up on the back of my neck.

"Patrick, you never told me I'd been invited to speak at the Sprained Wrist Association AGM. I know you wouldn't understand, but people with sprained wrists are excluded by society. I think we ought to make a speech about it."

The opening volley was designed to saturate my de-

fenses. While still distractedly craning out of the window
for a telltale sign of red carpet and a press posse, I would unconsciously assess the incoming missiles:

- She has deliberately chosen a bad moment for me. This
  kind of premeditation always spells trouble. Look out for
  the second salvo. (My God, I hope she doesn't know
  about that business with her new car...)
- She is accusing me of deliberately concealing an invitation from her because I disapprove of it or because I am
  too lazy to research it. (Both true on occasions, as she
  probably knows.)
- Why the Sprained Wrist Association, for goodness' sake?
  Aha—*cherchez* a handsome radial osteopath. Extra trouble: she loves to pretend you are jealous.
- Note that I am too insensitive to understand. This means
  I have missed a recent opportunity to be sympathetic,
  exacerbated by the fact that, unlike herself and people
  living with SWS (Sprained Wrist Syndrome), I have no
  idea what it is like to feel rejected.
- And now "we" have to make a speech. This means a
  heap of exploratory work with the Department of
  Health (again) and probably a ruined weekend while I
  draft the speech (again). The speech will then be rejected
  because—take your pick—she has gone off the os-
  teopath/the *Daily Mail* says SWS is all in the mind/the
  astrologer forbids speeches during the current transit of
  Pluto/the Prince is patron of the Sprained Knee Association and we are making a show of not competing at the
  moment.
- Worst of all, somebody has snitched on me. How else did
  she find out about the invitation? Surely not one of the
  girls in the office...somebody looking through my papers...maybe the butler...the driver...Oh no! So she
  must know about—
- "Patrick! And *when* were you going to tell me you'd *ruined* my new car?"

[CURTAIN]

Of course it helped, always having the last word.

*A*s time passed and I traveled with her more and more, I observed a phenomenon more usually associated with declining politicians and rock stars. The Princess found foreign tours stressful, both physically and mentally, yet she needed the buzz only they could provide. Tours also put her under unusually intense press scrutiny, because the traveling pack had no distractions other than her and the hotel bar, yet she delighted in the unmatched range of exotic and heart-tugging photo opportunities they provided. This persisted even when, as sometimes happened, the resulting press coverage back home was infuriatingly inaccurate and slanted.

When I challenged one of the traveling correspondents with a particularly misleading front-page story bearing his byline, he genuinely seemed to share my outrage. "It's the editors," he protested. "They rewrite my stuff to conform with their current line on the War of the Waleses."

This last remark came back to me later. The Princess's relations with the media were becoming a subject of growing interest to me, and to the public at large. I had already noticed that both she and her media pursuers had almost made a game out of satisfying their mutual requirement for each other (with truth as the first piece to leave the board), even though at times she would show flashes of resentment at press attention.

It was also dawning on me that there was something in her character that was attracted to this love-hate relationship. It was echoed elsewhere in her life. I often saw it in her attitude to her husband, or his family, or the public duties she did so well, and on each occasion it was the love half of the equation that seemed hardest for her to feel. Time and again, like an untrusting child, she doubted the dependability of the love she was shown. Small wonder, then, that she protected any affection she felt able to give—except to her children—with a portcullis of preconditions.

On a day-to-day basis, our job was to design her program in such a way that the press had the best possible chance to report her routine public duties favorably, without inconveniencing the organizations she was visiting. If those organizations benefited in the process—and some did in spectacular fashion—then so much the better. On a deeper level, however, a dangerous mutual dependence was certainly growing. The media stimulated the Princess's appetite for attention, but never satisfied her true requirement for love and security.

This produced some confusing results. A distressed Princess is famously remembered to have asked, "What have the tabloids ever done for me?" To this plaintively rhetorical question tabloid editors gave rather less rhetorical replies along the lines of, "We made you, Darlin'!" And so, in a sense, they had.

Unfortunately, it was not in a sense that gave her any feeling of genuine worth. After all, if being "made" is to have a life as thin as the paper it is printed on, it might make you doubt your very existence. I came to think that the media were a kind of family to her. Theirs was the language of a desensitized childhood—extravagant praise followed by harsh rebuke. Like a child coaxed onto its parent's lap for comfort, the pain of then being pushed carelessly aside was all the greater for her.

Although I only dimly understood the reasons for the Princess's childlike temperament, I knew they were deep and traumatic. They left her constantly in need of reassurance. Tragically, she cared less and less whether this reassurance was healthy, or where she found it. For her, words of comfort were even more essential than for the rest of us.

It was one reason why she was so good at dispensing them herself. How often her messages of kindness and encouragement must have seemed a mirror of those she would have liked to receive. Perhaps the most poignant difference was that from her the words were as genuine as she could make them, but those she received were avidly gathered up like flowers on a walkabout, unconditionally and indiscriminately. The words were what mattered, and she cared little whether they had been truly meant, or whether they came from policeman or President, butcher or baker, butler or playboy.

For me, however, especially in those early years, it was enough to know that she had to be jollied along with flattery, humor, gift-wrapped advice, and very visible loyalty—especially from men. I had only to master the formula, combined with an alert sense of self-preservation, to get through my brief appointment successfully.

*A*nother thing I noticed about the Princess as my apprenticeship came to an end was her tendency very vocally to dread overseas tours but then, as soon as one was over, to look forward eagerly to the next. Given the many extra stresses and strains imposed by touring, this mystified me.

Then I realized what the attraction was. Traveling press aside, tours provided her with an endless supply of new and interesting supporting casts. She liked foreigners and, of course, the only ones she met abroad were the ones who liked her. In fact, it must have seemed to her that they adored her, unreservedly and unconditionally. *They* did not read menacing broadsheet newspaper analyses of her waning relevance to the power of the British establishment. *They* did not stop to consider whether she manipulated London's popular media. *They* did not question her sincerity and motives in the way increasingly favored by her Pharisee critics back home.

It is hard to blame her if, in the end, she preferred the company of enthusiastic foreigners to the wan faces of rain-soaked, provincial England; or the simple gratitude of a limbless Pathan tribesman to the false smiles of London society; or the attentiveness of a playboy lover to the lizardlike watchfulness she felt scouring her from the drawing rooms of Gloucestershire or the smoking rooms of St. James's.

Noticing the quick approval she seemed to attract abroad, I wondered how much of the Princess's glamour was due to her innate qualities and how much she owed to the status she had acquired on marriage. The answer, I suppose, was an intricate mixture of both. Deprived of one—as she was when she effectively relinquished her royal status toward the end—the other had less chance to shine. Only the unique conjunction of inbred talent and historic opportunity could have created such a phenomenon.

Few film stars survive the transition from big screen to real life without losing some of their glamour on the way. Having been to more than my fair share of film premieres, I can vouch for the fact that in the flesh many actors do look surprisingly unheroic. It is the same with others in public life: to retain the importance we give them, they usually need to be surrounded by the trappings of office.

Royalty is famously no exception to this rule. The history of monarchy is one of clearly visible distinctions between them and us—from Henry VIII's outsize codpiece to the extra-width gold lace worn on today's royal uniforms. The necessity visibly to emphasize royal people's uniquely superior status has kept generations of courtiers happily employed, not least because of the fringe benefits that accumulate for themselves. I will not forget the hot flush of conceit that swept over me as I opened the little Gieves and Hawkes box and out tumbled my first pair of royal ciphers—little silver *D*s, one of which I wore with bursting pride on the left shoulder of my uniform on the rare occasions when I was still required to dress as a naval officer.

Unlike mere service equerries, the advantage of hereditary leaders is that, wherever they are and whatever they wear, they usually carry the genetic badge of office that marked their ancestors for greatness. This is one of many ways in which they differ from film stars. Nevertheless, even if they could quell a mob with a single Hanoverian glare, royal people still draw comfort and strength from the familiarity of grand surroundings.

The Princess could employ these props to dazzling effect, but her need for them differed subtly from conventional royal practice. For one thing, her inherent gifts created an aura that perfectly complemented her royal status (Ruby Wax remarked that the Princess had "charisma you can *surf* off"). Returning in the royal helicopter to Althorp or her old school, she would gleefully exclaim, "*This* is the way to arrive!" More often, however, she showed a touching disinterest in the opportunities she had to overawe impressionable people with the accoutrements of her office.

I was reminded of the truth of this one afternoon on a blustery Cambridge railway platform. I had accompanied her on a low-key visit to a drugs project in the city and, not uncommonly, for reasons of economy we were traveling by (very) ordinary train. For some reason I now forget, we were not a very happy band that day. Having given her best for the drugs project and its clientele, the Princess had little bonhomie left over for the detective and me.

Her body language was usually quite unambiguous and we had no difficulty in recognizing that she wanted to be left alone. This was a cue which, in the circumstances, we were rather mischievously happy to take. We retreated as far away as we dared—in my case into the station bookstall—and left her apparently alone among the commuters. Needless to say, we kept her under observation from our places of concealment, so I was able to monitor first her gratifying look of disquiet when she realized she really had shaken us off, and then the reaction of other travelers.

Confronted by what appeared to be the world's most photographed woman, statuesque in high heels and a pinstripe suit and apparently unattended on their familiar platform, their reflexes were instructive. A few just failed to notice. Rather more noticed but did not want to be *seen* to have noticed, probably out of a decent desire not to intrude on what was presumably a private appearance. Some backed off to a safe distance and then stared. A surprising number paused, looked her in the eye, and nodded different degrees of what was recognizably a bow before continuing their stroll along the platform.

The experience of being almost alone in a public place—and hence almost like an ordinary person—was one she repeated quite frequently. As well as offering a fleeting sense of normality, it did also allow her to enjoy the innocent pleasure of being the object of excited "is she or isn't she?" whispering among bystanders, most frequently in the Kensington High Street branch of Marks & Spencer where she was a familiar figure, especially in the food department.

It could be fun. One afternoon the Princess and I were driving to Burleigh. We were in a very unremarkable Ford, with no outriders or visible escort. We needed gasoline and she pulled into the next filling station. I did the man's task with the pump, followed by the man's other task with the credit card in the shop. By the cash register two boys were arguing about the identity of the woman in the driver's seat of the maroon Granada.

"No, it isn't!"

"Yes, it is!"

"No, it isn't! It can't be! She'd 'ave police motorbikes if it was Princess Di!"

"Don't you know it's rude to stare?" said the man behind the register. Still arguing, they disappeared back to their waiting mother, who was by now also looking rather intrigued by the woman adjusting her makeup in the next-door car.

As I finished paying, the man said, "Did anyone ever tell you your friend looks just like Princess Di?"

I followed his gaze back to the car, where the driver had put away her compact and was obviously keen to get back on the road. I furrowed my brow. "Now you come to mention it, in this light...I suppose there's a passing resemblance..."

"Looks just like her. She could make a fortune on the telly."

6

Toychest

*A*n old lag on the royal scene once gave me a very good piece of advice. "Never forget," he said over one of many brimming glasses, "to these people you're just a toy. They'll wind you up and watch you whizz all over the place and then, when your spring runs down, they'll throw you away and get another one."

In turn, I passed on a version of this guidance whenever new recruits fell into my hands. It was a gross exaggeration, of course, and it suggested a heartlessness about our royal family that was seldom my experience. Nonetheless, I thought—and still think—that it contained a grain of truth. Deference breeds indifference. Historically equipped with employees selected for their talent in the art of brown-nosing, there is little incentive for the royal recipient to experiment with more enlightened forms of personnel management.

In time, the respective postures become institutionalized. The servants seek ways to please, tendering advice with one eye on their pensions (I should know, I did it). The masters become jaded and indifferent, prepared eventually to swap a once-loved plaything for a new model with fresh batteries. The nursery cupboard is always well stocked with replacements, selected for safety and conformity. What is more, all the discarded puppets have conveniently signed confidentiality clauses, so there will be no trouble from *them*.

Every generation of toys thinks it will be different for them. Somehow they will escape the fate of all their predecessors and grow old in wisdom, honor, and their owners' esteem. Inevitably, however, most will be consigned to the charity box when the restless royal eye is caught by the next novelty.

You may think, rightly, that I was prematurely cynical, but the old lag had done me a favor by wiping the new toy's shining eagerness off my face. When I later relayed his lesson to those I thought would not have time to learn it for themselves, it saved them, I hope, the expenditure of energy necessary to court fleeting royal favor and the unhappiness caused by the inevitable eventual rejection.

It was obvious that some royal people had grown accustomed to the seasonal change of playthings and sometimes quite enjoyed it. After all, why should they be denied this harmless pleasure, since they are denied so much else? But at an early stage it dawned on me that the only thing more valuable—and more permanent—than a new toy would be a *toymaker*.

No sooner had I formed this theory than its truth was confirmed in a sharp little exchange. After three years of what was generally held to be exemplary duty as the Princess's equerry, my predecessor Richard Aylard had transferred to a post that was clearly on the Prince's side of the invisible divide running through our still joint office. In a typically nonpartisan gesture, he offered to cover for me on one of the Princess's engagements when I was unavailable. To my surprise his offer was immediately rejected. What could this good and faithful servant have done to incur such rapid alienation? Sadly I concluded that his sin must have been to transfer his allegiance, as she saw it, to her husband. The reason was probably immaterial. "Once gone, always gone," she said, and set her face resolutely against him.

I was naive enough to be flattered by this revelation. It was one of my boss's less endearing habits that she encouraged her current favorite toy to take satisfaction from the misfortunes of his or her predecessor. It was one of my less endearing habits that I fell for it, at least initially.

If nothing else, however, it validated my theory about the advantages of being a toymaker rather than a mere toy. From then on I made a special point of controlling as much as I could of the hiring and firing process—which, when I became her private secretary, was practically all of it. I would like to think my involvement tempered some of the Princess's more arbitrary attempts at personnel management. In the end, though, I could not escape the reality of royal service, which is that professional performance is less important than "chemistry" in determining the progress of your career (or lack of it).

From my observations of the royal family, I gradually came to the conclusion that inherited power values survival above responsibility. You might say that such considerations are irrelevant, since royalty has been shorn of all real power anyway, thanks to generations of people's representatives ready to risk their necks in the shearing. Yet it is perhaps because of this loss that some of today's royalty seems all the more anxious to exercise its power over the smaller domains now left to it, and these begin and end at home. To a dresser, a valet, a housemaid, a cook, a chauffeur, a butler, a lady-in-waiting, or even a private secretary, the royal master or mistress still holds the power of professional life or death. At least that would be the case, but for safeguards offered by postfeudal employment legislation and the spasmodic interest of the press.

This was even more true of the power acquired on marriage by the Princess. It was not that she was unfeeling, or lacking many of the qualities associated with effective leadership. Often the reverse was true. Rather, she had an iron resolve—understandable to a certain extent—to put her own interests above everything else in every situation. She subjected most decisions to a simple test: How will this action affect my reputation, power base, or convenience? It was further evidence of her subconscious need to assert her exclusive authority over as much and as many as lay within her reach.

She applied this test to people just as much as she did to decisions affecting her public profile. Cannily, she knew that the two areas sometimes overlapped. No Queen of Hearts—even in the making—could afford to spoil the public image with revelations about unsaintly behavior toward her own staff. Characteristically she would preempt such revelations with a simple denial. At the time of Anne Beckwith-Smith's "retirement," she had herself quoted as saying, "I don't sack anybody."

Perhaps only the Queen herself, famously loyal to her staff, could make such a claim. It was certainly not true of the Princess. The real significance of the remark is this: she actually convinced herself it was true. Put another way, she actually thought that having an old toy—sorry, long-serving cook—declared redundant (the usual way round the law) was not the same as having him sacked.

It was one of those remarks that she knew sounded good and that she would like to believe was true. Most of the time she conveniently forgot that it was not. After all, nobody was going to remind her. The curious thing was that so many people accepted such pronouncements about herself as if they *were* true. Thus her reputation was seen to be invincible, her domestic power base was strengthened, and her convenience was unaffected, as cooks were easily replaced.

Such wishful thinking seemed to become more unabashed as the years passed. There are many other examples that come to mind: "I will never complain again" (Nepal 1993); "I want to be Queen of people's hearts" (*Panorama* 1995); "I don't need to take advice from anyone" (*Le*

Monde 1997). Wide-eyed innocence became one of her favorite defensive ploys, acquired, I supposed, in childhood to protect her fragile self-confidence, especially when she knew she was in the wrong. The trouble was, she unblinkingly employed it in defiance of any unwelcome facts—and usually got away with it.

Megalomania is no more attractive for being played out on a small scale, at least from the viewpoint of those in the firing line, and they come no smaller than the pieces on the nursery floor whose time is up. Their sin might be no more than Richard's—a perceived allegiance to the "other side." Like his, it need have no bearing on professional competence. It could be merely that they knew too much (whatever their proven discretion), or that they laughed too little (however quietly dedicated), or that they spoke too much sense (however loyally expressed), or that they shared too little in her misery (whatever the cause of their happiness). Or—the worst crime of all—they had just become *boring*. An exaggeration? Hardly. As her chosen instrument I officiated at too many of these playroom executions to doubt her intentions.

I remember the first. In 1990, a secretary convicted *in absentia* of most of the high crimes listed above stood at my desk awaiting judgment. She knew the sack was hovering over her. As Wodehouse would say, she could practically hear the beating of its wings. This was part of the process. Very few victims were given their P45 out of the blue. Usually there was a softening-up period in which the transgressor would be frozen out of the Princess's affections. The warning signs were obvious.

"Is Charlotte on holiday *again*?" she would say to me.

"Yes, she is, Ma'am. In fact I sent you a note about it. You said you were quite happy. Is there a problem?"

"Oh no,"—innocently—"but she does seem to be having rather a lot of holidays … and we're *so* busy. It just seems so unfair on everybody else …" Her voice would trail off, leaving me to pick up a fairly typical clutch of veiled barbs:

- Charlotte is lazy. She may be taking no more than her holiday entitlement—or even less, it was not uncommon—but this inconvenient fact can be overlooked. Now, by royal command, she is lazy.
- I am incompetent. Why have I allowed a secretary to go on holiday when the diary is so busy? The fact that there is actually a lull in activity—hence the conscientious Charlotte's decision to take leave this week—can also be overlooked. This is a pincer movement, designed to intimidate me from taking the victim's side. Too often, I confess, I allowed it to silence me.
- The Princess, by contrast, is working *very* hard. You could dispute this, but only if you were ready to lose your job. In royal circles it is accepted as a matter of sacred truth that, by definition, all members of our modern royal family work terribly hard all the time—even if a cursory analysis of their daily existence might call this into question.
- She *cares* about the extra workload now shouldered by the other staff. Here was a classic example of "caring Di" behavior that was not quite what it seemed. By expressing concern for her remaining hardworking staff, she was actually isolating the absentee and preparing the ground for the execution to follow.

For added emphasis, the rest of the staff—even those notoriously less dedicated than Charlotte—would receive redoubled praise and interest from the Princess, now advancing on them with a careless laugh and a prepared ration of girly gossip.

It took a curious form of toadying to enjoy favors thus received, but some managed it. For most, though, it was enough just to keep your head down and hope that it was not going to be your turn as victim just yet. Perhaps it would not come at all. Such comforting thoughts came easily when the big blue eyes looked on you favorably. The gaze seemed full of trust and expectation then; quite incapable of measuring you for your professional coffin.

Being frozen out was a lingering death in which messages would be unacknowledged, memos ignored or even destroyed, and mere physical existence "blanked." This was especially easy when chances to ignore a desperate bow or curtsy were so abundant. For people chosen for their sense of loyalty, it was a torture few could bear for long. Many saved the Princess the trouble of sacking them and quietly took their leave, usually with great dignity.

I looked at the unhappy secretary standing by my desk, and she looked back at me. We both knew she had done nothing to warrant her dismissal. We both knew life would be unbearable for her if she stayed. I could not contain my revulsion; I had to get outside. I took her for a walk round Green Park and asked her how the parting could be made easier for her. References, medical insurance, gratuity—I promised, and delivered, them all. Her quiet tears diminished me even further.

I ran into her again some years later. Being the sort of person she was, she had quite forgiven my part in the shameful charade. Curiously, and not untypically, she had forgiven the Princess too. It is an astonishing fact that such forgivability was freely conferred on the Princess by a sacked secretary and a besotted world. It was surely her greatest and most exploited talent.

The executions continued throughout my time with the Princess: two ladies-in-waiting, a butler, a cook, three secretaries, a chauffeur, a housemaid, two dressers, and others I cannot now recall. Most went quietly. When the time came, few had any regrets. The Princess saw to that, which I suppose was a form of unintentional kindness, if a cruel one.

In its extreme forms the softening-up process could be actively hostile. In one case, the Princess started a rumor about a secretary's personal life, waited for it to gain currency and then cited it as damning evidence of unsuitability. (The secretary left, but only out of disgust.) In another she launched a bitterly resentful assault on a junior member of her staff whom she observed enjoying a happy relationship with another. (They are now married.)

She thought nothing of laying false trails, once accusing another junior employee of leaking secrets to the press when she knew that the only real perpetrator of such indiscretions was herself. "I saw him speaking to a photographer," she hissed to me between public smiles during an engagement. "He's always tipping them off. That's why I'm being photographed so much at the moment."

This seemed unlikely. To most royal employees, especially junior ones, the rat pack was to be feared and avoided—whereas I knew it often suited the Princess very nicely to be "surprised" by paparazzi. Depending on the location, it enabled her to send powerful messages to the British public, even if it was just that she looked great in gym gear.

"Take a look," she whispered urgently. "He's doing it again!"

From the window of the homeless hostel we were visiting I observed the accused driver approaching a notoriously zealous photographer. "I'll deal with it," I said, making for the door. I was propelled by curiosity, and by a desire to prove her wrong, if only to myself.

As I approached the pair from behind, I heard raised voices. The driver was administering a friendly warning. "And if you stand there with your stupid ladder I'll bloody well run you over…" A policeman overtook me, hurrying to the driver's support. I returned to my post, two paces behind the Princess.

Later, I went through the formality of reassuring her that her driver was to be trusted, but sadly this awkward fact went the same way as so many others that did not fit the scenario she was currently working on. Car journeys were frosty for weeks until a new target presented itself.

Her tantrums were the stuff of nursery vendettas. Her weapons were only grown-up versions of playground cattiness—the poisoned word, the sly rumor, sending to Coventry. As I labored one night with the long-suffering personnel officer over the tortuous administration of another mercy killing, I wondered at the deep well of bitterness that must lie within the unhappy Princess. Nothing else could explain her insatiable appetite for human sacrifices.

Such was the innate loyalty of most people in the Waleses' service, and such the mystique of happy normality that we tried to create around our bosses, that even this rather feudal system for staff motivation produced few audible murmurings from the lower deck. It was just accepted that life in royal service might not pay very much and might terminate abruptly, but it still carried enough attractions to make the risk worthwhile.

I was relieved to find that my role as occasional executioner was not held against me by the staff—or at least they were too kind to show it. The greatest opposition came from within myself. Loyal functionary that I was, I still felt uneasy at the fundamental injustice of so many of the dismissals.

Sometimes, however, the toys fought back. Soon after I resigned, a hitherto timorous housemaid was selected as the next victim. To everyone's surprise, she sued the Princess for unfair dismissal. To nobody's surprise, she won a generous out-of-court settlement. The incident attracted little attention, but I hope its significance was not lost on my former employer. Perhaps the humble housemaid taught her a lesson I never had the audacity to attempt. Of course, though, I had my mortgage to protect.

Taking into account all these factors about her relationship with her staff, it is not difficult to imagine the vehemence with which the Princess dismissed Richard's offer of help. The finality of her judgment was not lost on me, and if she could be unfeeling with her own staff, she could be merciless to those she perceived to be her enemies.

The list of enemies most certainly included any who worked for her husband. Being legitimate targets in her eyes, and temptingly defenseless, these were marked for special attention. Any she thought had crossed her—such as the chauffeur who took a shrewd, long-term career decision to switch to the Prince—were cast into the icy Siberia of her disapproval. She would pretend they did not exist, even as they made their loyal bow or curtsy, and they became leading players in the conspiracies that she increasingly saw formed against her. The fact that most of these plots did not exist outside her imagination was little consolation to those on the receiving end of her suspicion.

As I pondered the significance of Richard's exclusion, one thing was clear. However saintly her intentions and however justified her generous treatment in the press, my boss kept a knife in her handbag. It was long and jagged and quick, and I was going to do my damnedest to make sure it did not end up protruding from my back for a long time to come. That it eventually would, I think deep down I never doubted, but that painful experience was still six years in the future. As time passed, I also recognized that I could not rely on a repeat of Richard's promotion to a cozy refuge on the Prince's staff if my place in the Princess's toy cupboard started to look shaky. Opportunities to change horses midstream became increasingly rare as we felt our way into the uncharted waters of the Waleses' separation.

Perhaps it was hardly surprising that people became toys to her. For the first time in her life she was beginning to wield real power, even if it was only over a few people on her own staff. The power, however, came without responsibility. She did not have to deal with the consequences of her decisions.

Also, as I could already see, she was increasingly battling to make herself popular in her own right and so less traditionally royal. In the process she developed a tendency to pick on those least able to fight back. It takes no great insight to see this as a reaction to her own weakness. She felt powerless in the face of her superiors, the in-laws she saw as cold and hard, and she felt oppressed by work that in her eyes only exploited her. Her subordinates were the obvious target.

I had no evidence, but I increasingly felt that some un-conscious childhood memory was being endlessly replayed. The unfairness she felt, though painful, was at least familiar, and if ever its pain showed signs of easing up, she would reimpose it either in her imagination or by deliberate provocation. Like anyone setting out to find reasons to be unhappy or dissatisfied, she had no need to look very far. The people nearest to her—family (with the notable excep-tion of her children), staff, or friends—provided plenty of material. If, for tactical reasons, they did not fit the bill, there was always the diary, stuffed full—at her request—with endless demands on her good nature.

It became just part of my life that I saw this reality while the world saw the saint it naturally preferred. In the end, the contradictions in her character created unbearable tensions for many who were close to her. These were only magnified by the knowledge that such self-destructiveness was bound to infect the good she was capable of doing. Too many peo-ple's hopes rested on a belief that she was as wholesome as she looked. Trying to keep that image alive and at the same time contrive some purpose—even happiness—for her own life eventually became too frustrating for me and I resigned. In the same way, I imagine, her husband eventually felt un-able to resist the attractions of life with someone less psy-chologically demanding. In fact, the temptation must have been all the stronger for him, given his own tendency to morose introspection.

Away from the Palace intrigue, the Princess was busy on most days with public engagements in London or the provinces. They were the routine fare of a thousand court circulars. For a public still trusting in a royal happy ending, they were further proof that she was an integral part of the familiar and treasured face of our rock-solid ruling family.

This humdrum work in drizzly Britain contrasted sharply

with the color, drama, and glamour of the overseas tours
that she eventually came to prefer. Abroad, in the sunshine
and surrounded by impressionable foreigners, stardom came
easily, especially against so many exotic backdrops. Nevertheless, it was the work she did back home in the UK that
was the bedrock of her reputation, and it repeatedly pleased
and surprised me that it brought such obvious benefits to
the people and organizations she visited.

It made her feel tired, but from wholesome hard work. It
made her feel appreciated, however hard she might try to
dismiss it. It stimulated her intellectually, however thick she
claimed to be. It also confronted her over and over again
with the painful, ugly realities of life at the other end of the
social scale. For her amusement and interest, therefore, as
well as my own, I set out to keep her occupied in ways that
would stand her apart from her adopted family and encourage her to think differently about the people who came
under her influence.

It was no coincidence that, just as her private life was undergoing such traumatic upheavals, she increasingly wanted
her work in public to tend toward the grittier end of the
charity spectrum. This was a highly visible way of expressing her growing sense of independence from the traditional
royal way of doing things, but her reasons also went deeper
than that. Rightly or not, she felt an increasing affinity with
those who had suffered and particularly with those whose
illness or disability made them outcasts, at least metaphorically.

It was as though she was trying to say, "I may look OK
on the outside, but on the inside I know what it's like to be
rejected," and it was perhaps because victims are said subconsciously to recognize other victims that this proved such
a rewarding philosophy in planning her public engagements. The more she involved herself in "unfashionable"
causes—and the more intimately too—the more she felt appreciated, even loved, in return. One example of this tendency was her increasing involvement in AIDS charities,

and in one particular instance it gave her scope both to give and receive the affection she felt she so desperately lacked.

Adrian Ward-Jackson was known as an engaging and warmhearted figure in the art world who had been a driving force in marshaling the performing arts behind the cause of AIDS awareness and treatment. Less well known was the fact that, behind the outgoing and charming exterior, he was himself fighting a desperate battle against the disease. With another friend, Angela Serota, wife of the director of the Tate Gallery, the Princess found in Adrian the chance to focus enormous reserves of compassion, as well as a particular fascination with this disease, which appeared to her to draw its victims principally from the beautiful and talented. It was as if Adrian provided the opportunity for her to exercise on a personal level the compassion that so publicly linked her name with a cause she had done so much, since 1988, to make fashionable.

After a protracted illness, Adrian's final weeks and eventual death drew from the Princess an almost obsessive interest in the harsh realities of mortality. I remember the panic that ensued when she decided she wanted a personal pager to carry with her at all times so that Adrian could reach her day or night. Finding the right style of pager quickly took priority over every other consideration. It was maybe not surprising, therefore, that I reflected that perhaps the calls from Adrian's deathbed made her feel wanted in a way that less dramatic situations seldom could.

I noticed the same type of sublimated emotion in many of her activities on behalf of AIDS charities. As a cause, it had unmatched publicity value. The juxtaposition of sex and death made great copy and photographs of the glamorous Princess touching the gaunt men who were the image of the disease in its early days went right around the world. These images, and others of the Princess with AIDS-stricken children in America and Africa, made an incalculable contribution to greater understanding of the disease, those who lived with it, and those who cared for them. It was a prime example of the way the Princess acted as an agent of compassion, whatever her own motives, bringing unpalatable truths to life before our eyes and showing the way to make things better.

"I have to do it, Patrick," she told me. "Nobody else understands the rejection they feel!" I thought this was overdramatic. She had a tendency to assume an acquaintance with suffering that did not immediately seem to square with her life of unusual health and comfort. She believed it was true, however, and as events were to confirm, she had her own reasons for speaking with authority on being an outsider. This being her motivation, she was able to share an extraordinary understanding with patients of a disease that on the face of it represented the antithesis of her own pure and saintly image.

She was reluctant to share this virtuous spotlight, although she made an exception in the summer of 1991 when the American President was in town and she accompanied Barbara Bush to the AIDS unit at Middlesex Hospital. The two women set to work in a ward crowded with patients, officials, and relatives. On her home turf, the Princess sparkled as she deployed the unbeatable mixture of charm, humor, and controlled pathos that was her trademark. Mrs. Bush, far from home and of a different generation, adopted a more traditional, almost regal style. It was an impressive performance nonetheless, and in its own way every bit as sincere.

The two champions of compassion posed for pictures outside in the sunshine before the American motorcade departed in a phalanx of blue limos and Secret Service agents. Following in our own more modest convoy, I told the Princess how much I had admired the First Lady's professionalism. The Princess's agreement was tinged with pride in her own technique. "I like her a lot," she said, "but she hasn't got intuition with these patients. They need lots of TLC." TLC—Tender Loving Care—was a commodity in which she felt she had cornered the market. It became a favorite expression but seldom appeared, as on this occasion, without a hidden barb.

Of course, such images of compassion would not have been used to best effect unless there was an effective organization in existence to exploit in the most effective way the Princess's association with the good cause. Although during the last few years of her life the Princess's name was frequently linked to all sorts of AIDS organizations, in fact she was only ever patron of one—the National AIDS Trust under the direction first of Margaret Jay and then of Professor Michael Adler.

The NAT provided the Princess with a perfect vehicle for involving herself in almost any aspect of the disease and its treatment worldwide. Even when at her most enthusiastic, however, I knew she had reservations about her identification with the illness. It was not a matter of prejudice. Although squeamish about the mechanics of the virus's sexual transmission, she shared the royal family's generally tolerant view of homosexuality and perhaps more graphically than most demonstrated her interest and concern for the real person behind the outward image. Yet when the AIDS statistics obstinately refused to spiral out of control in the way so scarily predicted by certain experts at the beginning of the decade, and when pointed questions were asked about the amount spent on AIDS treatment per patient capita compared with other diseases such as cancer, she began to get cold feet. By 1995 she had relegated what had once been her great crusading cause to the role of helpful standby when a compliant victim was needed for the purpose of securing a timely or poignant photo call.

This in turn highlighted a dilemma faced by many of her favorite charities. The more she worked with them, the better they came to know her and the more they began to suspect that the motives for her involvement did not precisely match their own. This became most glaringly obvious after her dramatic withdrawal from public life in 1993, when easy ways back into the limelight were at a premium. By then, however, the charities concerned were experienced and tolerant enough to recognize their patron's value to them even when her need for favorable publicity apparently outweighed any strictly philanthropic motive.

Knowing this, was it therefore more honest to call upon her services less frequently? Or should they close their eyes to any lack of purity in her motivation and content themselves with being used in ways that they could ultimately exploit for the benefit of those they were caring for? Most opted for the latter, and it says volumes for the maturity of the relationship she built up with them that both sides were able to exploit the other and maintain an appearance of high mutual esteem, whatever the frustrations that lurked below the surface.

Always a good example of her gifts was the work she did with the leading alcohol, drugs, and mental health charity Turning Point. Although AIDS and land mines earned her the biggest headlines, it was actually her less reported association with Turning Point that absorbed more of her charitable engagements than any other.

The charity's style was informal and practical. Operating out of spartan offices in Smithfield, it brought a simple message of hope to those on the least fashionable margins of society. Its clients had usually fallen through every safety net that the family and state could provide. In their despair they had turned to alcohol and other drugs, while many lived lives of exile in secure hospitals such as Broadmoor and Rampton. They might have been thought outside the pale of traditional royal interest, but to the Princess they were fellow sufferers—and for those who looked for distraction or inspiration, she was happy to be a gracious source of both.

Accompanying the Princess on such charitable visits, I learned something about her attitude to suffering. Traditional objects of royal compassion, such as the very elderly, the very young, the bedbound, and the disabled, were in many ways a captive audience. Unless they actively refused to receive the light of the royal countenance, if they were in the right ward they would be visited come what may. I did know of a few instances of people refusing to meet the Princess, even from their hospital beds. There was sometimes an undercurrent of suspicion about her motives and a reluctance to play opposite her in what some thought was her own version of a medical drama in which she had cast herself as the undisputed star. Indeed, I remember it was possible at one point to cut out of certain newspapers a small slip of paper, like a kidney donor card, that said something like, "In the event of accident I do not wish to be visited by the Princess of Wales."

For the Princess, real satisfaction came from encountering sufferers such as drug addicts or mental patients who could vote with their feet if they did not want to meet her. She could always spot the person who hung back either through shyness or prejudice and took legitimate pride in persuading them to speak to her, which they often did with a candor that surprised themselves. "They can talk to me, Patrick, because I'm one of them!" she said. It was perhaps truer than she thought. Her belief that she shared with her charities' clients a common experience of suffering, especially rejection, was a constant source of motivation for her, and there was enough truth in it to make her an acknowledged icon of concern the world over.

I gradually grew to believe, however, that her success was often achieved *despite* her emotional empathy with victims rather than because of it. This was because, along with the scars that made her a fellow sufferer, there existed the neuroses that could make her a fellow destroyer too. More and more I realized that my job was to coax her along and smooth out the peaks and troughs in her feelings. Her emotional state was always fragile. As she grew in understanding of her own personality she would even joke, "Stand by for a mood swing, boys!" All the same, behind such disarming adult honesty I felt there was a damaged child, set loose in a tempting but dangerous world.

The temptations and dangers were unique because of the marriage she had made. Over much of her life, her word was law and there were few objects she could not have or people she could not influence. Yet from her adopted family she received little relevant guidance on how to cope with this, and even less sympathy when matters went awry. This is not a criticism that should be laid entirely at their door, however. An important aspect of her condition was her inability to accept the same care she tried to show others. At some deep level, her opinion of herself never rose high enough to permit it and she would eventually sabotage any relationship that threatened the reassuringly familiar pain of the status quo. This perhaps applied particularly to her relations with her mother-in-law the Queen. However eager she was to receive it, the Queen's approval never took root in the Princess. What lingered was the memory of the many more times when she felt it had been unfairly withheld.

A catalog of these destructive tendencies makes depressing reading, but no picture of the Princess would be complete without at least an attempt to identify the demons with which she wrestled. Only then, perhaps, is it possible fully to appreciate the effort she made to conquer them and the remarkable extent to which she succeeded. It is no secret that toward the end of her life some of her critics questioned her mental stability. Their invective might have been better channeled into recognition of her endurance in circumstances that would have driven a lesser person round the bend.

My efforts to encourage the Princess along a positive path met with more obstacles than I had anticipated. With her knack of humanizing even the most formal royal event, she had an unrivaled chance to persuade the many fascinating people she met to open up in a way they possibly would not have done with many of her in-laws. Since we lightheartedly thought of ourselves as being in "the happiness business," it seemed logical to try to find for the Princess the satisfaction and contentment she craved from the very work she was condemned (or privileged, depending on the mood) to go out and do several times a week. This, I thought, would at least create the chance for her to begin to enjoy herself through what she did best—bringing happiness to other people.

That was rather too radical, as it turned out. The attitude she inherited with marriage was that her work was tolerable at best and stern duty at worst. The concept of having *fun* while doing it was unfamiliar.

At first, it was not even a conscious strategy. For one thing, until I was promoted to private secretary in 1990, I did not have a free hand with her program. Also, in many ways what I was trying to achieve only reflected her own ambitions in charity work, her choice of public duties, and general style. All I was trying to do was to add into the equation some element of happiness for her. Even if she did not agree with this, it turned out to be a reliable foundation for all my subsequent work with her, and a simple guiding philosophy in the many days of doubt that were to come.

I could often see that worthwhile engagements, carried out in the course of duty, were also a source of pleasure and inspiration to her. She never accepted this view, sadly, and looked at me with contempt or pitying tolerance whenever I mentioned it. She preferred to believe that her work was a heavy burden, and one she carried with little thanks or appreciation.

This was so obviously untrue, as I pointed out to her, but the philosophy of duty as suffering—quickly learned from her husband—was a hard one to shift. It was so convenient. It made bad moods excusable and good moods heroic. It underlined the exclusiveness of royal virtues, since no one else was up to the job. It justified all the luxury and status that went with the territory, since lives of such sacrifice deserved appropriate compensation. Best of all, it provided a permanent excuse to complain about the unfairness of life.

The Princess was certainly alive to the material compensations of her position, which were clearly far from unfair. Perhaps surprisingly, she could be more acquisitive than her virtuous image might suggest. She never failed, for example, to spend the maximum allowed by the Foreign Office for dresses on overseas tours. The results were well worth it, of course, but the figures—which must have run to several hundred thousand pounds—were equally eye-catching.

She was also surprisingly proprietorial about gifts that came to her by virtue of her official position rather than to her as an individual. Lavish presents from foreign leaders, including a sports car from one Gulf state, were stockpiled even if they were of no real use. The perks of being royal are no problem to a royalist—I certainly had no trouble accepting the comparative crumbs that came my way—but the Princess's philosophy was one she clearly shared with the jackdaw. Her ultimate nest egg was the jewelry she had received as Princess of Wales, including some items from the Queen. This she said she would keep, as a reward for her "years of purgatory in this f——ing family."

Her public work therefore fitted into a complex pattern of private feelings. Most of the time she was professional enough to suppress her personal state of mind when in the public eye, although she was sometimes able to let it slip for dramatic effect. The visible appearance of stress in front of the cameras at certain crucial moments in her bid for public sympathy was no more an accident than the looks she wore for hospitals, funfairs, or garden parties.

Saint and martyr struggled within her for top billing. Later they were joined by an avenging Amazon as she did battle against her husband, and all the while, somewhere inside her a little girl also waited for her moment of attention. No wonder she said her marriage was crowded. Just sitting in the car with her was sometimes like dealing with a minibus of Princesses.

Her public engagements eventually became important for me only as the backdrop for her mood at the time. They acquired a sense of unreality, and not just because of the air of drama she inevitably gave them just by turning up. Living with her every day, reality was the personality she adopted in each one. Just as people became her toys, her public life became a sort of game.

In the year that followed my apprenticeship I had plenty of opportunity to watch her play this game with increasing skill. I also observed, over and over again, that regardless of her own complex motives, her involvement did a great deal of good for a great many causes.

The part of compassionate Princess was the one she played best. As I had already seen on my first awayday in Essex, she communicated an extraordinary sympathy to people in pain. She was also unmatched in her ability to bring a carefully measured vivacity to even the most depressing situations, and her patronage of Help the Aged gave her plenty of scope for displaying both talents.

I remember going with her one hot day to visit a geriatric ward in East London. Even though I had visited the place a few weeks earlier on the recce, I was still unprepared for the eye-watering blast of ammonia that hit us when we walked into the first room of incontinent old people. There were maybe twenty beds along each wall. Their occupants had been propped up on pillows and they stared in various states of incomprehension at the unexpected entertainment that was being provided for them. Others sat in chairs between the beds and in little groups along the route. Apart from a low murmuring between some of the more coherent occupants, a silence lay over the room that I thought could literally be described as deathly.

As well as the old people, there seemed to be dozens of staff, watching expectantly for something to happen. Behind me clustered a gaggle of hospital management and local politicians. The Mayor wore his chain and looked important. The Lord Lieutenant wore his sword and looked awkward. This was the best show in town and nobody wanted to miss a second of it.

The Princess metaphorically squared her shoulders and set to work. I watched in admiration as she systematically quartered the room, an innocent-looking girl among so many ancient, wasting bodies. In her sharply tailored, bright red suit, radiating health and energy against such a background of age and infirmity, she was like living proof of some youthful wonder drug.

Here and there a bright eye would engage her and a surprisingly youthful voice would emerge cheerfully from a tired old face, but the general tenor was depressing. I mentally kicked myself for a bad recce and silently blamed the hospital management for fielding patients upon whom senility's grip had tightened to such a deadening effect. The Princess gave no outward sign of sharing my small-minded lack of charity, although later she laughed about her new qualifications as a mortician. Instead she worked the fetid room like the professional she was, leaving happiness in her wake with anyone even barely conscious of what was happening.

On her tour she was accompanied rather too closely by a formidable matron dressed in blue and carrying in her face the weight of years of caring for people unable to give much in return. Such worthy escorts often unwittingly provided the Princess with the helpful contrast in appearance that her height, couture, energy, and beauty so photogenically accentuated. I overheard a muttered conversation between two of the patients who had just been visited, which went something like this:

"Oo was that then?"

"Oo was *wot* then?"

"Oo was that in the red?"

"I dunno. But she was a lot nicer than the one in the blue!"

The Princess made light of her talent for creating such happiness, although it never did any harm to flatter her— preferably with some originality. This was important as it seemed to be the only way to help her extract some personal satisfaction from what, on the face of it, was a pretty grinding routine of charming performances in depressing situations.

As soon as she was back in the car she might say, "God! Did you *smell* the pee? It was like being in a room full of tomcats!"

"Ma'am, you made a lot of people happy in there."

"Oh Patrick, you are loyal...but I don't think half of them even knew who I was."

"Actually, perhaps you're right, Ma'am. I wasn't going to tell you, but quite a few asked me when Princess Margaret was due to arrive."

"*Thank you,* Patrick. I'll make the jokes around here."

"Sorry, Ma'am. But seriously, I watched them after you'd moved on and whatever you'd said made them really happy. The Sister told me a visit from you was better than any medicine she could give them."

"Really? She said that? I thought she was a bossy old battle-axe."

"Honest."

"Hm..."

The idea that she might possess some form of healing power may have grown in her mind from such exchanges. I do not recall it dating from a specific incident, but it was well established by the time she was making headlines by touching AIDS patients in 1990 and there was no shortage of voices, more sycophantic even than mine, to encourage her belief in it. The proprietor of the Princess's current favorite restaurant—herself a deeply spiritual woman—was a particular advocate of this form of royal therapy, which I liked to think of as a benign echo of a more medieval faith in the power of kings. Anyway, if it helped my boss endure the sights, sounds, and smells of wards like the one in East London, there was surely no harm in it.

As time passed and she became more attracted to the idea, it gave us hangers-on some irreverent pleasure. Initially she was rather diffident about what she was doing, but after a while a practiced eye could spot the look of special saint-liness that accompanied her attempts at this truly "hands-on" form of treatment. "Look out!" we would whisper as the Princess bore down on an unsuspecting leper or AIDS patient. "We're laying on hands again!"

Sure enough, the photographers would be rewarded with a heartwarming image of the angelic figure, eyes de-murely downcast, hands firmly in contact with the untouch-able. To be fair, the scene was sometimes repeated—albeit briefly—even after the press pack had been shepherded out of the room.

No actual miracles were reported—but then, since so much healing takes place in the mind of the patient, who is to say that the unexpected physical expression of such kind-ness from a world figure did not somehow assist the occa-sional sufferer along the road to recovery? It did not seem to do any damage to the Princess either, except perhaps to her sense of humility.

Heaven knows, the sights, sounds, and smells she con-fronted needed some sort of antidote. Despite the often de-fiantly tasteless humor, I noticed that she did not acquire the emotional immunity with which most professional carers protect themselves. One of the reasons why she was so good at communicating with people in need was that her own need often made itself apparent to them at what seemed to be a subliminal level. This provided a pathway for her emo-tions to express themselves and it undoubtedly made her a charismatic visitor to the sick.

The idea that she had some kind of gift of healing re-mains very much open to question, of course. If she did possess such a gift, then it was completely unrefined, undis-ciplined, and undirected. Had it been recognized and devel-oped as the talent it sometimes seemed to be, I believe that her round of compassionate visiting would not have taken the toll it did on her emotional stamina. More importantly, direction and discipline might also have given her the sense of personal fulfillment necessary if she was to bear applying such a gift properly. Sadly, the lack of any appropriate direction and discipline forfeited for her any chance to explore or use a gift for which she seemed otherwise so eminently qualified. After all, as many believe, it is a gift that requires a level of personal spiritual development that I do not think she would ever have claimed to have reached.

In any case, the Princess's sights were soon set on more colorful and exciting work than visiting hospital patients in gray Britain. Solo overseas tours offered a glittering prospect of independent celebrity and in the years that followed I devoted increasing amounts of time and energy— not to mention taxpayers' money—to organizing a growing number of foreign expeditions. These became the basis of her rise to global icon status.

As is now well known, the talent she had for making people happy in British geriatric wards—or at British film premieres, for that matter—worked just as well in comparable foreign locations. In fact, it worked better and, to put it crudely, because solo foreign trips earned her more favorable recognition per hour worked, they came to dominate her program. She quickly acquired a taste for international celebrity and it was a game she mastered with increasing confidence.

7

꧂

Gameplay

*T*he Princess's first major solo tour—and mine—was to New York in the winter of 1989. I was sent out with a detective, Graham Smith, and a press secretary, Dickie Arbiter, as the advance party. Anne Beckwith-Smith was running the program, had already carried out the recce (a task made more onerous by the requirement also to recce Richard Branson's Necker Island, which HRH had borrowed for a family holiday), and would be arriving on Concorde three days later with the Princess. We were being sent to ease the way and, fresh from the instructive rigors of the Gulf, I could not wait to get on the plane.

I still held the complacent belief that Americans loved our royal family without serious qualification, despite having been harangued at a tender age by a Philadelphia taxi driver on the enduring evils of King George III. Now I began to learn that the taxi driver was only an outspoken member of a large group of Americans with a keen sense of history and no real love for the former colonial power. Drawing on my upbringing in an even younger republic, I felt some sympathy with their point of view and resolved to dispel my complacency forthwith, lest it be mistaken for the English arrogance that had caused the problem in the first place.

Some years later Ray Seitz, the American Ambassador in London, courteously described for me another good reason for caution. It had become an easy option, he said, for British fund-raisers to recruit a handful of "American Friends of (insert good cause here)" and sit back and wait for the money to roll in. It did so reliably, particularly if a royal patron—however minor—could be persuaded to fly over to visit the Friends and say a few encouraging words at a dinner. However, what he wryly characterized as these "Viking raids" on American goodwill (or gullibility) were becoming a little too frequent, he thought, and were straining the considerable pro-British sentiment that had survived the War of Independence.

In this, as in so much else, the Princess was to prove the exception. New York was already agog at the prospect of her visit, in what turned out to be the first stages of an enduring reciprocal love affair. As always when the love is true, the initial fascination promised to develop into a mutual regard that might have led to a more permanent relationship. There was never any shortage of speculation on this point, and if ever it showed signs of flagging, some enterprising realtor would stoke it up again, if only by sending me glossy details of apartments on the Upper East Side, or—a popular perennial—the Trump Tower. Sadly, having charted its progress from the start, it seems to me that this was probably one of those romances that was unlikely to survive the loss of the early enchantment, however long postponed. Eventually voracious New York and its society queens would surely have found devouring a real princess a challenge too tempting to resist.

Waiting to greet us at Kennedy airport was the irrepressible Sally O'Brien, a protocol officer sent from our Embassy in Washington and rightly regarded as the complete expert on the sometimes tricky subject of royal visits to the USA.

As we arrived at the Plaza Athénée on East Sixty-fourth Street, I was mentally trying to run through the recce checklist of items that had seemed so vital in the blazing heat of Arabia. What possible relevance could they have to the Big Apple in midwinter?

Feeling dazed, we followed in Sally's wake to find that the hotel had strained every sinew to help us. The royal suite was on two levels, elegantly furnished and with panoramic views of Manhattan. We commandeered the corresponding rooms on the other side of the building, giving Anne the upper floor of the suite and keeping the lower for a combined office/press-center/bar. In honor of his impending arrival from Washington we christened this the Cornish Suite after Francis Cornish, Counselor at the Embassy, former member of the Prince's office, and one of the most flamboyant and distinguished diplomats I have ever met.

He arrived some hours later in a flurry of snow and enthusiasm, and immediately ordered champagne. His carefree style and general bonhomie hid a razor-sharp professionalism beside which I felt, quite rightly, a complete amateur. He and Sally made a formidable team and between gulps they ran us through the program with an assurance that practically relegated me to the role of spectator. That's fine by me, I thought, and began to relax.

In its content, the program set many of the themes that were to recur in the Princess's public work all over the world, not least in her return visits to New York. There was fund-raising—for Birthright, one of her British charities. There was social concern—a visit to a community housing project called the Henry Street Center. There was commercial promotion for British exports—including a toy fair in the cavernous F.A.O. Schwarz toy store. There was culture—a performance by the Welsh National Opera (one of her patronages) at the Brooklyn Academy of Music, and a drinks reception for the American Foundation of the Royal Academy of Music (another patronage). There was also work on behalf of AIDS.

Years later, it is perhaps hard to believe that at the time of the Princess's first visit to New York AIDS was predicted to become a potential twentieth-century Black Death. To be fair, there were those who found that hard to believe even then. I was probably one of these skeptics, albeit a closet one for obvious reasons. Nonetheless, in the poorest quarters of American cities and, as the Princess went on to demonstrate, in Africa and South America too, the epidemic was tragically real enough.

At the time, however, we had a greater concern weighing on our minds. Demonstrations by Irish Republican sympathizers were not uncommon on royal visits to America, but for the Princess something special was being arranged. In numbers and vociferousness, the demonstrations planned to exploit her visit were expected to break all records.

Our friendly American security experts—never knowingly understated—were clearly taking the threat of disruption very seriously. CRACK POLICE TEAM KEEPS GUARD ON DI shouted the *Evening Standard*, alongside a picture of what looked like Robocop. Even Graham was looking unusually preoccupied as we shared a beer on our first night. The gloom deepened when we learned that the director of the AIDS unit that the Princess was due to visit was an avowed and outspoken critic of British policy in Ulster.

Suddenly I felt much less relaxed. In a reaction that became almost routine as the years passed, imaginary lurid headlines swam before my eyes: PRINCESS SNUBBED BY REPUBLICAN GRANNY or REPUBLICAN DOC WRECKS TOUR, and somewhere farther down the page a damning indictment of the Palace official responsible for the blunder, with a picture of me looking clueless to prove the point.

It would not always be so, but this time at least blessed help was at hand. I never quite discovered how he did it, but Francis achieved an unsung but in my book unsurpassed triumph of British diplomacy. On the day of the visit to the AIDS unit, before the world's cameras and microphones the demon doctor was seen chatting amicably with the future

British Queen, a Union Jack badge clearly visible on the lapel of her white coat.

Three days after our arrival, the advance party was back at Kennedy airport, shivering on the tarmac as we awaited the Concorde flight that was bringing the Princess from London. Ambassador and Lady Acland had traveled from Washington to greet her and at our backs a modest fifteen-car convoy sat in a fog of exhaust vapor as it prepared to whisk us downtown.

As soon as the Princess emerged from the aircraft's door, events followed at a breathless pace, as though seen on a video on fast forward. In London police escorts take pride in the discreet way they shepherd their charges through the densest traffic, a polite toot on a whistle being the citizen's only warning that he should kindly step aside. In New York I felt as if I were caught up in a mechanized marching band armed with ululating sirens as we blared our way through streets filled with homebound commuters. Traffic scattered before us and any who hesitated were treated to terrifying Brooklynese police invective at maximum volume over a bullhorn. "The yellow cab! DON'T EVEN THINK OF PULLING OUT!"

I cringed. Even though I saw the same performance repeated over the years, I still do not understand why an enraged populace did not rise up and dismantle the motorcade and its occupants with their bare hands. Of course, it could have had something to do with the blue pickup shadowing the royal limo. After a quick glance inside I could see that it might have won the world record for cramming the highest number of heavily armed agents into a small space. Oh well, I thought to myself, at least they know we're here.

The only engagement that evening was a reception to promote British textiles. The worthy event was good, standard royal stuff and the Princess took care to give the exporters and their guests their full money's worth. Outside, as crowds strained against the NYPD's blue wooden crowd barriers and flashbulbs and TV lights bathed the sidewalk in a high-energy glare, the scene was more like Hollywood on Oscar night. Celebrity met royalty in the world's brashest and most cynical city—no wonder it was love at first sight.

Back at the hotel the Princess, with a last smile for the cameras, was bowed into a lift by the manager, bowed out again thirty-six floors higher, and bowed finally to the door of her suite. There we left her, alone with the telephone and whatever fears or triumphs she felt the day had brought her. That was how it was done.

We left New York's finest to patrol the adjoining corridors and descended to our temporary office. Filled with a sudden sense of release, we noisily compared notes and laughed too loud. Anne issued her instructions for the morning and retired to bed. Dickie watched the TV bulletins of our arrival. Graham poured beer while I studied the room service menu. Francis ordered champagne.

Meanwhile, alone in her room, the Princess sat in the hotel bathrobe and watched late-night TV. When I told her that a thoughtful management had tuned her set not to receive any of the "adult" channels, she was theatrically disappointed. "Typical! I can't even *watch* sex. I might as well be a nun!"

*T*hey were still taking away the empties when I returned to the office next morning. Always an early riser, I was especially keen to tackle a real New York breakfast. I was joined by Graham and, while we waited for our orders, we stood companionably admiring the morning mist on the famous skyline and talked about the coming day's events. I was about to be forcibly reminded of the dangers that lay in wait round every corner.

The phone rang and I answered it. "May I speak to Princess Di, please?" said an American voice.

"I'm afraid that's not possible at the moment," I replied, sounding terribly pompous even to my own ears.

"Then who is this, please?" asked the voice.

"I'm Her Royal Highness's equerry, Patrick Jephson," I said, more pompous than ever.

Suddenly I was aware of a strange background noise, as if the caller was using a loudspeaker. Too late! "Well, Patrick, how does it feel to be talking live on New York's biggest breakfast radio show?" The receiver froze in my hand. My mouth opened and closed. My pomposity vanished in a paralysis of terror.

Just at that moment salvation appeared in the form of the press secretary, who had hurried in looking for breakfast. Putting my hand over the mouthpiece, I waved him over. "It's for you, Dickie," I said, reasoning that a former London Broadcasting Corporation professional broadcaster was the right man for the job. So it proved. Twenty minutes later he was still talking.

At 10:15 Anne and I assembled outside the Princess's suite. In the lift, in the lobby, in the street, and at our destination a huge number of people waited in readiness, each playing a part in a dozen separate but interlocking timetables. For some, like Doug the taciturn leader of our security detail, or the news crews clustered round the hotel door, it was just another routine job. For others, like the head of the housing project we were about to visit, it was the climax of weeks of preparation. For hundreds more, who gathered just for a glimpse of the glamorous visitor, it was a moment of excited anticipation. Here in this hotel corridor, however, at the center of so many concentric rings of activity, there was simply silence as we waited for the door to open and the Princess of Wales to set the whole machine in motion.

Of course there would be times when there was no such tranquillity, as dressers and valets bustled about their private kingdom, phones rang, and papers were nervously shuffled. Often, especially in later times, I would be invited to give a last-minute briefing, or just share gossip, or even adjudicate on the choice of shoes in the final seconds before the show hit the road. Even then I was always aware of the chain of events we were about to initiate. Every one of them would have to synchronize according to the plan if we were all to return at the end of the day in the happy daze of mutual congratulation that was, I now admit, a kind of drug.

Punctual to the minute, the door flew open and the Princess emerged in midstride. Galvanized by her energy, her penetrating gaze, and her speed over the ground, the waiting machine sprang into action. I took up my station in the fragrant wake, trying to look bored, and gave myself up to the inexorable passage of events.

Our drive to the housing project was a repeat of the previous night's convoy, although by this time I was beginning to feel more comfortable with our noisy progress. After all, if you cannot make a scene in New York, where can you? This was obviously also the motto of a glamorous contingent of Princess Di lookalikes who greeted us noisily as we emerged from the hotel. The couture and makeup were quite convincing, as was the authentically regal wrist action in their enthusiastic waving. It was only as the cars pulled away that I realized they were all in drag.

The engagement itself resembled its equivalent back home, right down to the point where I thought things were going so smoothly that I could slip away from the main action for a quiet cigarette. I was joined in my chosen stretch of deserted corridor by Doug, our security chief, his eyes wearing that vacant look that comes from listening to two radio conversations at once, one in each earpiece.

Communications were plainly proving a problem as he called for reports from his agents deployed around the building. "All units! This is Rattlesnake!" he hissed into his cuff, from which peeped a small, strangely obscene, pink plastic microphone. The vacant look returned as the voices spoke in his head—all except one, apparently. "Kowalski! Report my signal!" The absentee did not reply, however, and a further lengthy roll call ensued.

Stubbing out my illicit cigarette, I poked my head round the door of the room in which the Princess was meeting residents and a clutch of publicity-hungry politicians. I noticed the Mayor listening with intense sincerity. Eye contact was quickly made with Anne and Graham, who were in close attendance. Even without the benefit of Doug's technology, such nonverbal signaling—with a little practice—could convey a surprising amount of information. All is well, said Anne's eyes, but I am getting anxious about the time and we should be leaving soon.

For a second longer I paused in the doorway. A recently destitute resident of the project was recounting a fragment of her life story as the Princess listened intently. What a contrast that story made to the experiences of the young, aristocratic Englishwoman who sat next to her.

By the angle of her head, with each sympathetic nod, with every gentle prompt when the story faltered, the visitor gave notice that this was a private conversation. Around the two of them an invisible wall excluded the politicians, the officials, the photographers, and the police. We were all eavesdroppers to this most public of shared confidences. I saw this phenomenon countless times. The Princess could create an island of quiet intimacy on which she seemed to be alone with whoever she was speaking to at the time. The most nervous, displaced, or tongue-tied person found a new confidence in the private space she created.

I returned to Doug, who seemed to have solved his radio problem. "How's it goin' in there?" he asked.

"Fine," I said. "We'll be leaving soon."

He stiffened into action and spoke urgently into the sleeve of his Burberry. "All units! This is Rattlesnake! Empire will egress the facility momentarily!"

I just had to ask. "Exactly what does that *mean,* Doug?"

Not a flicker of amusement disturbed his steady gray eyes. "We'll be leaving soon," he said.

That night the Princess went to the opera—*Falstaff* at the Brooklyn Academy of Music, performed by the WNO, the Welsh National Opera. As departure time approached, Doug and I took our places by the door of her suite. In our short time together we had, I thought, developed a happy working relationship, mainly characterized by long silences as Doug stared into infinity while the voices chirruped in his ears. He was still in midtrance as the door opened.

Fashion correspondents from a hundred syrupy magazines have described the Princess's beauty and dress sense, but even they might have given up the task that night. She looked like the proverbial million dollars, distractingly bare-shouldered. Doug's trance deepened, the voices forgotten. As we bowed our good evenings, her hand unexpectedly reached out to touch an angular shape just visible under Doug's dress shirt (I had failed to spot it, of course).

"What's that, Doug?" she asked sweetly. Doug reddened. "Kevlar vest, Ma'am!"

The Princess smiled at him, mischievously quizzical. Her hand imperceptibly gestured to the seeming acres of lightly tanned royal skin on view. "Shouldn't I be wearing that?" she asked with wide-eyed innocence. Poor Doug was lost for words as we egressed the facility.

The drive to Brooklyn took forty-five minutes. As expected, a noisy party of demonstrators had assembled outside the Academy of Music, but they were swamped in numbers and volume by enthusiastic well-wishers. As we crowded into the Royal Box I discovered a recurring disadvantage to having the most exclusive seats in the house: unless you are in the front row you can usually hardly see the stage. I heard Mayor Koch's fulsome welcoming speech clearly enough, however, and although I knew little about opera, even I could tell that the WNO had done their patron proud.

After the final curtain the party from the Royal Box made a straggling progress through the cramped passageways and down the twisting stairs that led backstage. This was always a fascinating experience for me, repeated on many occasions. Excitement mixed with relief seemed to hover over the group of perspiring performers as the Princess moved slowly among them, talking quietly, laughing, sharing the drama that lingered after the audience had gone. Greasepaint and that special dusty backstage smell mingled with her perfume. TV lights cast sharp shadows in the sudden unnatural quiet. Evening gowns and patent shoes intruded diffidently onto a stage that still held the aura of the night's music.

Suddenly it was over and we were back outside. The cold New York night hit me in a sudden blast like a bitter gas. I was dizzy, momentarily lost. There were so many *people*. A bedlam of pushing journalists blocked the way to my car. The world seemed full of flashbulbs, grim-faced cops, and shouting fans. Then above the close cacophony I heard chanting. "Brits out! Brits out!"

Looking round, I saw the Princess and Anne being hurried into their car. Where was mine? I could see no familiar faces and in a second, sensing my hesitation, two of the grimmer-looking cops came toward me. Their breath cast plumes of vapor into the night air. What was I doing inside their police cordon looking lost?

I fumbled for my security badge as the biggest one fingered his Federal riot gun. He was so close I could hear the creaking of his boots as I scrabbled on the roadway to pick up the precious enamel pin. He peered at it with myopic suspicion as the convoy revved up. The chanting sounded closer now. This is ridiculous, I thought, panicking slightly.

"It's OK, officer, he's with me," said one of Doug's men, appearing beside us. He took my arm, looking urgently over his shoulder at the line of placards. "Come on, Commander. Time to move!" I agreed.

The inside of the Lincoln was pitch-black, the seat so low I felt I was sitting on the floor. I *was* sitting on the floor. Don't American cars smell strange? I thought irrelevantly, sliding surreptitiously up into my seat and hoping nobody had noticed. There was no interest in me, though, as I reclined in the darkness listening to the agents' conversation. We were still not moving and the agents seemed to share my anxiety that we should. In a moment of silence I asked what we were waiting for. "Cain't move till the Captain sezso."

It seemed that the Captain, like me, had been stuck in the crowd. In Britain, contact of the VIP's posterior with the limousine's upholstery is the automatic signal for immediate departure. Immobile in the growing clamor, I could keenly appreciate the wisdom of this practice. We were stuck fast aground in a sea of people.

After what seemed an eternity the Captain came on the radio. Something dramatic was called for. "OK, boys! Work the fenders!" So it was that the Princess and her convoy lumbered slowly out of Brooklyn bound for dinner in Manhattan, a dozen agents jogging alongside, puffing like steam engines in the chill air off the East River.

*L*ess than twenty-four hours later we were heading home, our speed now supersonic on the evening-scheduled Concorde. Across the narrow aisle the Princess worked daintily at a small patch of needlepoint.

Needlepoint? I looked again. It was not a trick of my imagination. Our supersonic airliner had not transformed into a time machine. Here was the media superstar of New York, the world's number-one celebrity Princess, lips pursed in concentration, reenacting a scene straight out of eighteenth-century Versailles. Another act was just what it was, however. After a while she became bored and the needlepoint was put away. I never saw it again.

Dickie and I sipped a companionable gin while the darkness outside whistled past at over a thousand miles per hour. In the cozy lighting it was a touchingly domestic scene after the triumphant tumult of the past few days.

I had a lot to reflect on as I considered the lessons learned on my first solo overseas trip in attendance. Many of the lessons learned stood me in good stead in the years that followed. Some were obvious. Memorize the program. Remember the really important faces, not just the faces of important people. Always try to leave a building *ahead* of the Princess, unless you want to be photographed with her (as some did), disrupt the hosts' farewells, and probably lose your car into the bargain. Also do not drop your security badge in front of heavily armed, nervous guards.

Some lessons were more domestic. Organize your clothes for the next day before you go to bed. Try to sleep at least two hours a night. Make sure your insides do not resort to audible mutiny at moments of tension, and—not unrelated—go easy on the hotel minibar. Some lessons were fundamental. Stay at least one jump ahead of events. Whatever the distractions, stay focused. If in doubt, just shut up and watch out.

I learned another valuable lesson before we reached Heathrow. Beware pressmen on planes. A tabloid reporter and his photographer had got themselves seats on our flight, which was clever, perfectly legal, and a potential nuisance. They were rewarded with a useful scoop as the Princess tossed them a few emotional words about her visit to the Harlem Pediatric AIDS Unit when they lingered by her seat. The next day it made front-page headlines—THE CHILD I CANNOT FORGET—and inside there was a two-page story under the heading "On Concorde: the vision of a dying boy haunts her still."

It was superficially great stuff, but the risks were obvious and most of them eventually came to pass. The greatest danger lay in the perception that exclusives were there for the taking, if you only had the energy to stroll up to the royal seat row. This led to resentment among less favored—or less intrusive—journalists. It encouraged sensationalism, not least because of the altitude, the false intimacy, and the chance of a direct quote. If unchecked it also caused traffic jams in crowded aircraft cabins. Ultimately, of course, it provided opportunities for direct briefing beyond the reach of Palace minders.

As the years passed, the Princess increasingly gave in to the temptation to do her own briefing. If, as I observed, the press were a kind of surrogate family to her, she did not only want to talk to them through go-betweens, especially if the go-betweens were paid by her husband or in-laws.

Eventually the Princess's impromptu press briefings became a feature of our homeward flights after overseas tours. Typically, I would wake from an exhausted sleep—it was usually the middle of the night—and see her seat empty. A knowing look from the personal protection officer was enough. Across the aisle, a snoring pile of blankets issued its own very public communiqué: the press secretary was off duty. Very sensible.

Sure enough, when I padded through the darkened cabin, I would find the Princess outside the galley, surrounded by a cluster of pressmen. A stewardess would often be hovering, unsure whether to push past the bodies blocking her way. It was like interrupting a high-school smoking club. Half a dozen familiar faces would turn to look at me. There would be a sudden silence.

I always tried to look pleasantly surprised. "Well! I thought there must be a better party going on back here."

The Princess would throw me a cold look, her hair unbrushed and her eyes looking tired without their customary makeup, dressed in her usual long-haul flying outfit—ski socks, leggings, and a baggy jumper. "Everything's all right, Patrick."

"Of course. Well, actually, I was just going to the loo..." They would all press flat against the bulkhead to let me squeeze past. The stewardess would spot her chance and slip by too.

Later still, the subject was taboo. It was part of the pantomime so that, the next day, we could all act surprised when we saw the headlines.

*I*n many ways, the years 1989 and 1990 marked the end of a state of innocence for the Princess's reputation. After that it was virtually impossible to keep the lid on the truth. During those years the public continued to be fed the comforting story that rumors of marital discord and general unhappiness were groundless, but meanwhile, the Princess was playing a complicated game in which her public appearances were both the means and the disguise by which she acted out her own needs and ambitions.

Anyone looking for evidence that all was well, at least superficially, could find it in the joint overseas tour program for the Prince and Princess. For the next two major trips, as in the Gulf, I was involved as deputy to the private secretary in charge.

Toward the end of 1989, in another of those violent contrasts that gave my life such a vivid sense of purpose but that also constantly uprooted it, I found myself miles from the comfortable routine of St. James's, doing my now familiar act of flying ahead of the Prince and Princess to make a last-minute check on the program and generally prepare the way—this time in Indonesia, where the royal couple were to spend some days before traveling on to Hong Kong.

"Do you know," our Ambassador said to me when I arrived in Jakarta, "if you superimpose the map of Indonesia on a map of Europe, from west to east it would stretch from Donegal to Tashkent." The geography of the place was certainly impressive. Unfortunately, my interest was in more mundane matters. As in the Gulf, the program was unraveling fast.

I was laboring under stupefying jet lag as the grim reality descended upon me. Outside the cool Embassy office, the oppressive heat of downtown Jakarta seemed to amplify the constant clamor of the city's frenzied traffic. Inside, the air-conditioned chill was deepened by the expression on the Ambassador's face. On balance I really preferred it when he spoke about geography.

One of the greatest threats that can face any overseas tour was now looming over the one that was due to start in two days' time. The program we had agreed on the recce—

which with some difficulty we had sold to our royal employers and which had been confirmed by the host's protocol department—had only now, at the eleventh hour, been seen by the President and his wife. It was ominously reported that they disapproved of certain aspects of the program. ("Why does Her Highness wish to see so many sick people? It is very sad for her. Surely she would rather enjoy a visit to a fashion show and cultural theme park?")

However belated, once known, their views became the only ones that mattered, at least in the eyes of their officials. For my part, the only views that mattered were those of my own boss, and she had only approved our plans after the recce with a truly regal condescension. When drawing up her program, I was always aware that she was just a hair's-breadth away from rejecting the plan I had constructed on such a delicate web of compromises with her hosts—if only to demonstrate a wish to control her own life. (It was a view with which I might have sympathized, if it had not threatened to create such a huge amount of extra work for me.) To incorporate all the changes "suggested" by the President, or in my case particularly his wife, would put me square in the firing line of the royal couple's severe displeasure.

I felt a rising panic and resorted to what any craven courtier would do in the circumstances. I blustered to the Ambassador and suggested that he sort things out with the President's office pretty quickly. Unenthusiastically, he lifted the telephone. I was joined by his wife, who listened critically to the string of capitulations that seemed to be the Ambassador's half of the conversation.

As he wearily put down the phone, he announced, "Well, I think that went OK."

His wife was unimpressed. "Oh, darling! You let him walk all over you," she said helpfully. My heart sank even lower. The Ambassador did not look very happy either.

The two days available to me to put the finishing touches to the program turned into a nightmarish cat-and-mouse bluffing game in which our hosts frustrated every pitiful attempt we could muster to oppose their changes to the program. As seemed to happen to me so often, I could see their point. I could not picture the courtiers at Buckingham Palace acting very differently if the roles were reversed.

"It's not your fault," said Graham Smith sympathetically, as we sipped beer by the poolside at the Mandarin Hotel. We both knew he was wrong. All the fears I had felt at a similar stage before the tour of the Middle East now returned to me with interest. When disaster finally struck, nobody would want the truth. They would simply want a culprit and, whoever shared my guilt, it was unlikely to be David Wright, John Riddell's energetic deputy, a career diplomat and the person with overall responsibility for the tour.

"More bad news," said the Ambassador when we saw him later. "The government guests to the various functions are beginning to pull out. The President's office is really putting the pressure on about the program." He looked at me accusingly. "At this rate hardly anybody is going to turn up to meet the Prince and Princess." The implications, not least to the British media, were not lost on me. "And," the Ambassador continued remorselessly, "the Indonesian Air Force delegation to the trade talks, which the Prince is supposed to be supporting, have also canceled. It's not looking good for the big export order."

He was beginning to look for a scapegoat and I felt his eye measuring me for the role. I had a horrid suspicion that I was acquiring all the qualifications. My fears were not much eased by an uncomfortable phone call with St. James's in which I tried to explain to David what was going wrong. In the royal business there are few more unpopular people than the bearers of bad tidings.

With only twelve hours to go before the Prince and Princess were due to leave England, I returned to the hotel to discover that at least something was going right. On the journey from the UK, Qantas—in every other way a brilliant airline—had managed to lose my ceremonial sword. I was due to wear it to greet the royal aircraft when it arrived in Jakarta the next day. Its loss and the subsequent protracted search had added a quite disproportionate twist to the knife I was already beginning to feel between my shoulder blades. I was heartened by the news that the sword had been found in Sydney and I would have it in time for the royal arrival.

Whether it was the next beer that Graham bought me, or the safe return of my beloved sword (it had accompanied my father throughout the Second World War), or whether I salvaged a sense of perspective about royal disfavor, I finally suggested to the Ambassador that we should give in. We would just have to make the best of it and forget the normal rules about recces and detailed plans.

In the hours that followed, with almost as much relief as I was feeling myself, the Ambassador reported a sudden resurgence of official interest in the various social functions arranged for the visitors. The royal rap when it came could surely be no worse than the anxiety I had been suffering in the last few days. Anyway, in the topsy-turvy world of royal justice, I knew that success or failure lay as much in the hands of the hairdresser as in the hands of the head of Indonesian protocol.

The next day I was out at Halim airport, pacing the red carpet and waiting for the VC-10 to arrive. At times during the previous two days I had pictured this moment in the direst terms. I had seen myself climbing the steps to the aircraft and greeting the Prince and Princess with the news that nobody was coming to their functions, nobody wanted to buy our exports, and I had lost my sword. For at least two of the preceding reasons, therefore, they might as well not bother getting off the airplane. Instead, here I was in the sunshine feeling quite relaxed. The band was playing happily. I was surrounded by smiling Air Force officers and the head of protocol beamed from his place beside the Indonesian Foreign Minister and his wife.

The VC-10 arrived on time, obliterating the band with its noise and dwarfing the reception committee with its commanding presence. I ran up the stairs and into the air-conditioned serenity of the royal compartment. The Prince was having imaginary fluff removed from his jacket by the ever-present valet. The Princess was fiddling with her earrings and peering out of the window.

She looked up and greeted me with a smile that banished my remaining doubts and anxieties. "Look," she said, "it's Patrick!" Everybody looked.

"Hello, Ma'am. Welcome to Indonesia. They've mucked up the program so much I was about to tell you to stay on the airplane."

She laughed. "OK," she said, "where will we go instead?"

My instant relief at her sunny mood was only slightly tempered by the suspicion that it was contrived as a contrast to her husband's concerned expression, but it was still an unexpected gift. With it, she set the tone of the tour. There was little outward sign of the tensions with the Prince that I had observed in the Gulf, though there was no sign of any particular warmth either. After New York, the Princess's emerging role as an international performer in her own right seemed to have overtaken the earlier pattern of petty competitiveness.

My earlier worries over the program vanished in the prevailing, if unfamiliar, mood of royal adaptability. Any blame was effortlessly transferred to faceless protocol officials. It was not always thus, but it made the point: attracting or avoiding royal displeasure was often just a matter of luck.

If the opening scenes of the tour had brought me panic and relief in equal measure, the next day produced emotions of a different kind. Thanks to our statesmanlike "compromise" over the program, many of the earlier planned engagements had survived. A large number of these reflected established areas of concern for the Prince or Princess, such as the environment or health issues. In an attempt to satisfy her curiosity about life and death in some of its more extreme forms and to reinforce her public image as a supporter of real issues in her own right, I had arranged for the Princess to visit a leprosy hospital at Sitanala, not far from Jakarta. In both objectives it succeeded beyond her wildest dreams.

From biblical times leprosy has had the power to chill the blood and a leper, real or metaphorical, has always been somebody to be shunned and excluded. Attitudes to leprosy at Sitanala Hospital were more enlightened and therefore, aside from the disfigurement and all-too-visible suffering, the visit was in most respects comparable to many others that the Princess had carried out to countless hospitals. In fact, perhaps because of the nature of the disease and the enlightened attitude that its treatment now enjoys, the atmosphere of the place was positively inspiring.

Through her later work with the British Leprosy Mission, the Princess came to know the disease quite well, to say nothing of the extraordinary courage both of its victims and those who defy so many prejudices to help them. It also seemed to bring to her mind a powerful comparison between the exclusion that was the experience throughout history of too many lepers and her own growing sense of exclusion from the family she had married into and the establishment of which it was the pinnacle.

In press terms, of course, it was a bonanza. Even before she left England the Princess was being urged in blaring tabloid headlines to abandon the planned visit. DON'T DO IT, DI! screamed one front page, and one tabloid doctor after another curdled the readers' blood with stories of the disfigurement and loss of limbs that would, they implied, inevitably follow for the beautiful Princess if she shook hands with a patient in the hospital.

I had, naturally, taken the trouble to check that this was not the case, which enabled the Princess to do herself no harm at all by being photographed making physical contact with the symbolically untouchable. The human touch that she displayed on this and many other occasions, perhaps most famously with AIDS patients, was of incalculable value to those who tried to educate the healthy many about the problems of the afflicted few.

That touch created an avalanche of publicity, all of it favorable for the Princess and, more importantly, for the causes she was supporting. Yet it seemed disproportionate. It *was* just a game after all. The world knew—and deep inside herself she also knew—that all she had done was to touch somebody and be photographed. There was no danger. There was no effort. There was not even anything to be said on this occasion, since the patient spoke no English.

Back at the presidential guest house she was unnaturally subdued. However distressing the day's images, a few jokes usually helped her cope with the stress, but not this time. She was reluctant to talk about it, but I had a couple of theories. Perhaps she was still affected by the disfigurement and bravery she had witnessed. It certainly still affected me. Or perhaps she was uncomfortably aware of the superficial nature of her visit—a few stories for the papers back home, and a saintly image acquired just by turning up.

From such misgivings, I believe, grew the Princess's desire to be more closely involved in the work she saw, even if the practical commitment required was often beyond her. As a compensation, her interest alone was sometimes enough to inspire others—or at least to attract media attention to a deserving cause. Her patronage, the Leprosy Mission, never failed to pay generous tribute to her contribution. Perhaps most memorably this happened at a House of Commons reception in 1991 when Jill Dando, another—largely unsung—champion of the lepers' cause, added her own appeal for leprosy's stigma to be forgotten.

One thing was for sure, however: as it accumulated over the years, such easy adulation did the Princess no favors. Receiving endless credit for other people's good works had a noticeably corrosive effect. She came to expect such praise; and it diminished far more than it uplifted—unless you were able genuinely to delight in other people's successes, that is, and the Princess, alas, found it as difficult as the rest of us to do that.

Nevertheless, to me the Princess's work with lepers stands as her greatest monument. It would be impossible to find a better example of her ability to transform attitudes, to help the ignorant accept the untouchable. There were no moral overtones to distract from the central message, as there sometimes were in the case of AIDS. This was goodness in a rare form, and if it also made a good photo opportunity, I should really only have been glad.

The heat and humidity of Indonesia over the following days were at the limit of the Princess's tolerance. Usually, under a shady hat, she managed to appear the picture of cool. Her loose-fitting cotton dresses looked enviably comfy, especially if you were wearing a suit and tie. In the provincial capital of Yogyakarta, however, she almost fainted while watching a traditional welcome ceremony in the blazing sun. Finding a seat, she struggled to keep her composure while her face ran with perspiration and mascara.

Other hazards lurked too. On the recce one of us had eaten a particular type of local nut. After it had spent an uneasy couple of hours in his stomach it reappeared, along with much else besides, in the back of a hot and airless Embassy minibus. The same sharp-eyed official was present at the Governor's lunch in Yogyakarta and was horrified to see a bowl of the same nuts sitting in front of the Princess. She reached out a hand to take a nut, but such were her powers of observation that even across a crowded room her eye was caught by her alarmed employee's body language.

It was hard to miss. Almost standing on his chair and waving his hands above his head, he dramatically mimed the action of swallowing the nut and then vomiting violently. She got the message—as did several hundred other people, including the Governor, seated next to her, who followed the performance with a furrowed brow. It was with a certain amount of relief that we set off in due course for Hong Kong.

*I*s this where they keep their bathing togs?" asked the Princess, peering into a recess in the colonnade.

"No, Ma'am. They swim in the traditional Roman style—naked!"

The Princess looked intrigued and then wrinkled her nose. "What do you keep in these pots?" she said, indicating a row of containers set conveniently at waist height.

"Urine!" came the reply, delivered with all the relish that comes from being legitimately allowed to talk dirty to royalty.

Walking toward the drug rehabilitation center's dining hall, I caught a glimpse through the trees of a pagoda far below on a rocky outcrop. Beyond it, the South China Sea sparkled in the sunlight. I could still just hear the music above the rattling of the bamboo trees in a sudden gust of sweet-scented breeze.

Hong Kong in 1989 still had almost a decade to run under British administration. A visit from the heir to the British throne and his wife was therefore (at least in theory) akin to the son of the big house visiting a far-flung corner of the family estate. To students of history or politics—and I was an amateur at both—or indeed to anyone with a romantic imagination, such a demonstration of proprietorship held quaint but intriguing imperial overtones.

Once just a pinprick in a world quarter bathed in the pink of British rule, by 1989 Hong Kong constituted in population terms by far the largest and most important part of all that remained of Britain's overseas possessions. I do not imagine that the vast majority of the population looked up from the main business of making money for long enough to register that we had even been in town—but for those who wanted to look, all the signs of a royal visit were there, complete with vestigial imperial trappings that, I suppose, brought forth reactions of nostalgia or contempt according to taste.

Having survived rather than triumphed in Indonesia, the royal couple flew on from Jakarta to Hong Kong's old Kai Tak airport in an impressively large and ancient aircraft of the Royal Air Force. They were received by His Excellency the Governor and then set out in the Governor's ceremonial barge—the *Lady Maureen*, also impressively large and antique—for the short voyage across one of the world's most spectacular natural harbors to the metropolis of Victoria, named after the Queen-Empress, the visiting heir's great-great-great-grandmother.

As dusk fell and lights blazed down from the skyscrapers that lined the surrounding hills, helicopters of the Royal Air Force could be seen collecting Their Royal Highnesses' considerable quantities of baggage and whisking them with an impressive clatter of rotors and expenditure of government fuel to Her Majesty's naval base. There Her Majesty's Yacht *Britannia*, her beautiful lines bathed from stem to stern in golden floodlighting, was waiting to receive the royal suitcases and shortly also the royal visitors. Meanwhile, patrol boats of the Royal Navy and the Royal Hong Kong Police kept a watchful eye out for unsympathetic gatecrashers.

At Queen's Pier a spectacular welcome awaited. The General Commanding British Forces in the colony presented the commanding officer of the Hong Kong Regiment (the Volunteers), a guard of honor gave the Royal Salute, and the band of the Royal Hong Kong Police played a rousing version of the national anthem. Then, while a specially composed musical tribute brought a lump to the throat, hundreds of Chinese schoolchildren danced an elaborate welcome, military standards were dipped in salute, and the royal visitors received traditional tributes from a dancing lion that knelt at their feet in homage.

During the next few days the Prince and Princess were busy with a program that took them all over the colony.

From the Governor's residence to remote corners of the New Territories, the visitors enjoyed a formidably organized postimperial tour.

So it was that the Princess found herself having the surreal experience of visiting the island drug rehabilitation center run by Dr. Barry Hollinrake on the island of Shek Kwu Chau and, in particular, admiring the center's "Roman" baths. She had never seen anything like this. The superintendent was plainly dedicated to the task of returning reformed addicts to society as useful members of their community, but he had chosen methods that perhaps matched his own rather eccentric style.

The rocky, cone-shaped island rose out of the South China Sea among countless others in the southwestern Hong Kong archipelago. On its summit space had been cleared for a helicopter landing pad and from there a twisting road meandered through thick foliage to the main settlement. All the accommodation, the medical center, the assembly hall, the kitchens, and every other building had been constructed by the island's inmates, who contributed whatever skills they had to the common need, in the style of all the best cooperatives.

Small groups of inhabitants observed the Princess's arrival inscrutably. The predominant uniform seemed to be blue shorts tied up with string and white T-shirts. They murmured quietly among themselves as they watched this latest manifestation of colonial rule. Dr. Hollinrake led the Princess into the center's gardens to show her the island's crowning engineering achievement. Under a canopy of green fronds and surrounded by carefully tended plants in huge earthenware pots, the inhabitants had constructed an exact replica of an ancient Roman bath, complete with colonnades and statues and numerous Latin inscriptions.

I stared at these for a few moments with all the effortless familiarity of one who had narrowly achieved a Latin O level twenty years previously. "I put those in to confuse future archaeologists," said Dr. Hollinrake, smirking contentedly. Chinese music twanged and trilled quietly from loud-speakers concealed among the bushes.

"What a wonderfully peaceful place you've made here," said the Princess. "I'm not surprised your rehabilitation program is such a success."

"The philosophy is simple, Ma'am," replied Dr. Hollinrake. "Once my clients are removed from the temptations and troubles of the mainland, in most cases the cause of their addiction is also removed."

Suddenly misty-eyed, the Princess looked wistfully at the inmates now crowding into the hall to watch a ritual dragon dance performed in her honor. I was only guessing from the expression on her face, but how many of them, I wondered, might imagine that for just an instant they were envied by the Princess of Wales?

*I*n organizational terms, the best thing about reaching Hong Kong was the floating palace that was waiting for us alongside in the naval base HMS *Tamar*. For a weary tour party far from home, the royal yacht was a haven of tranquillity and comfort. Now decommissioned, in 1989 *Britannia* was still very much a floating home from home, steeped in the ambience and technology of 1950s Britain. Accustomed to the simpler surroundings of a cramped anti-submarine frigate, I perhaps enjoyed the comforts of the yacht more than some of my companions. "*This* is the way to go to sea," I thought to myself as I sank into what must have been one of the softest bunks afloat.

On the evening after their arrival, as was customary, the Prince and Princess held a reception and dinner party on board for the colony's great and good. After the outward calm of Indonesia, there now seemed to be only an uneasy truce between the royal couple. They did what was expected of them in front of both cameras and guests, but I saw no repeat of either the tentative intimacy or the overt estrangement that had been noticeable on the Gulf tour.

The strain was telling on them both, however. The Princess in particular was counting down the hours until she flew home. As in the Gulf, she was returning to London before the Prince. He was due to stay on in Hong Kong for a few days' holiday and to lay the wreath at the colony's Remembrance Day service. As in the Gulf, I was also staying behind.

"God, Patrick!" she said to me. "I can't *wait* to get on that plane. Get home and see my boys."

"Yes, Ma'am."

"Pity you can't come back with me. I expect you'll be dragged round housing schemes..."

"Something like that, Ma'am."

"...and Chinese medicine shops. Looking for tigers' bits. Ha!"

The necessity to reconcile their differing styles—at working a room crowded with guests, for example—demanded a hundred little concessions from each of them just to begin and end at the same time. Making concessions was not always at the top of their agenda. Once again, as I observed that evening on *Britannia*, the Princess's tactic was to outcharm, outchat, and outflirt her husband. He was left to look pedestrian and dull by comparison, as people—especially tall, handsome men—seemed to gravitate in her direction. Even the women tended to find her a distraction as they surreptitiously compared their war paint with hers. That was far from being the whole picture, of course. The fact was that the Prince's calm dignity valuably offset his wife's more eye-catching style, but it must have looked different through his eyes and we all knew he found it provocative. That, after all, was the intention.

*A*s in the Gulf, I rather enviously watched my boss and the rest of the advance return party settle themselves into a homeward-bound jumbo jet. Once again I returned on my own to the Prince and his personal staff, feeling rather subdued.

My spirits were improved by the knowledge that the next few days almost counted as holiday. Instead of the doubtful delights of Saudi Arabia, this time we faced only the appealing prospect of cruising in the royal yacht round the eastern islands of the Hong Kong group before returning to Victoria for the Remembrance Sunday services at the Cenotaph on the waterfront. The yacht anchored in Double Haven, a natural harbor surrounded by picturesque islets and with a view onto the mainland of the New Territories so devoid of human habitation that it seemed impossible that downtown Hong Kong lay just a few miles round the corner. Our holiday mood took its cue from the Prince, who as usual spent much of his time at his easel. The covering illustration for one of his published collections of watercolors dates from this time.

It turned out to be another valuable opportunity to see something of the Prince's personality, so different from that of the Princess. With her, there was a sense that you had to read the music as you went along and hope not to hit too many wrong notes. By contrast, with the Prince the performance followed a recognizable score, the orchestra was not expected to extemporize much, and solo performers seldom held the stage for long, to the relief of performer and royal audience alike.

On our return to Victoria, the public ceremonies to mark Remembrance Day proved to be a good example of the colonial power's continuing ability to put on a good show to impress everyone taking part, as well as any watching media, if not to any great extent the local population.

To my delight Governor Wilson wore his full ceremonial uniform for the occasion, including his ostrich-plumed hat, while his ADC wore a solar topee that could have come straight from the Raj. The Prince, in Royal Navy Captain's uniform, and I, a respectful distance behind him holding his wreath, were positioned behind the Governor who symbolically represented the Queen.

The Prince was not greatly impressed with this. I was surprised by the strength of his objections to the Governor's insistence on performing his part in the proceedings as if he were the monarch. As her representative, he was technically entitled to do this, but the monarch's son seemed to think that the Governor's hairsplitting adherence to protocol was unnecessary and inappropriate. Here, after all, was the next best thing to the sovereign, present in person and embodying all the necessary regal qualities.

The Governor stuck to his guns, however, and laid his own wreath on behalf of the Prince's mother. I was then supposed to make the long and lonely march to where the Prince was standing on his allocated mark, a couple of paces behind His Excellency. I had to salute and hand him his wreath, turn about and march back to my place without dropping my sword.

To the uninitiated, this is not as straightforward as it looks. By long tradition, when in their scabbards naval swords swing on the end of two lengths of leather strap attached to the sword belt. Gathering up the sword to the correct position for marching is a complicated maneuver, known as "flicking up," that has to be conducted with fingertip precision. Not even a single nervous downward glance is allowed and it is only too easy for the whole clattering apparatus to become tangled in your legs. At the thought of such a disaster befalling me in front of the large and interested audience I broke out in a cold sweat.

"Thank you," said the Prince politely when I handed him the wreath. Then, as he watched me salute, his look turned to one of sympathy as I prepared to maneuver my sword. At least, I chose to interpret it as sympathy. He certainly knew the hazards of the drill I was performing—and sensibly avoided attempting it himself. My luck was in. My sword obeyed me and the Royal Navy drill book's sanctity was preserved.

Our final night on the yacht saw us all dining informally with the Prince, who then treated us to some of his prized collection of Spike Milligan videos. I sat in the flickering darkness listening to the Prince's loud guffaws, which were faithfully echoed by the assorted courtiers and yacht officers present. It was surprising how many of them suddenly seemed to remember how sidesplittingly funny *The Goon Show* had been.

The tour had a revealing postscript. As we were approaching the coast of England in our VC-10, and just when we thought there was nothing left to do but climb into the bus for London, the weather added its contribution to the tour's tests on the Prince's good nature. Fog at our destination, Lyneham, meant that it was impossible to land there.

A hurried conference with the crew concluded that Glasgow was the best alternative. Radio phone calls were made to the startled Chief Constable of the Strathclyde police, warning him to prepare for the imminent arrival of the Prince of Wales and his accompanying party, inbound from the Orient and in search of anonymity and a bed for what remained of the night.

Thus the Prince found himself eating an unfamiliar breakfast in a Glasgow airport hotel while a cold, gray dawn broke over Scotland's second city. It was the morning of his forty-first birthday; he had uncomplainingly suffered a tedious disruption to his itinerary; and only a handful of people ever knew he was there.

As I contemplated my own bowl of porridge, I wondered how his wife would have reacted to such a disturbance of her plans. The intervention of mere forces of nature would hardly have served as an adequate excuse for what she would more than likely have portrayed as an almighty foul-up. Her sense of injustice at the sheer unfairness of it all would have been uncontainable. In this assumption I was only partly right, as it turned out. There were occasions in later years, including a risky visit to

Northern Ireland, when her imperturbability in the face of similar meteorological provocation surprised me.

*T*he Far Eastern tour and the one to Hungary which followed it in mid-1990 were the last grand gestures of togetherness. Henceforth, where the Prince and Princess went and why they went there became less important for the watching media than how they coped with the ordeal of being in each other's company.

Despite this increasing pressure, the Hungary tour was a publicity success for them both as individuals. Ironically, it also produced some misleadingly optimistic comments about how well they seemed to be getting on. It was an exciting time to visit Budapest. The communist regime had melted away between the time of our recce and the start of the tour. In the early summer sunshine the whole country seemed to be having a party, and the press would not have been human if they had not felt the romance that seemed to lie over the city like early morning mist on the Danube.

Authoritarianism was in full retreat, as our police discovered during discussions with their Hungarian counterparts when they tried to suggest some very necessary crowd control for the planned walkabouts. "We are a free people," they were told, "and we will stand wherever we like." It was impossible to argue with the sentiment, even though it proved its limitations in dealing with enthusiastic crowds when the Prince and Princess were in town.

There was an unusually large number of joint engagements, and enough romantic photo opportunities to satisfy even the most soft-focus *Hello!* photographer. The Prince and Princess were seen looking wistfully across the Danube from the Fisherman's Bastion, inspecting vegetables in the traditional covered market, and looking for all the world as if they were on holiday together as they sat on the upper deck of a riverboat during a cruise on the last day of the tour.

This led to a small rash of excited reports in the press that the Waleses had put their marital difficulties behind them. How wrong could you be, I said to myself as I read the misguided speculation. To be fair to the press, you did have to be very close to the action—and very cynical—to understand the guerrilla warfare that was being waged below the surface.

Behind the apparent togetherness of the Hungary tour, there had been no real rapprochement. What we were seeing was a professional performance from two individual performers, not the media's dream of a revived love affair. There was no real teamwork in their public appearances—a knowing eye on the walkabouts told you that. Nor was there any letup in the minor point-scoring, at least on the Princess's side, as she sought and found the cameras' sympathy in the arrival ceremony while she held the President's wife's hand, or on the romantic *pusta* plain as she posed with daredevil horsemen, or in her detachment from the Prince's effusive support for Kenneth Branagh and Emma Thompson as they brought Shakespeare's *King Lear* to Budapest.

Point-scoring was still on her mind as we set off the next day on a busy round of joint engagements. It was in the hubbub of the covered market that the Princess sprang one of her occasional surprises, designed to test the ingenuity and resourcefulness of her equerry and to attract the sympathy of anybody else within earshot.

"Patrick," she hissed, "I've got to go to the loo!"

Since, at that moment, we were hemmed in on all sides by a crowd of produce vendors, photographers, politicians, and police, the task of even asking for a lavatory, let alone finding one that was presentable, had me momentarily nonplussed. Then a happy inspiration struck me. "Ma'am, the next engagement is at the St. Mathias Church. I'll be there ahead of you to check out the plumbing and meet you on arrival. Nobody will notice if you slip away for a couple of minutes there."

Without waiting for her to disagree, I disappeared into the crowds and commandeered one of the spare cars, in which I raced at high speed to the church. The difficulties of arriving at a major ecclesiastical establishment that is in the final stages of preparing to receive distinguished foreign visitors became apparent as soon as I tried to negotiate my way past the security cordon, which seemed suddenly to have remembered some of the cooperative charm that had marked its totalitarian past.

Having with difficulty overcome this hurdle, I then had to find a suitable recipient for my urgent piece of news. Given the delicacy of the subject matter, this took some time. I was in a state of ill-suppressed panic when I was shown eventually to a distinctly elementary facility, down a dim side passage and seemingly guarded by a roomful of nuns, through which I had to pass on my lightning inspection.

I puffed back to the main door just in time to see the Prince and Princess arrive. I signaled at her urgently with my eyebrows and she made a beeline for where I was standing, leaving a bemused Prince looking questioningly over his shoulder as he carried on with the official receiving line.

Needless to say, this digression from the established program caught the attention of the hawklike British media, who were thus well placed and well primed to photograph the Princess as she paused in devout prayer on her way back from sharing one of the less mystical experiences of the nuns' life.

From the shadows a discreet distance away I watched the saintly figure bowed in prayer, and admiration overcame any irritation I might have been feeling. In the noisy background the spiritual Prince was being shown the finer architectural points of the church, while his notoriously disco-mad wife knelt in a pew, apparently lost in reverent contemplation. I just hoped she was giving appropriate thanks to the Almighty for Hungarian ecclesiastical sanitary conveniences.

As always, there was enough sincerity in her actions to allay casual suspicion as to her real motives. To my mind, however, there was no doubting her underlying intentions—to attract attention, to signal an independence from her marriage, and to exert by guile and gamesmanship the strength she felt unable to express openly. Foreign tours, no less than home engagements, were vehicles for a subliminal message: I am not a dumb clotheshorse, a junior player in a marriage that frustrates me; I am a figure in my own right, and none too scrupulous.

8

Jump at Shadows

*B*ack in England, the same unscrupulousness was becoming more apparent in her public duties and private relationships. The energy that the Princess used in creating such a world of intrigue and suspicion might, of course, have been used more productively to sustain her popular support of good causes. Used positively, it might also have helped her feel generally more content, but being content was not a natural state for her. Given the chance, she always preferred to plot and maneuver.

A prime target for these instincts was the Duchess of York. During 1989 and 1990 the two of them were often bracketed together, both in the public mind and in the disapproving eyes of some senior courtiers. This was always to the Princess's detriment. Being senior—as the wife of the heir—and having already established a better record of public service than the Duchess, she actually needed only to emphasize the differences between herself and her sister-in-law in order to achieve a comfortable superiority. The process should have been made even easier by the simple fact that the media had cast the Princess as the epitome of stylish elegance, while they portrayed the Duchess as, well, someone rather less photogenic. Improbable as it now seems, however, at that time the Princess was paranoid that Fergie was winning the popularity battle.

The rivalry the Princess introduced into the relationship spoke volumes about her sense of insecurity. It also emphasized a little known fact. Fergie was in reality a much stronger personality than the Princess and was always able to influence her moods, often for better, but sometimes for worse.

As the wife of the Queen's favorite son, Fergie enjoyed a closeness with the monarch that the Princess never felt she shared. This closeness was a constant source of jealousy and suspicion. It meant that the Princess could never fully accept Fergie's freely offered friendship. Instead, she traded on it to acquire information and to build up a spurious sense of sisterly solidarity.

The Duchess's own marriage was in its painful final stages during those years. This gave the Princess a chance to share the dangerously thrilling idea of royal divorce, while coolly watching someone else go first into the fiery furnace of family ostracism and media condemnation. The situation afforded her considerable *schadenfreude*—always a pleasing sensation—as well as some practical tips on avoiding any adverse media consequences of her growing taste for independence, such as the importance of keeping up a consistent program of hard work and being efficiently discreet about affairs.

"Who do you think will get the blame for the Yorks' bust-up?" she once asked me, revealing her own sense of priorities in the process.

I was not at all sure what answer to give. The whole issue of royal separation or divorce was still officially unthinkable, but some of us were unofficially thinking the unthinkable every day, without really knowing what to do about it. We were just the staff. We simply hoped against hope that our employers would sort themselves out. We did not want to get involved—it was too dangerous.

She needed to look no farther than Fergie to see how absolute would be the Windsors' alienation when provoked, and provocation—either deliberate through media manipulation or incidental through the popularity she attracted—was increasingly what they must have perceived in her actions. It must privately have been what her husband felt too, from a date long before I joined. Since neither of them found compromise easy, the eventual outcome should have been no surprise. That it was not more widely anticipated demonstrates one of the royal family's greatest assets: at that time people still seemed to have an infinite capacity to believe the best of it.

Little by little I developed a personal policy of doing what I could to soften the Princess's landing when the crash happened. It was self-interest, really. After all, I was strapped into the cockpit with her. Now my policy—and my faithfulness—was being put to the test. My answer to any question about the Yorks' marriage would be filed in the Princess's memory under "Loyalty." It was a crowded section and my dossier was constantly under review. Too damning, and I would be written off as part of the unfeeling establishment. Too approving and I might as well be the footman. I paused, hoping to look judicious while actually racking my brains.

Somewhere in my head a voice was telling me just to say what I really thought: that the whole thing was a ghastly mess and she would be a bloody fool to have any similar notions. Just get on with your lovely life, Ma'am, turn a blind eye to what hurts you and *stop making such a fuss*. The voice was a stranger, though, not to be trusted. I fell into the familiar habit of weighing my words.

I guessed that the Duchess would come off worst, but something stopped me from giving my boss this answer, perhaps because I knew it was exactly what she wanted to hear. Instead I adopted my stuffy courtier look—not easy to accomplish in profile in the back of a Jaguar—and said, "Hard to say, Ma'am, but I think people will only blame either of them if it looks like the children are being exploited to gain popularity in the press."

This piece of pomposity was received in disapproving silence. Already I could guess that the most powerful weapon in the Princess's impending battle with her in-laws, namely her reputation as a devoted mother, was being secretly sharpened up in readiness. The question about the Yorks was further unwelcome evidence to me that such a battle was only a matter of time. Like so many people approaching marital disaster, she hesitated on the brink, not sure of her ground, anxiously gathering opinions to bolster her own uncertainty. Who could blame her, after all? Her husband and his family were not enemies to be made lightly, yet enemies they were inexorably becoming as the Princess diverged ever farther from their ideal model.

From watching Fergie's experience, she might also conclude that from neither her potential suitors nor even her closest friends could she expect the strength of support she would need for a successful independence campaign. Her future was in her own hands, in the hands of general public opinion, and in the hands of those to whom she entrusted small parts of it—such as me.

As the Yorks' separation continued to unfold in public, the Princess's role as spectator and coconspirator grew more and more absorbing. She would avidly scan the newspapers for clues as to the trend in Fergie's popularity and seemed to feel little dismay that it appeared to be in free fall. Meanwhile, there were daily phone calls between the sisters-in-law, from snatches of which I got a taste of the intrigue afoot. Even then, however, the Princess seemed only to see herself as a player in an exciting and illicit game, the ringleader of which shared little of her own sense of self-preservation.

The true story of Fergie sending the Princess a copy of the video *The Great Escape* hints at the schoolgirlish plotting that was going on. Those of us who knew what was happening were able to dismiss it as such, if uneasily. Despite the childish antics, my boss nonetheless never lost her coolly detached ability to assess Fergie's tortuous path to freedom, or the pitfalls that awaited her when she too took the plunge.

Here was further evidence of the Princess's talent for matching her oscillating moods with a calculating analysis of public opinion. She could run rings round the hidebound royal establishment and dupe a willing press into endorsing her squeaky-clean image. Meanwhile, unknown to most watchers—and carefully kept from her staff—her relationship with James Hewitt was passionately resumed, and already she was secretly cooperating with a little-known court correspondent called Andrew Morton. No wonder she watched Fergie's downward progress with a mixture of fascination and dread.

In these circumstances, anything that might dispel so many nagging uncertainties—and provide a lot of fun along the way—was bound to be popular with both women, and it was around this time that their shared interest in clairvoyance acquired an importance bordering on obsession. Characteristically, it was the Duchess who made the running, acquiring regular bulletins about the future, which she shared with the Princess. Some of these she then passed on to me.

"You'll never guess, Patrick! Fergie's magic woman—she's really brilliant—has said that my husband's going to have the worst day of his life next week!"

"Really?" I replied, with heavy sincerity. "Any tips for the 3:30 at Kempton?" This she dismissed as the predictable response of a mere man—and a man blind to her psychic potential at that.

My tactful skepticism never deterred her for long. Next week the seer had stepped up the drama factor accordingly. Well, I thought, at least she knows her market. "Patrick! Fergie's witch-woman says my husband is going to be killed! She's seen mountains and a helicopter..."

This time my skepticism was even less tactful, but the

Princess was not to be denied her supernatural thrills and retained a faith in clairvoyance that appears to have lasted to the end of her life, despite the public debunking of the Duchess's most notorious fortune-teller, Madame Vasso.

Keen to share her delight at recruiting a royal client, Madame Vasso invited a tabloid newspaper to write all about it, including a reference to the efficacy of her famous blue pyramid. Incredulous snorts arose from many breakfast tables as the news was absorbed, and at last my skepticism raised a laugh from the Princess. "I don't know what all the fuss is about, Ma'am. I use my blue pyramid all the time and it works brilliantly!" Her laughter was as much over Fergie's embarrassment as my attempt at humor. Once again she had kept her head down as the impetuous Duchess set off on a dangerous but intriguing track, and she had been able to watch the subsequent derailment from a safe distance.

One of the last and potentially most damaging fantasies the Princess acquired from such unconventional sources was the belief that her husband would not succeed to the throne—either through death or disinclination—and that his place would be taken by the Duke of York as Regent. This outcome plainly held attractions for the sisters-in-law and the Princess seldom lost an opportunity to extol the Duke's kingly qualities—and, it has to be said, the fine figure he cut, especially in tropical naval uniform. "In those white shorts, he's really rather dishy..."

In retrospect, the apparent relish with which she contemplated the disasters predicted for the royal family might show the Princess in a poor light. Even at the time, it struck me as rather tasteless, as I rather ineffectually tried to tell her. The fact was, however, that she believed herself beleaguered in the face of overwhelming numbers of heartless enemies, among whom she increasingly numbered her husband and his family. In this state of mind, help from any quarter was likely to be welcomed. Moreover, it was part of her vulnerability that—such was her selective attitude to more conventional advice—the more disreputable rescuers could expect the most avid hearing.

Running through it all was her mistrust of Fergie. No matter what misfortunes publicly befell her sister-in-law, the Princess would still torture herself with the thought that she might yet become a real rival rather than just a useful counterpoint to her own good fortune. Precisely because she must have known at heart that it was as much good fortune as any superior virtue that kept the popularity scales tipped in her favor, the Princess's self-doubt always lurked close by.

Some years later, when relations with Fergie were notably strained, she had me arrange a secret meeting with John F. Kennedy Jr. while we were visiting New York. The Princess's wish to meet America's most eligible bachelor owed more than a bit to the fact that he was at the time a particular pinup of Fergie's. Nothing came of the Princess's meeting with him. They passed a pleasant enough hour in her suite at the Carlyle discussing, among other things, the burden of fame and the intrusiveness of the media. It was perhaps not the best moment, therefore, for John to request that the Princess appear on the first cover of his new magazine *George*. Being a cover girl was something she normally enjoyed, but refusing an invitation was sometimes more satisfactorily provocative. Sure enough, after a theatrical glance in my direction, she politely declined the offer.

*W*hen she was in the grip of the insecurity caused by Fergie rivalry, the Princess whipped herself—and her staff—into a pointless campaign of public competition. We would suddenly find ourselves soliciting engagements just to keep the statistics favorable to the Princess. It made me squirm to tout for business in this way.

"Patrick," she would say in her morning phone call, "I really think we must do something *quickly* for... (here she might quote a cause championed in the morning tabloids).

D'you think you could tell them I might be free to help them tomorrow?"

At other times, particularly when stung by one of her sister-in-law's rare media successes—"Caring Fergie backs research into Motor Neurone Disease" was the sort of thing that sparked a reaction—her response could be uncompromisingly direct. "Patrick! We seem to be reading rather a lot about the red-haired lady..." she would say, and I would dutifully rake up a spontaneous caring counterstrike.

Luckily for me and my conscience, and for the Princess's image, there were usually quite enough genuine invitations to make these bouts of cynical exploitation fairly rare. I knew the media suspected what was going on, but they preferred to give their profitable golden goose the benefit of the doubt, at least initially.

Most of the patronages that benefited were quite realistic enough not to feel that any serious principles were being compromised. If they were happy, I reasoned, why should I ostentatiously hold my nose in disapproval? Charitably, I assumed the Princess had already reached the same conclusion, which would explain her lack of visible scruples about exploiting good causes in this way. No doubt she added to this a belief—not unreasonable—that she was a pretty good cause in her own right.

The Princess's tendency to seek extra publicity for such half-baked reasons was always heightened at times of enforced inactivity. I came to anticipate her more bizarre proposals either during or immediately after her many holidays, or during the weeks she spent incarcerated with the rest of the royal family at Balmoral in the summer or at Sandringham at Christmas. Her intentions were sharpened by her wish to draw a distinction between the perceived idleness of her in-laws and her own tireless dedication to the needs of her constituency. In this instance her constituency comprised as much the headline writers of Fleet Street as the occupants of the hospitals and care centers that were the unwitting beneficiaries of her boredom.

It would go something like this. I might be at home one evening when the Balmoral operator would ring to tell me that Her Royal Highness was on the line. Briefly pausing in whatever domestic activity was occupying me at the time, I would grab my notepad and appointment book—the essential two tools of my trade—while the Princess was put through.

"Patrick! I thought you'd like an update from my ivory tower."

"Ma'am, yes, what news from the front line?"

A giggle, then, "I'll go mad if I don't get a break from this place. Isn't there something we could do? The country needs to know that not everybody is on holiday and I thought perhaps you might have some ideas about somewhere that needed visiting."

With practice, I learned to curb my cynicism and instead have a list of reliable, standby engagements ready to activate at a moment's notice. Inevitably, this list was drawn from organizations that I knew could be relied upon to produce a good show at the drop of a hat, so regional projects of Barnardo's, Help the Aged, the Red Cross, Relate, and similarly quick-witted charities would sometimes receive the unexpected pleasure of a royal visit. These charities also had the advantage of tacitly understanding my dilemma and responding swiftly to what was, after all, one of the easier prices to pay for having a patron of such media-pleasing qualities. Hospitals, particularly those with which she had an established link, such as Great Ormond Street or the Royal Marsden, also proved to be helpful sources of impromptu engagements.

There were many doors that readily opened for her to provide an emotional refuge from the barren wastes of "holidays" and provide wholesome activity and favorable media coverage without asking questions. Their motives were, quite legitimately, sometimes a wish to attract attention to themselves, particularly if seasonal fluctuations of either income or activity could be brought to the attention of the public in this way. Sometimes they were also more worldly and compassionate in simply recognizing a young woman's need to escape from confinement with often stressful company and instead to be with people who genuinely needed her as much as she needed them.

At times, either out of overfamiliarity with my list of reliable standbys or because of a wish to exercise her office at a time when they might also have expected to be on holiday, she would suggest something rather more ambitious. Occasionally this produced very worthwhile results, such as the time one summer when she flew unnoticed on a commercial flight to visit a hospice in Blackpool, repeating the exercise a few days later in Hull.

At her request, both establishments treated the Princess as they would any other volunteer—or so they claimed. Dressed in an auxiliary's uniform, she assisted with various mundane, domestic chores and, more importantly, spent time with patients whose lives could be measured in days or weeks at most. This was especially appreciated by her because, in contrast to a normal public engagement, this time she was unhurried by an equerry standing in the doorway anxiously looking at his watch. Although we maintained strict security, it was no surprise to find that the news happily leaked out after the event to reassure both her admirers and detractors that the Princess was continuing her good work. Also, although she would not dream of pointing it out herself, while she was working certain people she could mention were decimating Scottish wildlife.

Not all such impromptu outings passed without a hitch. As the coordinators of all royal visits to their counties, Lords Lieutenant were not always amused by engagements that cropped up outside the normal, sedate programming process. Nor were they always entirely sure that they understood why a Princess who always claimed to be overworked could somehow suddenly appear to have time to spare to visit their patch in search of deserving causes. Soothing such troubled minds was very much my responsibility. Even when I felt I had accomplished the task with the necessary reassuring blarney, however, I never lost the feeling that we were causing a lot of extra work in order to appease a requirement that we could not truthfully share with our hosts.

The quality of the engagement was also less predictable in these off-the-cuff circumstances, whatever its novelty value. In addition, I was always conscious that curious and not altogether approving eyes were being cast at us by the Princess's other patronages, many of whom had longstanding invitations still unhonored but were waiting patiently in line for their turn. Eventually, the newspapers began to scent that they too were being manipulated and my colleagues in other households grew offended by the sight of so many sacrosanct holidays being defiled.

The Princess was oblivious to my concerns. In fact, I seemed to spend large amounts of my life ensuring that she remained oblivious to my concerns on a great many things. This may have been because I believed that nine times out of ten she would do precisely as she pleased in any case. My simple duty both to myself and to her was therefore to ensure that as few people as possible got hurt in the process. This made me feel trapped at times, but I consoled myself with the hope that, with luck, some of us might manage to emerge with credit at the end.

Eventually she felt emboldened by the success of her short-notice engagements to the point where she felt she could act almost literally on impulse to bring them about. Sometimes she concealed her self-publicizing motives by finding an excuse in a topical news story. When she was in this mood, it only took a *Daily Mail* report of a brave child in a "mercy dash" for a lifesaving operation in the USA to produce a surprise "caring" letter or signed photograph for the distraught family. Such touching concern could then be revealed by the dazed but grateful parents and the watching world could renew its faith that—even on this most superficial level—at least one member of our royal family had a heart.

There were many examples of this sort of opportunism, and they were not all completely cynical. When she wrote the caring letter—or, more likely, had me draft it for her—her concern was genuine enough, but the quest for self-interest often came out on top. This was certainly the case with her wish, dutifully reported in the *Daily Mail*, to visit victims of the Warrington bombing in early 1993.

Unmoved by such publicly displayed concern—if not by the sentiment itself, which she surely shared—the Queen made her own choice of representative and sent the Prince instead. Undeterred, the Princess wrote directly to the Parry family, whose son Tim had been killed and to whom her letter obviously meant a great deal. Predictably, the letter became public. The kindness of her gesture was as genuine as the tragedy of the circumstances deserved; it was just that there was a further, secondary agenda to the one presented more or less artlessly to the public. It was less noble, but it served a vital psychological function for the Princess. It helped her believe that she was *wanted*, and there was never going to be any shortage of opportunities for a public figure of her popularity to extract the desired level of gratification from such gestures.

Over time, she developed a formula for these gestures. All she was trying to express, she maintained, was her wish to serve the higher concerns of humanity and the emotional needs of the nation as a whole. Such was her transparent sincerity that many people believed her, first among them herself. In reality, such idealism existed mostly in the eyes of the recipient. In the Princess its main value was as a smoke screen, helping both her and me to avert our eyes from the void in her life which, in the absence of a settled marriage, she was partly able to fill with work, wherever it came from. As a distraction from this very personal agenda, the Princess was able to enhance her image by invoking a naive idealism in others. The watching public seemed happy to set aside any suspicion that it was being led by the nose, just for the reward of seeing the Princess express a popular emotion. For her part, no emotion was too facile, so long as it was popular. This was the test.

Despite this, I knew that the impression I had formed on that first outing to Essex—that she genuinely cared—was not untrue. It was the instinctive reaction of any sensitive adult, heightened by a strong maternal instinct and a personal acquaintance with pain, all powerfully communicated by the most expressive eyes in the business. Not even the best actress could sustain such a convincing show of compassion for so long; nor would those on the receiving end be so easily fooled. Some of it had to be real.

Over time, however, I observed that this gift of empathy with suffering people could become confused with hunger for the unconditional love and understanding that she felt she needed for herself. Feed this internal hunger with unlimited media opportunities to appeal to greater humanitarian principles, and a balanced understanding of her own motives becomes all the more vital. That the task was beyond her was not entirely her fault. Much of it was mine.

All this was yet to become clear. The picture only emerged as the years passed and my knowledge of her deepened. At the time all I could try to do was to make sense of the contradictory evidence of my own eyes, while every engagement, every tour, and often every glance or casual remark added to the mosaic of emotions that I saw at work in her.

Watching her, I came to feel that almost anything can be sanctioned, or overlooked, for the sake of a great principle. Royalty, being at its best a kind of manifestation of an ideal, is given enormous latitude to claim idealism for itself, no matter how hackneyed its chosen subject, how undisciplined its thinking, or how self-serving its motives. The truth seems to be that many of us prefer to think of our royal family acting out of principle in a way we have learned not to expect from our politicians. The trouble is, however, that by borrowing tricks from spin-conscious politicians some royal people have taken a major step away from their traditional and most highly prized function—to exercise the privilege of acting out of principle rather than out of a desire (or need) to secure short-term popularity. From there it is only a short step to hypocrisy, as I discovered late one night in a railway lavatory.

It was Christmas 1995, not long after the painful *Panorama* interview. Despite repeated reminders from me and others, the Princess had made no plans to take up any of the offers of seasonal hospitality that had been sent to her. She was lonely and bored. She felt unloved and unappreciated, and I believe it was sadly some form of consolation to her to bring this unhappiness sharply to the attention of any who might be planning a rather more conventionally happy holiday.

Having left London to go on leave with all outstanding business, as I thought, completed at the office, I received an urgent pager message to call my boss. As was my custom, I made my way unenthusiastically to the First Class lavatory, locked myself in securely, and dialed the Palace number. The Princess's first words confirmed the suspicion I had held for the previous two weeks.

"Patrick, I'm so sorry to bother you when you're away on your hols, but I think it's really important we go to Calcutta to see Mother Teresa for Christmas. She'd love it. It would be a marvelous way of using all this wretched publicity of mine to draw attention to the wonderful work she's doing."

"That's a hell of an idea, Ma'am, but—"

"We don't need to tell anyone. I could just go with a policeman and offer to help with caring for the people who are dying."

"Where would you stay? In Mother's house with the Sisters?"

"Well, I don't think *that* would do. No, we have to find a hotel..."

"Ma'am, this is going to have to be done properly. I'm sorry always to sound so unenthusiastic, but if you arrive in

Calcutta in a blaze of publicity in the middle of the Christmas holidays without us even having told the High Commissioner, a lot of people will be very embarrassed and the benefit of your visit for Mother Teresa would be spoiled."

"But Patrick, they'll try and stop us. They don't understand what these people *need*..."

I had a sudden inspiration. "Let me ring Mother and see what she can do from her end. I'll call you back as soon as I've spoken to her."

I looked in my address book under Mother Teresa and there was the number. Standing swaying in the loo (the aroma did rouse some distant Indian memories, now I came to think of it), trying to ignore the intrusive clickety-clack in the background, and losing the signal every couple of minutes as we went under a bridge, I rang Calcutta. I was put through to the nun who was, I suppose, Mother Teresa's private secretary equivalent, a very formidable American who, despite the fact that she had such a high spiritual calling, was very much a person of the world and took no nonsense from anybody.

"The Princess of Wales has said that she would be willing to come and visit Mother's work over the Christmas holiday," I said to her. "It's something which on a personal level I think she would find very fulfilling, but she has also pointed out to me that the publicity it's bound to attract might well benefit Mother's wonderful work."

I heard a muffled snort, or it may just have been interference on the line. "Patrick, this *is* good news; and so unexpected. Just let me spend a minute or two thinking about it and discussing it with Mother and then let me call you back."

About fifteen minutes later—we were somewhere between Westbury and Castle Cary by then—the American voice confirmed that my plan had worked. "Patrick," she said, "Mother asks that you send her thanks and blessings to Her Highness and is delighted to hear that she wishes to help with our work in this way. But she says there's no need for the Princess to come all the way to Calcutta, because as it happens our Order has recently opened two alcohol rehabilitation projects in a suburb of London called 'Southwark.' Mother feels that, if the Princess would like to help us with our work, it would surely be more convenient for her to visit these centers instead of making the journey all the way to India."

With a sigh of relief I said, "Thank you, Sister, very much."

I thought I heard a chuckle. "God bless you, Patrick, and have a happy Christmas."

I had a bracing cup of Great Western tea and nerved myself for the call I now had to make to the Princess to report my failure. With as much regret and sympathy as I could put into my voice, I relayed the essential message I had received from Calcutta. There was a long, hurt, and unloved silence at the other end of the line before the train plunged into a tunnel and the phone mercifully went dead. I am afraid the alcohol projects never did get their visit.

9

❧

Hot and Cold

*F*urther evidence that an age of innocence was slipping away from us came in my growing realization that the Princess's place in the royal machinery was no longer beyond doubt. So far as the world was concerned, of course, she was still very much the future Queen. Her role as a mainstream royal operator—a senior board member of the royal "firm"—is worth emphasizing in this respect. For anyone reviewing the events of 1989–90 and even into 1991, there is ample evidence of her role as a hardworking member of the royal team. This was very reassuring at the time, particularly for those who were beginning to believe the rising tide of stories about marital strains hidden from public view, although there were also growing signs of independence and assertiveness.

The royal family is a federation of semi-independent households, each one reflecting the character of the royal people it exists to serve. Those of us who worked for the Waleses were still, at least in theory, members of a unified household, but the Princess's increasing wish to stamp her own personality on her public life inevitably put her on a divergent path from the organization that had been set up for her husband, to whom it largely still owed its first loyalty. Other members of the federation, particularly its leadership, could only view the emergence of a new and possibly incompatible body as potentially destabilizing, if not actually alien. It became my job as private secretary to do what I could to minimize these concerns.

It was a time of transition. The Princess's stardom had not yet parted company with the reality of her achievements. It was still possible to believe only the best of her without having to set aside serious doubts about her motives. Unless, that is, you had inside knowledge of her well-established ability to manipulate public appearances to serve her need for personal recognition. Spin-doctoring—on behalf of the Princess or her husband—was not yet obtrusive either, so when Lesley Garner wrote the following fairly typical appreciation in the *Telegraph* on June 17, 1989, her remarks could be taken as genuinely representative.

> If ever The Princess of Wales was just a frivolous Sloane, she has surely changed beyond recognition. As a working mother approaching her 28th birthday, she is patron or president of more than 40 bodies. She works hard, gets on brilliantly with people from all walks of life and, most importantly, she is prepared to tackle the least attractive causes... The young woman who dresses so beautifully and who lives such a privileged and apparently sheltered life probably understands as much about the major social problems that face us as anybody... The Mouse that Roared indeed.

It was high summer for her admirers. You could delight in her successes without even slightly compromising your loyalties as a monarchist—quite the opposite, in fact. Here was a Princess who many people thought could and surely would make the best possible sort of Queen for the twenty-first century. I was not alone in picturing her ultimately as the far-distant inheritor of the kind of affection currently reserved for the Queen Mother.

At that time it was also still possible to see her continuing in a traditional royal role. Her choice of engagements had not yet descended to the kind of cherry-picking that marked her final years. She still uncomplainingly carried out many public duties, not because they might enhance a particular aspect of her popularity but because they were just that—duties. Ironically, because they showed her as a mainstream royal figure, and because she carried them off with such style, these duties earned her the kind of unspectacular, reliable public approval that became so important in the years when the institution was trying to marginalize her.

She never recognized the debt she owed to these examples of routine, worthy royal work. Their setting was typically a gray industrial town, their audience typically the very old, the very young, the desperately poor and sad. These people felt that nobody spoke for them, but she made them feel they were not forgotten. Yet, when she had the chance, these engagements—along with the patronages they represented—were progressively discarded from her appointment calendar as she found easier popularity and more entertaining work to take their place. This was tragically wasted potential, both for her and for the monarchy, though at the time neither side perceived it.

Two contrasting engagements from this period come to mind. For me they show a final glimpse of the Princess in the role intended for her—royal, dutiful, and conformist. The first was a visit in the summer of 1989 to the Royal Naval College at Dartmouth in Devon, where the Princess had been asked to take the salute at Lord High Admiral's Divisions, the Navy's version of a pass-in-review. It was a typical royal engagement, albeit more colorful and ceremonial than an awayday in yet another provincial town. In a bright red tricorn hat and matching suit with brass buttons, the Princess was the Day-Glo focus of attention in a sea of massed, dark blue ranks.

She was, as always, very professional about remembering the part she had to play in the proceedings. Before venturing out to take the salute, she was given a briefing in the Captain's office on the intricacies of the parade to come. She listened with serious attention, only causing some consternation at the end, when she asked with wide-eyed innocence, "And will they do it all again if I ask them to?"

Then she emerged laughing into the sunshine, where the entire College was paraded in review order under the admiring gaze of their friends and families, who had come to witness their great day.

"Look at all those uniforms!" she breathed, her eyes roving up and down the ranks of men standing rigidly at attention.

"Hmm," said the Captain. "And royal weather for you too, Ma'am."

"Of course," came the reply. "The sun always shines on the righteous!"

A Royal Guard was drawn up under the dais ready to give the Royal Salute. The band played, the Guard commander shouted his hoarse commands, and with impressive precision several hundred swords and rifles were flourished in a symbolic act of respect. The statuesque, strikingly female figure in red looked down at the beautiful tableau of military symmetry and very gently inclined her head in acknowledgment. Queen Mary herself could not have done it better, in the days when the College sent young officers to serve the most powerful Navy in the world.

If Dartmouth showed once again the Princess's continuing potential as a popular combination of "old" and "new" royalty, a very different engagement from the same period showed the potential she still shared with her husband to be what the ordinary people of the country wanted them to be. It was a rare joint engagement at home in Britain. The town of Northampton had long been planning to honor its famous daughter and on June 8, 1989, the Princess was formally created a Freeman of the Town. Arrangements for the day were fiendishly complicated, involving the Prince and Princess arriving from different directions and departing separately as well.

The whole day was an excellent example of the goodwill, efficiency, and simple loyalty that lies behind so many royal provincial visits. There was a church service at which the Prince read the lesson, a civic ceremony at which the Princess made a pretty speech in reply to the honor the town gave her, a march past by the Army, a huge lunch, a tour of the museum, and a squelching walkabout in pouring rain. The watching public loved it all.

By then, however, the Princess was in a foul mood. Her umbrella had broken in the wind and rain, her hair was wet, and her shoes were leaking. To cap it all, we ended the afternoon with tea at Althorp, her ancestral home. Waiting to greet her was her stepmother Raine, in those days mercilessly demonized by the Princess. "You watch," she had said before we arrived, "she does the lowest curtsy in England." But the Princess was denied her fun. That afternoon Raine's curtsies and conversation were all for the Prince.

Presiding behind the teapot, the Countess dispensed Earl Grey and dazzling smiles to the little group sitting awkwardly round the tea table. Amidst the imposing splendor of Althorp, we made a bedraggled group. Reaction to the tensions of the day was setting in, especially for the new Freeman of Northampton, who had lapsed into a sullen silence. The Prince was coping well as he parried his stepmother-in-law's unctuous offer of miniature éclairs. The lady-in-waiting caught my eye and grimaced imperceptibly. The table groaned under the weight of dainty cakes and tiny sandwiches. Even nibbling suddenly seemed an impossible effort.

Only the Princess's father seemed oblivious to the mood of deepening gloom. He left the table and returned a moment later flourishing a bottle of Scotch. He spoke in breathy gasps, the legacy of a stroke. It was surprisingly endearing. Pointing the bottle at the Prince, he said, "Sir! Warm you up!" The Prince declined in mock horror—at least, I think it was mock. Undeterred, Johnny thrust the bottle at me, winking broadly as he filled my teacup to the brim. Then he poured himself a similar dose and we raised our cups. Soon a warm glow began to suffuse at least two members of the chilly gathering.

As soon as decency permitted, the Prince departed by helicopter for an architectural assignment. The Princess returned to London by car. Once again they had put duty before their private feelings and produced a performance for the townspeople that should have reaffirmed their faith in the security of the royal marriage.

Touchingly, I thought, it also represented a major effort on the part of the Prince to honor his wife's big day. He could not have enjoyed the rain either, and he was never at his best when being upstaged by his wife. This had been before her hometown audience too. Even though I had hardly seen them mutter a word to each other, as we sat in the mother of all traffic jams on the M1 I wondered if perhaps, after all, my royal employers could yet find a way to work happily together.

It was so much wishful thinking. All the day had proved, in fact, was what a strain it was for the Prince and Princess to share the limelight. What a grim day it must have been for her too, I realized: unhappy childhood memories, a stepmother she thought had stolen her father, a husband she could not bear to be with and who could not bear to be with her, a ceremony full of empty words of praise she felt she did not deserve, and—the last straw—her favorite umbrella broken.

There was little chance of happiness in all this. Over the next two years such unhappy experiences accumulated, and eventually separate lives came to seem the only way of breaking the spiral of growing discontent between the Princess and her husband. In the summer of 1991 this spiral received an extra and very public twist. During golfing practice at Ludgrove School, Prince William was accidentally hit on the head with a club, causing a depressed fracture of the skull. As the world now knows, he fortunately made a complete recovery, but for a few hours there was real fear that he might have suffered some significant neurological injury. Nobody felt this fear more, naturally, than his parents. It was in the ways they expressed it that the differences between them were laid bare.

The Prince, as was widely reported, having checked that William was not in serious danger, carried on with his scheduled engagements. In publicity terms it was a pity that these included an opera at Covent Garden followed by an overnight train journey to Yorkshire. This was all the ammunition his critics needed to paint him as heartless and remote, not to mention a cultural snob for good measure. I think even the Princess was surprised by the venomous way in which the tabloid press condemned the Prince as an uncaring father. They certainly said more hurtful things about his alleged shortcomings than I heard her voice aloud on this occasion. Nonetheless, she did not let that stop her falling into her natural role as distressed mother, worried to distraction about her injured son.

"He might have brain damage!" she told me on her mobile phone from Great Ormond Street, her voice quivering with anxiety. I sensed also a strange exultation, confirmed later when I met her at the hospital. She had hardly slept all night, having kept vigil at her son's bedside. She was careworn, disheveled (by her standards), and very vulnerable—but this was real life at last, a real crisis in which she would receive nothing but sympathy. "And you know, Patrick, you can identify so much more easily with other people's suffering when you've been there yourself." I could only agree.

In her eyes, of course, "being there" was exactly what the Prince had failed to do. She thus further strengthened her position within the marriage as the most (visibly) caring parent. Although I never heard her reproach him for his absence, psychologically it gave her an important advantage in the marital battle to come as it played into the hands of the Prince's own demons of duty and guilt. It reminded me again that almost every royal tragedy I witnessed was not the result of wicked things done by bad people. Most were the result of good left *undone* by people who lacked the necessary inclination, or sagacity, or sense of self-preservation— or good advisers, I later reflected in a habitual fit of self-doubt.

As so often when she was involved, following William's accident there were many whose lives were touched by the Princess in ways that could never have been planned by the most imaginative media adviser. For a start, there were the parents and children whom she visited during her own unexpected stay at the hospital and whose worries she could now share with a rare sincerity. Another surprise beneficiary was Headway, the head injuries charity whose work she supported—with much helpful publicity—for years afterward, even to the extent of hijacking one of their fundraising lunches as the setting for her melodramatic "Time and Space" speech in 1993.

For those of us looking for charity a bit closer to home, however, this was a time of further disappointments. Another twist in the marriage's spiral of decline was provided by the Prince's plans to celebrate his wife's thirtieth birthday in July 1991. The Princess chose to view his plans for a big party at Highgrove with suspicion. She possibly had grounds for this, knowing that the Prince seemed to be in need of his staff's advice on what he should do to mark what might have been a relaxed family event but that would inevitably be a focus of media interest.

I belonged to the "anything for a quiet life" school of marital management, as perhaps did the Prince, but a quiet life was not what the sad Princess was accustomed to; nor did she like the idea of others enjoying the benefits of such an alien concept. She preferred to interpret the planned celebrations as an attempt by her husband's supporters to portray him as a devoted husband, which, by then, she no longer believed him to be. "I won't be part of his charade!" she said when I tactfully suggested that it might be a good idea to go along with the plan.

Predictably, she publicly snubbed her husband's offer and thus earned a reputation for emotional honesty at whatever cost. As she well knew, the main cost was to the Prince's image, but this was just another example of a predicament that was becoming familiar to him. He was damned for offering a party, and would have been doubly damned if he had not.

This sharp and public disagreement was also the most visible sign so far that the rifts in the marriage ran deep. In their most obvious bid yet to damage the Princess, "friends" of the Prince contrived a doom-laden front-page story in the *Daily Mail* for July 2, 1991, that marked the lowest ebb so far in the gathering War of the Waleses. CHARLES AND DIANA: CAUSE FOR CONCERN it intoned solemnly. The reader might have been forgiven for wondering if there had been an assassination attempt or an outbreak of plague at St. James's Palace. Reading on, it became apparent that this call for national anxiety was justified by something far worse. The friends were "furious" on the Prince's behalf that his wife had rejected his offer of... a birthday party.

I was very glad indeed to have the chance to get away from this cycle of suspicion and recrimination and concentrate on the kind of work that most people—including me—thought that royal officials were paid to do.

September 1991 finally saw plans approved for the Princess to make a solo visit to Pakistan—a major development of her public role as a high-profile member of the royal team. It was the greatest confirmation, and the greatest test, of her royal credentials.

Until then, my only involvement in major overseas tours

had been as equerry, really just second-in-command to the private secretary, however indispensable I had felt myself to be. In the interim I had taken charge of a handful of short overseas visits by the Princess, mostly to Europe. For me Pakistan was the big one—my first major overseas tour for which I alone carried full responsibility.

It was not going to be a pushover. Pakistan is a proud nation, as I had discovered during my recce the previous year. From its period under British rule it had inherited a strong sense of protocol and a Byzantine Foreign Office littered with traps for the innocent and unwary visitor. In addition there were daunting logistical challenges involved in simply moving about such a geographically diverse country. Complications of climate and custom also had to be taken into account, as well as the ever-present scrutiny of what was regularly the largest of all traveling royal press parties.

In my favor I had many strong cards to play. First and foremost was the enthusiastic hospitality of our Pakistani hosts. There was also what seemed to be an infinite variety of tempting program options in which I had almost a free hand. From the snowcapped valleys of Chitral in the Himalayas to the sweltering public health projects of Lahore, there were enough potential engagements to fill a hundred tours. I also had the advantage of working for a Princess who was almost as keen as me to jump on the airplane.

In the increasingly sensitive political atmosphere back home, I had secured a clear-cut mandate from the Foreign Office for the Princess to make such a high-profile solo visit. Opinion on the royal home front was at least neutral, if, I felt, rather watchful. Not too many tears would be shed if this groundbreaking solo tour disappeared into the inside pages of the tabloids. In fact it was to invade the front pages of the broadsheets, a place claimed by most of the Princess's tours ever afterward. Our own Foreign Office's enthusiasm owed much to the influence of our High Commissioner in Islamabad, the irrepressible Nicholas Barrington, whose encyclopedic knowledge of Pakistan and wholehearted commitment to the success of the tour proved decisive in making it such a triumph.

That success was certainly not cheaply won, at least in terms of my nervous energy. I knew that for me personally the tour was a make-or-break milestone. Failure would destroy the mutual trust that I was beginning to develop with my boss and that lies at the root of any effective relationship between a private secretary and his principal. For her part, even though she was used to playing for high stakes, Pakistan was a crucial moment for the Princess too, in her quest for a new, independent, and substantial public role. As she was kind enough to say in her letter of thanks to me after the tour, I therefore put my heart and soul into making sure it would work.

We flew on a scheduled British Airways flight to Muscat, where a BAe-146 of the Queen's Flight had prepositioned to carry us on the last leg of the journey to Islamabad. Even getting that far was not without incident. Perhaps oppressed by pretour nerves, the Princess retreated to a corner of our cabin on the scheduled 767 and did not emerge from her self-imposed isolation until we arrived for a refueling stop at Dhahran in Saudi Arabia.

To my consternation I saw that a red carpet had been laid on the tarmac and what was very obviously a royal welcoming committee had assembled at the foot of the aircraft steps. We had made no requests for any sort of official recognition of our transit stop and I knew it would not be welcome to the Princess. With uncharacteristically tousled hair and sleepy face, she peered over her British Airways blanket for just long enough to tell me, "You'd better sort this out, Patrick."

I duly descended to confer with the officials now looking anxiously up at the airplane from which royalty stubbornly failed to materialize. Our hosts plainly reckoned that, although a poor substitute for the real thing, I was better than no guest at all, so I spent the hour or so of our refueling stop being entertained literally royally in the VIP terminal, where the full paraphernalia of a buffet and other refreshments had been laid on. As I tucked into the caviar, exotic salad, and foie gras, I began to wish that I had not so recently done justice to a BA dinner. I felt my country's honor was at stake, however, so I dutifully loaded up my plate. Judging by their own groaning plates, my hosts were equally anxious not to let a single quail's egg go to waste.

My conscience improved when I spoke to the local Governor's chief of staff, who explained that it was quite normal to make such arrangements when any member of the ruling family or indeed any visiting ruling family passed through the airport. Such were the accepted whims of royalty, that, whether or not the Princess disembarked to see the preparations that had been made for her, no offense would be taken. A little later I duly staggered back to the plane and whispered this reassuring message to the sleeping Princess. It seemed a pity to wake her.

Mercifully, by the time we had settled into the familiar surroundings of the Queen's Flight 146 that awaited us after an overnight stop in Muscat, the Princess was beginning to exhibit that blend of confidence, enthusiasm, and quick-wittedness that she would need in large measure during the days that followed and that made her such an accomplished royal performer.

The little red and white jet made good progress over the Arabian Sea and along the length of Pakistan, and she descended in it as if it were a chariot on an expectant and excited Islamabad. As we waited for the doors to open, she looked out of her window and surveyed the scene. This time it was all for *her*—the waiting High Commissioner, the Government Ministers, the red carpet, the girls with baskets of rose petals, and the line of politely clapping officials. This time the small talk in the chilly VIP lounge would be for *her* to control and she had read enough of her briefing to ensure that, of all the subjects to be discussed, shopping would definitely not be among them.

I imagine every private secretary who ever organized a

royal tour must at times have wished for a magic book of instructions that, if faithfully followed, would produce a reliably successful result. Helpful guidelines were indeed prepared, but they were only for the use of Embassies. Others had haphazardly accumulated for typists or domestic staff. For the private secretary there was no single source of distilled wisdom gleaned from decades of royal tours, or if there was I never saw it. Instead, being naturally a bit of a bureaucrat, I tried to distill my own.

Much like many better private secretaries before me, no doubt, I never reduced it to the single set of foolproof gems that between them would hold the answer to every potential tour calamity. This was mostly because, in the case of the Waleses and particularly in the case of the Princess, our tour programs had to be as adaptable as possible to take account of the capriciousness of our employers' moods.

In the end, apart from a few straightforward domestic fixtures, such as her reluctance to begin the day's engagements before 10:00 A.M., there was only one rule that mattered: make it work. For the Princess, the main measure as to whether or not an event had worked was the judgment passed on it by the next day's papers. If this seems rather cynical and further evidence of the Princess's obsession with her newspaper image, then that is probably no more than the truth. I reconciled myself to this rather unelevated principle by reflecting that if the Princess's good works were not seen, then they were largely useless.

Her pursuit of private virtue was one thing, but when in public I was determined that she should get maximum credit not just for herself but for the causes she brought to the public's attention. This perhaps reinforced what I already knew. She was not in herself a saint or blessed with an unusual amount of human compassion, but she represented how much compassion was needed in the world and some of the ways in which it could most effectively be directed.

This was no time, I reasoned, for her to hide her light under a bushel. Beginning with Pakistan, I tried to arrange all the programs for her tours with an eye to what would make it easiest for the inevitable accompanying press to do their job. I knew that if the first day's engagements gave the photographers some good snaps "in the can" and the reporters some stories that positively highlighted the main themes of the visit, then half the battle was won.

After arriving in Pakistan, therefore, the Princess went straight from the airport to her first engagement. *Message:* "I am an energetic working woman keen to get down to business straightaway."

The first engagement was in fact to lay a wreath at the Commonwealth War Cemetery in Rawalpindi. *Message:* "I am representing the Queen on this visit. As well as the status this confers, I also want to make it plain that I am firmly aligned with the monarchy's traditional role of presenting themes of continuity and respect for past sacrifice."

The next stop was a center for the hard-of-hearing. *Message:* "Despite this, once the opening formalities are accomplished, I want to get down to work doing what I do best—showing my concern for the sick."

Then it was on to the High Commission to shake hands with British diplomatic staff and their families. *Message:* "We're always expected to do this, so I'm going to get it over and done with right at the beginning."

Finally the Princess retired to her quarters to prepare for the evening's official dinner. *Message:* "This should have given my dresser plenty of time to unpack the hairbrushes..."

At the Prime Minister's dinner that evening, the Princess proposed a toast and made a speech and generally flew the flag for British diplomacy with an assurance that would have brought sorrow to all—and there were not a few—who would have liked her to be portrayed on her solo mission as an empty-headed lightweight, more accustomed to pop concerts and clothes shops than the volatile politics of the subcontinent.

The next day saw more of the same with what I hoped

was a judicious blend of commercial promotion—in this case in aid of the British telecommunications industry—mainstream medical and welfare engagements—mostly concerned with women's and young people's issues—and formal ceremony—provided by her attendance at the President's dinner.

On the third day, however, the effects of unfamiliar food, the weather, and the constraints of an intense program that required unfamiliar amounts of application and self-discipline began to tell. Showing a side of herself that was all too familiar, the Princess fell into habits of sulkiness and passive defiance that might conceivably have been tolerated and even justified in certain circumstances back home. Seeing their appearance in the middle of our most ambitious and exposed expedition so far, however, filled me with apprehension and no little degree of irritation. Moodiness was a trait she generally regarded as unforgivable in others—notably her husband—and she would take voluble pride in being too professional to succumb to it herself. Why could she not see, I whined to myself impotently, that she could put all her achievements at risk by indulging in the type of petulant emotion that would have earned most three-year-olds no pudding and an early bed?

The situation came to a head as we sat on the humid nighttime tarmac at Lahore airport with Nicholas Barrington, waiting to return to Islamabad for a dinner the Princess was due to host at the High Commission. As she sat morosely in her corner seat in the aircraft, I could see from a hundred small signs that she had given up for the day. Her mouth was set in an obstinate pout, her shoulders hunched as she turned away from us, and suddenly she had found something fascinating to look at in the darkness outside her porthole. This was big trouble. I had always suspected that, despite her habitual professionalism, given a sufficiently obstinate mood she might just refuse to play anymore.

The same impression was growing on the High Commissioner, who, being committed to his duty and also a bachelor, was visibly at a loss to understand what was going wrong. I could almost hear him wondering, à la Professor Henry Higgins, why a woman can't be more like a man.

Just as I was beginning to nerve myself for the task of reconciling these two irreconcilable forces, word came from the flight deck that there was a severe thunderstorm over Islamabad and we would have to stay on the ground in Lahore and wait for it to pass.

Nicholas and I were both filled with strong emotions. He wanted the thunderstorm to pass quickly so that we could get back to his beautiful residence for the most prestigious dinner of the Islamabad year. In sharp contrast, I wanted the storm to stay exactly where it was and so give the Princess the perfect excuse for missing the dinner altogether and taking the early night she obviously needed.

To escape the heavily charged atmosphere that she had built up around her, we excused ourselves and went to stand under the wing of the 146 to shelter from the rain, which was now beginning to splash in warm, heavy drops onto the aluminum above our heads. With my heart in my mouth, I watched a slight figure in RAF blue slowly walking toward us from the airport's meteorological office. Luckily our Captain did not know that, whatever the weatherman said, he was going to disappoint either the Princess or the High Commissioner. It was a dramatic moment. As a sudden, heavier burst of rain pattered on the engine casings I saw the Princess's profile silhouetted at the lighted window and prayed fervently to the local gods of thunder and lightning.

The Squadron Leader came to a halt in front of us and pushed back his cap. "I'm very sorry," he said. "We're going to be stuck on the ground here for some time yet. The storm isn't forecast to move from Islamabad for a couple of hours at least."

"God, what *rotten* luck!" I said rather too quickly. I dared not look at Nicholas, but heard his carefully controlled exhalation.

I got back into the royal compartment just ahead of him.

Fixing our now very irritated-looking Princess with as good a stare as I could muster, I announced, "*Very* bad news, Ma'am. I'm afraid we're going to have to wait here and miss your dinner at the residence."

She visibly brightened, but remembered herself enough to say, "Oh Nicholas, I *am* sorry. How very disappointing for you."

There was no mistaking her sudden chirpiness as we got off the plane. Nicholas manfully swallowed his feelings and we spent a raucous hour drinking tea and telling stories in the VIP terminal while his assistant made some urgent phone calls.

As I was saying goodnight to her back at her room in the residence, she said to me, "That thunderstorm was a bit of luck. I don't think I could have faced another grown-up evening like that."

"Yes, Ma'am," I agreed, "but..." and I trailed off.

She stopped kicking off her shoes and looked at me. Then she repeated what was becoming a bit of a catch-phrase. "I know, Patrick. What you're saying is, 'Just shut up, Diana, and do your job.'" I left her laughing to get on with her own phone calls.

Downstairs Nicholas presided mournfully over empty tables full of linen, crystal, and silver, meticulously prepared for a grand dinner that would now not take place. It had been, I knew, a labor of love, for him and his staff. With the help of the PPOs and some senior High Commission staff, we managed to have a very merry stag dinner and all felt much better.

The next day spirits soared again as we headed off to the Northwest Frontier. From Michni Point high in the Khyber Pass, the future British Queen looked down into Afghanistan from the furthermost rampart of what had been the frontier of British India. The future British Queen... and her hairdresser.

Early that morning I had been congratulating myself on that clever trick with the thunderstorm—and trying to wish away a minor hangover—when, typically, a royal whim disturbed the clublike tranquillity of the High Commissioner's breakfast table. Reluctantly I put down my black coffee and presented myself as requested at the Princess's bedroom, where she was finishing her own more modest breakfast of grapefruit and whole wheat toast.

"Patrick!" she said brightly. "Did you boys have fun last night?"

Careful. Fun was, theoretically, impossible without her presence. "Ah well, you know, Ma'am. We missed you. But we had to keep His Ex company..."

"I bet you did." Her eyes searched my face and general appearance for signs of last night's excesses. My head throbbed alarmingly, but I seemed to pass the inspection. Thank God for naval training, I thought, wondering what was coming next.

"Would you like me to run through today's program?" I asked. That usually flushed it out.

"No, thanks, I've read all my briefing, and I can always look at it again on the plane if I run out of things to say to the Minister." As a courtesy, she was accompanied everywhere by a member of the Pakistani Government. "Anyway, everything you organize seems to run so smoothly!" This was terrible. Compliments usually had a price tag attached. I waited for it to make an appearance. "Patrick, why aren't Sam and Helen coming with us today?"

It sounded innocent enough. Sam and Helen were, respectively, the hairdresser and the dresser. Both were vital figures in my universe, since they were crucial in delivering to me each day a Princess ready to do the work I inflicted on her. Their place was back at base, however, ready to welcome their mistress home with a smile after a hard day at the royal coalmine. In fact, they usually preferred it that way, having most of the day free to sit by the pool or take up the shopping and local sightseeing I had arranged for them as part of my recce.

The Princess's sudden inquiry was for one of two reasons, I quickly concluded. Either Sam and Helen had already grown tired of the High Commission's recreational opportunities and had used their unrivaled access to lobby for a more exciting trip (they seemed happy enough, so I assumed it was not a sign of discontent from them), or the Princess was amusing herself with a request that was not unreasonable on the surface—it demonstrated her famous concern for her staff's welfare, after all—but that she knew could potentially cause havoc with my carefully prepared passenger lists, seating plans, catering arrangements, and general program fine-tuning.

This might be a backhanded compliment to my organizational powers. If so, it was one I could cheerfully have done without. Or, the unworthy thought occurred to me, it might be revenge for last night's quality lad time. It was not beyond her. She had probably heard the singing.

Either way, it was a fastball, as she well knew. There was only one way to play it, so I knocked it back to her for the easy catch she wanted. "Of course they can come, Ma'am. Easy. The more the merrier."

"I thought so too. Now, which d'you think I should wear?" She held up two pastel-colored jackets that to my eye looked virtually identical.

"You always look good in pink, Ma'am."

"D'you think so? Really? I'll wear the pink, then, if you like it."

I had passed the test. If she had gone for the green, I would have started a difficult day knowing that I was already in the doghouse—and so would everybody else who understood our charming code.

The day turned out to be a huge success. The men of the Khyber Rifles gave her exactly the sort of unaffected masculine welcome that was always guaranteed to put her in top form and the front pages of the next day's London papers all carried the picture of a laughing Princess wearing her newly acquired Pakistani military headgear. Just out of camera shot were a smiling Sam and Helen, who then and often afterward repaid my extra work with far greater favors in terms of my relations with their mistress than I could ever do them.

The weather once again played into our hands, the cloud cover being below limits for the Hercules chartered by the press party to fly them into the remote Himalayan valley. By contrast, our sprightly 146 handled this aeronautical obstacle course with ease. We took the precaution of graciously giving a seat in the royal plane to the photographer from the Press Association so that he could cover what I knew would be an engagement filled with photogenic potential.

Flying back to Islamabad at the end of a long but happy day, the Minister in attendance—a courtly Anglophile some forty years the Princess's senior—was so moved by the emotion of the occasion that he confided to his royal guest, "You know, Your Royal Highness, this country has never been the same since you left."

His reference to the last days of the Raj fell on bemused ears. "Hold on," she laughed. "We haven't even gone yet!"

That night she gave a reception for the traveling British press party in the garden of the residence. Once a standard feature of the Waleses' overseas tours, the Prince had dropped the practice some years previously, thinking, I believe, that his hospitality had been abused when remarks he thought had been made in private became unexpectedly public the next day. The Princess, on the other hand, revived the custom with enthusiasm. The familiar faces that had followed us around the country in heat and rain now reappeared in suits and ties, unencumbered by telephoto lenses and tape recorders and all looking freshly scrubbed.

Press receptions were included in all her subsequent tours and she saved some of her best performances for them. It was effort well rewarded. She seldom took the opportunity to do more than josh and banter with the people she loved to hate, however. The real briefing took place later to a selected few in the airplane on the way home, while her watchdogs safely slept. This also became something of a habit, though why she bothered, having—as I later discovered—spent all that summer speaking into a Dictaphone for the benefit of Andrew Morton's planned book, I was never quite sure. You might say, perhaps, that fame was her drug and these flirtatious, dangerous men were lover and pusher combined.

The Princess returned to England in triumph. It had been an exhausting trip, but in terms of establishing her in the public mind and in the eyes of her detractors closer to home as a semi-independent force to be reckoned with, it had succeeded beyond her expectations. The news spread through Whitehall. "The Princess of Wales took Pakistan by storm," enthused Nicholas's official tour report.

For the next four years, until she became unjustly tarnished as a "loose cannon," the Foreign Office never lacked enthusiasm for entrusting her with similar overseas missions. In return, she gave them great value—never committing an undiplomatic gaffe and always stoking up immense amounts of goodwill. Her journey from Lahore airport to the city center had been lined by crowds six deep. "More even than for the Chinese President!" an excited official told me. "And then we had to bring them in buses." This kind of comment became familiar to me, all over the world, wherever the Princess went.

I knew, nonetheless, how close we had come to disaster. That hot night on the tarmac at Lahore might have ended with a major diplomatic embarrassment without the intervention of a friendly thunderstorm. It had been just the most scary of a dozen little incidents in which her outward professionalism only narrowly succeeded in hiding the temperamental little girl that lived inside the glamorous Princess.

I knew also that the enthusiasm emanating from Pakistan and Whitehall would not find much of an echo in the corridors of St. James's Palace. As a priority, I wanted to reinforce her position as a fully integrated member of the royal family. There was no safety for her—or me—in simply indulging her occasional flashes of defiant independence. Somehow I had to find a way to let her *feel* independent while staying securely part of the main organization.

*O*ne obviously productive way for the Princess to assert herself as a senior member of the royal family was to carve a niche as the young and female voice of individual common sense. A promising route to this end was to make more serious speeches on issues, such as AIDS, drug abuse, and mental illness, that challenged comfortable concepts of what were suitable subjects for royal involvement—especially when the speaker was more readily associated with a glamorous lifestyle and had no great reputation for intellectual insight.

She had done little public speaking in her early days as Princess, but by the time she went to Pakistan that was certainly no longer the case and she was improving all the time. For someone so articulate without a script, she was at first surprisingly underconfident when reading aloud to an audience. Her first few halting efforts had benefited from the advice of experts such as Lord Attenborough. The first real breakthrough came in the summer of 1989, when I wrote her speech for the twenty-fifth anniversary celebrations of the charity Turning Point.

Intellectually it was no great challenge. All I had to do was imagine what I would want to hear from the Princess of Wales if I were an ordinary listener with no connections to royalty or drug abuse at all. The charity, as usual, provided briefing notes about their work in an unfamiliar world that even I could plagiarize quite effectively.

She delivered the speech in a firm and steady voice with just the right amount of girlish hesitancy to secure the audience's sympathetic and unwavering attention. She extolled family values and warned of the dangers of addiction. It was good, straightforward stuff and the next day the papers were full of it. A fairly typical comment came from the *Daily Express* on May 19: "Diana's six minute speech to the Turning Point charity for drug and alcohol abuse was a powerful, poised and polished performance. It proved once and for all that she is more than just a pretty face to adorn magazine covers." Another commentator said, "The future Queen emerged for the first time as a powerful public orator campaigning against those twin evils in the most important speech of her eight years as a member of the Royal Family."

In those pioneering days the Princess gave me the credit for this sort of coverage, which was music to her ears. Such positive reports fueled her ambition to carve out an independent life for herself. Needless to say, they fueled my ambition too. I had never written a major speech before and, knowing that my boss had not contributed a word to it herself, I took very private satisfaction from such complimentary reactions. Even when she later grew reluctant to swallow my drafts whole, the satisfaction remained.

The small milestone of that first successful speech was marked in tangible form by the Princess with typically impulsive generosity. The next day's Bag brought a small package for me. Inside were a pair of expensive cuff links and a note which read:

> *Dear Patrick,*
> *Something v small to thank you so much for all the time and effort you put into the Turning Point speech. I can't begin to tell you how much I appreciated your help.*
>
> > *Diana*

In the years to come there would be more cuff links and other presents and many, many more notes. The Princess was a prolific note-writer, and took pride in responding quickly to incoming correspondence and in writing the many thank-you letters that her life required. Although they were sometimes overflowery and she could not resist borrowing contrived phrases from other people's letters, their intention was simply to convey a straightforward emotion—gratitude, sympathy, irritation, laughter.

Rather like her many acts of kindness, when she wrote them she was entirely sincere, but I sometimes thought that once they had left her desk they ceased to exist for her. They captured the moment perfectly, but were not intended to be a permanent record of her feelings. It was as though, in her world, such expressions of feeling were pushed out of an emotional hatch, which was then clanged shut again for safety.

Given the constant calls on her emotional reserves, it is not surprising that she should develop such a self-protective carapace. She had to look no further than her in-laws, however, to see how it could become an almost permanent fixture. It is much in her favor that right to the end of her life she was still willing to open this hatch—perhaps more in hope than real expectation, and despite the fact that it only increased her vulnerability.

With the possible exception of the speech she gave on the subject of eating disorders a few years later, she did not seem to feel a genuine, personal commitment to any of the subjects about which she pronounced. The emotional hatch stayed firmly shut on these occasions and the speeches served a different purpose. Throughout her career, the Princess of Wales's speeches sometimes attracted criticism, more often attracted praise, but always attracted attention. As the author of many of those speeches, I quite enjoyed this, but for her, I rather suspect, the attention was their principal appeal.

The speech was a prime means of attracting attention—to a good cause, certainly, but also to herself. The emotion she expressed, with rare exceptions, was for public consumption only. Speechmaking, like walking around hospitals, was another means of conveying a sentiment and reinforcing an image. The words were not wrung from her soul—she never begged me to use my larger vocabulary to match the intensity of her feelings, or to communicate a deeply felt message. My vocabulary was there to make her sound like what people wanted her to be—the voice of common sense and recognizably royal, as well as young and unstuffy.

Very few public speakers have the satisfaction of speaking with genuine sincerity all the time, of course. She was not a politician running for office. She was a conduit for other people's images of what she ought to be, and if in the process she enjoyed public adulation and a vicarious expertise, there was surely no harm in that. Any benefit or satisfaction she got from making her long, lonely marches to the podium were paid for through the nervousness she suffered beforehand and the effort she took to prepare herself for the ordeal.

She became increasingly possessive of the extravagant praise her speeches regularly attracted, although it must have occurred to her that this credit was earned at least as much by the words as by her skill in delivering them—and she had not written the words. It was fine by me. Private secretaries exist to contrive credit for their bosses, and not just by writing speeches. They share in it too, albeit privately. The Princess, however, seemed to feel that this necessary and time-honored professional protocol was an affront to her dignity. Her response, characteristically, was to sow dissent.

I soon felt I had invented a monster that had got out of control, as she cast about for novelty in her contributors. She was not always impressed, either, by my attempts to persuade her that the relevant government department was the correct starting point in her quest for authoritative things to say. Just as I had ridden roughshod over the sensitivities of those in the office who might have expected to draft her speeches, so she in turn let me suffer the discomfort of having strangers and outsiders put words in her mouth.

Long and sometimes incoherent drafts would appear in the return Bag, haphazardly typed on unfamiliar paper. Some seemed to have been written by the current therapist and were stuffed full of New Age clichés. Some bore the mark of Richard Kay's easy style, recognizable from his day job as court correspondent at the *Daily Mail*. Others, on medical subjects, I guessed came from her close friend and (not that I knew it at the time) Andrew Morton's collaborator, Dr. James Coldhurst. Her regiments, on the rare occasions when she addressed them, had the benefit of the thoughts of Acting Major Hewitt—fair counterpoint, I supposed, for the thoughts of Lieutenant Commander Jephson. Other audiences heard the ardent offerings of her speech trainer, Peter Settelen.

Intriguingly, one day I found a draft written on what was unmistakably office paper. The Princess had successfully recruited an ally in the Prince's camp, his deputy private secretary Peter Westmacott, and flattered him greatly by supplementing his duties with, among other things, part-time speechwriting for her. Peter's draft was at least suitable for royal use, but it took a long time to persuade her that such scheming—however exciting—was unnecessary. I was not so proud that I would have minded the involvement of other contributors. In fact, provided their material was literate and reasonably uncontroversial, I welcomed it.

It was not unusual for her to test loyalties—and prove her power—by attempting to provoke professional jealousy. It was an emotion she was so familiar with herself that it must have felt soothing to be the cause of it in others. I was not immune, but I had learned enough to realize that if I visibly succumbed to the temptation, it would be fatal. Eventually, as with most nursery amusements, she tired of this game and my stoicism was rewarded. In a development that marked a growing maturity for both of us, she would collect the offerings of her various unofficial speechdrafters and give them to me for editing, polishing, and on occasions completely rewriting.

As well as speeches, I was beginning to draft more and more of the Princess's correspondence, briefings, introductions, and forewords. From then until the day I left, there was almost nothing that appeared in public over her signature—

and much in private, too—that I had not written. Sometimes I felt as if I were literally writing the script of her public life.

*M*eanwhile, as well as attempting to carve out an independent niche for herself, the Princess was still a willing and welcome volunteer to deputize for other members of the royal family when occasion required. She always reacted enthusiastically to a call for a volunteer to stand in. As well as a desire to help—and also a desire to cut a favorable image as the rescuer of an otherwise doomed engagement—I detected another and more touching motive behind the Princess's habitual eagerness to assist on such occasions. By stepping into the breach, she would earn the gratitude of the family into which she had married. Since such gratitude was seldom forthcoming for any other reason, she valued it all the more. At an unconscious level, it may also have appealed to her desire to be recognized as an integral part of a larger family.

This most visible reminder of her continuing position in the royal framework was strongly underlined when she stood in for the most "establishment" member of the royal family, the Queen Mother, at an engagement in Westminster Cathedral.

As has been reported elsewhere—not least in the transcripts of the "Squidgygate" tapes—the Princess's attitude to the royal family's matriarch was ambivalent. She recognized the Queen Mother's strength as the most powerful operator on the royal chessboard, especially in the influence she wielded over the Prince. Perhaps for this reason, however, she also feared and therefore privately criticized her. She would sometimes speak with satisfaction of the disruptive effects of the court mourning that would follow the older woman's death, and speculate fairly irreverently on the choice of black clothes available to her. She seemed also, even if only subconsciously, to sense the vacuum such a death would leave in national life and her own potential to fill the gap in the country's affections. It was not hard to imagine her, sixty years hence, exercising a similar degree of control over a future royal family, for whom she represented a precious link with a golden past.

While the Princess played her part flawlessly as a conventional royal performer at the engagement in Westminster Cathedral, the experience also opened up the possibility of a more spiritual answer to the public and private pressures that were gathering around her. Mainstream, traditional royal duty has always involved religion. There was surely potential for combining public duty with personal enlightenment—and the Princess, as I had begun to sense, had a vague but unmistakable spiritual hunger about her.

The engagement entailed going to the Cathedral for a Festival of Flowers and Music in aid of the Cardinal Hume Center, a charity working on the front line in the war against youth homelessness. On the face of it this was an entirely standard royal engagement, familiar, and traditional in its theme and structure. Having been planned for a guest some sixty years older than herself, the visit was more sedate and contained far more formal presentations than would normally have been the Princess's personal preference. In contrast to some of the more frenetic engagements she carried out in unstructured and informal circumstances, often with people to whom a natural deference was quite unfamiliar, this time the Princess was forced to go at somebody else's pace and I think that, despite herself, she found the old style had its attractions.

The Roman Catholic Cathedral seemed cavernous and dark. In the background the organ played softly and the air carried the heady perfume of incense. The Princess's route around the great building was lined on every side by beautiful flower arrangements and quietly respectful, even reverential, guests. At her side, the tall figure of the Cardinal fell naturally into the role of fatherly guide.

After touring the Cathedral he gave her coffee in the

Archbishop's House, where she also met people from the Cardinal Hume Center. That engagement, attended by the Princess only by chance, forged a relationship with the Cardinal's homeless charities in London that lasted for the rest of her life.

The link with the homeless center gave her a further opportunity to practice a type of royal visit that she made her own—engagements planned and conducted in secret but subsequently, and sometimes simultaneously, publicized through favored parts of the media. It has since been copied by other royal people, but the Princess pioneered it in particular cases where advance publicity would have ruined the entire effect. This was especially true with homelessness projects, where the whole benefit—for visitor and visited alike—depended on her presence being kept secret.

The impression created publicly of good works modestly carried out did no harm either, nor did the news that William and Harry sometimes accompanied her on trips to see the rougher end of the social scale. This publicity bolstered her image as tutor to the boys in matters of real life, in contrast to their father's apparent preference for traditional, and elitist, country pursuits.

There has been much speculation about the Princess's interest in spiritual matters in general and in the Roman Catholic Church in particular. The story of the Westminster Cathedral engagement perhaps provides an illustrative introduction to the subject, and one that shows the Princess in a particularly good light.

From that visit to Westminster Cathedral, undertaken on behalf of somebody else and in its content and style not really to her taste, grew a link with an unsung charity working with people in desperate need. It was a link that the Princess followed up with minimal publicity, but with considerable personal interest and financial support. Some years later, as administrator of her Charities Trust, I made a very substantial donation on her instructions to one of the Cardinal's charities. It was perhaps her single most selfless act of charity that I encountered. Moreover, its message was particularly welcome. Despite the superficiality of much of her charity involvement—however diligently performed—there were exceptions that proved the rule. The Cardinal's quiet but practical holiness made a deep impression on her and she would have given a great deal to be able to emulate it, and to know the peace of mind that was its reward.

The visit to the Cathedral was still very much in my mind when, after an illness of great suffering, my father died of cancer. I came back from the hospital after a night at his bedside, filled with every sort of confused emotion and utterly exhausted. In the immediate aftermath of his death my brother and stepmother and I were numbed with shock, which I suppose is grief's merciful anesthetic. As they began the practical business of informing relatives and arranging the funeral, I sat in my father's garden in the early morning Hampshire sunshine.

In my hand I carried my office-issue mobile phone, in those days the size of a small briefcase. Like so many before and after me, in a moment of deep personal anguish the thought of telling the Princess of Wales about it was somehow soothing. As my boss, I knew her well enough to understand that she could not enlighten me about the meaning of life, or life after death, or the purpose of suffering. Instead, I perceived that the comfort she gave came less from the person she was than from the permission she somehow gave that would allow me to begin to grieve. That is the best I can do to describe what I felt as I sat on the grass and tried to form in my mind the words that I would use when I spoke to her.

Another way of looking at it might be to say that she had the gift of creating a neutral, safe space between herself and whoever she was talking to, into which that person's fears and hopes could be safely placed. She could not heal suffering any more than a priest can forgive sin, but the analogy is perhaps not so outrageous if you consider that providence finds recruits in the most unlikely places, even palaces.

When I eventually spoke to her, therefore, the words for once came from the heart and so, I believe, did her reply. Afterward I realized that the comfort and strength I had undoubtedly received did not come from the Princess herself, but equally I realized that without her I might have searched and searched and not found that comfort at all, while all the time my sadness sank slowly and painfully into the darkness of my mind.

That incident marked another small milestone in my relationship with the Princess. Death being no respecter of social status, it had enabled us to communicate with a rare equality. It was a level of communication that would return often in the years ahead, but especially at times of crisis for her, not least following the death of her own father.

Here was yet another sign of the Princess's potential: time and again, good was achieved through her mere involvement. At a subconscious level, I believe she was aware of the virtue of what she was doing—not just for the Cardinal's charity or for me, but in all her humanitarian work—but it was done by instinct rather than as a formalized response to any structured religious influence on her life. Sadly, she did not feel the happiness she deserved from the good work she did. The compassion she showed others was too often just compensation for the attention she seemed to feel she had always been denied herself. In addition, because she was a catalyst rather than a direct cause of good, she did not develop the disciplined thinking necessary for spiritual growth, or feel the satisfaction that might have been of solid benefit to her in return.

I think it was an instinctive need to redress this imbalance that led her to seek spiritual answers from her various therapists and astrologers—but they demanded little in the way of disciplined thinking either, or if they did, their services were quickly dispensed with. Maybe that was why she made so little progress with her occasional signs of interest in acquiring more formal religious knowledge. She preferred to find her religion in other people and, like some other royal travelers, took special comfort from encountering particular shining examples on her journey.

Certainly the Cardinal made a very deep impression on her that day at Westminster Cathedral, not just as a tall and reassuring companion in the public eye, but also as the embodiment of a life devoted to the welfare of others, uncluttered by all the demands of the world to which she felt victim. "That man," she commented later, "he's so holy—and just like a great big teddy bear. I love his ears!"

However cynical, manipulative, or self-indulgent her motives might sometimes have been for doing some of the good things for which she received such credit, in the *act* of doing them there was no cynicism at all. I saw the same transient sincerity in her exaggerated thanks and huge output of notes expressing warm appreciation. People who had no knowledge of her other than as recipients of her concern or gratitude were in no doubt about what they felt she gave to them. It is the same quality we can see even now, years later, in contemporary news photographs of the Princess doing her routine work of bringing hope and comfort to people in need. It was given and received at a level beyond speech and I do not think it can ever be explained properly in simply human terms.

In my time with her, however, she never found the faith that might have given her strength in moments of real doubt and loneliness. It was probably the only way in which she could have gained genuine satisfaction and happiness from the good that was so often laid at her door. Here, perhaps, was the greatest lost potential of all. The Princess's quest for personal fulfillment grew increasingly desperate. In the absence of a solid faith that could comfort her, she took refuge in impulsive bouts of mysticism and psychology. Without a reliable framework of knowledge and support, or wise guidance she was prepared to trust, these too were bound to fail her.

10

☞☜

Roses

I was right in thinking that the Princess's triumph in Pakistan would not win much acclaim in Palace corridors back home. The reason, perhaps, was that foreign tours were traditionally not popular with royal people. Aware that all-expenses-paid trips to exotic destinations might be misinterpreted as frivolous jaunts, we tended to portray overseas tours as stern duties to be stoically endured. There was plenty of evidence to justify such a view, given the real discomfort and inconvenience these expeditions usually involved. The sight of the Princess apparently enjoying film-star status against exotic backdrops was at odds with this established image, and it did not seem to sit easily with the often unglamorous reality of routine diplomacy and British trade promotion that lay at the heart of traditional royal tour programs.

Having won the popularity contest at home, was this media-hungry young woman now going to turn her superficial charm on foreign audiences? I could hear the unspoken question—followed in my imagination by a rather thin-lipped resolve to stand back and watch how long it would take her to slip up on her self-imposed solo high-wire act.

My attitude was overly cynical, as I can see in retrospect. Nobody uttered such comments, at least not in my hearing. It was also true, however, that nobody in the Palace uttered much in the way of appreciation to the Princess herself, and she felt its absence—especially from her in-laws—more keenly than they might have suspected.

Over time, as she obstinately refused to fall off her high wire, the abundance of recognition she received from all other directions only accentuated their reticence. This in turn roused her competitive instincts and each new tour became a test of her ability to outshine the last. This was the unwelcome, and largely avoidable, outcome of letting her feel that she was slipping from the irksome but reassuring embrace of royal comradeship. Being royal is, after all, one of the loneliest jobs in the world and mutual support must be vital. I knew they would not change—royal people do not—and I knew also, without a doubt, that the Princess's world was going to change very soon indeed.

Meanwhile, duty was beginning to take second place to star quality as the guiding principle in the Princess's public image and in her personal motivation. As if to challenge her nearest and dearest, she worked hard and thrived on it. Almost every day the familiar Jaguar, with three outriders and a police backup car, would sweep out of Kensington Palace.

The little convoy passed quickly beneath the unseeing lenses of tourists craning to get a picture of what they imagined might be her bedroom window, oblivious of the real Princess passing within inches at child's-eye level. Usually it was the children who spotted her first, tugging at the sleeve of a parent determinedly pointing the family Pentax at the palace facade.

If the adult responded quickly enough, and stooped to peer through the car window, he might catch a fleeting glimpse of the famous profile and even earn himself a quick wave in the process. If he saw her lips move, it was no more informative than watching a fish in an aquarium—silent behind the glass she could say anything she liked and often did.

"Patrick! My God! *Why* do men that shape insist on wearing tartan trousers? And did you *see* that child's snotty nose? Hello! Hello!" she would mouth. "Goodbye... Ooh! *He's* rather dishy!"

"Shall we drop you here, Ma'am? We could always pick you up on the way back."

"Ha ha, Patrick. Look, there's one for you... God! What an old dog... *Hello* (cheesy smile)... Oh *look*! It's Princess Margaret's chauffeur (lowers window)... Hello Griffin! How's the cold? I hope you're feeling better (said with genuine feeling)... Goodbye..."

Her powers of observation were phenomenal. Even the sharp-eyed PPO riding in the front seat would sometimes be slower than the Princess to spot a familiar face in a crowd or walking along the pavement. The pedestrians of Kensington High Street might have been astonished by the royal scrutiny so often directed at them from the back of the anonymous-looking Jaguar.

On other occasions it was motorists who were picked up on her constantly scanning sensors. One day, returning from a light shopping expedition to Marks & Spencer and her regular chat with the news vendor outside the tube station, she spotted the venerable journalist Sir John Junor's Range Rover stationary in the traffic. Seeing a rare opportunity to score a point, she dodged across the road to surprise him.

Never her natural ally—and instinctively more prone to extol her husband at her expense—the doyen of columnists was momentarily flabbergasted to find the Princess of Wales cheerily greeting him through the window. Her immediate success was evident in his subsequent description of the encounter—"charming"—and he never again employed his acerbic pen against her.

I complimented her on her initiative, but, with an increasingly familiar flash of worldliness, she was dismissive.

"They can't cope with the real thing," she replied coolly. "They're all the same. Haven't the guts to tell you to your face."

She was right, I reflected, uncomfortably aware that the same accusation could often have been leveled at me. On the other hand, I thought, brightening up, she was no mean character assassin herself.

*S*ymbolically, at the opening of the decade that would see her divorce, the familiar territory of her marriage and early royal years was becoming increasingly foreign to the Princess and she set out to identify herself with surroundings that gave the greatest possible contrast to her previous image. The time of transition was moving inexorably toward a time of unalterable change.

This was when it began to become clearer to the watching world—and to her lurking critics—that she was setting her own path, well before the solo triumph in Pakistan. Although she was, as we have seen, still an expert at mainstream, conventional royal events, from 1990 onward her growing talent lay in giving them a new twist. Even when this was unconscious or even accidental, the event in question was indelibly marked by her involvement.

Hospitals, for example, are traditional royal territory, but not hospitals for the criminally insane—as became obvious from the media reaction when the Princess started visiting them. There was much lurid speculation about which depraved killers she was doubtless going to meet. The fact that she met no criminal "celebrities" during any of her visits did not deter a regular accompaniment of "beauty and the beast" tabloid stories. The Princess was not deterred either. I sometimes allowed myself the uncharitable thought that beauties generally look at their best alongside beasts anyway.

So it was that one day we found ourselves driving through the gates of Rampton Hospital, home of some of the most notorious, criminally insane inmates in the country. I often wondered about the attraction of these institutions to the Princess. If nothing else, visits to such forbidding places demonstrated a rare commitment to the cause—though whether the cause was the public one of helping to support her charity Turning Point or some private one of her own was never quite certain, not even in her own mind.

For no very obvious reason, however, there was one thing she was sure about. "The poor patients in these places," she said, "they're all brutalized by the staff!" Subsequent scandals at Rampton made this a remarkably prescient comment, but at the time I thought it showed a curious readiness to identify with the perceived victim. It offered a remarkable insight into her view of the world, in that she could apparently disregard the proven ability of most of these "victims" to inflict more brutality on others than they would ever experience themselves in the hospital.

With the Princess I eventually visited all of the Special Hospital Authority's establishments, some of them such as Broadmoor more than once. The crimes amassed by their inmates would have had the most seasoned tabloid editor reaching for his dictionary of hyperbole. Hearing the great security gates clang behind her never failed to send a frisson of forbidden pleasure down the Princess's back. It was like a modern version of going to watch the inmates of Bedlam. Every raw emotion, every extreme of human behavior was represented behind these high walls. It was the ultimate vicarious shock-trip.

Such sentiments would have been deeply offensive to the professional and compassionate men and women who ran such institutions and who, over the years, I came to admire and respect greatly. They would also, no doubt, have deeply offended most of the patients we came to visit, whose attempts to rehabilitate themselves and return to normal life pushed most royal problems—and my own—into the shade.

At Rampton the Princess spent most of her time in the

women's wing. The wards we went into were suspiciously tidy, the floors polished, the paintwork fresh, the seat covers unstained, the lavatories unswamped, the air unthick with cigarettes, fried food, and BO. The patients themselves, for the most part, sat around in attitudes of resignation.

Visiting a craft lesson, the Princess saw young women patients drawing cards for Mother's Day. Doing our best to impede the other hangers-on who tended to crowd closer than she liked, we left her to walk among the patients unescorted. Here and there she sat down and spoke for a while with girls no older than herself, but whose faces bore the mark of years in the grip and company of dreadful things.

As usual, the best way of judging the Princess's effect on people was not to look at those to whom she was speaking but at those to whom she had spoken some minutes before. These women were under instructions to carry on with their work, not least because of my insistence on the recce that everything should look as uncontrived as possible. At the tables she had already visited, however, further work was impossible. The girls whispered to each other about their impressions, giggling and snatching further furtive glances. Others just stared mesmerized and not always adoringly at the retreating figure who had visited them from another world.

One girl at a table close to me just let her head drop. Silent tears ran down her cheeks and her half-finished card lay abandoned on the table in front of her. In large, irregular letters I read the message, "A mum is someone who loves you no matter what you've done."

We were a very subdued little group as the helicopter flew us back to the real world of Kensington Palace. The Princess retreated into her corner seat and flicked unseeingly through magazines. I had never known her so withdrawn.

As the Wessex whirred and clattered low over Notting Hill, I formed a theory about what I was seeing in the Princess's reaction to the sights of the day. There ought to be a name for the condition, suffered by many royal people, that is brought on by repeated exposure to other people's good works. Its symptoms are a fixed expression of deep concern and an inner feeling of profound uselessness. Cure is almost unknown, since quarantine—the only effective treatment—would put too many people out of business.

Away from such radical and emotionally demanding engagements, the Princess continued to excel at rather more traditional royal duties. Even then, however, she could increasingly be expected to transform them with personal touches and minor deviations from standard royal practice, vividly illustrated by a visit she undertook to the Royal Hampshire Regiment on duty in Northern Ireland.

Although she became less and less enthusiastic about conventional royal work, she was generally easier to persuade when asked to visit either of the two British Army regiments for which she had the honorary title of Colonel-in-Chief. For one thing, Army officers held a special appeal for her, and for another, such engagements could provide excellent publicity, a fact that was certainly borne out on this occasion.

At the time, the political and security situation in the province was highly unsettled and any royal visit to what was practically a war zone had to be arranged in the greatest secrecy. This added an extra and not unwelcome touch of drama to the planning for what was in any case, from my point of view, a fascinating insight into the role of an infantry battalion in the uniquely demanding circumstances of helping to enforce law and order in Londonderry in 1990.

The weather could not have been more uncooperative. As we disembarked from the royal aircraft at RAF Aldergrove, freezing sleet was blowing almost horizontally across the airfield. The sense of having accidentally arrived on the set of a James Bond movie was irresistible as I looked out at the dark, camouflaged helicopters, their rotors turning, that waited to escort us on the next leg of the journey, the hunched shapes of the armed guards posted around the apron, and the small line of military top brass waiting formally to receive the royal visitor, buttoned up to their necks in greatcoats, the slush almost covering their boots.

Hovering in the background was a tall figure talking into a discreet radio. He looked as if he might have played in the second row for an Ulster soccer team at one time. In fact he was the officer in charge of all VIP security in the troubled province. During the many visits that followed, the sight of this genial bear of a man never failed to impart to me a feeling of utter reassurance. As I grew to know him and his wife in subsequent meetings, I slowly came to understand the daily danger that his job forced him and his family to confront. Of all the brave men and women in all the security forces I encountered around the world during my time with the Princess, this man stood literally head and shoulders taller. To me he also symbolized a whole breed of people whose help was essential if the royal show was to create the desired impact, who received little recognition for what they did, and who, in their modesty, would have dismissed my view that their association with it brought more honor to the institution for which I worked than anything I would ever contribute.

The helicopter rotors turned in vain. As we disembarked from the plane, the decision was taken that the weather was too bad to fly the sixty-odd miles to Londonderry and we would have to make the journey by car. The trip was made at high speed, in a small convoy of vehicles, through country thought to be potentially dangerous and in atrocious weather. I sat in one of the RUC cars, listening to a complicated security operation unfolding with minimum fuss over the radio. For the last few miles we picked up an escort of soldiers from the Princess's regiment and soon the great corrugated-iron gates of Ebrington Barracks clanged shut behind us.

The Princess spent all day watching members of her regiment demonstrate the training needed to carry out their internal security duties in streets where the urban terrorist threat was a constant reality. She listened to technical briefings about their daily operations, heard about the dangers they faced and the successes they had achieved. She met the soldiers in their barracks, the NCOs in their bar, and had lunch with the officers in their mess. She clearly found the whole process quite enlightening, but her main concern, of course, was to cheer up the troops.

In this she succeeded better than any other visiting celebrity. It does not take a great genius to work out the therapeutic effect of dangling a beautiful Princess in front of a captive audience of several hundred fighting-fit young men. The effect, I might add, was mutual and heightened by the Princess's inspired decision to wear standard-issue camouflage combat dress throughout.

Eventually we made the long trek back to Aldergrove. It was getting dark and the wind and sleet showed no sign of abating. I began to worry about the flight home. Sure enough, at the airport we were told that conditions were too bad to fly, at least for the next few hours. Unbeknown to us, in England storms had been wreaking havoc the length and breadth of the country and very little flying, least of all royal flying, was taking place.

We borrowed a room in the RAF mess, for the Princess, myself, and a handful of close security officers. A steward lit the fire and somebody drew the curtains against the gathering gloom of the winter night. It was one of those touch-and-go situations, in which the royal foot could metaphorically be stamped in frustration at not being able to end a long and tiring day in the expected comfort of one's own aircraft, prior to returning to the comfort of one's own Palace. Alternatively, as sometimes happened, it might have the opposite effect, when distinctions between royalty and commoner could become blurred in the face of what we could pretend was a common adversity.

While the Princess was deciding which of these options she would choose, I sent for a bottle of Bushmills, on the basis that there was no point in us all being miserable and an outbreak of conviviality among those around her might produce the desired result in her own internal debate.

Hardly had the whiskey arrived when her mind was made up. "Gather round, boys!" she said, picking a chair by the hearth. So she sat in the flickering firelight while the strong, silent men of the Royal Ulster Constabulary moved closer to the warmth and sipped their whiskey.

They talked of their work, their worries, their families. All were subjects about which she herself must have harbored anxious thoughts, yet she was content to sit, with her own glass in her hand, listening intently, offering words of encouragement and whenever she possibly could—and even when I swore she positively could not—finding something in what we discussed to laugh about. After that evening, in a tradition that was entirely her own, the Princess would present her regular bodyguard with a bottle of Bushmills during every visit she made to Ulster.

If mental hospitals marked one extreme of the Princess's range of work and "meeting the troops" came somewhere in the middle, at the other extreme was her growing popularity as a guest at diplomatic events. She relished the chance to exercise her increasing supply of firsthand overseas impressions—to say nothing of her supply of chic cocktail dresses. At Rampton, in the soldiers' mess hall and in all the smarter Embassies, she had the right word for everyone, or so it seemed.

The French Ambassador, an enthusiastic supporter of the arts, lent his residence for a fund-raising dinner for the English National Ballet, of which the Princess was a very active patron. Securing such a prestigious venue for its fundraiser was typical of the ENB's resourceful approach to gathering support and typical, too, of its imaginative use of its patron's pulling power.

As we arrived at the residence's grand entrance the sounds of a party in full swing, complete with jazz band, could be heard inside, and there was the Ambassador himself, bowing low and preparing to dispense his legendary Gallic charm. The Princess rewarded his efforts with some legendary charm of her own and they ascended the steps to the grand salon in what appeared to be convivial conversation.

The band was playing at full tilt at the top of the steps and I saw the Ambassador lean even closer to the Princess in order to hear her reply to some question he had put to her. Suddenly he recoiled, as elegantly as his Gallic charm would permit. He seemed to have gone paler and a look of quizzical uncertainty spread across his face.

As soon as I had a chance, I discreetly asked the flustered Princess what had gone wrong. "Oh God, how embarrassing!" she said. "On the way in I'd been admiring the huge white Christmas decorations that were hanging from the hall ceiling." I had noticed them too and unusually, although they were every sort of festive shape, every one of them was white. "On the way up the stairs," she went on, "I thought he was asking me about the decorations, but I misheard him. Actually he was asking me about the *band*. He asked me if I thought they were any good. 'Oh yes,' I replied. 'Marvelous. And they're all so beautifully *white* too...'"

I sat thoughtfully at my old desk in St. James's Palace and watched Anne's secretary finish boxing up her personal files. It was late January 1990. Under new arrangements I was to become the Princess's assistant private secretary, supplanting Anne in most of her duties. It was a daunting prospect.

I had been aware for some months that the Princess was contemplating a change at the top of her private office. A member of household—nominally the top tier of royal employees—received no more shrift than a housemaid when the royal eye grew weary of his or her anxiously smiling face.

With her usual wide-eyed innocence, the Princess had set about undermining Anne's position as her senior adviser (John Riddell, the private secretary she shared with the Prince, though theoretically Anne's superior, had little regular contact with his boss's wife) by the effective but unattractive means of making her job increasingly impossible. This she achieved by distancing herself personally and in day-to-day business in a dozen small ways, each individually no more than a nuisance, but in combination a deadly expression of lost confidence. Phone calls became frostier, written proposals received grudging or unhelpful replies, and the light of the royal countenance was generally turned in other directions.

This time the light was turned toward me. I was still naive enough to be flattered and unscrupulous enough to become the Princess's passive accomplice in a game of musical chairs that, I suppose, has had its echoes in every court since our ancestors decided that they could not cope without a royal family. Anne, being devoted to the Princess but having no illusions about her skill with the knife, wisely saw the blow coming and resigned.

In a gesture that could appear generous—and which I am sure did wonders for her conscience—the Princess asked Anne to remain in the largely honorary role of principal lady-in-waiting. As such she would always be a commanding presence in royal circles, but her departure nevertheless marked the end of an era and I was not going to be the only one who would miss her benign but critical eye on our day-to-day proceedings, or the clarity with which she saw right and wrong in a world where little was really as it seemed.

Whatever her personal feelings about leaving St. James's Palace, and I believe relief was among them, Anne showed me nothing but generosity and helpfulness. After our brief turnover of current business, I installed myself in her elegant office and with a sudden, unbidden envy watched her collect her remaining belongings and depart, as one commentator put it, "like a skater making her dignified departure from the royal ice rink."

I had already seen several bright young hopefuls move into new offices in royal Palaces and I was to see many more. For sure, we knew our lease on our enviable little bit of Palace was a transient one, but this time, we told ourselves, it *would* be different. We could arrange our books, settle in, feel at home. We could install our families in their grand new accommodation, in my case a tiny house in Notting Hill Gate. We could commission our personal stationery, admire the car and its parking space. We could preen at garden parties, stride the red-carpeted corridors, and pretend to be statesmanlike in the face of shock-horror tabloid headlines. Best of all, we could adopt an attitude of maddening inscrutability whenever anyone, from a taxi driver to a mother-in-law, asked us any question on any royal matter, however inconsequential.

Especially in those early days, I probably embodied every one of these vanities and I offer belated thanks to my friends and family who endured them. The truth was that our offices were overdecorated, our status was overblown, our perks overgenerous, and our loyalties overtaxed.

I did not see it like that at the time, of course. For one thing, I was too busy conferring with the Princess's interior design consultant, Dudley Poplak, about the redecoration of my office. The first priority was to get that lavatory soundproofed... The Royal Library at Windsor provided yards of impressive-looking old books to fill my new floor-to-ceiling bookcase. The Royal Collection provided portraits of Princesses of Wales past, under whose haughty eyes I idled away many minutes admiring my new curtains and carpet—not to mention my new desk, which could easily have doubled as a landing pad for one of the royal helicopters in which I could now confidently expect to fly regularly, far into the distant future.

As further proof of my inflated importance, the Princess appointed a new equerry to take on my old duties. How I enjoyed the selection process from my new position inside the members' enclosure, and how I enjoyed the arrival of my new subordinate. Squadron Leader David Barton had been my opposite number years before when we had both worked in Plymouth as ADCs to senior officers. He was unflappable, efficient, loyal, and good-humored. Best of all, he stood well over six and a half feet in his elegantly cut Air Force uniform, a factor in the selection process to which the Princess may just have given an extra ounce of importance.

I gave David all the advice I could, amassed over my several years at the Palace, and warned him among other things that, regardless of outward appearances, words could hardly describe the depth of our employers' indifference to us as people. This may have been overstating it slightly, but I was anxious to avoid the consequences for me of an equerry who might understandably fall victim to red carpet fever, or in some other way become besotted with his beautiful mistress, or at the very least suffer the depression that could set in from the occasional bouts of rejection that would inevitably come his way.

I was also anxious, if I was honest, to avoid him becoming too comfortable behind his smart new desk. Whatever I tried to tell myself, I had let self-interest take too large a hand in my own transition from temporary equerry to permanent household member and, as the only potential loser in any contest, I did not want David to feel inclined to follow my example. Nor, for that matter, did I want him to become a tempting target for the Princess's desire to manipulate even those most dedicated to serving her. I had readily fallen in with her rather unattractive machinations to unseat Anne and knew very well that she would not hesitate to employ similar tactics against me if, or when, the mood took her.

It says something for the attractions of the job, or for my cockiness, that not even that daily prospect was enough to make me want to find safer employment, perhaps as a lion tamer. The best safeguard against becoming the object of any such plot was to make myself an indispensable part of any long-term plan she eventually evolved for her future or, in its absence, to make myself the indispensable source of such plans. The other safeguard was to foster an atmosphere of friendly interdependence among our small team in which information was freely exchanged, thus denying the Princess one of the more elementary methods of dividing her staff by benefiting today's favorite with information tomorrow's scapegoat might have needed to avoid incurring further censure.

The role of messenger about plans for the future was given to me almost unconsciously by the Princess. My mere appointment gave the message to her husband that she, not he, would now exercise control over whom she hired and fired. The Prince had no input (or no visible input) in David Barton's selection, whereas his had been the casting vote when I had been chosen as equerry only two years previously.

The message to the other Palaces and to the wider world was also there, if they cared to look for it. With the departure of Anne Beckwith-Smith and John Riddell—who left a few months later—the Princess could no longer be counted upon to acquiesce when it came to conforming to conventional ways of doing royal business.

The message to her own constituency of organizations, charities, and admirers was that her office had a new face and in many ways a new philosophy. In my self-confident mood I did not share Anne's instinctive wish to form a united front with the Prince's staff whenever possible.

Personally, I felt my position was like that of the driver of a speedboat. The Princess's public popularity and senior position in the royal hierarchy represented enormous potential horsepower. Steering the thing was a team effort, in which the Princess told me roughly where she wanted to go and I worked out what I thought was the best way of getting there. There were only three certainties in this: (1) after any mishap it would be found that my hands were on the wheel; (2) the Princess would probably change our destination in midvoyage, but (3) wherever it was, we were going there at breakneck speed. Without straining the analogy, I might add that later on it began to get very dark and stormy and we had very few lighthouses to show us the way.

To reinforce the message of a new start, I instituted a program of weekly meetings that the Princess would attend at my office in St. James's Palace, along with the equerry, the press secretary, the head of security, and any others I thought might amuse her with their input. At our next lunch, Anne received this information with polite amusement. "I don't see that lasting very long," she said and in this, as in so much else, she was absolutely right. It did not last very long. By then, however, with the weekly meetings and a number of other obvious pieces of window dressing, such as relocating all her secretaries into one room from their dispersed locations around the office, I think the message had been made clear enough. The Princess was under new management—her own.

This was an exciting thought. Nonetheless, as the official with the job of turning it into reality, I had no illusions that hazards lay in wait round every corner. I was also uncomfortably aware that every failure was newsworthy. To keep myself constantly alert, it helped to imagine that I had an invisible companion watching everything I said, did, and wrote. He was the editor of the *Sun*.

I had hardly settled into my new office when I was sharply reminded of the pitfalls in store. I had arranged for the Princess to spend a day carrying out engagements in Edinburgh, concluding with a concert at the Usher Hall. Still flexing my organizational muscles, I had ordered up the royal train, to take us north in style and to provide a convenient base in which the Princess could change and prepare for the evening engagement.

The royal train was used regularly by the Prince, but the Princess said it had unhappy associations for her and she seldom suggested we should use it. As we pulled out of King's Cross, however, and I explored the delights of the private secretary's compartment, not to mention the train's other unique attractions such as the royal accommodation, the dining carriage, and the household compartment, I could not help hoping that her reservations about using the train could be overcome in time.

Having seen the Princess retire safely to her quarters for the night, the rest of our small party fell to exploring the train's supplies of good brandy and expensive cigars. It may have been these, or some fault with the air-conditioning in my cabin, but I woke early the next morning in the grip of one of the worst hangovers of my entire life. I was convinced that its treatment required a day of complete bed rest, subdued lighting, gentle music, and nourishment by intravenous drip. Instead I knew that in a couple of hours I would have to begin a long day of grueling engagements, at a time in my career when anything less than a faultless performance might have dire, long-term consequences. Summoning up years of training, I somehow managed to shower, shave, and dress before making my way unsteadily to the household dining car.

Sometimes, I recalled, my abused system would respond to shock treatment. The royal train's fried breakfasts were legendary—and probably the greatest alimentary shock on wheels. Grimly resolving to be cured or die in the attempt, I ordered the full works, but when it arrived, in all its artery-threatening glory, surrounded by a thin pool of grease that lapped gently at the edges of my plate, my stomach threatened imminent rebellion and the carriage started a slow spin.

A rather hurt steward removed my plate and returned to see if there was anything I would like instead. Remembering another sovereign cure, I asked if by any chance he had some plain yogurt on the train. "No, sir. I'm afraid we don't," he said, looking suddenly very crestfallen. Feeling rather crestfallen myself, I retired to a quiet corner with a bottle of mineral water and massaged my forehead between sips.

Soon I became aware that we had stopped in a large city. Through gritty eyes I could recognize that it was not yet Edinburgh, thank goodness, but it was somewhere pretty big. Newcastle? I closed my eyes again, deciding there were better people than me in charge of driving the train, especially in my present condition. Soon we were moving again and the throbbing in my temples began to ease.

Silently the steward reappeared at my side. "I got your yogurt, sir!" he said with an air of triumph. There on the table sat six cartons of yogurt, all of them sweet and fruity, which I knew would do nothing to calm the incipient mutiny in my insides. It was undeniably yogurt nevertheless, and as I thanked the steward I was silently cursing him for having overreacted to my request. To keep him happy, I gamely ate two of the glutinous concoctions and felt, if anything, slightly worse.

Somehow I survived our day in Edinburgh with both my job and my liver intact, but the next morning my darkest fears were realized. As if in divine retribution, a prominent tabloid newspaper story reported that the Princess of Wales had commanded the royal train to make an unscheduled stop in Newcastle so that a harassed member of the train staff could make an urgent purchase of yogurt. The paper went on to remark that this was further proof, if any were needed, that the Princess was impulsive and imperious in her unreasonable demands and, more than likely, that she was pregnant as well.

Even on their own, each of these allegations would have been enough to put the Princess in a foul enough mood to start chopping off heads. Put together, they earned me a very uncomfortable day while she considered my rather implausible explanation. Back at base, I stomped around the office trying to look unconcerned and failing miserably. I even eyed the appointments section of *The Times*, but gave up when I realized that I was probably not qualified for *anything* at all useful.

Then, as suddenly as it had blown up, the storm merci-

fully passed. Such were her moods. I did not have long to
wait for the next, however.

*A*t around this time, relations between the Prince and
Princess were undergoing another downturn. As was often
the case, just as trouble was brewing behind the scenes, the
public image as interpreted by the media was determinedly
optimistic. That summer—1990—the Prince had fallen
while playing polo and suffered severe injuries to his arm.
While he was hospitalized in Nottingham, the Princess
filled in at short notice for some of the engagements he had
been forced to cancel and also made some highly publicized
visits to his sickbed. The combined image of brave royal
trouper and concerned wife was impossible to resist.

Unfortunately, any sentiment of wifely duty that may
have lain behind her actions was quickly redressed in the
Princess's mind, and in the minds of other observers, by the
reactions of the Prince's own staff to his injury. Quite apart
from the lady physiotherapist, who for some time was an indispensable part of the recovery effort, his close personal
staff clustered round in a way that would have done credit
to a flock of broody hens.

The extraordinary degree of male concern shown by his
staff to the hospitalized Prince drew mild derision from his
wife. She felt excluded by their protectiveness, which she
interpreted as overfamiliar. "They'll be dressing up as nurses
next!" she snorted. It was true that, ironically, some of the
Prince's men felt free to express a devotion to their master
that might have sounded odd coming from a male member
of her own staff. Several aspired to share his exquisite taste,
too, and the Prince's warrant-holders found a ready market
among his staff for everything from shirts to eau de cologne.

Whether it was the intention or not, such closing of
ranks served to fuel the sense in the Princess's mind and in
the office generally that the Prince's misfortune was a pri-

vate matter and others should keep out. It also earned him a great deal of sympathy and caused the appearance of glowing references to his physical courage on the field of play—none of which seemed to cheer her up very much.

It was therefore a good moment to dangle something in front of her that would be high profile and symbolically independent. One of her more glamorous patronages had the ideal proposal. The London City Ballet had for years been struggling to match its remarkable artistic success with similar triumphs in the field of fund-raising, but it was a hard slog. When the opportunity arose in the autumn of 1990 to earn some serious money with a royal fundraising dinner in Washington, D.C., they were therefore quick to ask for their patron's involvement and she was just as quick to accept the invitation.

Her eagerness and mine may have had something to do with our enthusiastic recollections of the triumph in New York, but, as others have also learned to their cost, New York and Washington are very different cities, with very different attitudes to the sort of glitz represented by visiting Princesses.

Apparently out of the blue, Washington's smart social commentators started to give the Princess's visit decidedly mixed billing. The *Washington Post* quoted Georgette Mossbacher, a Washington society hostess, as saying, "The British organizers of the Gala erred by failing to consult local community members." She and her formidable sisterhood of "community members" began to find they had no space in their busy engagement calendars for a mere royal gala dinner. Suddenly it was noted that everything, from the catering to the gilt chairs that would be used at the banquet, had been shipped from England. What was the matter with this Princess, the murmurers implied, that she did not like Washington food and could not bring herself to sit on real American furniture?

Smoke signals from our own Foreign Office reminded me of the advice we had been given to think very carefully before undertaking fundraising events of any kind in the

USA. Other households began to mutter. My brother private secretaries—an intimidating trade union—began to look reproachfully at the Princess's plans as their own American "Viking raids" for charity cash came under scrutiny. The White House, where we hoped to have coffee with Mrs. Bush, also seemed to be having cold feet. Nobody would confirm our appointment.

It was a classic example of how good intentions and an apparently perfectly correct use of royal patronage could precipitate a minor media landslide that left us all with the uneasy feeling that the ground was shifting under our feet. With the disaster-sensitive antennae that seemed to be a courtier's stock-in-trade, my colleagues began to be sympathetic. Then I really started to worry.

The Princess herself switched moods violently and apparently overnight. From enthusiastically looking forward to what she imagined would be another New York-style triumph, she became apprehensive about potential bad publicity and began to look around in a predatory way for scapegoats before the act even began. With my severance from the Navy now absolute, my Duchy house not yet ready for occupation, and a series of recent close escapes, I began to feel that I was already facing my final hours. The speedboat of my new job seemed to be heading inexorably for the rocks. It was time to act decisively if I was not to find myself washed up on the beach with the other flotsam.

Early one evening I picked up the telephone to the Palace switchboard and heard myself nervously barking, in the worst B-movie style, "Get me the White House!" Somehow in the days that followed, not least with the help of the irrepressible Francis Cornish—still at the Embassy in Washington—and with the cooperation of the ballet company and its sponsors, we completed the necessary surgery to the program in the nick of time. The hostesses found room in their calendars again, the First Lady and then the President himself sent word that they hoped the Princess would visit with them. Everybody forgot about the English chairs.

As we boarded Concorde, it was with the feeling that our chestnuts had been pulled out of the fire, if only just. There were still dangers ahead, however. Some of the slower London tabloids were still reporting Washington's anticipated coolness to the visit and it was one of these two-page spreads that an aghast lady-in-waiting dramatically drew to the Princess's attention with wide-eyed horror as we sat in the airplane. I could cheerfully have strangled her, had she not been sitting on the opposite side of the aisle. With friends like these... I tensed, ready for the explosion.

It never came, surprisingly, and the Princess kept her nerve. She seemed to realize that this was no time for a traditional display of royal petulance. In fact, it was the first of many occasions when we both knew we had stuck our necks out and the best way to minimize any recriminations was to plow on and look serene. Sadly, though, she forgot this lesson more often than she remembered it. Petulance in adversity is a hard habit to break.

The supersonic jet arrived in Washington on time. There was the familiar figure of the Ambassador to greet us, together with the even more welcome figure of the Princess's PPO Graham Smith, who had gone ahead to coordinate arrangements with the Secret Service. There, too, were the Secret Service agents, looking reassuringly as if they had come straight from central casting and named, I swear, Lenny, Lonny, Danny, and Randy.

The gala that evening was a great success. Nobody mentioned the chairs and everybody seemed to enjoy the food. The Princess, in a scarlet silk, cowl-necked dress reminiscent of Greek goddesses, at last attracted the kind of acclaim she was used to. Such was her star quality that the reality of her presence—as opposed to catty previews—usually had that effect.

Across the crowded dance floor I caught a glimpse of her doing a sedate twirl with Michael Ashcroft. As the principal benefactor of the London City Ballet, this was no less than his due. For her part, the patron seemed to be enjoying her-

self, although her attitude to rich benefactors as a class was
ambivalent. She recognized the immense help they gave to
good causes, often making the difference between life and
death for vital projects. She also observed, however, that for
many, involvement in her charities was a means of acquiring the remaining intangible assets that money could not
buy: gratitude, recognition, and—perhaps—a knighthood.
"They'd put their money in a dustbin if I asked them to,"
she said on an unusually jaundiced day.

Nonetheless, there was no disguising the fact that the
success of the Washington trip owed much to the prompt
generosity of both Michael Ashcroft and John Hughes, the
LCB's chairman. By guaranteeing generous donations to
the local charity benefiting from the ballet evening—
Grandma's House children's AIDS center—they helped
draw the remaining sting of the capital's skeptical social
commentators.

Very late that night, Graham Smith and I sat drinking
whiskey in the room I had been allocated at the Ambassador's residence. I tried to find inspiration in any lingering
presence of its most famous former occupant, Winston
Churchill, but it took Graham to point out a distant parallel
with the famed bulldog spirit.

I was complaining about the tightrope act I already felt
my job was becoming. Graham did not disagree, but then
he observed, "This could have been a disaster, but you told her
the truth about the risks we were running and it made her
determined to fight to make it a success. You've got to tell it
to her straight—not many of you lot have the guts to do
that. Then she may bite your head off at the time, but she'll
respect you for it later."

Like practically everything else the PPOs said, this was
good advice and it told me something about the Princess
that I was already beginning to suspect. She had no com-
punction about hitting below the belt—and she never accepted defeat. For someone so often obsessed with the
fickle winds of popularity, once her mind was made up she

was coldly determined and would fight tenaciously to protect her own interests, as her opponents eventually discovered.

The next day, the Princess visited Grandma's House, a home for underprivileged children, all of whom were expected to die from AIDS before they reached their teens. The picture of the Princess surrounded by so many hopeful, upturned faces was repeated a thousand times all over the world, but that particular memory still brings a lump to the throat.

From there, still glowing with virtue, we traveled in an impressive motorcade to the White House for tea with the President and Mrs. Bush. Like a number of other powerful older women, Mrs. Bush seemed to feel a protective, almost motherly attitude toward the Princess. She ushered us round on a tour of the famous building, chatting away. The atmosphere was relaxed and friendly, the house decorated in sunny shades of yellow. "Not the most sensible color to choose," admitted Mrs. Bush, "when you've got spaniels in the house. Nancy Reagan would have a *fit*."

Part of the way through our tour, she somehow managed to lose her bearings. We emerged unexpectedly from a side door into the area where the tourists were lining up for their own guided tour. For a moment the two women stood uncertainly in front of the startled crowd. As recognition slowly dawned, the double takes were worth the whole trip.

Later we sat down to tea. Dainty cakes were handed round. A photographer flashed discreetly in the background and flitted out. The Princess and the First Lady talked about AIDS and children and spaniels and AIDS and ballet and AIDS...

President Bush stirred restlessly in his chair. Even seated, he radiated energy and enthusiasm. On the other side of the world Saddam Hussein was preparing to invade Kuwait and the President's next meeting was to discuss the growing crisis. Suddenly he turned to the Princess and briskly asked her what the British public's attitude was to the prospect of war in the Middle East.

For a horrible moment it was obvious that the Princess's mind had gone blank. I felt the Ambassador stiffen next to me, but she was beyond our reach. "Um," she said. Then, "I think it's all very worrying." You could always tell when she had been caught on the hop, because her voice reverted to an exaggerated Sloane Ranger drawl.

There was an uncomfortable pause. Noiselessly, an aide appeared at the doorway. "Mr. President? The Joint Chiefs are ready."

President Bush took his cue. "Well," he said, seeming to get out of his armchair and shake our hands in one smooth movement, "guess I'd better go save the world!"

*B*ack in London a note arrived for me in the Bag:

Thank you very much for fighting my corner with the folk in Washington. It's greatly appreciated.

D.

That was all right, then.

It was not all right for long, however. Another ordeal was on its way, and this one was much bigger than my yogurt crisis, bigger even than the Washington ballet gala crisis. That winter, every other issue was dwarfed by the growing preparations for war in the Gulf. The Princess's reaction to such a great national drama presented new problems for me. It also revealed a devastating personal drama of her own.

From bases all over the United Kingdom and from Germany, what seemed to be the greater part of the country's fighting strength was flying off to the heat and sand of Arabia, still so vivid in my memory from our tour there. Now, with war in the Gulf a certainty, I saw a chance for the Princess to reinforce her continuing place at the royal top table. She should go to the desert to cheer up the troops, I told my superiors. To myself and the Princess only, I added an additional reason: such a trip would symbolically reinforce her position as future Queen by showing her actively supporting the forces of the Crown as they prepared for battle. How better to prove to a skeptical establishment that the Princess was ideally qualified to represent the younger generation's support for our brave boys? And how better to cheer up the brave boys getting ready to fight in the desert than with some youthful glamour? The choice seemed obvious—to me, anyway.

The Princess was enthusiastic about my plan for many laudable reasons and for a few others as well, as I discovered. These turned out to be mainly to do with Captain James Hewitt, already practicing gunnery with his regiment on an Arabian beach.

Meanwhile, the Prince's advisers had come up with a similar idea and, showing a glimpse of their growing skill at lobbying, succeeded in persuading Buckingham Palace to propose their man to go and be photographed among the Chieftain crews. This he duly did. Rather tamely, the Princess was sent instead to raise morale at the offices of the Gulf Help Line, which had been set up to provide reassurance to relatives of those Saddam was keeping as human shields in Kuwait. Shortly before Christmas 1990, she was also sent to Germany to comfort the families whose menfolk had gone to war.

Denied her photo opportunity with the troops, she seethed. For some time after the Washington trip I felt my fortunes with the Princess had recovered, but what she saw as my failure to get her to the war zone put me straight back in the doghouse. Once again I felt the chill of being the flavor of *last* month.

All the signs were there—a flatness in her voice, an avoidance of eye contact except when administering a scold, the very obvious redistribution of favors toward others, including former enemies, and a cool indifference to every program suggestion I made. My morale plummeted. I was heading for the rocks again. My gloom was deepened by the knowledge that she was the sole arbiter over whether what I did was right or wrong, even if what I produced was exactly what she had asked for.

After spending an afternoon in a bleak barracks in northern Germany, surrounded by bravely cheerful women and children, I looked out of the car window at the black branches of the trees against the snow-covered ground. The gray gloom gathered. My macabre mood suffered an unexpected downward twist as I realized that we were passing the site of Belsen concentration camp. *What was the matter? What could I do to put things right? God, I wish I'd stayed in the Navy.*

Worse was to come. The frigid silence in the car was suddenly broken. The Princess was using the special voice that was calculated to remind you that everybody else was now her new best friend. "Graham," she said, "you'll never guess who's been sent to the Gulf."

"No, Ma'am," said Graham, turning round in the front seat.

"James Hewitt."

"Oh," said Graham, carefully noncommittal.

"Oh *God*!" I said to myself.

It was like a revelation. This explained everything. My boss was gripped by concern for her beloved, an emotion doubled by remorse. So far as I knew, she had abruptly cut her links with him more than a year previously, much to the relief of those few of us who had even an inkling of the friendship's true depth. Now her remorse would be redoubled by his imminent exposure—at least in theory—to Saddam's bullets. That explained her sudden personal interest in the impending war. It soon grew into an obsession.

I was numb with shock and a sudden comprehension of her coolness toward me. I understood just enough of the skewed dynamics of her emotions to know that James's reappearance spelled trouble for me.

I certainly did not feel—and never had felt—the re-motest attraction to the woman who to the world may have been the definition of desirability but to me was only ever my boss. I knew her too well for any of that. Nevertheless, having chosen me as her main, long-term source of male support and advice, the Princess had also cast me in the role of fall guy in any imaginary competition for favors of an-other sort. As I repeatedly saw—such as in her pointless plotting over speechwriting duties—it added to the excite-ment of her life to feel that she had kept a secret from me. I did not mind that too much, but I certainly minded when I realized that she was equally excited by the idea that I might disapprove of her friendships with other men, that I might be jealous. Given the aridity of her love life, to have rivals for her affections—even imaginary ones—must have been wonderfully soothing to her fragile sense of self-worth.

A whole new list of dreadful possibilities was raised by this piece of news and began to run unstoppably through my head like a computer printout. I was the perfect scape-goat for the unrequited passion that was now reignited in her mind. Not only was the man she adored now preparing to die a hero's death in the desert, but her distinctly un-heroic and arguably rather less dashing paid companion—me—was happy to plan his holidays while she had to face the ordeal of a royal family Christmas entirely unsupported.

Of course, I had known about James Hewitt. About eighteen months earlier—in July 1989—the Princess had invited me, as she put it, to "help out" with a lunch that she was giving privately at Kensington Palace. This in itself was not particularly unusual. I was increasingly called in to act as a sort of surrogate host for her entertaining. This could be professionally hazardous—it was necessary to develop an intuitive awareness of her conversational requirements from minute to minute—but it was also a good way of keeping track of her current attitudes to people and events.

This lunch was different. The guests comprised some senior officers from the barracks in Windsor where the

Princess had been learning to ride, a General who was also a prospective private secretary to the Prince, and, on my right, a taciturn but beautifully groomed Captain with strikingly colored hair. She had already introduced us.

At that time James Hewitt and the Princess were more than two years into a passionate romance. Among a tight-knit circle of close staff it was common knowledge, a knowledge borne with sympathetic understanding but constant anxiety that its public exposure was inevitable sooner or later. That anxiety was heightened by the kind of effort at innocent social contact—such as this lunch and her sons' riding lessons with James at Windsor—that gives illicit lovers such a thrill but fools practically nobody. I imagine a similar anxiety existed among the Prince's staff as they quietly accommodated his need for Mrs. Parker Bowles.

The Princess respected our tacitly supportive conspiracy and we all happily pretended that nothing was happening. This was easier than it sounds in the atmosphere in which we lived. We were very practiced at presenting an image of outward respectability while coping behind the scenes with the harsh reality of the Waleses' foundering marriage. The worst strain inevitably fell on the PPOs, but even under this hardest of tests their loyalty and discretion never wavered.

Not long after that lunch James was due to depart for Army duty in Germany. In the face of the impending separation, the Princess felt deserted and reacted self-protectively to what she unconsciously saw as a rejection. This tendency was only exacerbated by the royalty that overlaid her childhood traits and that encourages the belief that wishes are usually to be treated as commands. She therefore took care to reject him first, ending the relationship as she ended so many—by ignoring him so pointedly and for so long that in the end, mystified and hurt, he quietly withdrew, leaving her own hands clean and her conscience appeased.

The ensuing separation lasted until the prospect of James's imminent involvement in the Gulf War triggered an intense resumption of the Princess's interest. It was this that

I had just witnessed in the car and, from his monosyllabic response, I knew that Graham's heart was sinking almost as fast as mine.

I thought back to that happy lunch in the summer of 1989. For obvious reasons, the Princess had studiously avoided paying too much attention to the diffident Captain, concentrating her unusually animated chatter on the senior guests. They responded with ponderous civility. Thus left on the margins, as the two youngest officers present we naturally fell into conversation. I found him rather nervous, very polite, and good company. I could not disagree with people who said that he lacked any great intellect, but to be fair, as a junior cavalry officer his talents were necessarily more practical. I certainly could not fault his coolness. Considering the high-octane mixture of anxiety and passion that must have been struggling beneath his snappy suit, it would not have been surprising if he had burst into flames on the spot.

As has been widely reported since, his affair with the Princess erupted again on his return from the Gulf and never, I think, truly evaporated. Their opposite personalities created too strong an attraction. Although by every outward sign—and by a huge conscious effort—the Princess relegated their passion to a distant friendship soon after the war's end, I believe the elemental psychological link remained.

That link, and her attempts to cut or replace it, lay at the heart of many of the Princess's apparently impulsive actions. The huge energy required to sustain the affair now had nowhere to go but into attempts to build her new, independent life as a public figure in her own right.

In addition, ending her feelings for James demanded a concentration of emotional effort that perhaps helped her to identify and resolve many of her own internal demons. It appeared to encourage her to think of herself as a confident, self-sufficient person, freed at least partly from the need for constant reassurance. It also enabled her to share the pain she detected in others. It also, however, fueled her need for revenge against people and experiences that she felt had treated her unjustly.

In the contacts I had with him in the years that followed, most of them at times of great stress, I had no reason to change my opinion of James or of his good nature. Nonetheless, as the sad details of his affair with the Princess became public, he was confirmed as just the most prominent member of a long list of impressionable men only too ready to believe that a distracted Princess's interest in them was actually safe and healthy affection.

I had noticed as long ago as our first outing to Essex that the Princess's attitude to sex and relationships was as distinctive—and as worrying—as her attitude to many other of life's great conundrums. The framework in which she pictured love certainly seemed to have been conditioned by long-suppressed traumas in her early life. In the opinion of a senior relationship counselor who knew the Princess, her experiences in childhood, including the protracted pain of her parents' acrimonious divorce, had permanently damaged her ability to give and receive love. I had certainly observed her deep unwillingness to make a commitment either in relationships or in her work. I also recalled her precipitate withdrawal from introductory training as a marriage guidance counselor—training that would quickly have revealed such early experiences. "God, they had me in pieces!" was all she would say.

I do not believe she would have wanted her experiences to be ignored, or felt it a disservice to her memory to record what I saw. She so often expressed her own pain by identifying with others in areas such as mental illness, addiction, and eating disorders. There was no doubting the affinity she felt with the women she encountered in mental hospitals, homeless hostels, and women's refuges. Then there was the bulimia. The idea that fellow victims subconsciously recognize each other's experiences is widely acknowledged by therapists.

Equally compulsive was her need to control people and

relationships. *In extremis,* she reverted to a fantasy version of events to perpetuate the illusion of controlling them. This was matched by a need for power over everything that affected her life. She built and defended a strong power base by using her innate strength of character, hugely enhanced by her acquired royal status.

The constant search for affection that resulted was cruelly matched by an inability to accept true devotion when it was offered, no matter how generously. No matter, either, whether it was offered by a kindhearted man or a besotted world. Only in her devotion to her children, and in their unconditional love for her, did she seem to find release.

In the end, she reacted to men's interest in her by protecting herself in the only way she knew how—by avidly consuming what was offered, then throwing away the empty husk with cold and apparently heartless rejection. Faced with this attitude, the attempts of men like her husband, James, and others to heal such deep-seated hurt were bound to fail. Worse, such attempts would be treated by the Princess as signs of weakness, and in her mind, strength was paramount in relationships. She longed to feel safe in the affections of a strong and confident man, yet her contradictory need to control everything made this practically impossible. From this paradox developed the erratic use of her own power and, ultimately, her preference for men she could perceive as inferior.

It is, perhaps, supremely ironic that it was infamously the Prince who publicly questioned the nature of love during their syrupy engagement interview. The Princess was emphatic that she felt it and, inwardly, was perhaps expressing an even greater need for it. Unfortunately, if love is a language, she was speaking Greek and the men who came closest to her all spoke Latin.

11

✿

Guns

*I*n the first months of 1991, the world's media was gripped by Gulf War fever. The Princess was gripped by it too, and by her own volatile cocktail of romantic emotions. She sat in Kensington Palace, writing letters to the front line. She was scathing in her attacks on those she felt did not share her personal identification with the loved ones who could only watch and wait, with the added frustration that her feelings were supposed to be secret.

She looked up from her desk, eyes red-rimmed and loaded with reproach. "What is it, Patrick?" From a corner of the room her TV blared reports about allied air strikes. It was permanently tuned to the satellite news channel. She made no move to turn down the volume.

"I wonder if we could go through some of these invitations, Ma'am."

Her eyes blazed. "I can't *think* of doing normal work while this war's going on. I don't know how *anybody* can. These men are waiting to die." She had a happy inspiration. "And it's disrespectful to their families!"

"But, Ma'am, there's nothing frivolous in these invitations. Nothing that would look bad here, or from the Gulf."

Her face was set in an expression of defiant suffering. Suddenly I was impatient. This had been going on for weeks. "Look here, Ma'am. We're *all* very worried. I've got friends out there too." This was true. "But life has to go on here as well. I mean, our parents went through *years* of this in the last war, and this one hasn't even started properly yet. When it's all over people are going to remember who carried on working despite the worry..."

It was no good. In a world of so much false emotion, here was a *real* crisis and she was going to experience it to the full. What was more, I was not who or what she wanted, and the comforting familiarity of routine work would have robbed her of the dramatic tension that I supposed she felt as love.

Her understanding of love was probably less complete than would normally be the case for a woman of her age. It is, after all, the trickiest of all subjects even for well-adjusted people, and that was a state I do not think even she would have claimed for herself. Given this fact, the prospect of the object of her affections suffering a violent death, however unlikely it might appear to me, stoked her lurking neuroses into a blaze of suspicion and undirected activity. When a gift of jade earrings, sent from James, was misdirected to the office and subsequently went missing, the unrestrained fury of her reaction was quite unsettling.

"Patrick! I *know* they've been stolen!" Her eyes flickered over my face accusingly. For a mad second I even thought she was checking my ears for the missing items.

Wearily I went along with her overreaction and, as so often in moments of difficulty, sought the professional advice of the PPOs. After an uncomfortable investigation (in which the shadow of royal suspicion fell on her anxious and innocent secretaries) the missing gift miraculously came to light. If it had not, I reflected in a desperate moment, she might well have inflicted on her staff the time-honored

Roman practice of decimation—had there been enough of us.

The ground war duly came and then was over in a matter of hours. British casualties were mercifully light and suddenly the Princess's inflamed sentiments had to readjust to the rather more mundane prospect of James's safe return.

Her unspoken contempt for my failure to go and die instead still had some way to run, however. I had evolved the philosophy that nothing I said or did should betray for a second, to her or to her eyes and ears in the office, that I was anything other than totally indifferent to her feelings of antipathy toward me. This, I hoped, would either drive her to commit some unpardonable offense against me, or help her quickly conclude that I could be more use to her alive than undead.

Meanwhile, I suffered private agonies of doubt. The absolute requirement to keep a stiff upper lip—for the staff, for my family, and for my own self-respect—took an enormous effort to sustain. Again I contemplated *The Times* appointments section. I quickly realized, however, that it was better to go forward than try to extract myself from what was still, on paper, one of the most desirable jobs in the world. So I told myself, and the few close friends I allowed to share my worries, that I was happily digging my garden and that when she wanted me, she could come to the door and send for me. Otherwise I would get on with my own life and do my best to enjoy its many blessings.

The tactic worked, both then and subsequently, whenever an outbreak of similar hostilities was threatened. Above all else she hated to be ignored and there was nothing more frustrating for her than to find her thunderbolts falling on ears that were apparently deaf.

It was an unedifying experience. We were, after all, supposed to be a force for good in a society that desperately needed the unaffected care of the beautiful Princess. It was another reminder of the contrast between the public and private faces. I had no deep philosophical objection to this.

I knew the Princess was not perfect and she had to find her own way of coping with the stresses placed on her. My job was to absorb any flak that came my way and help her see the positive side of her own predicament. If I could not stand the heat... The alternative was never far from our minds when she made life difficult.

As I was slowly readmitted to her unpredictable favors, the final scales fell from my eyes. The Princess was never going to give me a quiet life. Our relationship would be that of two people thrown together by various degrees of adversity. In the final analysis, I could expect no loyalty from her. I did feel needed by her, though, and in turn I tried to develop the unspectacular dependability in running her public life that was necessary to balance her tortuous private emotions.

The heated domestic politics of the time could have been designed to inflame the most stable Princess. We were also learning that mere public success did not necessarily make her life any easier on the home front. I pondered the realization that her very popularity meant that certain types of independent action, notably overseas tours, were bound to become areas of potential conflict. The near disaster of Washington had only strengthened the arm of those who wished to see her fledgling independence curtailed. It was evidence—albeit not conclusive—that she could be an embarrassment as well as an asset abroad.

Mind you, with painful regularity she herself found ways of strengthening the arm of her doubters. As I labored under the burden of her disapproval, I was still able to perceive a further potential embarrassment in her attitude to public duties. She had allowed herself to become obsessed with the Gulf War. Every attempt to make her do something unconnected with the war, or something that might conceivably be interpreted as recreational, drew her violent opposition. As so often in history, a real war was the perfect excuse for those behind the lines to dispense gleefully with irksome routine. Her calendar was cleared wholesale.

It was hardly surprising, therefore, that the powers that be in Buckingham Palace and at the Foreign Office chose not to send the popular Princess to identify herself with the great wave of patriotic sentiment directed toward our boys in the Gulf. She had an unwelcome personal motive for going and would, in any case, steal too much limelight. She must stand to one side while the Prince duly donned uniform and went to perform his duty.

It was a pity, I reflected later, that this policy could not have been refined and packaged in a way that might have made its implementation more successful. Openness was not the chosen method, sadly. Instead, by trial and error, the Princess and her staff learned the limits of her freedom. Not that there was a plot against her—in some ways that would actually have been preferable. At least plotters have a clear view of their objectives. Rather, I think it was hoped that any damage she did could be contained by piecemeal restrictions and much wishing for the best.

With greater foresight, the Gulf War could have created the opportunity to use the Princess's strengths directly in the service of the Crown, in exchange for a commitment from her to put that service ahead of any other ambitions she had. There were, of course, many other such opportunities, almost until her divorce, but they were not recognized either. Even if they had been recognized, they would have required a departure from customary ways of thinking that was just too abrupt.

These opportunities may well have been missed because I, with the closest vantage point, did not point them out sufficiently vigorously. That said, the organization of which I was a part—and the Princess too, however unwillingly—had a natural aversion to vigorous pointing out, and history will surely prove that such an aversion has been one of its greatest strengths, if at times its least attractive.

The Iraqi cease-fire at the end of February 1991 also signaled a thawing of hostilities between myself and my boss. While it was possible to fall from favor in an apparently vertical plummet of sudden unpopularity, negotiating one's way out of purgatory took rather longer. The process of rehabilitation was hampered by the fact that the Princess did not find it easy to admit that she might have been wrong, at least in matters of real importance. Nor, I suppose, did I. A wary couple of months followed in which my presence was increasingly acknowledged once again and the work of the office, which had suffered during her preoccupation and my ostracism, resumed its normal tempo.

One further trick remained to be pulled from the Gulf War box. She instructed me, in a rather spare note, to make arrangements so that she could entertain the relatives of those killed in the conflict to tea and sympathy.

As a humanitarian gesture it was superficially irreproachable, but its subtext, as I well knew, had more to do with the Princess's wish to salvage some of the media spotlight that had been lost to her during the course of the war. It would also, I thought unkindly but probably accurately, be a popular move with the returning soldiery, one in particular.

With minimal research, I confirmed what I already suspected from reports in the news. Of the fourteen who had died, only two or three had suffered deaths that might be described as uncontroversial. I sent her a note saying this and was not very surprised to hear no more on the subject.

*T*he Prince's success in being portrayed as the only member of the royal family to brave the war zone rankled the Princess, and her vengeful mood set the scene for the spring and summer that followed.

She had opted to go to the St. David's Day celebrations at Llandaff Cathedral on March 1 and planned to take Prince William with her, on what would be his first public engagement in the principality. It was a PR masterstroke, very simple in its conception and almost impossible to counter. Belatedly, the Prince added himself to the event and a convincing show of unity was staged. The only problem was that the Prince's schedule had not been designed to accommodate a morning in Wales, so he had to leave straight after the service by helicopter to go to another engagement while his wife and eldest son stayed on to enjoy scenes of mass popularity in Cardiff city center.

For part of the trip I shared a car with Sir Christopher Airy. Christopher had replaced John Riddell as private secretary to both the Prince and Princess less than a year before. With a distinguished Army background and a rigid sense of duty and precedent, Christopher would have been ideally suited to the gentlemanly atmosphere of Buckingham Palace. Unfortunately, a different philosophy reigned at St. James's, in which the qualities that had served him so well as General Officer Commanding London District were of painfully little relevance. He quickly—and all too obviously—felt out of place in an organization already in the process of disintegration.

I sat next to the courtly figure as it waved genially, and quite inappropriately, to the Welsh crowds. I could see why it was common knowledge in the office that the shadows were already gathering around him. Having myself connived at Anne's resignation a year earlier, I was in no position to hold my nose at the unsavory ways in which Christopher's demise was being engineered. In time-honored fashion, ambitious subordinates were making the most of their better access to the royal ear. It was typical of our happy life at St. James's, however, that the General was probably one of the last people to realize what was happening.

The underlying tensions of the day were plainly as unwelcome to him as they were to the rest of us, and he consoled himself by remarking over and over again on the size and enthusiasm of the crowds. This was a bad sign, I thought, arrogant in my own professionalism. The crowds, large or small, should be the least important part of a private secretary's job.

By the time I went to Salisbury for the day with the Princess in April, my rehabilitation was almost complete. This probably had less to do with the Princess's rediscovery of what a nice chap I really was than with her realization that I was undeniably the devil she knew and had, indeed, even selected. Plans to replace me, which must have crossed her mind during my exile, had retreated. Her hopes of securing employment for James Hewitt, which I suspected was one of her motives, took a further blow with Christopher Airy's dismissal just a short month or so after the Cardiff fiasco. Christopher had been a guest at that long-ago KP lunch when I met James and I think he had a kindly understanding of the pitfalls of young officers' romantic attachments. In her emotionally charged mind at the time, I could imagine the Princess trying to wheedle a favor for her beloved out of the impressionable old boy.

The day of Christopher's abrupt departure revealed him at his dignified best as he exhorted the office staff to be loyal to the Prince (though, forgetfully, not to the Princess as well, I noted with some wry amusement). Seldom can euthanasia have been administered with such a blunt needle, however.

To nobody's surprise, except perhaps briefly his own, in May 1991, following a period of increasing influence as comptroller, Richard Aylard now assumed the title of private secretary—but to whom?

Although never on close terms, Richard and I shared a similar naval background and understood many of each other's problems. Having served the Princess as equerry for several years, he had a valuable insight into much of her thinking and later on he frequently used his knowledge to urge moderation in his boss's attitude to his wife during the stormy process of separation.

Sadly, Richard was a marked man in the Princess's eyes for having, as she saw it, crossed to the enemy camp. Coupled with Richard's enthusiasm for working with the media and his energetic and arguably overdue attempts to galvanize some morale and efficiency into the Prince's office, this made it relatively easy for her to see him as a schemer, always ready to aid and abet—if not actually conceive—moves to downgrade her. It was never likely that she would accept him as joint private secretary to herself and the Prince, which had happily been the arrangement with Richard's predecessors since the early days of the marriage.

I had already effectively been doing the job—without the pay—for a number of months by this time, so the obvious choice was to appoint me as her own private secretary and, for all practical purposes, complete the separation of the office into two. There followed an uncomfortable few weeks while the Princess debated with herself whether I was sufficiently restored in her favors to warrant such a promotion. I, meanwhile, made quiet plans to resign if she chose any other course of action. In the end she decided in my favor.

Thereafter, however well Richard and I maintained civilized relations, the joint office was inexorably set on division. Since this administrative schism reflected an increasingly bitter marital feud, the Princess and I would also soon be struggling to hold on to the status she had acquired on marriage. The poisoning effect on relations within the office was slow and insidious. As time passed, our attempts to recreate the old spirit of teamwork—staff parties, office coordination meetings and the like—declined into a prickly charade of mutual suspicion.

My appointment marked the end of my first and longest period of estrangement from the Princess until my resignation in 1996. Certainly there were occasional bouts of frostiness in the intervening years, but I think we had both learned from the experience of the winter of 1990–91. She apparently reconciled herself to the thought that the trouble of replacing me was more than the trouble of keeping me, especially as relations with her husband's office hardened, and I learned the painful way that my happiness was my own responsibility. In the end, she had enough to cope with keeping herself going without having to worry about my delicate feelings. Henceforth, I tried, albeit with limited success, to cultivate a degree of self-protective detachment.

The division of the office was accomplished with remarkably little publicity. Richard and I would probably not have chosen each other as companions on a desert island, but we shared a common understanding of the realities of our situation and I wrote him a short note promising my cooperation in what were plainly going to be troubled times ahead. Although we sometimes subsequently found ourselves at odds, when the chips were really down, such as at the time of the couple's separation in 1992, we found we were able to work together with surprising unanimity.

In the course of the previous year, such a gap had already opened up in the way the two staffs worked that it only took a few secretaries to move desks and me to have my stationery reprinted for the transformation to be virtually complete. Common services such as the accountant and the organization of joint events continued to give us the facade of a combined operation, which prevented media mischief-making at what was a very vulnerable time. The Princess's staff kept their offices in St. James's Palace and I helped myself to another pay raise.

The Princess would still only visit erratically, except during a brief period when I tried to introduce regular meetings to help reinforce the image of a working woman in control of her own affairs. Her visits were always exciting for the secretaries and almost despite herself I think she found them a welcome change of scene. They also brought her into contact with her husband's staff—a mixed blessing for both visitor and visited alike.

It would go something like this. If it was one of the regular, planned visits, I always made careful preparations, mindful of the well-tried maxim about reducing the risk of surprises. The hall porters, for example, were told when she was expected, which enabled them to keep a space clear for her car. The green-fingered housekeeper lovingly tended the straggly foliage in my office. I casually mentioned the imminent visit to Richard, so that he could prepare himself and his staff (and the Prince, if he was around) for any impromptu walkabout.

The women cleared incriminating paperwork from desktops and stowed it safely away from curious royal eyes, and then spent slightly longer making imaginary improvements to their appearance. The equerry rechecked his lists of forthcoming engagements and rehearsed what he thought she would like to hear about them. The press secretary braced himself.

Meanwhile, I thought hard about the agenda for the meeting. It already contained standard subjects such as program, media, correspondence, and domestic administration, but under "Any Other Business" I could introduce subjects ranging from the latest famine to befall the Sudan and whether we should get involved, to the latest scandal to befall a Government Minister and whether she would want to share a speaking platform with him.

Alongside these weighty matters, we sometimes strayed onto things that sprang more readily into the Princess's mind. Had we read the story in the paper about the girl making medical history as a guinea pig for a lifesaving new treatment? She really wanted to send her a personal message. Would I draft something? Had I seen that program about homelessness on TV last night? Would I phone the producer and see if we could send a private donation from her Charities Trust? Didn't I have any other coffee cups? These ones would give my visitors a *very* bad impression. One of the girls could choose new ones from Thomas Goode in Mayfair and send her the bill . . .

When she arrived in Ambassador's Court, therefore, we were ready. My office was the best lookout post in the Palace and I had time to see her car draw up and still run downstairs to meet her in the hall. She seemed to blow in on a breeze of vigor and enthusiasm, tall, laughing, and confident. She's been getting ready too, I thought. The hall porters bowed like the ex-Guardsmen they were. The housekeeper curtsied. I stumbled up the stairs. She laughed. We all laughed.

In my office the sun was streaming through my lookout window. Steaming coffee and expensive polish mingled with the scent of freshly laundered Princess. The new cups sparkled and so did the blushing secretary who was still artfully arranging them when we arrived. All six and a half feet of commando equerry inclined himself in the Princess's direction. The press secretary winked.

Amazingly, my spindly weeping fig had cheered up under the housekeeper's ministrations. Even the pencils were sharp, next to the crisp white blocks of embossed notepaper. As we took our seats and everybody turned to me, waiting for me to speak, I thought, not for the last time: this *must* be the best job in the world . . . now what do I say?

*E*very five or six weeks a note would come from the Princess suggesting that it might be time for another "A Team" lunch. This was her way of thanking her male staff—me—and her policemen for the ordeals we endured in looking after her.

We were the "A Team," while her husband's staff were, inevitably, the "B Team." This fairly harmless piece of morale-boosting was the Princess's own idea, dating back to a time when she really felt she had hardly any representation in what was from the outset an office overwhelmingly designed to cater for the Prince's needs. By 1991, however, such childish fun was beginning to grate and the use of the terms "A Team"/"B Team" was officially discouraged—a sure sign, we felt, that they were more appropriate than ever.

Once I had become her private secretary, the new equerry was included in the lunches, and occasionally a secretary or lady-in-waiting. To keep up the cozy image of the Princess and "her boys," she classified any additional female guests as honorary men for the occasion.

This seems a good moment to pay a brief tribute to the Princess's policemen, or personal protection officers to give them their proper name. During my years with the Princess I must have worked closely with about a dozen of them. Four senior PPOs worked weekly shifts with her, supported by backup teams of varying sizes. Their professional roots lay in the Metropolitan Police, from which they were chosen through aptitude and ability for royalty and diplomatic protection duties. As well as being seasoned by years of policing the capital, they also underwent innumerable courses, including training with the Special Air Service.

These men, and occasionally women, were a breed apart. From my faltering first steps in England to what I hoped was the practiced professionalism of our later recces around the world, they gave me support, friendship, and invaluable advice. Their generosity in this and so many other ways was matched only by the consummate assurance with which they carried out their duties, one of which—though we never discussed it—was to take any bullet intended for their vulnerable charge. They were loyal, discreet, wise, and brave, and I never fathomed the Princess's eventual desire to cast aside their protection, let alone replace it with the well-meaning amateurishness of hired substitutes.

Our occasional "A Team" lunches were a chance to provide an all-male escort for the world's most famous lady-who-lunched in any one of London's top restaurants that we cared to choose. You might therefore imagine that I was the most enthusiastic of her guests—and you would be right, but only just. It was always a pretty contented crew who settled down at the bar of Tante Claire, Bibendum, Cecconi, or Clarke's, or any of a dozen other favored establishments.

We usually timed it so that we had some flying speed under our belts before the Princess's car swept up to the curb. She was always at her best in exclusively male company and I think her pleasure was heightened by the knowledge that, unlike so many of the meals she took either as part of her public duties or in pursuit of her convoluted pri-

vate friendships, this was one where the company was genuinely grateful, genuinely discreet, and for whom she had to
pretend to be nothing more than their boss.

Of course, none of us was foolish enough to believe that
just because we were all off-duty, so was the critical royal
eye. Playing a starring part in an "A Team" lunch one week
was no guarantee against summary ostracism and even enforced resignation the next. Nevertheless, we all entered
into the spirit of the thing and traded gossip and dirty jokes
at a pace that even her customary lunching companions
might have envied.

Her car would return promptly at 2:30 and she would
make a scene-stealing exit, accompanied by the hapless duty
policeman who, being armed, had not joined in our plun-
dering of the upper reaches of the wine list. Their departure
was the signal for waistbands to be eased, ties loosened, and
serious demands placed on the restaurant's supplies of co-
gnac and cigars.

I usually left them to it after a while, in order to be back
at my desk before the inevitable phone call from Kensington Palace. She would almost always check to find out how
long we had stayed after her departure. If it was too long—
and there was no reliable way of measuring it—she would
feel exploited and resentful. This was the flip side of much
of her generosity. At least it had the benefit of making me
sober up pretty quickly after any lunchtime excess. It also
gave me a chance to write our joint thank-you letter, which
custom demanded ought to land on her desk before the
Chablis had even finished working its way into the blood-
stream. It was for this reason that I usually wrote the letter
with a steady hand some hours before the lunch took place.
Luckily, I also remembered not to put it in the midday Bag.

We were an increasingly foreign body at St. James's
Palace and from time to time the host organism would try

to expel us. I knew, however, that for her office to retreat to
the cozy security of Kensington Palace would condemn the
Princess to being sidelined from the great debates that were
soon to ensue between St. James's and Buckingham Palace
about the future of the Waleses. It would enable us to be
dismissed and the world to be given the impression that we
had gone away to occupy ourselves with trivial things in a
peripheral palace. This objective was only finally achieved
after my resignation—with, I believe, the consequences I
had predicted.

Staying at St. James's Palace also enabled me to keep an
eye on the internal politics of the Prince's office. I was
aware that during my period of banishment the Princess
had recruited an ally in the Prince's camp. To my chagrin, as
I mentioned earlier, she had enlisted the help of his deputy
private secretary, Peter Westmacott, in drafting one of her
more important speeches. Creating this channel of communication, so attractively illicit in nature, seemed to satisfy
one of the Princess's major enthusiasms, which was to
spread her affections and sow mistrust as widely as she
could. Both at St. James's and later, when he had been
posted to the Embassy at Washington, I believe Peter performed many valuable services for the Princess. He did me
a big favor too, by teaching me the futility of taking the bait
of jealousy, which she was apt to dangle in front of any
whom she thought dependent on her benign disposition.

The opening salvo in a war of media briefings was fired
by Andrew Morton in the *Sunday Times* in May 1991. In an
article which, among other things, praised the professional
diplomats who were saddled with the impossible task of
serving the Prince, Morton castigated the heir as unfeeling,
hypocritical, self-indulgent, and a danger to the future of
the monarchy. To my eyes, the article read very much like
the Princess on her favorite subject.

The furor over Prince William's head injury from a golf
club stirred up the war of words in June. Not long after
that, at the beginning of July, the Prince's camp hit back

with a front-page story in the *Daily Mail* headed CHARLES
AND DIANA: CAUSE FOR CONCERN, in which Nigel Dempster wrote at length, attacking the Princess's alleged petulance and ingratitude over the Prince's plans to mark her
thirtieth birthday. It was a naked example of briefing by
"friends," elevated by its portentous headline to the point
where national concern over the Waleses' marriage and
who was to blame for its failure appeared quite legitimate.

I think this was the first time that the two armies came
truly into the open. Its significance for me was not that the
marriage of the Prince and Princess was in trouble. I had
known *that* practically since I had joined. To me, it was far
more important to realize that the issues at stake were
whose fault it would be when it happened and what would
be done with the Princess after it had happened. It was also
vital to appreciate that, whatever means the Princess might
find to put her case, the Prince's "friends" would not hesitate to return her fire tenfold. In addition, without being
unduly concerned with scruples ourselves, the hostility of
their intentions demonstrated a depressing ability to overlook the moral responsibilities of the office they were
loudly seeking to defend.

Another indication that the gloves were coming off in
what was still at that stage merely the skirmish of the
Waleses had come with a schedule clash slightly earlier in
the summer. The Princess was due to attend a combined
National AIDS Trust and National Children's Bureau conference. The invitation, once accepted, was subsequently
upgraded to include a request that the Princess should also
address the conference. Her reaction was enthusiastic. She
was getting the hang of speechmaking and enjoyed the impact she was able to create, which far exceeded anything she
achieved by just turning up and being photographed.

In passing on the request I also warned her that the
Prince was due to make a major speech on the same day.
Strictly speaking he took precedence, mainly because he
had accepted an invitation to speak before she had. To make

speeches on the same day would be seen by the media at
best as poor coordination between the Waleses' offices. At
worst it would look like a deliberate act of rivalry, of the
kind on which Andrew Morton was so soon to capitalize in
his *Sunday Times* article.

My reservations carried no weight with her—indeed,
they seemed only to reinforce the *froideur* that still existed
between us at that time. I got on with writing the speech, a
task that occupied most of my Easter holidays. The media
explosion duly came, but its main victim, I regret, was the
hapless Christopher Airy, who was accused of poor schedule
coordination. In terms of public impact there was really no
contest. In a competition between AIDS and standards of
English in schools, AIDS was always going to win the battle
for column inches.

By this stage the Prince and Princess were conducting
almost separate existences as independent stars of the royal
stage. Competition—never acknowledged as such—increasingly affected their dealings with each other. That clash
of speeches was just one example among many. The old
routines of office life continued as in the days of innocence,
at least in part, at least for a while longer, but we labored
under a growing realization that our increasingly unjoint
household was no longer coping with the demands of our
two diverging bosses.

The engagements calendar was always a minefield. Every
six months the small mountain of invitations that had been
sent in from around the country and around the world were
processed by the Prince's and Princess's staffs—filtered, as-
sessed, studied with jaundiced eyes, and, in the great majority of cases, politely rejected. The few that made it through
the filtering process, maybe one in ten, found their way into
the draft programs prepared by the private secretaries for
consideration at the twice-yearly program planning meeting.

By the time I arrived at St. James's the PGM meetings, as
they were known (nobody quite knew what the initials

stood for), had become bloated gatherings of close courtiers and other hangers-on, all anxious to be seen to be involved in what were recognized as the most important strategic planning sessions of the year. I imagined that the routine had begun originally with the young Prince and a few close advisers sorting out how he wanted his life to be for the next six months. Now in his forties, the Prince came into the room where the PGM was held and saw more than twenty people waiting for him, including his polo manager, his press secretary, his senior policeman, and all his senior office staff—and his wife with her staff of two, a private secretary and an equerry. With the Prince and Princess sitting opposite each other in the middle of a long table, flanked by these unequal teams of support staff, an agonized progress through the coming year's proposed appointment calendar was conducted under the baton of the Prince's private secretary.

From 1990 I was responsible for the Princess's input to these meetings and by then I had had plenty of opportunity to work out that they were not suitable occasions for reaching any conclusions about anything at all. In the week leading up to each meeting I therefore sat up late at night, surrounded by piles of files, scribbling draft programs in the smart, blank appointment diary pages that we used in the Palace.

To a tinkering bureaucrat such as myself, this was both an onerous chore and a bit of a hobby. I would take whole suitcases of files home in the evening or away for the weekend and, through a process of osmosis and intuition mixed with a semiscientific analysis of the Princess's likely preferences, I hashed out a series of draft programs from which she could choose. In my mind's eye the heaps of widely varied invitations represented a stampeding herd of cattle that I somehow had to transform into the neat little tins of corned beef that I served up as part of a persuasively typed proposed program.

Every six months I tuned my own mechanism for the

production process and every couple of years I reinvented it completely. I tried to be ultrademocratic, sharing royal favors equally between the patronages that had first claim on her time. I studied county maps of the United Kingdom and tried to ensure an even geographical spread for her appearances. Then I filled in the gaps with interesting-looking daytime engagements in London. The whole tapestry was woven around the great fixed state events such as the Queen's Birthday Parade, the garden parties, Armistice Day, and Ascot. Space also had to be allowed for overseas tours, although dates for these were seldom available at the time of the program meeting, which made for extra planning work (a crystal ball was handy too).

With our business thus pretty much done and dusted before the meeting even began, the Princess was able to look forward to it as a kind of entertainment in which her husband's staff were nervously put through their hoops as they pitched for their own slice of his overcrowded calendar. His staff were divided into separate portfolios—industry, architecture, art, and music, etc.—and there was therefore a degree of competition between the assistant private secretaries to gain the right level of prominence for their own subjects.

The Prince's private secretary refereed the contest, but had a much more difficult task than I had. No matter how much preparatory work his staff had done, the Prince never really seemed to focus on his forthcoming calendar until the day of the meeting and even then, it sometimes seemed, only intermittently, especially if the weather was nice and there was a view of the garden through an open window.

On one occasion the meeting was being held in his ground-floor office in St. James's Palace. Not untypically, the Prince jumped up and announced that he was going to open a window. He had failed to notice that the shadow of a large tour bus had fallen onto the net curtains and as he opened the window he was confronted, at a distance of no more than four feet, by fifty camera-wielding Japanese tourists disembarking from the bus. Their look of frozen disbelief at seeing what they must have thought was some sort of hallucination was a treat to behold.

The meeting could be a cause of considerable tension, especially as stresses between the Prince and Princess became more obvious. With most of our own planning done and nothing to do but spectate while the Prince's staff made their carefully prepared proposals, the Princess frequently became bored. She would sometimes lighten the moment with scribbled, irreverent notes that she surreptitiously passed to me, *sotto voce* asides to those next to her, or ill-suppressed giggles.

The Prince bore any irritation at these distractions patiently, even when, tiring of notes and whispers, she started to intervene in the deliberations about his calendar. Her contributions were usually astute and reflected her own instinctive knowledge of what would please the public. Once or twice she crisply urged him to cut through Palace red tape to resolve a problem of coordination with other households by making a direct personal call to the Queen—which he did, there and then. Apart from these rare interventions, however, she would sit and fidget while the process ground interminably on. Tension would rise as the few joint engagements were discussed and I could see the apprehension in the eyes of the Prince's staff, watching her as one might watch a temperamental animal whose next move—whether to snarl or purr—was quite unpredictable.

There were, of course, several opportunities for silent, internal amusement, perhaps the best being when the Prince inquired about the state of progress with a program for a complicated overseas tour. All eyes turned to the equerry whose unenviable task it often was to pick up this sort of loose ball.

The imperturbable Commander in question probably had an IQ greater than the combined total of all others in the room. He looked at the Prince unblinkingly and said, "It's inchoate, Sir."

There was a general knitting of brows, including those of the Prince, but only for a moment. "Right," said His Royal

Highness. A pause followed while we all cleared our throats
and thanked God for an equerry who had swallowed a dictionary.

Momentarily flustered, the hapless private secretary—
Christopher Airy at that time—then marched confidently
onto some very thin ice. As he occasionally did, the Prince
was now rhetorically asking his unfeeling staff and the
world beyond why he was yet again obliged to attend some
state occasion. Oblivious of the danger, Christopher informed him that it was "his duty."

The Prince stiffened and there was a perceptible intake
of breath around the table. "Oh *is* it?" he asked, with heavy
sarcasm. Christopher could only nod. Duty was sacred to
him and no doubt it seemed incomprehensible that it could
be a subject for debate. The rest of the meeting passed in the
sudden, pervasive chill of royal displeasure. Even the
Princess had lost the urge to giggle.

There were many differing interpretations of the notion
of duty on view at the Palace. My own institutionalized upbringing and natural sense of deference let me see as duty
almost anything rather joyless but grimly necessary. (Any
joy that was encountered unexpectedly in the process could
be part of the duty as well, of course.) At first, this aligned
me with traditional thinking at the Palace. Duty was what
we did, and the simpler the better.

By contrast, the Princess's view of duty was anything but
simple. The concept appealed to her in that it provided a
sense of abstract sacrifice as she endured the trials of her
daily life. It gave to mundane public events at least an appearance of higher purpose.

The label of duty was thus applied pretty indiscriminately. As time went on, I found myself faced with two uncomfortable truths. The first was the discovery that it was
fatal to introduce the word "duty" to a royal ear if there was
any suggestion that its owner did not understand the subject
better than you ever would. Duty was what we did. Duty
was what they *lived*.

The second discovery gave my conscience an occasional tweak. Most of the time, most of what I did for the Princess had a simple moral value that made it a natural companion for my own rather overdeveloped sense of duty. Her public life symbolized all the virtues applicable to a socially concerned young mother—and a few more besides—so, by association, I received regular injections of moral certainty about what I was doing. This was deeply comforting to one of my rather Calvinist upbringing, but it did not really withstand a rigorous moral audit. Our royal family stands for many good things, but, with rare exceptions, working for it is not a soul-enriching vocation. At least, it was not for me, and I was perhaps less coy than others about admitting its many moments of pleasure.

As the program planning meetings grew more edgy, an increasingly contentious undercurrent was the involvement of William and Harry in public engagements. Their theoretical potential as pawns in the Waleses' game of rivalry was loudly decried on all sides, but it did not stop it happening.

The Prince was perhaps slow to recognize the value of being seen to be introducing the boys onto the public stage—or, more likely, he jealously guarded their privacy. His wife, on the other hand, suffered few such inhibitions, quite reasonably holding the view that their education in their future duties—particularly on matters of social concern such as homelessness—could not start soon enough. If in the process she could also be seen to be modernizing the whole task of educating royal Princes in their often unenviable role, then that was fine by her.

When I joined the Princess, both young Princes were less than seven years old. They and their organization were collectively known as "the nursery." It was almost a court in its own right. There were bedrooms, playrooms, a kitchen, and a dining room snug under the eaves of KP. There were full-time and part-time nannies, policemen, a shared driver, and a separate routine of school runs, parties, shopping, and trips to the cinema. Every Friday morning almost the whole apparatus would transport itself a hundred miles to the west, to spend the weekend at Highgrove in Gloucestershire. There a duplicate set of rooms awaited, together with all the attractions and diversions of life on a small, picture-postcard country estate.

This self-contained routine needed little interference from new and junior courtiers and I saw little of William and Harry at that time, except for chance encounters in KP. That suited me. Noisy small boys—which these certainly were—were an alien species to me, at least since the time I had been one myself. These ones were third and fourth in line to the throne and so were, at least potentially, to be revered and feared accordingly. Nevertheless, their day-to-day status was that of children first and royalty second.

My aversion to addressing anyone as "Sir," let alone "Your Royal Highness," at least until they were old enough to shave, seemed to put me in tune with accepted practice. Others were understandably less certain. I will not forget in a hurry the distinguished, but perhaps overpunctilious cavalry Colonel who bowed low in front of Prince Harry and greeted him with a ringing military "Sir!" The look of bemused delight on the three-year-old Prince's face almost made him fall off his tricycle.

Given that they were still so young, and given her frequently expressed wish to be in control of their care, the Princess naturally assumed priority in parental dealings with "my boys," as she called them. In that, she was just like most mothers. In the same quite unexceptional way, her husband's work commitments and disposition perhaps aligned him with the many fathers who are content to let the mother's influence take precedence, in the early years at least.

In common with most aristocratic English families, the Waleses' contact with their children was primarily social rather than a necessity. Every normal chore of parenthood, from laundry, cooking, and housework to transport, educa-

Mercy Dash—visiting a friend dying of AIDS, August 1991.

"If the cap fits . . ."—
Pakistan tour.

Captain James Hewitt.

Returning to England for her father's funeral, March 1992.

"The eye of the storm"—separation day, December 9, 1992.

Queen and future queen at Buckingham Palace,
November 1993.

"Time and Space"—
Grosvenor House,
December 3, 1993.

Will "Captain" Carling.

Risky pursuit—unguarded in Beauchamp Place.

"Good-bye to all that"—with Henry Kissinger and
Colin Powell, New York, December 1995.

tion, security, and finance, was taken care of by others. Had she so wished, the Princess could have opted to be far less involved in the practicalities of motherhood—yet she was not averse to the extensive domestic organization taking the strain when public duty or private convenience intervened.

This option being available, and quite normal in her experience, she can hardly be criticized for taking it. Nonetheless, it does add a degree of balance to the popular image of idealized motherhood that has grown up around her. This was an image she was happy to encourage, of course, with well-timed photo coups such as the Alton Towers water splash or the much publicized reunion with her sons on the upper deck of *Britannia* in Canada. Less visible that day, but no less sincere, was their father's greeting, which followed in private. Equally shielded from intruding eyes has been all the time he has spent with them on outdoor pursuits on the royal estates.

From these few observations I was already able to draw some inferences about the Princess's relationship with her sons. Her affection for them was unmistakable. She was warm, expressive, and tactile. Very obviously, she wanted neither her boys nor anybody else to be in any doubt about her love for them. If this determination was sometimes expressed overenthusiastically, that was usually because they gave her so much to be enthusiastic about. It may also have been because she did not want them to suffer through any lack of visibly expressed love.

Less often, it was also designed to assert a publicly recognized degree of ownership. Her position as an ineradicable part of the Windsor line was now a genetic fact. Unfortunately, she perceived that this obvious truth was unwelcome to some. It was no secret toward the end of her life that reactionary elements in the royal establishment were questioning her desirability as a mentor in the art of kingship. It was therefore small wonder that she sometimes saw a valuable role for her sons as the living, breathing proof of her suitability to raise Princes. She certainly felt she had little to learn on the subject from recent history.

*E*venings away from her children were usually taken up with work. Throughout this period of change and jostling for position, the Princess's patronage of the arts was growing. Night after night I would accompany her to Covent Garden, the Albert Hall, Sadler's Wells, the Coliseum, the Barbican, and a dozen other venues as she carried out her duties as a conscientious patron of a whole variety of artistic organizations.

Quite apart from their cultural attractions, such occasions were always a great excuse for putting on the grandest style—the jewelry, the latest dress—and playing to perfection the role of glamorous Princess out on the town, eclipsing any glitterati who had also ventured out that night. Conveniently, most of the performances the Princess attended were also in aid of one or other of her charities, so there was a reassuring element of selfless dedication to good causes to leaven the general air of self-indulgence.

Stars came to bathe in her reflected light and, it is true, she bathed in theirs. Her initial attitude when meeting top-division celebrities was exaggeratedly calm, as if encountering a rival or competitor. This would be rapidly replaced by coquettish banter once mutual recognition of each other's rarefied status had been exchanged.

Such was her own, innate star quality that she had little difficulty establishing her ascendancy. For one thing, many of those she met were men and therefore easy prey. For another, her stardom—unlike most of theirs—had not been grafted on by Hollywood publicity machines, a process that often left exposed the uncertain actor beneath the on-screen image. And for another, she was so much taller than most of them.

This happy fact was hard to miss, especially when she

met Michael Douglas at the premiere of *Wall Street*. "Patrick! Did you notice—his trousers were six inches too long!"

Others were more royal than royalty. Barbra Streisand would only be photographed with the Princess if the cameras had a shot of her left—or was it her right?—profile. "All through the film she kept asking me if I liked it..."

Some stars just made her feel at ease. Elton John and Liza Minnelli were particular favorites. "They understand what it's like to be famous. They just accept me." Clint Eastwood was another. After the premiere of *The Fugitive*, he hosted a private supper party at the Savoy. "A girl's dream date," she said, and spent a rapt evening basking in his reserved charm—and his height.

Clint Eastwood later shared her thorough approval with Tom Hanks, and probably for similar reasons. Hanks appeared at a special preview screening of *Apollo XIII* in aid of Turning Point and, unusually, gave a short speech in support of the work of the charity, about which he had taken the trouble to acquaint himself. This earned him high marks in her book, to which he added at the subsequent dinner in the Greenhouse by revealing himself to be as modest as he was talented. Surrounded so often by people who forgot their modesty in her presence—if they ever had any to forget—she found this especially attractive.

One evening she attended a royal gala preview performance of *Bits and Pieces* by Wayne Sleep. The Princess's love of dance is well known and she often reminded us that she would have liked to be a ballet dancer had she not grown so tall. This was a standing joke between herself and the diminutive Wayne. "And I've got *huge* feet!" she would complain, waving the offending extremities around as if to invite contradiction. The preview evening was full of exuberant fun, not least when the Princess went backstage afterward. In introducing the company, Wayne almost eclipsed the dramatic performance he had produced on stage. That engagement was a rare example of one where the Princess genuinely entered into the spirit of the performance she was seeing.

For her own pleasure in private she played the piano with enthusiasm, if without much technical brilliance, and the sounds of opera or great choral works were as likely to echo through the private apartments at KP as any offering by the pop groups she was popularly believed to love. I sat through enough evenings of worthy cultural activity to grow to laugh at the irony of portraying her as the disco-mad Princess while her husband was the solemn man of classical music. In my last year with her I calculated that he had actually attended more pop concerts than she had. This was not necessarily because he liked pop music more than she did, merely that she had such an aversion to the tabloid label of "Disco Di" that she would go to almost any lengths to prove it was obsolete.

As if she herself were a film star, when dealing with the Princess it was generally necessary to allow some latitude for the artistic temperament. The essential aim was to spot potential sources of royal displeasure and preempt the trouble by taking appropriate avoiding action.

This was my chance to forestall ominous remarks such as, "If I'd known the Duchess of X was going to be here I'd never have worn this dress," or, "Why didn't you tell me that man was going to be there?" or, worst of all, "I simply don't know why I had to visit that place/meet all those people/stand in front of the cameras for so long/get home so late..."

Allow such comments to accumulate, however charmingly delivered, and you knew you were dicing with disfavor. When that happened, it was always useful to be able to point out respectfully that all such questions had been answered in the briefing notes you had sent up in the Bag the previous night. In exceptional cases, however, even the black-and-white evidence of your foresight could be dismissed by a royal employer unwilling to change an opinion for the sake of a few facts.

With this ever-present danger in the back of my mind, I would always take great care over the briefing notes. I invariably asked for comprehensive briefing material from the host organizations, which I would then repackage into a familiar format—extensively rewritten if necessary—for the Princess to study the evening before the engagement.

Assembling the briefing and extracting the important bits for a covering *aide-mémoire* was an art that developed with practice. If I could find any to put in, jokes were always a welcome addition and helped prolong the sometimes fleeting royal attention span. "On YRH's right at lunch will be Minister X. As you may have noticed (press clipping attached) he's in a spot of bother at the moment, so better not talk about actresses...unless you really want to, of course." I lived in daily dread of such a scurrilous—and often libelous—document falling into the wrong hands.

The risk was slight, as it happened. The Princess was usually very security conscious and took care to keep such sensitive documents safely stuffed in her handbag or handed them to me to carry. When one day, uncharacteristically, she did leave a wad of this typewritten dynamite in the seat pocket of an airliner, it took the combined efforts of three police forces and the air traffic control staff to get it retrieved from the flight, which was preparing to take a full load of passengers back to London. Quite properly, everybody—including me—agreed that it was my fault.

Genuine innocence counted for little when guilt could be sprayed casually at you like hair lacquer. Then you were in real trouble. As you suffered your punishment (usually an icy ostracism, but it could get worse) you could silently rail at the injustice of a system that did not even have a higher authority to whom you could appeal. Royal infallibility was just a medieval myth, of course, but only when they admitted it first. After all, who was going to tell the glamorous

Princess with the world at her feet that she had got it wrong?

The star image was inescapable. She may not consciously have invited it, but having been invested with it by the public, she slipped effortlessly into its world of distorted values and perspectives. For one thing, it underlined how different she was from her in-laws, some of whom—notably her husband—actively courted celebrities when it suited them. The difference was, she outshone them all, as anyone who saw her in the company of supermodels would testify.

As supermodels would certainly appreciate, no star image is complete without a collection of stunning photographs, and the Princess gave increasing consideration to hers. Not long after I became her private secretary, I found myself arranging a formal photo shoot.

I have already described the importance attached to the gifts that were handed out at the end of overseas tours. Usually these were portrait photographs, signed and dated in the royal hand and issued in one of three sizes, depending on the perceived importance of the recipient. In Ambassadors' residences, administrative offices, and private homes all over the world, collections of these prized objects were accumulated on pianos and mantelpieces, to draw discreet gasps of admiration from impressionable visitors—or discreet winces, as the case may be.

The Princess also presented such photographs to commanding officers of her affiliated Armed Forces units when they moved on to new appointments, to retiring directors of her charities when they called to take their leave, and, on a fairly random basis, to almost anyone who incurred her gratitude or admiration or whom she thought might be an influential recruit. The same applied to other objects in her small range of gifts, including her distinctive blue cuff links that can even now be seen decorating important wrists in corridors of power all over the world.

As far as her employees were concerned, these gifts only made an appearance when it was time to take our leave. No matter how acrimonious the parting, or its cause, the convention was that with a photograph of herself, a set of cuff links, or even a briefcase in especially favored farewells, all debts were paid and bygones would be bygones. The expression "You nearly had your cuff links there, mate" was our equivalent of the civilian employee being threatened with his walking papers.

The portrait photographs had to be changed on a regular basis because, in addition to the above uses, they were also available for purchase (not as gifts, note) to charities and other organizations that the Princess favored with a visit. Almost as a condition of departure the Princess had to sign one of these photographs, together with a visitors' book, before she could leave any building she had been inspecting.

Someone as conscious of her image as the Princess took very great care over the selection of photographer, and equally close and critical interest in the results of their time together. Snowdon, Demarchelier, Donovan, Moore, and a handful of others all had their turn at composing the ultimate portrait of the world's most photographed woman. Some succeeded better than others but none, I felt, as well as the unposed shots snapped by news photographers during day-to-day engagements.

As time went by, the process became more sophisticated and before long, what had been quite brief sessions had acquired all the accoutrements of a full-blown fashion shoot. Hairdressers, makeup women, lighting technicians—all had a part to play, as well as the master lensman himself and, of course, all the resources of a professional studio. A whole day had to be allocated for this exacting process, and why not? The results went on to give enormous pleasure to Ambassadors, charity workers, and media-hyped child-heroes around the world. As she would probably have been the first to admit, the whole business also gave the Princess a lot of fun. She was so often described by her critics as a brainless clotheshorse, obsessed with her appearance and the contents of her wardrobe, and here at last was a day when she *could* play at being the dumb fashion model of their sniping remarks.

She was very democratic about making the final decisions. Within a few days of the shoot, large boxes of contact sheets would be delivered to KP for her perusal and usually within the hour they arrived in the office, so the women could share in the enjoyable task of picking out the three or four winners that would go on to be our standard portrait shots.

The only snag was that, as time passed, one or two of the selected few would fall into disfavor. There was always a fair chance that the portrait I had so presciently slipped into my briefcase, so that she could make the all-important spontaneous presentation when the mood took her, would be one of those she had grown to detest. Disposing of these rejects kept the office incinerator busy for some time.

Unless they really offended her, portrait photographers usually remained in the Princess's good books. In the case of someone like Patrick Demarchelier, the favor was extended as she gave him permission to reproduce her pictures in his arty photo books. The chemistry they created produced some of the most inspired images ever taken of her.

Not so lucky, however, were most of the royal portrait painters. For them there was no exciting wardrobe selection, or experiments with makeup, wind machines, or lighting. All they demanded was a regal background, clothes to match the image they had in mind, patience, immobility, and enormous amounts of time. It was not always a winning combination as far as the Princess was concerned.

The results were for others to judge, but I thought some captured certain aspects of her complex personality quite well. Perhaps most notable was Nelson Shanks's 1995 portrait of a woman pausing at the door of some unknown destiny. It is tempting to conclude that the photographer, working fast, inevitably found sympathy for someone so immediately pleasing to the lens. The artist, on the other hand, with a protracted mission to capture the inner person, had a more demanding task and in pursuing it might too often have stumbled on royal defenses and shortcomings hidden from the less penetrating eye.

12

❧

Sphinx

Nelson Shanks's image of unknown destiny was still three years in the future. At the beginning of 1992 no such doubt, theoretically, existed about the Princess's long-term role. It was still possible to believe that the Prince and Princess of Wales could reach an accommodation that would enable the public appearance of togetherness to be maintained.

After all, we had by now amicably arranged the separation of their offices and they themselves had fallen into a routine that saw the Prince spend as much time as possible at Highgrove and the Princess do the same at Kensington Palace. Although KP was surprisingly small, a bit of clever internal redesign—with the cooperation of their neighbors—could even have enabled them to carry on under the same roof a life of public respectability and private acceptance of each other's need for time apart.

It was not to be. The story of the year is one of inexorable decline from the relatively optimistic pragmatism of its opening to the open bloodshed and separation which marked its end. This was the *annus horribilis*.

My own observation was that the Prince had in fact arranged his life so that it would have been relatively easy to create the rather worldly but realistic arrangement I have described above. It was, after all, one to which his ancestors had been accustomed, and many wives—particularly those of a certain English tradition—might have taken the opportunity to devote themselves to the children and public good works as a substitute for cozy domesticity, if not with gratitude then at least with public stoicism. Such an arrangement would also have allowed both partners the benefit of a blind eye being turned to any extramarital affairs, if that was their wish.

For a number of reasons, the Princess did not conform with this pattern. At one level she was still the idealistic girl, still in love with the idea of being in love and at times still seeming desperately anxious to preserve the appearance of stability that even a dysfunctional marriage could allow. Also, not least due to her work as patron of Relate, she had a keen appreciation of the effects such a separation would have on the children.

In addition she found it irresistible to play the wronged wife. As I often saw, however, her lines lacked conviction. "Really, my husband's just a child. Honestly, it's as if I had *three* boys..." Acting out this role set up a particularly confusing internal conflict for her as she contemplated the reality of her affair with James Hewitt. To surrender the moral high ground was bad enough, but to surrender it for a love that failed was intolerable. She was suffering the guilt of having had an affair, but, unlike her husband, she no longer had the object of her affections to console her.

What usually came out on top was her sense of having suffered a cruel injustice. This was particularly easy to sustain while the public remained ignorant of her own transgressions, but her favored role of innocent victim was at daily risk of exposure and this put her under enormous pressure. After "Squidgygate" and various other salacious revelations, that sense of injustice grew.

She knew that the royal family was not a byword for marital virtue, yet she felt she was being singled out and pilloried for having made her own small bid for happiness. She frequently made claims about her in-laws' romantic activities that I chose to take with a pinch of salt. In any case, the stories lost their impact when repeated several times with added embellishments. The more lurid they became, the more bitter I knew she was feeling about what she saw as others' invulnerability to the sort of media scrutiny she increasingly faced.

There was also a strong streak of stubbornness in her that would have opposed on principle anything the Prince suggested. Finally, it was beginning to dawn on her that, however much the Prince and his supporters might try to intimidate her—which they did—she still had some powerful cards to play. Her aces were her children, her media value, her public image of caring good works, and the great groundswell of opinion that held that she was more sinned against than sinning. As the year progressed and the marital battle lines were drawn up, she was canny enough to delay showing her hand until her opponents, in frustration and overconfidence, had revealed theirs.

After the skirmishes of 1991, 1992 saw battle joined. It was a battle in which the Prince's legions, though numerically superior, became bogged down in a swamp of self-righteousness. They were encumbered with prejudice and self-importance and would have liked to extricate themselves by appropriating the Crown's authority. The Crown, however, remained obstinately aloof from the fray. Throughout the separation—as the Prince's lawyers tried to limit the Princess's independence, as his "friends" briefed the press against her, and as his staff grew more condescending toward us—the Queen's office stayed resolutely impartial. The Prince was an unwilling leader of such supporters. He repeatedly let it be known through Richard Aylard that they acted without his consent, although it did seem that he was able to turn a blind eye to many of the attacks made on the Princess on his behalf.

Against such an enemy the Princess was styled in my mind like Boadicea—flawed but imperious; lightly armed and outnumbered, but able to strike without warning when opportunity offered and then melt into the thick cover provided by press popularity. Even then I knew that, however many battles we might win, we would be sure to lose the war in the end. Yet one look at the forces being deployed against the Princess in her doomed bid for independence made me happy to align myself with the revolutionaries.

For all the squandered chances, the self-indulgence, the stupidity, and the occasional downright wickedness, there was something heroic about her, just as there was something essentially brutal and intolerant about those gathered against her. For me she represented a feminine vulnerability combined with a dogged determination to survive against whatever odds she faced and, although I was well aware that neither side could claim a monopoly of virtue, that made it an easy decision to throw myself into the fray in support of her. To this I could add my romantic belief that history always had room for valiant last stands, whatever the strategic folly that had landed the heroic few in such trouble in the first place.

If this all sounds rather overprincipled, then it probably was, but I had a vague idea that the monarchy was supposed to be all about principle anyway, that its main function was to represent certain core national values. Essentially I saw these as something to do with the strong protecting the weak, natural justice outweighing blind precedent, and humility getting more than a passing nod along the way. I saw more of these values—just—around the Princess than I did around her husband. I felt she had not received protection from those from whom she could have expected it. I observed that attempts to restrict her activities were at odds with her obvious ability to do a good job for the monarchy when suitably encouraged. I also saw a surprisingly honest humility in her attempts to discover her role that was lacking in the high-handedness of her detractors, most of whom should have known better. It was as simple as that.

Two other factors influenced my decision and contributed to the freedom I felt from any serious doubt about my course of action. The first was my belief that the concepts of monarchy which I so high-mindedly saw in the Princess were still best embodied in her mother-in-law the Queen. This was a belief I was happy to see that I shared with the Princess, who in all the disintegration that was to follow I never heard refer to the Queen in anything other than respectful terms. "The Top Lady has to put up with such a lot," she said to me more than once, "and she always tries to be helpful."

This was crucially important to me. If I had felt that my first loyalty to the Queen was jeopardized by my second loyalty to the Princess, I could not have done what I did. It was only when those two loyalties became irreconcilable toward the end of 1995 that I realized I would have to go. In 1992, however, it was a source of constant encouragement to me to find that the Queen and her office remained true to my concept of the principles of monarchy—just as it strengthened my resolution to find those principles being kidnapped as camouflage for those who plotted against the Princess on behalf of the Prince.

The second factor was even simpler. Although I did feel that the Princess represented a cause for which I was prepared to crusade, it was also true that at the time I had nowhere else to go. After the brush with resignation I had experienced the previous year, I had no wish to subject myself again to the horrible uncertainties I had felt then.

The forces the Princess was up against were most crudely exposed at the end of the *annus horribilis* when, in the course of negotiating a separation agreement from her husband, attempts were made to limit her access to the very royal infrastructure that enabled her to do the job expected of her by the public. These were accompanied by attempts to downgrade her status as a royal individual in her own right. Frustrating such moves became for me practically a pleasure. The hypocrisy and injustice from which they sprang ultimately provided all the motivation I needed to crusade under the Princess's banner.

*T*he first major event of the year, a joint tour of India, provided a microcosm of what was to come. The Prince did what was expected of him and what he did so well, promoting British exports, the work of the British Council, and the environmental and health issues that meant so much to him. The Princess meanwhile launched a daring guerrilla raid on the Taj Mahal and captured it and the world's hearts just by sitting down and being photographed in front of it. She then underlined her victory by maneuvering just as skillfully to avoid the kiss her husband aimed at her cheek when receiving a polo trophy from her.

I did not accompany the Prince and Princess on this tour. By now my boss had in David Barton an experienced and efficient equerry, while the Prince had his own strong team. I learned enough on the phone, however, to realize that this tour had plumbed new depths of animosity behind the scenes as well as on the public stage.

The Princess responded to her own unhappiness by projecting it onto her luckless team, who experienced her wintry side under the blazing Indian sun. Between photo calls, including the first of many emotive shots with Mother Teresa, she fell into a familiar pattern of looking for, and inevitably discovering, things with which to find fault, while icily rebuffing her loyal staff's attempts to show their support. The lady-in-waiting for the tour, Laura Lonsdale, was still new in the job and, from all I could gather, earned every penny of her dress allowance.

I remained in London, taking maximum advantage of the breathing space the Princess's absence always created. It was a chance to recce in peace and to take rather longer lunches than usual, in the fairly certain knowledge that the pager that I wore like an electronically tagged suspect would not suddenly start bleeping in a way that I came to dread. Even so, by her usual sixth sense, I always felt my boss was convinced that while she had been away the mice had been behaving like rats.

Nothing could have been farther from the truth. In fact, by staying in London I found myself well placed to observe an ominous new development. As a beleaguered town might notice with foreboding the progression in incoming bombardment from long-range bombing to close-range artillery, so we noticed the involvement of the Prince's lawyers as a sign that the enemy was no longer distant but had advanced to within visual range.

The Prince's advisers were already anticipating the legal battles that would lie ahead as separation loomed. In what I interpreted as an attempt to overawe the Princess's fledgling organization, Richard curtly advised me that they had already approached Lord Goodman, who, as a Law Lord of formidable years, reputation, and ferocity, might very credibly have been expected to blow any resistance out of the water by his very presence.

Forewarned is forearmed. In what was a foretaste of the type of tactics we would have to use, I took the opportunity through a friendly intermediary of calling on Lord Goodman in his flat. The ostensible reason was to discuss a possible commission for a portrait to be painted of the Princess, because among other things the good Lord was almost as eminent in the world of art as in the world of law. On this pretext I hoped to add some balance to whatever he had been told about the Princess and her office. This might at least make him a less reliable weapon for those who wanted to train him in her direction like a piece of heavy legal artillery.

During my visit I noticed a signed portrait photograph of the Duchess of York standing on a side table. "Oh yes," said Lord Goodman, "very unfortunate. I did give her some advice, but I'm afraid she didn't take it." He got rather unsteadily to his feet, padded across the room in his slippers, and removed the photograph with an air of finality. He politely gave me the impression that this was not symptomatic of a generally disapproving attitude to young royal wives. His references to the Princess at least suggested that he would not take at face value much of what he was hearing as briefing from "the other side." It was about all I could hope.

I duly reported my legal reconnaissance to the Princess. Then, on her instructions, I cast about for suitable divorce lawyers and found several who were unsurprisingly keen to take her on as a client. In the end she found her own in the genial figure of Paul Butner of Wright, Son and Pepper.

When I first spoke to him—inevitably on my mobile phone from a filling station on the A303—he was in Istanbul preparing to depart for his stag night with what sounded like the cast of a Turkish *Carmen* in the background. Seldom without a dangling cigarette in his hand or a look of world-weary tolerance on his benign features, the Princess found him an unlikely but ideal champion to set about the task of legal jousting with her opponents.

She quickly learned (others, to their cost, took longer) that his slightly crumpled appearance and absentminded manner were not to be mistaken for mental lethargy. A plain-talking divorcé with grown-up daughters, he had surprisingly little trouble in empathizing with her position as he cast an unruffled eye over the legal talent being assembled to oppose him. Any signs of overbearing pomposity on their part, and there were a few, very quickly inspired in him a natural defiance on his client's behalf and scant respect for those sent to intimidate him. His client's interests were what mattered to him most and let the constitutional niceties find their own place in the list of moral priorities.

We were thus as well prepared as we could be for the serious business of separation that finally erupted in the autumn. Meanwhile, Lord Goodman's remarks about the Duchess of York stuck in my mind. The incident reminded me, if I needed it, that the Princess's association with the Duchess was never to her advantage. The Princess was not unaware of the risk to her own reputation, but she had to play a difficult balancing act. She needed to remain close enough to the Duchess to be the recipient of confidences, while at the same time putting increasing distance between them in the public's eyes.

The Princess had realized that she was in danger of becoming a straw to which the drowning Duchess might try to cling. Once she realized that Fergie no longer had special access to the Queen—an access of which the Princess had always been suspicious anyway—and that she no longer had helpful Windsor family intelligence to relay, her mind was made up. In a pattern that was now all too familiar, she allowed the axe to fall on a friendship that had outlived its usefulness. It was, after all, a battle for the survival of the fittest, and the Princess's apparent unkindness displayed a brutal pragmatism that was to serve her well in many ways.

The Princess had good reason to be worried. The threat from people who might tar her with the same brush as the Duchess was a real one. In an article in the London *Evening Standard* in January 1992, Peter Mackay devoted three out of four columns to deploring the well-documented faux pas of the Duchess of York. He then included the Princess in his criticism, for no greater justification than that she had enjoyed a friendship with a man that was open to misunderstanding and had spent long periods apart from her husband.

While both facts were undeniably true, they created an understandable resentment in the Princess at a time when her husband's contribution to the strains in their marriage could still be disregarded by commentators on the grounds that their main purpose was to protect the monarchy. This sort of hypocrisy cut the Princess very deeply. At a time when her devotion to her public duties was becoming more and more irreproachable—always the best way to preempt criticism—to be castigated *en masse* with "the younger royals" (code for the daughters-in-law thought by many to be the source of all the royal family's troubles) fanned a flame of injustice deep inside her that was not going to be smothered by the crude tactics of exile so bluntly applied against her sister-in-law.

If she were in any doubt about how blunt these tactics could be, the Princess had only to consider the infamous briefing given by the Queen's press secretary to the BBC that January in which he revealed that "the knives are out" for the Duchess at Buckingham Palace. Although the Duchess could exercise considerable influence over the Princess, my boss's instinct for self-preservation was stronger. She cannily watched what happened to Fergie and resolved not to fall victim to Buckingham Palace's anger herself.

She realized that the best counter to criticism from that quarter was to establish a popularity with the public that would make it impossible for her opponents in the Palace to sideline her without putting their own reputations at risk. In the event, this did not deter some of them for whom misplaced loyalty to the Queen sanctioned distinctly ignoble tactics as they tried to rid the institution of a figure whose unpredictability they increasingly grew to mistrust.

Be that as it may, for the Princess the best tactic was undoubtedly more hard work. She was good at what she did, therefore her popularity grew. Although she was not averse to briefing selected journalists when it suited her, such a program of transparently diligent public service required no campaign of media manipulation on her part. Her activities spoke for themselves. Happily, I was successful in filling her calendar with engagements that were calculated not only to show her at her best but also at her most royal, and this frustrated even further those of her detractors who wanted to portray her as an empty-headed clotheshorse.

Contrary to the image some tried to create for her, she obstinately refused to go to pop concerts, be photographed leaving late-night restaurants, take a succession of freebie holidays, or generally live a life of flippant pleasure. Instead her life became increasingly constrained in private at this time—not just because of the limitations suffered by all famous people, but also because she imposed on herself a regime that would make it difficult for her detractors to write her off as an inconsequential, self-indulgent bimbo lucky enough to have ensnared the heir to the throne.

This became a continuing pattern for my remaining years with her. As her private life became more and more restrained, her public work became more important as the visible expression of her independent existence. This did not necessarily imply a higher degree of saintliness in her public good works—the sincerity of her actions was a matter of daily variation depending on the mood she was in, and she always had an eye to the next day's headlines. Her conscientious professionalism became even more pronounced, however, even when she scaled down her public engagements toward the end of 1993. She remained an unsurpassed royal performer even when her own doubts about her future role prejudiced any credible, long-term personal strategy.

In order to appeal to the public over the heads of the old establishment beginning to gather like predators around her, the Princess needed to look the part and feel good within herself. While she may have denied herself many other pleasures, therefore, she did not economize on her wardrobe or her grooming expenses (except, touchingly, certain types of makeup that she always bought from a standard Boots range). It was no surprise, either, that this period saw an acceleration in her keep-fit campaign. Nor, such were the times, was it a surprise to find that the costs involved were somehow leaked from the Prince's accounts.

*F*or the rest of the year the Princess carried out a pattern of engagements that put her in the royal spotlight as never before. March saw her returning to Hungary, this time for a solo visit in support of her patronage of the English National Ballet. She also paid a repeat visit to the world-renowned Peto Institute, where she had an emotional meeting with British families to whom the Institute offered practically the last hope for their crippled children.

As in Pakistan the year before, however, the really significant elements of her program lay in those parts of it that underlined her status as the mother of the future King and as a future Queen herself. Thus after the ballet she had a private supper with the President and his wife. The next morning she opened the new offices of the British Council, a task more normally associated with her husband. She called on the Prime Minister at the Hungarian Parliament building and she attended an export-boosting reception for British and Hungarian businessmen. Only then did she fly to a remote part of the country on the borders of war-worn Croatia, where she spent a harrowing couple of hours touring a refugee camp in freezing drizzle.

A welcome novelty on this trip, and the forerunner of a practice that was to become routine, was the Princess's decision to bring her elder sister Sarah along as lady-in-waiting. Unaccustomed to royal habits and procedures—a positive advantage—Sarah took a good-natured but questioning interest in the way we operated. It helped to protect us from creeping complacency, the occupational hazard of our trade. In addition, while she always showed a proper public deference toward her sister—and a healthy respect for her temper—she felt no need to toady, which made her something of a rarity. Her inexhaustible fund of risqué jokes made her especially valuable in moments of low royal morale. She smoked enthusiastically in the royal presence (and practically everywhere else) and provided a touch of family solidarity for a Princess growing increasingly distant from her in-laws. "Aunt Sarah" was an immediate success.

After flexing her powers of statesmanship in Hungary, the Princess returned to England and was soon exercising her other great powers as a wife and mother during one of the last of the increasingly awkward family holidays that she and the Prince were to take together. Even as she nimbly upstaged him during the ski-slope photo calls, however, her next role as grieving daughter was thrust upon her.

News came to the skiing party that her father had died in hospital. The shock caused a violent outpouring of emotion, of which her husband bore the brunt. The death of a parent is perhaps one of the most powerful triggers that can legitimately allow the release of the inhibitions imposed so powerfully by English upper-class culture, and something in the Princess allowed her to give her distress free rein.

The holiday party returned to England, riven with the Princess's grief. The anger that accompanied it seemed inexplicable, except that it seemed merged in her mind with resentment against the Prince. I quickly became aware of this when I called on her to offer my sympathy. I had already written to her, recalling her kindness to me when my own father had died a couple of years previously and reminding her of the advice she had given me then: to accept the grief and, in time, look forward to reliving happier memories.

There was a warmth in her greeting that made much further talk unnecessary. It was one of those rare moments when our relationship lost its professional detachment and became instead an exchange of genuine feelings, uncompromised by the intricate codes and games of our day-to-day contact.

It soon became apparent, however, that she resented her husband's sympathy. Her anger reminded me of her reaction to the Prince's thirtieth birthday party offer the previous summer. Behind his plans to attend the funeral she saw only the machinations of his PR advisers. "This funeral's going to be turned into a charade. It's so *false!*" She determinedly thwarted all the Prince's well-meant attempts to appear as the supporting husband. Judicious planning and the Prince's use of a helicopter rather than a separate car preserved the outward appearance of togetherness, but the Princess made her feelings plain enough in the photographs that appeared the next day. From her body language it was very obvious that, emotionally, she was on her own.

Such a spasm of feelings left her drained for several days. I kept my distance. When she resumed work the following week it was as though the experience of so much genuine emotion had been cathartic. The first major loss of a close relative added a maturity to her feelings of sympathy for others. Whatever the cost in personal pain—and in the Prince's public image—the ordeal left her with a new understanding of bereavement that I saw reflected in her public work. The professionally sympathetic Princess had acquired an extra layer of sincerity.

As time went on, the strategy of constantly reminding the public of the Princess's royal status certainly had its critics. It became one of the most frustrating aspects of my own life that very often the most severe critic was the Princess herself. This was not because she disapproved of the overall objective, which as she could see even in her most obdurate moments was going to empower her considerably. Rather it was because, in carrying out the strategy, she had to impose a degree of self-discipline that was not part of her natural makeup.

She could be enthusiastic when I first proposed a certain series of engagements and then turn against them, to the point of pulling out of them altogether, if the mood took her. These about-faces would be accompanied by a smoke screen of reproach—"What were you *thinking* of when you let me agree to this?" and sometimes self-pity—"All anybody does is take from me. Take, take, take. There'll soon be nothing left! Who gives *me* anything?" The fact that she was just as capable of saying this when receiving prestigious awards or the adulation of the crowd at Wembley did little to reduce its impact when delivered with blazing eyes and an accusatory glare.

It was one of the less endearing consequences of being

used to getting your own way most of the time. In her position, however, self-discipline was almost the only kind she was going to get. Its absence in someone not raised to duty and self-denial was scary. It was a tribute to her ultimately sound sense of self-preservation that she could take such obstinacy to the brink of calamity—sometimes having to be persuaded out of her car to perform at a great public event—but still come through as the professional she had learned to become.

Her sense of self-discipline and purpose was at its wobbliest whenever she caught the scent of potential controversy or mixed publicity. Like the highly strung thoroughbred she so often resembled, her nostrils were always alert to such signs of impending danger. A comprehensive lungful of it arrived in the month after her father died. In an unaccustomed PR coup and with, I admit, a little partisan support from a certain naval member of her staff, the Princess had agreed to become sponsor of the Navy's first Trident nuclear ballistic missile submarine, HMS *Vanguard*.

At a time when the Campaign for Nuclear Disarmament was still a voluble force, the implications of such an association were obvious. The naming of the submarine by the Princess was irresistible as a rallying point for what was left of the shrinking antinuclear movement. As a means of portraying the Princess as a senior royal figure undeterred by the fickle winds of such controversy in pursuit of her duty to uphold the safety of the realm, it was also pretty irresistible to me. When two such sharply opposing forces met there was bound to be an explosion, and when it came I was unhappily standing on ground zero.

The naming ceremony took place at the Vickers yard at Barrow-in-Furness on April 30, 1992. As an engineering accomplishment and as a demonstration of awesome firepower I found the Trident program fascinating, but not even this blinded me to the fact that it was going to be a pretty tough day.

On the recce I discovered that we would have to land the helicopter on a remote part of the site and travel by car to the headquarters and scene of the ceremony, partly along public roads. The police seemed suspiciously confident that they had anticipated every eventuality, and perhaps naively I thought no more about it until warning signs in the press and in the Princess's mailbag woke me out of my patriotic daze to the realization that there was real trouble ahead.

The feeling was accentuated by the Princess's sudden discovery within herself of a strong antinuclear streak. Even a long and closely worded memorandum on the theory and practice of mutually assured destruction and nuclear deterrence—with a line or two about her brave sailors for good measure—failed to shake her suspicion that what she was doing might very well earn her criticism from some previously friendly quarters.

She was dead right. Many of those who saw the Princess as the embodiment of compassion found it hard to reconcile this picture with one of the Princess as the embodiment of nuclear annihilation. Nonetheless, if she really was going to be the people's Princess—and this was some years before the expression was coined—she was going to have to appeal to *all* the people, and that included the tens of thousands whose livelihoods depended on the defense industry. It also included, I rather pompously pointed out to her, the hundreds of men who would serve in HMS *Vanguard* and who might at a pinch have to fight and die in her as well.

Whether it was because of the force of my argument or because she shrewdly calculated that to pull out would cause even worse controversy, the Princess agreed to go through with the engagement. We were still a tense little crowd, though, as we set off in the helicopter for the long journey north. Turbulence always seemed worse in a helicopter, but I had additional reason to feel queasy. Unknown to the Princess, I had discouraged the then Defense Minister Jonathan Aitken from sharing the helicopter because I did not want him to detect any lack of resolution in the star performer at the start of a day that was likely to test resolution all round before it was over.

Having safely arrived at the remote landing site, we set off by car for the Vickers headquarters building. As we pulled into the public road I could see that it was lined with people. It was always like that, wherever the Princess went. Here and there a few policemen struggled cheerfully to hold back the enthusiastic crowd.

Then, with a cold feeling in my stomach, I realized that this crowd was not at all friendly and the police, while certainly struggling, were anything but cheerful. The Princess realized it as well and an icy, accusatory chill settled over us. Sitting low down in the back of the wallowing limousine, I felt horribly vulnerable. I also felt horribly sympathetic, because if I felt like this, how on earth did the slim figure sitting rigidly next to me feel? "Shame!" screamed the crowd.

I noticed that most of the protesters were women. The sight of their uncontrolled anger, their contorted faces, their gesticulating arms, and their shapeless bodies hidden under duffle coats and shawls in the cold weather touched a chord of real horror within me. This was far worse than the incident the year before when, mistaking her for the Prime Minister, a crowd of student demonstrators had chased the Princess's car down the Embankment near the Houses of Parliament.

Putting on my best business-as-usual voice, I turned reassuringly to the Princess and said, "Ma'am, after the cabaret's over we'll arrive at the headquarters building, where you'll be met by Lord Chalfont." She nodded very slightly in acknowledgment, her eyes round with apprehension as the crowd continued to boo and bay.

At last the entrance to the headquarters building came into view. I could see the welcoming committee on the steps and the police cordon that, though obviously under pressure, seemed to be keeping the immediate area clear for our arrival. As the car pulled up to the pavement the Princess already had her hand on the door handle, anxious to escape from the Daimler that for a few awful minutes had suddenly seemed like a tumbrel.

At that moment a terrifying face thrust itself at her. With a yelp of fear she pulled her door shut and the face pressed itself hideously against the glass. The protester was young and male, with long, dreadlocked hair and a face painted to look like a leering skull. I was getting ready to run all the way back to London when the Princess turned to me with a nervous laugh and very steadily said, "Patrick, I don't think that's Lord Chalfont."

After the protester had been hauled off and the normal civilities had been exchanged in the doorway, the Princess retired to powder her nose and I retired to smoke a cigarette between trembling fingers. I felt as if we had fought our way into a Wild West fort, only to realize that we would have to fight our way back out again. Through the glass doors I could see the senior police officers having a flustered conference on the pavement. The garrison seemed to be as rattled as I was.

We moved on to the next item on the program, which was to drive down to the submarine where the Princess would perform the christening ceremony. By then, unfortunately, the bus carrying the VIP guests had been halted by demonstrators staging a mass "die-in" by lying on the road in front of it. When the Princess arrived on the casing of the great submarine, where the bottle of home-brewed beer hung ready to be smashed against the conning tower, she was accompanied by the naval chaplain and a very small group of nervous male companions and we found ourselves in front of a ceremonial grandstand full of empty seats, in clear view of a road bridge alive with shouting protesters.

The experience still comes back to me in nightmares. As we huddled in the wind, the Princess struggled to hold on to her hat, the chaplain struggled to hold on to his cassock, and I felt quite sure that I was struggling to hold on to my job. If a medal were awarded for light small talk above and beyond the call of duty and in the face of the enemy, the

Princess would surely have won it that day, although a few others might also have received an honorable mention in dispatches. Slowly our nuclear winter thawed as the grandstand filled with the delayed dignitaries and high-ranking NATO officers. The brief ceremony passed off without further incident, to everyone's relief.

By the time we returned to Kensington Palace that evening the mood had changed again. Instead of being an exploited victim of a military-industrial complex, the Cold War, and an unthinking private secretary, the Princess had become the ice-cool hero of the hour who had safely shepherded her little flock through an ordeal for which we were all much the wiser. In addition, the Princess's selfless dedication to traditional mainstream royal duty even in the face of physical danger had been publicized in a way that had exceeded my most optimistic expectations.

The PPO and I retired to the basement wine bar opposite the gates of Kensington Palace and toasted our survival. We found time to toast our boss too, whose resolve when it mattered had once again proved unsinkable. As a postscript to the incident, it is important also to mention that the Princess and HMS *Vanguard* went on to enjoy a happy relationship characterized by regular mutual expressions of admiration.

*A*fter the excitements of Barrow, just over a week was to pass before the Princess departed for another important solo tour, this time to Egypt. It was a week that even at the time I recognized as a new high-water mark in the schizophrenic nature of my life. Late one night, weaving my way as usual round Hyde Park Corner on my way home, I considered the dramas crowding into my mind. It was hard to know how to sort them into some kind of priority order.

On the one hand I had a front-row seat in the royal soap opera, which by this point was building itself into an epic

worthy of TV at its most melodramatic. A welter of speculation was beginning to break out about the impending
publication of a new royal book by the journalist Andrew
Morton. It would be pure dynamite, apparently, promising
as it did to catalog with irrefutable proof the tribulations inflicted on the helpless Princess by the unfeeling family into
which she had married.

On the other hand the cast of characters in the impending drama were also just the human beings with whom I
worked on a daily basis and who for me seldom acquired
the inflated stature or attributes, both good and bad, that I
read about in the papers every day. As a media feeding
frenzy began to gather pace over speculation about the future of the Waleses' marriage and the significance of Mrs.
Camilla Parker Bowles in the plot, I and the rest of the
Princess's staff carried on with whatever we could contrive
to call life as normal.

It was quite possible to bury ourselves in work while the
media drank its fill from the cup of royal scandal and intrigue. For us the story provided no more than a flickering
backdrop to the day-to-day necessities of running the office
of the world's most famous woman. Allowing it to invade
our daily chores would quickly have induced hysterics, in
me at least, and driven our herbal tea consumption to dangerous levels. My working routine was still filled with mundane considerations such as recces, working lunches,
nonworking lunches, planning meetings for future engagements, doctor's appointments for the Princess's inocula-
tions, and arrangements for the departure of one royal
equerry and the integration of his replacement.

This last item highlighted one of those idiosyncrasies
that demonstrate that royal service still sometimes owes
more to feudalism than modern management practice.
David Barton left to return to the Air Force with promotion and honor all round, except any acknowledgment from
the source of all honor, the monarch herself. It was always a
curious anomaly to me that equerries to the Princess of

Wales could be expected to take time out from their military duties and submit themselves and their young families to all the rigors of court life in the service of one of the most high-profile and hard-working members of the royal family, and yet received no official recognition for their service in the form of the humblest class of the Royal Victorian Order.

This is the Queen's own order with which she recognizes loyal service, whether good, not so good, or indifferent. The Princess's equerry's opposite number on the Prince's staff received an award from the Order as a matter of course when he left his post. For carrying out the same job—and even, arguably, a more difficult one—the Princess's man could expect nothing other than the Princess's own thanks and an economical farewell party in the Palace billiard room. Why was this, when, on tour at least, he had alternated duties with the Prince's equerry on an identical basis?

According to Napoleon, men are governed by such trinkets. Although the RVO was modestly passed off within the household—at least in front of colleagues—as a slightly embarrassing reminder of the passage of time, there was a glaring disparity in the case of the St. James's Palace equerries, and it could easily rankle.

Not, I hasten to add, with the Princess's equerries themselves—being men of stature both metaphorically and physically, they treated such baubles with the indifference they deserved. The Princess noticed the difference, however, and could not understand why her staff, who undoubtedly worked as hard and as loyally as any in royal service, should not have been recognized in the same way as their contemporaries in other households. Needless to say, the disparity was noticed more widely too, and in a world that was increasingly looking for evidence of the Princess's estrangement from the royal mainstream, it did not help the cause of unity.

I occasionally sought an explanation for this apparent injustice, but none was ever forthcoming from the secretive cabal that advised Her Majesty on such matters. As an indicator of the attitude we sometimes felt we were up against, it perhaps serves a useful purpose.

Incidentally, anyone caring to check will notice that I was awarded a humble version of the order in 1995—not for any act of outstanding loyalty or service, but simply because my name had come to the top of the list. The honor it represented was not lost on me, though its effect was diminished by my knowledge of the injustice described above, and by my knowledge that I lacked the guts to decline it on principle.

I digress, however. On Sunday, May 10, 1992, the Princess of Wales flew to Egypt. The pretext for the visit was an invitation from the President's wife, Mrs. Mubarak, to visit various charitable projects on the banks of the Nile. So far as the watching world was concerned, this was a fully fledged royal visit, attracting a press pack of more than fifty and the formal recognition of the country's head of state. In fact, that formal recognition was kept unconfirmed out of diplomatic deference to Palace sensitivities, but it was never really in any doubt.

The Princess's Egyptian visit was high profile, glamorous, photogenic, and a fine example of her ambassadorial role, of which I think most British people approved. The same appeared to be true of most Egyptians. The visit also proved to be an early example of the stratagems that had to be employed to thwart those who would clip the Princess's wings and confine her to the habitat of fashion shows and nursery schools that they thought suitable for her.

I did not feel encouraged by Buckingham Palace to involve heads of state in the Princess's program for overseas visits, even if such reticence puzzled our hosts and—often— our Ambassador on the spot. In turn, such ambivalence about her status encouraged the impression that high-profile overseas tours were better suited to senior members of the royal family whose public image and private inclinations more closely suited a certain type of establishment picture of the monarchy. Ironically, as the Princess set out on what was by any measure a testing representational mission on behalf of British interests in the Middle East, her aircraft—paid for by the taxpayer—was shared by the Prince and a party of friends *en route* to what was variously reported as his seventh or eighth holiday of the year.

Diverting the aircraft to Turkey in order to deliver the holiday party added considerably to the Princess's flying time. It meant that as we approached Cairo in the darkness after a long flight—during which the emotional tension of her situation had reduced the Princess to a prolonged bout of sobbing—I felt justified in wondering whether the Prince would have diverted his own aircraft *en route* to an official tour to oblige his wife and *her* friends. It did seem rather unlikely.

For enthusiasts of such detail, it is perhaps worth noting that at the end of the Princess's tour the same aircraft had to make a double journey, returning to Turkey to collect the holidaymakers because their timings did not dovetail with the end of the Princess's Egyptian visit. Not surprisingly, such apparent profligacy made unwelcome headlines.

It could be argued, of course, that the Princess's tears on the outward flight were no more than she deserved. As she knew at the time, but as I only suspected, she had given full cooperation to Andrew Morton's book, still some weeks from publication but already showing every sign of living up to its advance publicity of shaking the monarchy to its roots. The tears that I interpreted as frustration and unhappiness at her predicament—and it was quite possibly her intention that they should be seen in that way—might instead have been out of pure trepidation at the thought of the revelations about to be unleashed.

Either way, my immediate concern was rather more practical. Waiting for us less than an hour away lay the ancient kingdom of the Pharaohs, crossroads of Middle Eastern trade, culture, and politics. Knowing as I did that it would provide for the Princess a backdrop of spectacular wonders including the Pyramids, the Sphinx, and the temples of Luxor, I was filled with trepidation of my own as I contemplated the hunched figure sitting opposite me in the royal cabin. How on earth was she going to be ready to face the trials of the week ahead, not to mention the scrutiny of the press?

I gave in to the irresistible temptation to allow this professional concern to descend in my own mind into sheer self-pity. After all the work that had been put in on the recce, after all that I was personally staking on her success, how dare she succumb now to a bout of feminine weakness?

It was as if she had been reading my mind. I would not have been surprised if she had. The sniffles opposite me stopped abruptly. Once again the Princess disappeared to the royal lavatory—beckoned, I assumed, by the bulimia that was always prone to beset her at such moments of tension. My spirits sank even lower.

She emerged some minutes later a transformed woman. The puffy eyes had been bathed with water and freshly made up. The hair had been adjusted with fingertip precision. The leggings and sweatshirt of the long journey had given way to a sharply cut suit and power heels. "Don't worry," she said. "I'm not going to let you down." Pressing the bell for the steward, she ordered champagne.

It was true. No matter how close she came to the edge of losing courage, she always produced the last-minute effort of will that could turn imminent disaster into serene triumph. To me it was one of her heroic qualities—even if, at the time, I would gladly have swapped it for dull dependability. I summoned the troops from the forward cabin and we drank to her success. Then, while the others vied with each other to tell the crudest joke, I tried to make her concentrate on her briefing for the arrival ceremony.

I need not have worried. The arrival ceremony, the departure ceremony, and everything in between she played with consummate professionalism, poise, and devotion to duty. I wondered if her opponents really understood the bloody-minded determination of the woman they were seeking to banish to the backwaters of royal life.

The lasting images of her Egyptian tour are of the Princess standing in front of various famous antiquities looking lonely and wistful. There was an unavoidable echo of similar images from the Indian tour, when the Princess had sat alone and forlorn in front of the Taj Mahal. This time, however, there was something about her stance and the angle of her chin that marked her transition from theatrically abandoned wife to capable international campaigner for a few lucky causes, the British nation being one of them.

As in Hungary and Pakistan, I had planned her program so that it bore all the traditional hallmarks of a conventional royal tour. We had the private meeting with the head of state, the encouragement of British commercial interests, a visit to the British Council, and the laying of a wreath at the Commonwealth war cemetery. The tour also carried the special stamp of the Princess herself in its concentration on children's medical charities and centers for the addicted and disabled. In fact, it was only out of respect for understandable Egyptian pride in the relatively high quality of their health services that we did not press for visits to even more compelling centers of disease and disadvantage. With only the most minor hiccups, the tour progressed on a wave of gratifying success, thanks in large part to the characteristic efficiency and imagination of the British Ambassador and his staff, and the uncompromising efficiency of the Egyptian protocol and police departments.

As often happened, fortune smiled on the Princess in unforeseen ways. During her call on President Mubarak it quickly became apparent to the handful of aides in attendance that the President and the Princess got on famously. Their animated meeting overran to an extent that for any other engagement I would have considered alarming, especially as Mr. Mubarak's next caller—President Menem of Argentina—was expected at any moment.

Another piece of good fortune, albeit at the expense of some temporary inconvenience to the photographer concerned, occurred when Fleet Street's most famous royal photographer, Arthur Edwards of the *Sun*, contracted one of the tummy upsets for which Cairo is renowned. He had the compensation of being visited by the Princess's own doctor, Surgeon Commander Robin Clark, whom I would not have swapped for his weight in gold, either on this or subsequent tours. By symbolically scoring a hit with the President and the pressman through adroit use of the gifts she had been given, the Princess achieved in one day the kind of success that marked her as an envoy whose effectiveness bore little relation to her qualification by age or experience.

The hiccups may have been few, but I think we must have offended one of the minor Nile deities to suffer one particular series of upsets. It so happened that on the day that the Princess visited the Pyramids the Egyptian police, in an excess of enthusiasm, had closed many of the famous monuments in the interests of security for longer than might otherwise have been considered strictly necessary. Thus, although the photographers got some wonderful pictures of the Princess standing on the Sphinx's paws, a large crowd of tourists were excluded from the site.

Even though I was concentrating on the timing of the event, and in particular whether we would leave the Pyramids before President Menem arrived, I was conscious of raised French voices on the other side of the police barrier. They certainly seemed dissatisfied with the alternative entertainment that was being offered. As we sped off in a cloud of dust I complacently thought to myself, "Ah well, can't win 'em all."

A couple of days later, during a breathtaking visit to the island of Phillae on the Nile above the Aswan Dam, our paths crossed again. Once more the *entente cordiale* was the chief victim. As the Princess's boat approached the landing stage a French tourist boat appeared on a converging course, heading for the same spot. With a blare of sirens and much gesticulating, our escorting police launch ordered the other boat to lie off and wait. By sheer ill chance, it was the same group of French tourists whose visit to the Sphinx we had disrupted. As some of the accompanying British press gleefully reported, a chorus of boos and even snatches of the Marseillaise were clearly audible across the enchanted waters of the Nile while we scrambled ashore.

"Oh well," I thought, "that proves you really *can't* win 'em all." Surely, I told myself, this would be our last encounter with the disgruntled tourists.

I was in for a horrible shock. On our last day in Cairo we paid a visit to that showpiece of the Egyptian Department of Antiquities, the fabulous Egyptian Museum. Always thronged with tourists, the labyrinthine corridors of the museum had been carefully cordoned off along a prepared route so that the Princess could make an unimpeded progress around the main exhibits. That was the plan, at least.

Unfortunately, the museum's director had not been present on the recce and appeared to feel that the planned route gave the Princess an inadequate impression of the true splendor of the range of exhibits on display. To my alarm he suddenly steered the Princess off on a route of his own.

In a flash the crowd had closed in around us. Where once there had been order and decorum and an opportunity to marvel at the relics on display, now there was just a hubbub of jostling figures, a tide in which the Princess was swept along, occasionally casting pleading glances in the direction of me and the policeman. Short of shooting the museum director on the spot—a fate that at that moment I felt was too good for him—there was little we could do.

The police, reacting as best they could to the situation, tried to anticipate the director's general line of advance and clear rooms ahead of our arrival. It was surely the work of some deity's curse that the first room from which they chose forcibly to evict the innocent public happened to be occupied by the same party of French tourists who had dogged our steps at the Sphinx and at Phillae.

As was so often the case, the Princess was quicker off the mark than I. While the Gallic protests mounted, the Princess fixed me with a glare and said, "I must apologize to them. What shall I *say*?"

As usual in such emergencies, my mind went blank. Somewhere, though, a small voice was complaining that this was a hell of a time to choose for a French oral exam. "Er," I ventured. "*Je suis très desolée...*" Luckily for me, the Ambassador took charge at that point, giving an effective demonstration of why French is still regarded as the essential worldwide language of diplomacy.

Later that day the Princess flew to Luxor, where she visited the great temple of Karnak. By this stage thoroughly rattled, I arranged for an Embassy scout to go ahead of us by Land Rover to all the main sites on our route, checking for French tourists lying in wait. It was a great relief to find that the curse appeared to have been lifted.

Later that evening—our last in Cairo—there was a distinct outbreak of morale as we realized that we had almost reached the end of a tour that had begun with such apprehension but had ended with such success. The Princess was therefore at the top of her form as she joined the reception we had arranged for the traveling British press party. As in Pakistan, this was the Princess's opportunity to mingle with those who would communicate her thoughts and views to a wider audience than could ever have been achieved by the osmosis that was the traditional way of conveying a royal message.

Ashley Walton, who attended the reception, was quoted in the *Sunday Times* on May 17, 1992, as saying, "It is a mark of her confidence that even after all the recent publicity about her marriage she is prepared to walk into a room of tabloid hacks. Charles could never have done it but then he isn't really interested in people. The transformation in Diana has been quite incredible. Diana will never be a great intellectual but she is a very shrewd, sharp woman with amazing strength of character." Or in the words of another commentator from the same article, "Nobody should underestimate the Princess of Wales—she is a calculating and clever woman." Quite right, I thought—and just as well too, given the many who would rather have written her off as a self-obsessed clotheshorse.

After the press reception, spirits rose even higher and we all repaired in what fancy dress we could manage to the poolside in the Ambassador's garden. One by one the members of our party were thrown fully clothed into the pool, with the decorous exception of the lady-in-waiting. She gamely helped to fish the survivors out of the deep end, which was soon bobbing with discarded jackets and funny hats.

Eventually we caught our boss and threw her in too. As she performed a graceful arc through the night sky it occurred to me that this might have been a jape too far... Suddenly subdued, we watched the little patch of bubbles that marked the spot where the Princess had disappeared into the water. Just as I thought she must have hit her head on the bottom and I would have some serious explaining to do, she reappeared shouting good-natured threats and snorting like a dolphin.

This was the pool that had been made infamous on the first day of the tour when a group of British photographers had illegally gained access to a rooftop adjoining the Embassy, from where they had taken illicit pictures of the Princess taking her morning swim in a distinctly unsexy black swimsuit. In a foretaste of the subsequent sneak gym pictures scandal, it was even suggested that she had connived at the intrusion. I was skeptical. It was not that she was incapable of such a stratagem, but that swimsuit banished my doubts.

Nevertheless, she was stung by the suggestion and vented her anger on the press secretary Dickie Arbiter, who in turn issued draconian banning orders on the culprits. She did not like that either, once she realized that she risked some temporary unpopularity among the pack.

"Dickie totally overreacted," she confided to me.

"They invaded your privacy," I said. "He had to make a point." I knew, though, that Dickie could not win in this situation.

"But now he's upset them. Nobody else understands the press like I do." This was arguably true, at least in matters concerning herself. Her long-suffering press secretaries, however, seldom knew from minute to minute what media-relations script she was working from, or what private stratagems she was cooking up. All they knew for certain was that they would get it in the neck when a news story incurred her displeasure.

Later that night I sat down in the office we had been lent in the Embassy, at the desk from which Cromer had virtually ruled Egypt in the early years of the century when Egyptian monarchs reigned by the will of British military and diplomatic power. After our departure the next resident of the Embassy's splendid guest suite was going to be the Foreign Secretary Douglas Hurd, who was due to visit Cairo on a Middle East peace mission whose importance would certainly dwarf our own.

Aware of the Princess's high regard for the Foreign Secretary, and suspecting it might already be partly reciprocated, I thought that leaving him a letter would only enhance her image as a tangible asset to British diplomacy, worth entrusting with more such tours in future. I enjoyed drafting this sort of thing on my boss's behalf. The mental exercise of pretending to be a thirty-year-old Princess without a single O level conveying her thoughts to a distinguished statesman made up for a lot of being chased around by disgruntled French tourists.

After some general remarks about how much she had enjoyed her visit and how impressed she had been by the work of the humanitarian agencies she had seen, the Princess reported on the content of her call on the President and dwelt at some length on the helpfulness and efficiency of the Ambassador and his staff. It concluded, "I do hope my short tour will have made some contribution to your aims. Please be in no doubt of my gratitude for the opportunity such a visit gives me to broaden my own horizons, or my readiness to give my support to our foreign policy in any way you think would be helpful."

It was perhaps significant, and certainly gratifying, that in his tribute after her death Douglas Hurd quoted from this letter as evidence of the Princess's appreciation of her responsibilities as a roving ambassador for her country. After Pakistan, Hungary, and now Egypt—to say nothing of the USA—I thought her qualifications for the job spoke for themselves. Never once, by word or deed, did she give any valid ammunition to those who liked to describe her as a diplomatic "loose cannon."

As I sometimes found to my frustration, however, it was impossible to maintain the elevated tone for very long. As I have mentioned, the aircraft that brought the Princess back to England was then to return to Turkey to collect the Prince and his party. I watched without much pleasure, but also without much protest, as the Princess encouraged certain subversive elements in our party while they prepared a ribald message in cutout newspaper lettering, which they left taped to a bulkhead to welcome the aircraft's next passengers.

However much it offended me—and it could certainly have offended many more if they had known about it—her occasional lapses into her own brand of juvenile delinquency were probably the smallest price anyone could expect to pay for a star of such untapped potential. Even as I tut-tutted to myself and self-righteously mourned my boss's continual refusal to turn into a Completely Perfect Princess, I had only to remind myself that she had just pulled off a remarkable triumph in defiance of her doubters, without much tangible support from the organization she represented to recognize what she was really worth. She had also performed successfully despite the crippling anxieties that must have been gnawing at her insides while she awaited the outcome of the Morton explosion and all that it meant for her future.

My dismay at the forthcoming revelations—which would have been even greater had I known of her active involvement—was tempered by a story she had quietly told me on tour. In retrospect, that was probably why she had shared it with me. She spoke of the evening when she had confronted Camilla Parker Bowles at a party and pleaded with her to leave her husband alone. The response had been stony, from her antagonist and her husband, and the Princess had fled in tears.

I was deeply moved, as was no doubt the intention. All my protective instincts bristled in her defense. The story, moreover, had been told without self-pity and without malice, at least toward her husband. Even the antagonism she clearly felt toward her rival—it was the first time I had heard her use the name "Rottweiler"—was not to last beyond the separation.

It was as if, confronted yet again by the genuine emotions of such an encounter, she forgot the sort of petty vindictiveness that she so often directed at her own supporters. In the last analysis, she could be genuinely magnanimous to those who had hurt her, while simultaneously organizing the symbolic disemboweling of a loyal subordinate. It was hard to escape the feeling that the little people bore the brunt of the anger she felt toward her real tormentors.

Meanwhile, the Princess was returning from the success of Egypt to the uncertain sanctuary of her husband's house in Gloucestershire. I was going home to do my best to forget for a short while about everything to do with the royal family.

13

❧

Truth or Dare

*A*s some perceptive watchers could see at the time, and as anyone can see with hindsight, an explosive chain of events awaited only a spark to set it off. The Princess now effectively had her own office, her own press spokesman, and virtually—in view of her husband's lengthy absences—her own palace. She appeared to be finding a mission as a high-profile overseas ambassador for her country, as well as being the embodiment of glamorous compassion at home. She had a massive media following that she was able to choreograph with little help from others. The public perceived her as a model mother, a hardworking member of the royal team, and a potentially powerful future Queen. Morton's book would add to this the picture of a troubled woman fighting for survival in the face of her husband's treachery and his family's indifference to her plight.

Ranged against her in tabloid myth and often in reality too was an establishment that, if it was to remain true to itself, would have to align itself to the heir to the throne in any circumstances in which the succession might be threatened. The members of this establishment were the monarchy's natural supporters, both out of inclination and out of self-interest. However, what they were beginning to learn about the true nature of the institution to which they willingly gave their deference was already unsettling some.

The same conviction that naively but compellingly made me see the Princess as more sinned against than sinning was growing in the minds of others no longer willing to accept at face value the axiom that right must lie only with those who by accident of birth find themselves as royalty. For me and many others in the establishment—to whom royalty was their natural focus and often their very *raison d'être*— this was an unwelcome discovery. As so often, the Princess acted as a catalyst in helping even the most unimaginative people to see the world differently. Thus the editor of one conservative broadsheet was heard to say that he was in the Prince's camp because this was how a member of the establishment should react, but he was there without any heartfelt conviction.

Meanwhile, the monarch herself and her private office left no stone unturned in their determination to be neutral in the escalating War of the Waleses. This statesmanlike impartiality frustrated some of the old guard who might have wished that the Queen would come round to their point of view. Some even presumed that they could speak with her authority. To my knowledge, however, *nobody* spoke against the Princess with the authority of the Queen. Those who did were motivated by their own convictions or prejudices, or, in a few cases, out of some perverted sense of loyalty to the Prince.

The chain reaction of explosions may only have needed a spark to ignite it, but in briefing Andrew Morton as she did the Princess opted to use a blowtorch. People started to get burned as soon as serialization of *Diana: Her True Story* began in the *Sunday Times* in the weeks preceding the June publication date. The impact of the book was harmful to the royal family, but for the Princess it was catastrophic. However gratifying it may have been to her sense of vic-

timhood, any view in which detached logic played a part—
and this, to be fair, was not her strong point—would have
shown her that all efforts I and others might make to reinforce her image as an independent but still royal operator
were now ultimately bound to fail.

The urge to command attention by any means remains
for me the most likely motive behind her cooperation. It
was a recurring temptation for her. With this she played
into the hands of people for whom she was little more than
a prospective bestseller. Once she had cast herself as victim,
getting her story across was her priority at whatever cost. If
people knew her story, her argument went, then their support and understanding would follow automatically and so,
crucially, would their affection. For this end she was ready
to risk *anything*. Even her normally acute sense of self-
preservation could be bypassed temporarily. It was not a
death wish exactly; she was just blind to the consequences,
so driven was she by the need to be noticed.

She succeeded in this, of course, but only in the long
term and only with those who were her natural supporters
anyway. The benefit was never going to be worth the cost
she paid, let alone the cost she exacted on the institution
into which she had married. That consideration was never
going to worry her much, however.

The damage done by the book went too deep to enable
a reconciliation to take place, not just between the Princess
and her husband but also between the Princess and the role
she had made for herself. Long before the disastrous
Panorama interview, she had already become a "Queen of
Hearts," carrying the hopes placed upon her by many millions of people. Now this role could exist only as a saccharine gesture, unsupported by the authority she would have
wielded from within the royal fold.

After Morton's revelations, any success or satisfaction she
created by operating independently would inevitably be
short-lived. This was partly because the Princess did not
have the stature or the intellectual capacity wisely to em-

ploy the opportunities she now had, whatever her other gifts, and partly because the establishment would now be compelled to expel her as a dangerous foreign body. Worst of all, the image of a Princess who could stoop to share ordinary people's suffering could only be damaged by the new image of a Princess who also stooped to wash her dirty linen on the front pages.

The damage was not limited to a single, cataclysmic event. It was a slow-acting poison. From my perspective, the process that began with Morton ended three and a half years later with the awful *Panorama* interview. During those years the Princess breathed the heady but tainted oxygen of success and independence and then, with her judgment fatally impaired, she embarked on a course ruled by her own impulsive nature that would inevitably take her farther and farther away from the royal support structure. Without that structure she could only be vulnerable to those whose motives seldom began or ended with her welfare.

I was part of that royal support structure, of course, and I willingly stuck with her on the independent course she was beginning uncertainly to plot for herself. In some ways my motives were the same as hers. I was not quite sure where she was going, but I knew that it would be an exciting ride. I knew also that I stood a better chance than most of influencing her thoughts so that, whatever lay ahead, she would do minimal damage to herself and the organization I felt bound to protect.

This sometimes seemed to me like a risky leap in the dark, but I still had a blind belief that at least in her public work the course the Princess chose was likely to follow the directions of my own wobbly moral compass. In cruder terms, I also found her opponents' hypocrisy increasingly loathsome and I had little of the inherited English concern for hierarchical distinctions that might have made it easier for me to bear.

The Princess chose not to let me in on the whole secret of her cooperation with Morton. In many ways this was a blessing. Credible deniability is sometimes a great comfort to a private secretary. It may even have been her intention to spare me the discomfort of conflicting loyalties. At least my ignorance enabled me to fight valiantly in her defense.

Another motive for her secrecy might have been that she just did not trust me. This is slightly less likely than it appears at first, however, given the astonishing confidences she shared with me on other matters.

A third possible motive also persists, at least in my own mind. I believe she was in many ways ashamed of her cooperation with Morton. She was not a natural rebel. Certainly she was angry, but she was also surprisingly timid. As the enormity of the events she had set in motion began to dawn on her, a wish to deny any involvement took root. Whatever her views about my other shortcomings, she knew at least that I was loyal. She also knew, however, that I was not slow to bring questions of principle into our discussions about her future program, her relations with the other members of the royal family, and her responsibilities as an extraordinarily gifted and privileged person. What tough questions might I have posed to her, had I known what she was doing?

I do not think she can have found it an uplifting experience to pour out her emotions into Andrew Morton's Dictaphone. In fact, I believe she felt quite sullied by it. She was never normally slow to take credit for good news, but whenever the book's huge success was mentioned she took no visible satisfaction. Instead she became evasive and uncharacteristically reticent. As a form of emotional bulimia, this was something to be hidden away, to be indulged like another dark and self-destructive urge.

It was perhaps significant that the chosen go-between who passed the Princess's tapes to Morton was her friend James Coldhurst. As a doctor he had some influence over the Princess's attitude to medical issues. As a concerned friend, his encouragement of such revelations—as a kind of emotional purging—might tacitly have helped them seem therapeutic. As it happened, however, the main beneficiary appeared to be the Princess's denial reflex. In my experience, shame is not an emotion with which royal people are very familiar. Certainly, the more people urged the Princess to experience it in the wake of Morton, the less inclined she was to do so.

Nevertheless, there was no doubting her regret and confusion when she realized that her panicky denials of involvement with the author had caused her brother-in-law Sir Robert Fellowes to mislead the Press Complaints Commission under Lord McGregor. In a well-documented incident, Lord McGregor publicly admonished the press for "dabbling their fingers in the stuff of other people's souls." Andrew Knight, executive chairman of News International, shared a friend with the Princess who had told him the true origin of the revelations in Morton's book. This was communicated to Lord McGregor, along with the information that the next day there would be photographs in the tabloid papers publicly endorsing the Princess's friendship with Carolyn Bartholomew, a key contributor to the book. Lord McGregor could thus only conclude that either he had been deliberately misled by Fellowes, or Fellowes did not know what was going on.

The truth was that Fellowes had been misled by his sister-in-law and by her private secretary, both of whom denied she had anything to do with the Morton book. It will come as little comfort to Sir Robert to know that he was not the only private secretary who had been misled in this way. I had beaten him to it, although as the official most closely responsible, my willing credulity was the greater lapse.

My understanding of the self-destructive forces at work within the Princess was likewise greater than Sir Robert's. Even had I known the truth of her involvement, my answer to the Queen's private secretary—and thus to the Queen herself—might still have been the same. Such was my loyalty to my leader at that time, even though she had comprehensively misled me.

I duly gave my support to an internal press office briefing that said something like this: "The Princess of Wales has not given access/cooperation to the author on the production of this book for either the text or the photographs or in any other way. Her Highness is certainly not checking a copy of the text as alleged in one paper." All these assurances turned out to be false.

So did the assurances I received from the Princess in an illustrative little incident, the significance of which only dawned on my overcrowded brain as I descended the KP stairs afterward. It was still early in the Morton saga, when a pretense of normal routine could still be continued. I had been with her in her sitting room, wading through routine correspondence and program details. She looked drawn and distracted, but I sensed a suppressed excitement within her. The unspoken subject dominating her mind and mine was the question of her complicity in The Book.

At last I was able to put away my piles of papers, diary, and notebook. "Ma'am," I ventured, "I had a long session with Robert and the others in BP this morning..."

"Poor you! Are they all jumping up and down?"

"Well, they're worried. Nobody wants to think you helped Morton."

"I've *never* spoken to him. And why would I want to damage my children's future?"

"Exactly. That's just what I told Robert."

"This family had this book coming to them. I can't help it if people don't like what they read."

We looked at each other. Now she had color in her cheeks and her eyes held mine with a challenge. It was one of those moments—one of many—when I had a choice. I could either accept the truth as she was giving it to me, or I could question her integrity to her face and so destroy the whole basis of our relationship. Like an ailing marriage, it depended on the outward appearance of mutual trust to have any purpose at all.

It was not a difficult decision. I did not have the evidence to refute what she told me (many people went half mad trying to find it), and I did not fancy being sacked. It was a truce. She would pretend to have told me the truth and I would pretend to believe her.

As it turned out, what she had told me *was* true—as far as it went. She was quite good at that sort of verbal contortionism, her favorite ploy being to deflect an awkward question with one of her own. Being who she was, that gave her an unbeatable server's advantage in this sort of unwholesome game of moral Ping-Pong. It could be confusing, though, trying to remember what I was and was not supposed to know.

"Well," I said after a pause, "the press office is publicly denying that you had anything to do with it."

"Good," she replied, though the fire was now gone from her eyes. It was time to leave. By a twist of our curious etiquette, I was not supposed to make her prolong the act.

As I thoughtfully made my way downstairs, my mind was filled with the significance of what I had just learned. Her denial was the best confirmation I was ever going to get. OK then: her denial would be my denial. That was simple. But what about that business with the Bartholomew photographs? There could have been no clearer endorsement of Carolyn's contribution to the book. (The press had been mysteriously tipped off by a woman with "a posh voice" that the Princess was going to visit Carolyn Bartholomew and so give her a powerful endorsement as one of Morton's most candid contributors.)

"Patrick!"

She was leaning over the banisters above me. I stopped and looked up. "Yes, Ma'am?"

"What do people think of me going to see Carolyn like that? All those photographers popping up?" It was uncanny. Once again she had read my mind. Careful now.

"I think they see you as a very supportive friend."

"And the photographers?"

"Well, they follow you everywhere, don't they?"

"Yes, they certainly do!"

Throughout the saga of the Morton book, I was aware that the allegations it contained—which if even half true demonstrated an astonishing degree of negligence on the part of the royal family's senior management—were always at least partly obscured by this question of the Princess's co-operation. It was as if the means of transmission rather than the message itself was all that mattered. It was not important that something might be seriously amiss, but only that anybody should have the temerity to blow the whistle on it. It was not important whether the Princess had been misled or mistreated at various stages during her time in the institution's care, but only whether that institution might be accused of having even temporarily misled the press watchdog.

The revelations in *Diana: Her True Story* were almost entirely true, although they were certainly not the complete truth. Truth of any kind, however, seemed to be the last thing that mattered inside the royal crucible I now found myself occupying. There was outrage that the Princess should even tacitly have lent her support to such a breach of the pact of secrecy, and there was a reflex outpouring of sympathy for the Prince that he should have suffered such cruel indignity.

By contrast, I reacted in the opposite way. To me it was practically immaterial whether the Princess had cooperated or not. What mattered to me were the implications of what the book said about her experiences in the past and her predicament in the future. A magnanimous response from the establishment she now tremulously realized she had mortally offended might have been the best incentive yet for the Princess to come back into line. The only effective reply to such a gigantic piece of whistle-blowing was to demonstrate a very visible concern to respond positively to any truth that the book contained and to undertake a privately conciliatory approach to the Princess herself. This would have demanded superhuman restraint and imagination from the royal establishment and was therefore an unrealistic expectation.

In some quarters, notably the Queen's office, there was an extraordinary degree of understanding for the Princess, and for me as the poor sod in the middle. In the end, however, the organization suffered the worst of all worlds. The Princess continued to be portrayed as wronged, isolated, and defiant. The Prince was seen as petty and vindictive or just humiliated. Buckingham Palace appeared to be unable to keep its house in order and at a loss to know what all the fuss was about.

"Come on, Patrick!" was a fairly typical accusation along the red-carpeted corridors. "We know she did it. It's incomprehensible, unforgivable ... I'm just sorry for the poor Prince." Then came the afterthought (sometimes), "And for you, of course."

"There is *no* evidence that she did it!" I would retort, hoping to God that none was about to come to light. "Anyway, that's not the point ..." But it was the only point, at least as far as the institution was concerned. Only a few perceptive individuals heeded the main message of the book and declined to be distracted by acrimony over the source of the details it reported. By then, sadly, it was all too late.

As the June 7 publication date for *Diana: Her True Story* approached, I became acutely aware of the Princess's agitated state of mind. One day I received an odd and unexpected instruction from her to find out immediately how the charity Turning Point would be able to cope with a sudden donation running to some tens of thousands of pounds. Knowing that the author was not involved, could the charity be trusted to use it in any way that was discreet? Could they be trusted not to ask where it came from?

It only took me one call to the charity to establish that they could set her mind at rest on these questions and would be more than happy to put the windfall to excellent use on behalf of their clients with alcohol, drug, and mental health problems. The Princess did not mention the subject again, however, so after a couple of days I asked her who the charity should thank for such largesse when it appeared.

She was evasive and plainly did not like being reminded of what in retrospect seemed to me to have been a panicky attempt to find a respectable resting place for cash arising from contributions to Morton's book.

Further evidence of the Princess's jitters came rather more predictably with a sudden request for me to arrange additional engagements on dates adjacent to the day of publication. Thus the surprised staff and patients at the Royal Marsden Hospital and St. Joseph's Hospice and the young homeless at Centrepoint all became the unsuspecting beneficiaries of the Princess's reflex response to a situation that put her good image under threat.

It was a clear example of a phenomenon I already associated with her. Time and again I saw the Princess arrive at a hospice, a drugs center, or a homelessness project and perform a great service for the people she visited, for the organization that was helping them, for the local community, and for the institution of monarchy too. Her motive in agreeing to the visit might have been far from selfless, however. Sometimes she was there for some distinctly narrow purpose to do with her own perception of her public profile, or even to satisfy a personal vendetta as she attempted to upstage the Prince. Be that as it may, her role as a vehicle for the relief of suffering and the good she achieved for the people she visited remained untainted by her questionable motives (as, largely, did the good she achieved for her media image). For those of us who saw both sides of the coin, it was a remarkable achievement.

*N*ot long after the Morton missile had been launched, the perfect opportunity arose for the Princess to demonstrate that, even if she was the perpetrator of the book's revelations, her value as a top-rank royal performer had to be set against any blame that might rebound on her. In addition, if she was the victim either of the book or the unfeeling family it portrayed, she was strong, determined, and glamorous enough to survive the ordeal with her head held high.

With some encouragement, not least from me, the Northern Ireland Office—with whom I always fostered close relations—let it be known that the Secretary of State would like the Princess to be guest of honor at his annual garden party at Hillsborough Castle. Sir Patrick Mayhew was a distant relative of the Princess and, although not normally a keen volunteer for garden parties, she quickly grasped the value of such an invitation at a moment when her status might be in dire need of shoring up.

Thus on June 29, 1992, the Princess returned to Belfast, this time in the middle of a heat wave. After a couple of engagements in the city center, she carried out a spectacularly successful walkabout in the Falls Road, in a part of the city synonymous with the grimmest aspects of the province's twenty-three-year experience of urban terrorism. The unscripted arrival of the glamorous Princess produced a spontaneous outpouring of welcoming emotion that moved even the most cynical observer and paid dividends in the next day's papers.

The *Daily Mail* estimated that 20,000 onlookers came to "shout for Diana." DIANA STEALS ULSTER HEARTS proclaimed the *Belfast Newsletter*. THE BRAVEST WALKABOUT OF ALL said *Today*, noting the fact that details of the Princess's program had been leaked in a serious security breach the night before her visit. WE WANT DI! shouted the front page of the *Daily Mirror*, followed by the subtitle "Frontline Belfast with a Message for the Royals."

Such printed adulation for the Princess was not entirely unknown, of course, but in its unanimity and in the attention it drew to her courage in the face of a known security threat it was unusually helpful. Behind Palace walls the finger of accusation was being pointed firmly at the Princess over the Morton book, so this was undoubtedly a providential media windfall.

Almost more significant to me was a little-noticed report

in a Dublin newspaper, which deserves quoting at greater length because of the evidence it gives of the Princess's transnational appeal. On the subject of the British royal family there can be few more skeptical readerships in the world than those of the Irish Republic's Sunday newspapers. Yet Anne Cadwallander wrote in the *Irish Press* on June 30, 1992:

> Princess Diana braved thousands of peering eyes yesterday to shake the hands of hordes of curious strangers...as speculation about the future of her marriage reached new heights. Her eyes seemed to say it all. "Look, you all know what I am going through, please be kind." And kind they were. Polite, smiling and kind.
>
> There could not have been a single one of the two thousand people she met who had not seen some parts of THAT book about THAT marriage. But not a word about it passed their lips as they bowed and exchanged polite words with the Princess of sighs...
>
> Earlier in Belfast city center there had been what was described as "pandemonium" when the Princess went walk-about. One photographer even got his forehead gashed...Then she was away again, lifting her royal hand in a final gracious wave to the watching press. And you know, some of us just could not resist waving back.

In her letter of thanks to the Secretary of State after the garden party, the Princess reminded him of her "ardent hope" that the search for peace should have a successful outcome. She also underlined her own willingness to assist in any way she could. As might be expected, this was an offer with a not wholly unselfish hidden meaning. As with her letter to the Foreign Secretary after the Egypt tour, however, even on face value alone it was thought quite valid enough to deserve a positive response.

At a time when her very future in the royal family was under question, the Princess had successfully reminded leaders in two critical areas of national policy that even as the subject of exaggerated media reports she could make a useful contribution—particularly in areas where a touch of feminine glamour and maternal emotion could achieve worthwhile results. At the same time she had reminded the growing ranks of muttering opponents within the British establishment that it might just be safer to keep her on board the royal family's leaky ship. If jettisoned, she might very well not sink in public esteem as quickly as the obliging Duchess of York.

It quickly became apparent that such opponents were prepared to use almost any weapon against her. On the same day as the papers published their ecstatic reports of her success in Northern Ireland, others carried stories that could only have been planted by her enemies, clearly suggesting that the Princess suffered from mental instability.

Reports of the Princess's occasional mental brittleness came as no surprise to me and many others who worked or lived closely with her. I suppose the difference was that, for those of us who were sympathetic to her, the real story was not that she was occasionally mercurial in her thoughts and emotions but that she had not years ago retreated to a life of seclusion and contemplation as a result of nervous strain. I had only to recall the unforgettable picture of the Princess among the crowds in the Falls Road to feel a slow-burning scorn for those who had directed such a slur at her from the safety of their anonymous briefings.

Perhaps this was why I, and maybe some others, managed a thoroughly reprehensible smirk at a cartoon in a popular tabloid that showed the Prince of Wales in conversation with his pot plants: "I need hardly tell you how worried I am about my wife's state of mind."

In terms of my day-to-day work, the Princess's emotional unpredictability was just another challenging aspect of the job. Slowly and painfully, I developed structures and routines for dealing with it. This was so that my main duty to the Princess—to organize her public life—did not slip below my secondary duty, which was less official but could roughly be translated as doing what I could to ensure that she was in the best frame of mind to undertake the public tasks I had set up for her.

An apocryphal story used to circulate about a private secretary advising his royal boss to be cautious about some new enthusiasm. It perhaps illustrates the sort of professional challenges faced by any functionary for whom the collective noun might be "a grovel." Applied to my own situation, the imaginary conversation goes like this:

"Patrick! I've had a brilliant idea!"

"Ye-e-es, Ma'am?"

"I've decided to run naked down Piccadilly!"

"That *is* a brilliant idea, Ma'am. Tell me, would you like me to stop the traffic first?"

Her moods seemed to change as often as the weather. Although with practice I hoped to have some chance of influencing these moods, the task seemed at times about as easy as diverting the course of a thunderstorm or prolonging a beautiful summer evening. To stretch the meteorological metaphor, the Princess's moods could also be deceptive. What might look like a benign overcast could contain sudden blizzards, while within viewing distance a more fortunate stretch of landscape could be bathed in unexpected sunshine.

What gave the game of forecasting its special thrill was wondering which moods were genuine and which were assumed in order to achieve a particular purpose. Sometimes, manipulative though she could be, I think the Princess herself got confused. Certainly the transition from victim of cruel injustice to Boadicea with a headache could be accomplished in an instant.

Shortly after the earliest Morton revelations hit the headlines, I was with the Princess on a visit to Merseyside. I was in the car immediately behind her in the convoy when news came over the radio that a diversion was urgently required to find a lavatory. My first thought, typically, was of the disruption this would cause to my carefully scheduled program. My second thought was that she must be pulling a stunt in order to win sympathy from the publicity that would inevitably result from such a departure from the published program. This seemed more likely, given her need for extra public sympathy in the fevered climate that prevailed at the time. Only then did I wonder if there might be something actually the matter with her.

As I had seen in Budapest and on many other occasions, unscheduled loo stops were not unknown, but unscheduled loo stops for the sole purpose of going to the loo *were* virtually unknown. There was almost always a message to be passed to the watching world, and this was no exception.

After hurried discussion with the typically unflappable Merseyside police, we diverted to a small airfield where I strode into the headquarters of the local flying club to tell a startled chief instructor that his lavatory was required at once by the Princess of Wales. His reaction to what might have been some sort of elaborate hoax spoke volumes for his unflappability. With scarcely a moment's delay, not only the ladies' loo but also a retiring room were immediately provided.

The Princess hurried in, eyes downcast, and took up occupation with her lady-in-waiting for what seemed like an age. It gave me time to thank the chief instructor and reflect to myself that if this was how he handled emergencies on the ground I would not mind being his pupil in the air.

Eventually we were back on the road, trying to catch up with our now seriously disrupted schedule. You may think me callous, but I still could not bring myself to believe there was anything seriously the matter with my boss. I knew her well enough by now to interpret the downcast gaze as a sign not of demure shyness but rather as a simple reluctance to have to meet the eye of anybody who might see something there to question.

By the time we reached our next destination, the air of apprehensive concern was almost palpable. In response to a speech of welcome vibrant with genuine emotion, she contrived—again with downcast eyes—to shed a tear, and the mood both in the hall and in the media coverage that followed was of almost unreserved sympathy. It was another masterful performance and I mentally saluted it as such.

Lest I be thought terminally cynical, I should add that I also detected how close to the surface the Princess's inner conflicts and unhappiness came that day. I often saw these and other stronger emotions at work in her, however, and no matter how much of her mind and actions they affected, one part of her—and it was a steely and determined part—somehow never completely relinquished control.

If this seems confusing now, I can only say that it was at the time as well. There was only one helpful rule of thumb: see every apparent mood in its context. So she was upset and had to make an unscheduled loo stop—reasonable enough until you realized the current media value of the image of a fragile Princess publicly wrestling with the private demons of her marriage. A happy mood was the same. There was the Princess, without a care in the world, graciously acknowledging public adulation—while her husband agonized over organic agriculture or went foxhunting; or (a message for internal consumption only) while a hapless lady-in-waiting digested a series of privately delivered slights.

When a totally genuine emotion overcame her, as with her anxiety over Prince William's head injury or her grief at the death of her father, there was a sense almost of relief. Here at last was something real for her to experience, unlike the endless repertoire of public faces, or the equally comprehensive range of personae she adopted when pursuing a private objective, such as the recruitment of a new supporter or the isolation of a soon-to-be-ex-friend.

It is worth repeating that, despite the playacting, the Princess's frequent outward expressions of care and concern

were not mere cynicism. Frequently they were disturbingly
sincere, especially in the presence of very sick children. It
was just that she usually also had an eye open for the inevitable camera and took care not to miss an opportunity
for the watching world to share her feelings of sympathy. It
was possible to argue that this was in itself a perfectly adequate justification for her public existence. She invariably
did more good than harm, whatever complicated inner
script she was following at the time.

Soon the summer's usual twin ordeals were looming ever
closer. First was the Wales family holiday aboard a yacht lent
by the Greek shipowner John Latsis (also our neighbor in
St. James's). Then came the annual holiday at Balmoral with
other members of the royal family. For the Princess the two
holidays were a landmark in her relations with her husband
and his family.

Bizarre as it may now sound, the press were encouraged—not, I might add, by the Princess's office—to report
the Latsis cruise as a second honeymoon. The Balmoral residence, as it always had, would convey a sense of family togetherness and continuity. Hopefully it would show the
holidaying British public that the royal family was together
in its favorite surroundings of glens and braes and that all
was really well with the world.

In reality, the royal world was changing fast. Never again
would the Prince and Princess be required publicly to deny
the reality of their estrangement. Never again would the
Princess feel that she had to go along with such charades
without any means of escape. Unwittingly or not, the Morton revelations were the Princess's Rubicon. There was no
way of repairing the damage they had done.

The only task she had set herself was to decide how far
she wanted to go with her quest for independence and public recognition. Her views on this matter depended on her

nerve, which fluctuated alarmingly from day to day. Sometimes she was full of bravado: "I'm really strong, Patrick! People don't *realize* how strong I am!" At other times she was distinctly apprehensive: "I'm just sitting here not knowing where the next explosion is coming from." Or she would simply ask, for the umpteenth time: "What are the papers saying?"

The infrastructure was already in place to support her role as an independent royal figure. I had also made long-term plans for further solo overseas visits, as well as following up an idea to coalesce her leading patronages into an informal advisory committee—effectively a potential nucleus for a new Princess of Wales's Trust. The opportunities were all there, and I think this knowledge strengthened her in the private ordeals she faced when she was alone with the royal family in the weeks immediately after the Morton revelations.

During that year's Ascot Meeting, she spoke regularly to me of her sense of isolation both at Windsor Castle and in the public displays of togetherness in the Royal Box, and I had a strong impression at the time of the degree to which the senior households underestimated her. They did not truly appreciate her importance as the mother of the future King and as an applauded royal figure in her own right, but this was something that I do not think ever came easily to them. More importantly, they drastically miscalculated her abilities as a fighter and survivor.

From a position to which deference has always been paid, it must be only too easy to see manipulation and instability in any attempt to change the status quo. The Princess never lacked respect for the offices held by her husband and his family. As she memorably said, they were, after all, offices to which her own children were born. Nonetheless, on a person-to-person basis she could call upon her own noble lineage, her sense of injustice, and all her many other talents in resolving to fight when family diplomacy failed.

The failure of her adopted family to provide regular words of encouragement and reassurance—at least in a form that worked on her—made it easier for her to feel besieged. From this position it was only a short step to the kind of guerrilla tactics—press manipulation, calendar rivalry, and emotional blackmail—that she increasingly favored in her battle for survival.

The fact that the Princess may have needed an inordinate amount of indulgent handling must have been alien for the Queen and others of a generation that prized above all else the ability to control emotion and suppress spontaneity. However, such an attitude—to which I had also been raised and which claimed to uphold so many of the great British strengths that had withstood all the tests that Empire and war could bring—missed the point. To borrow a word so often ascribed to royal activities, I felt it was their *duty* to make whatever effort was necessary on a personal basis to understand the Princess of Wales and then to persist *ad infinitum* in affectionate attempts to lead her into safer paths. Whatever else I learned about her nature in eight years, I was quite sure of this: when handled with honesty, respect, and affection, her response would be cooperative and loyal. It would be appreciative too.

In various forms, this sermon was constantly in the back of my mind that summer. I preached it on several occasions to patient members of the Queen's office, who demonstrated their own good nature not just in hearing me out but also, I believe, in agreeing with me. Their apparent impotence only added to my own.

In the private family meetings that followed the serialization of *Diana: Her True Story*, the Princess inevitably felt the full weight of the accusations made against her. She was, after all, the outsider. She received several well-intended letters from Prince Philip at this time, but appeared to register only what she chose to hear as their unsympathetic tone. "He thinks I'm just in it for the publicity!" she complained to me.

Once again, it seemed that the messenger not the message was her in-laws' principal concern. Unfortunately, what the Princess saw as overbearing attempts to whip her into line only strengthened her defiance. She was very good at defiance. It is often a sign of emotional immaturity, as I think it was in the Princess's case. Allied with her other attributes, however, and strengthened by the hypocrisy of which she felt the victim, it made her a bad enemy.

Bearing all these factors in mind, it seemed to me that the Morton furor had a silver lining. At last the truth was in the open, even if that truth were only that the Prince and Princess were now irreconcilable. Surely some action must now be taken to resolve the situation.

On the morning after the serialization began, the Princess rang me privately and said, "The Prince and I have decided to separate."

My first reaction was one of relief. "Good," I said, and really meant it.

Other reactions followed as the implications of the news sank in. I was speaking on my car phone while negotiating the middle lane of Hyde Park Corner in the rush hour. Somewhere a distant part of my mind—that bit that did the steering and braking—registered how alert my fellow commuters were that morning, as I somehow avoided adding "collision" to the word "constitution" at the top of my list of immediate priorities.

By the time I reached the office I had got as far as thinking that, although "Her Royal Highness Diana, Princess of Wales" definitely had quite a good ring to it, I was equally sure that, both for the sake of the monarchy and for her own personal happiness, this might be the time to leave the stage completely. Fired as I was with a crusader's righteous passion on her behalf—and, somewhere lower down the scale, slightly concerned for my own future—I nevertheless saw this as a golden opportunity that might not return, publicly to finish the job that Morton had started. She could choose to sweep from the stage with her head held high, her enemies in shame and confusion behind her, and a new life of fascinating possibilities ahead of her.

Later in the day I phoned her. "Look, Ma'am. If I come

into work tomorrow and there's a note from you on my desk saying, 'Patrick, I've decided to run away with Mr. Perfect. Please sort everything out,' then I'll be only too glad. So long as you send for me afterward."

She laughed. The relief was evident in her own voice too. "No, Patrick," she said. "We've got work to do." That being the way the wind was blowing, I settled to the task of finding her the sort of work she wanted while lending her what sympathy and advice it was in me to give.

I did not accompany the Princess on the family cruise aboard the Latsis yacht, but it was by all accounts a holiday in name only. She sat in self-imposed isolation or with her children, avoiding the other guests who were overwhelmingly drawn from her husband's circle. She knew, she told me, that her husband was taking radio phone calls from Camilla Parker Bowles. She even claimed inadvertently to have listened in on one.

Knowledge of that relationship seemed no longer to pain her. Rather, it seemed a vindication of her stand and therefore something of a relief. It was also a kind of permit, as she began to see her own departure from the marital straight and narrow as in some way more excusable than her husband's. She had almost perfected the appearance of hurt innocence, which she kept up more or less until she felt able to shoulder her share of the guilt in *Panorama* three years later. Meanwhile, her references to Camilla Parker Bowles as "the Rottweiler" became fewer and she could still find in her heart the generosity to say of her husband, "I wish he could be happy. He'd be far better off going somewhere and painting. That's what he'd like. In Italy or somewhere."

Soon after the cruise, in August 1992, I teamed up with the Princess for a very successful engagement in Glasgow on behalf of a Scottish alcohol treatment charity. After the stresses of the holiday it was visibly a relief for her to be back at work, if only briefly, before the next ordeal began at Balmoral. After the engagement I accompanied the Princess on her flight to Aberdeen, where I would leave her to travel on to Balmoral while I returned to London. Also on board the plane were the Prince and the Duchess of York, as well as the children.

The Duchess had recently returned from France and was running just ahead of the publicity surrounding the infamous toe-sucking photographs. The atmosphere inside the small aircraft can be imagined. A black gloom settled over the royal compartment. The Duchess devoted her natural vivacity to lightening it, but she only seemed to make things worse. The Prince retreated into paperwork and the Princess stared fixedly out of the window or at the *Daily Mail*, while Fergie organized a kind of hide-and-seek for the young Princes and Princesses. As airborne recreation, the game had its limitations.

In Aberdeen I watched the royal people climb into their cars and set off in the direction of Balmoral. I knew my boss was heading into a lion's den, but my sympathy for her was elbowed aside by a sudden and overwhelming urge to acquaint myself with the Aberdeen airport bar. Utilitarian as my surroundings were, a martini at the Savoy would not have been more welcome.

No sooner had I embarked on my own brief holiday in the West Country—I did not dare go abroad in the circumstances—than the phone began to ring. It was the Palace press office. There was a vague rumor about some tapes.

I had heard this rumor before and dismissed it as just another among so many ghastly whisperings, gobbets of disinformation, and black propaganda that were by then my daily diet. This time, however, the rumors were true and "Squidgygate" burst upon us.

With a mixture of horrified prurience and fascination, anyone who could read a newspaper could follow the Princess's unhappy mobile-phone discussion—illicitly recorded nearly three years earlier—with a male admirer, generally accepted to be James Gilbey. She had never spoken to me directly about him, but I knew he was a "best friend" whose precise status I was happy to leave a bit vague.

It was an unedifying conversation to read, revealing an all-too-human Princess with an adolescent's vocabulary and an angry child's sense of injustice at her treatment by the royal family (notoriously described by her as "this f——ing family," an expression I had heard often enough to recognize its authenticity). Being so out of date, the recording was an uncomfortable throwback to a time when she was just coming to terms with her situation but had not yet found the courage or means to do something about it.

Given our peculiar way of dealing with matters of truth, I never bothered to ask the Princess if the tapes were authentic. Although I was at pains never to confirm it, everybody at the Palace knew they were the genuine article. If I had any doubts, I had only to call the Squidgygate phone line helpfully provided by the *Sun* to hear my boss's familiar tones. During our daily phone calls the Princess and I laughed about it. "Hope you're able to charge the call to the office!" she said.

Every morning brought a new rash of allegations and revelations. Incarcerated as she was in the north of Scotland—"like a rabbit" she said, trapped in her "lonely turret"—she was unable to see the London newspapers before the dubious delights of meeting the other residents of the castle at breakfast. Every day, therefore, I rose at 5:30 to fetch all the papers from the early train at a country station in Devon. Then I stood in a call box outside the newsagent's, breathing in the evidence of last night's boozy occupant and reading to the Princess as calmly as I could the printed transcript of her intimate conversation with James Gilbey and the damning chorus of comment that accompanied it.

On these occasions her mood could be anything but composed. She was alternately despairing, defiant, or lost in self-pity. Any crusading feelings I had gave way to simple sympathy for someone younger than me buried in misery and surrounded by the very people to whom she should have been able to turn for help but knew she could not.

One day I rashly set off for the beach, hoping that for perhaps ten hours the phone would not ring. I was wrong. Three miles down the road my pager summoned me to another public call box. "Patrick!" said the Princess in a shrill voice. "I want to talk to the Prime Minister!"

I watched a lone buzzard circling high over the sunlit Devon fields. What freedom, I thought enviously as my brain tried to produce the right reply. In its absence I came out with the private secretary's Sir Humphrey-ish standby. "Ye-e-e-s, Ma'am," I said slowly. "Is there anything in particular you'd like to say to him?"

Her voice grew shriller as her exasperation mounted at my failure to catch the obvious. "About this *family*, of course..." She became incoherent. She had better not talk to the Prime Minister like this, I thought.

I adopted my most soothing and therefore probably my most irritating bedside manner. "I understand, Ma'am, but perhaps you'd let me speak to the Prime Minister's office first. I know Alex Allan [the private secretary] quite well and perhaps I could brief him on what it is exactly that you think the Prime Minister can do to help. Shall I call you back in, say, an hour?"

"All right," she said, her voice dropping back to something like its normal pitch.

I drove on toward the beach and in due course stopped at a Happy Eater. The phone box smelled better than the restaurant. It was therefore an easy choice to do as my conscience dictated and make my call before attending to the sudden, urgent requirement for lunch.

"Well, Ma'am. Have you decided what it is exactly you'd like to say to the Prime Minister?" It was no surprise to learn that she had not. All of a sudden, however, there was a load of other, more important things she wanted to be done quickly. I never did made it to the beach that day, nor for many afterward.

The fallout from Squidgygate turned the rest of that un-happy summer into a protracted rehabilitation exercise, both for the Princess's image and her personal equilibrium. In the event, perhaps surprisingly, both survived pretty well. She certainly fared better than her husband did when his own telephone intimacies were revealed in the "Camilla-gate" tape early in 1993.

Of course, few people who came into contact with the Princess—especially those who were trying to obtain favors from her—were likely to reveal any adverse reaction to the tapes. Most seemed happy to act as though it had never happened and, privately, most accepted that it was none of their business. Who, after all, could honestly relish the idea of their phone conversations from the distant past being splashed all over the papers?

In the furor that followed the decision by some papers to print extracts from the conversation—and they were natu-rally the most cringe-making bits—proceeds from the ac-companying phone line were offered to several of the Princess's charities. To their eternal credit, all refused. David French, the head of Relate, led the stand for decency. "We have to show we have a moral compass in all this," he said.

Undoubtedly, the scandal hastened the decline of the Princess's pristine image. In its place, however, grew some-thing more durable: here was a young woman with flaws who nevertheless aspired to something better. Rather like her bulimia, a secret some might regard as shameful actually became a scar that she bore with an acceptance of her own fallibility.

Crucially, the Squidgygate drama also revealed her to be unhappy in love. The sentimental British public—or at least the media that served its tastes—might enjoy the process of finding out about this fact, but they were not ready to con-demn her for it. If anything, they were more likely to blame the people most obviously responsible for it. For this rea-son, outside a narrow circle of existing supporters who saw in the revelations some vindication for their man, the

Prince did not benefit from his wife's embarrassment. The fact that he was shown in his own subsequent tape scandal to be in a happy relationship himself only made the public reaction more disapproving.

Two independent accounts of this period make interesting reading now, so many years after that confusing, emotionally charged summer. In the heat of the moment, I may sometimes have fallen short of the professional objectivity that I thought was not only my best qualification for the post of private secretary but also my best tool in my quest to make a success of it. It was hard sometimes not to become emotionally involved in such a dramatic saga. Luckily, however, it contained so many elements of farce—I had only to picture myself spelling out lines from the Squidgygate transcripts on the crackling phone line to Balmoral—that it was usually possible to return to the real world of mortgages and gas bills with a laugh of sheer disbelief. Nonetheless, in circumstances devoid of most reliable outside reference points, it was a relief to find some independent commentary that could lend credibility to my gut-feelings about the Princess and her situation.

The first was from the August 1992 edition of *Life* magazine. Under the heading ALONE TOGETHER, Robert Lacey made some very acute observations, not least an assertion that *Diana: Her True Story* was "the Princess's personal petition for divorce...as one-sided and unfair as such documents usually are." "But," he said, "many parts of its story must be considered authentic." He went on, "She considers her marriage dead and she wants the world to know about it—even at the risk of jeopardizing her Royal position... she has *not* lived happily ever after." Like many others, Lacey saw *Her True Story* as the end of a fairy tale—an image that now had to be replaced with a picture of bleak, "almost gothic" tragedy.

He put the current frenzy in some sort of royal context: "Diana is being criticized by traditionalists for breaching a cardinal protocol—Royal folk don't blab. Yet a look at the history of the Monarchy's relationship with the media suggests that Diana could be forgiven for not fully understanding the rules of the complex and often devious game." He went on to describe how both the Queen Mother, with her prewar media courtship as Duchess of York, and the present-day Queen, with films such as *Royal Family*, had been involved in "calculated surrenders of cherished Royal privacy." He also listed instances of active collaboration with biographers by Prince Philip, Princess Margaret, the Prince of Wales, the Duke of York, Princess Michael, and the Duchess of York. Then he commented:

> Diana's original encouragement of her True Story might have been excused as one rash sally in a war that has had Royal partisans on both sides. But the Princess's refusal to disavow the book adds up in Royal eyes to a clear case of treason... The Princess will not make an easy target... She has been a trouper—caring, brave and natural with an extraordinary ability to reach out and touch people's hearts.

His final analysis of the cause of the marital breakdown takes some beating: "Two emotionally needy people have come together and have discovered they have only demands to make."

Another independent observer, the magazine the *Economist*, made its point with satire, providing a company brief on the House of Windsor in its August 29, 1992, edition. Describing it as a fairly typical British firm, the article went on to note that the company's management "has diversified into younger brands and raised the firm's profile to a new emphasis on public relations." The management were hoping to increase customer awareness and prevent the possibility that "customers might switch to a cheaper Presidential product." However, "high brand awareness can cause problems when quality is in doubt." About the Princess, the article said:

Current difficulties with The Princess of Wales illustrate a different problem created by the dash into the entertainment business. The Princess was promoted so heavily that many customers transferred their loyalty to this one product at the expense of the rest of the range... If she were to leave there would be trouble for Windsor. She has outperformed the rest of the range so dramatically that she could carry the customers with her.

One final commentary on the events of that summer comes from a rather less impartial source, but for me it was the best and most significant of the lot as I searched for reassurance that I was doing the right thing:

I did so want you to know how much your support, encouragement and guidance has meant to me, particularly during the last two months... I do admire you enormously, not least for having to cope with a lady Boss, but you do it with a unique quality which I trust implicitly!

As with most of her missives, this one came "with love from Diana." *Love*, I thought, *whatever that means*.

*D*arkening our horizon was the planned joint tour to Korea, due to take place at the beginning of November 1992. Her Majesty's Ambassador to Seoul at that time was David Wright, who had led our joint tour to Indonesia and Hong Kong with such aplomb. Despite the eventual success of that tour, it had suffered its fair share of stressful dramas and David had borne the brunt of them. Now he was volunteering for a repeat dose. I could not quite understand why he had not invented almost any excuse to prevent such a visit occurring during his ambassadorship. His good nature and optimism certainly exceeded mine.

I was fortunate in that the only contribution the
Princess's office would make to the tour was the presence
of Anne Beckwith-Smith as lady-in-waiting. I was pretty
sure that by fielding our strongest player we were doing
everything that could be done in the circumstances to support our boss through what were plainly going to be difficult days.

Then, in a sudden and deeply unwelcome development
only days before they were due to depart, the Princess decided in the name of "honesty" that she could not accompany the Prince on a tour that she saw as nothing more than
a charade. In this, of course, she was very largely correct, but
as I grimly coped with the fallout I reflected that it was a
singularly inappropriate moment to discover one of the
fundamental truths about royal tours in general.

Such was the overheated atmosphere of the time that I
wrote a long and carefully argued note to her. Whatever
point about her marriage she was trying to make, I said, she
could make it far better if she was not at the same time risk-
ing being seen as the wrecker of a diplomatic initiative of
national importance. If she did not do her bit in representing the country this time, how could we ever win Foreign
Office support for her own overseas tour plans later on?

It was strong stuff and I concluded by saying that had I
not been so blunt with her, she would be justified in sacking me for dereliction of duty. If she still decided not to go,
she would pretty soon want to sack me in any case. In fact,
I was on fairly safe ground here, as I already knew that the
Queen was prepared to tell the Princess where her duty lay.
I would like to think that my veiled threat of resignation
helped to change the Princess's mind, but you may prefer to
believe that it was the Queen's personal intervention that
tipped the balance. Whatever the reason, the Princess reluctantly set out for Korea with the Prince as planned.

She had hardly touched down in Seoul when the familiar pattern of highly charged phone calls began, as the

Princess used me—and many others, I am sure—as an outlet for the frustration and isolation she felt. Taking advantage of the "cat's away" atmosphere at St. James's, I had sneaked off to the Land Rover factory to take up a long-postponed invitation to see the production line. Inevitably, just as the guided tour was about to start, my pager emitted its dreaded bleep. Some internal organ in the vicinity of my waistband always seemed to know instinctively that it was she.

"Patrick! *Why* am I on this trip? It's so *dishonest!* I *knew* I shouldn't have come..."

I realized that, whatever other reasons she may have given for not wanting to accompany the Prince to Korea (the thought had crossed my mind that she only wanted to seize the opportunity to embarrass him), she might also have wanted to avoid being cut off from her network of supporters and friends at such a critical time. Since most of the support she derived from this network came over the phone line anyway, however—often in fervent but not very considered terms—mere distance probably counted for little. More probably it was separation from her children that took the greatest toll, especially when uncritical love—or any love, in fact—was in such short supply closer to hand.

This factor, as much as disenchantment with her tour partner, might account for some of the doleful looks that characterized almost all the photographs emerging from Korea. Some newspaper editors subsequently admitted that they had deliberately chosen the most miserable pictures to give credence to their harsh predictions about the imminent demise of the Waleses' marriage. Once again, unnecessary energy was wasted on remonstrating with the newspapers on their unhelpful choice of illustrations. Cynical it may have been, but even had they searched hard for the few photographs that could have been interpreted as showing the couple happy in each other's company, I do not believe it would have made a jot of difference to events over the following few weeks.

As others have commented, if the first ten months of
1992 had seen the press pack licking its lips at the prospect
of the banquet in store, with the Korean tour they moved in
for the kill. By the time the Waleses had returned to London for the annual Remembrance Day observations, the
tabloids had their stories ready. A MARRIAGE IN NAME ONLY
said the *Daily Mail* and, with its reporters drawing on their
typically "excellent" sources, the tone was set for the tenor
of royal reporting in the four weeks that remained before
official announcement of the separation.

Much was made in some of the papers about the
Princess's appearance above the Cenotaph with the
Princess Royal and the Queen Mother, standing at their
traditional vantage point on the Foreign Office balcony. Either by use of a clever camera angle—or, it was alleged,
clever computer gimmickry—the Princess appeared to be
standing significantly apart from the others. Again such
speculation was irrelevant. With or without trick photogra-
phy, the gap between the figures on the balcony was spiritual and emotional rather than physical.

Given the increasingly fraught atmosphere, it was a relief
to set out for Paris a couple of days after Remembrance
Day on the Princess's next solo tour. Friday, November
13—a date that might have promised ill omens—turned out
to mark the start of a particularly rewarding trip. Its indis-
putable success finally threw down the gauntlet to those
who might figuratively have wished the Princess to "get to
a nunnery."

As the official responsible for the tour, I was painfully
conscious of the subplot of Palace politics that would deter-
mine its perceived success or failure quite as much as anything that happened in front of the adoring crowds in Paris.
The French media had already decided which side it supported. *Paris-Match* carried a front-page Demarchelier pho-

tograph along with the exhortation, COURAGE PRINCESSE! Not for the first or last time, we set off on our ambassadorial mission uncomfortably conscious that success abroad was unlikely to translate into universal approval at home.

"We'll show them!" said the Princess, determined blue eyes staring fixedly out of the window of the royal jet. She seemed to be speaking to the whole city as we climbed into the sky above London. In fact, I knew her words were more specifically intended for the occupants of a group of buildings at the end of the Mall, for the newsrooms of the capital, and for certain residents of country houses in Gloucestershire.

Interestingly, she had also said "we." I had come to recognize that simple pronoun as a code word of huge significance. This was not the royal "we" so beloved of dumb comedians. It was an invitation to a conspiracy. It was an offer of triumph or guilt by association with her one-woman crusade for independence. That "we" gave her courage and recruited other consciences to share her doubts. It often gave me nightmares, but by now it was far too late for me to get off the roller coaster that her life had become. I was too closely associated with this turbulent Princess to expect the offer of a safe, alternative position in the royal machine—and anyway, the terror of the ride had become a powerful drug. I was hooked.

The Paris tour, though only lasting three days, turned out to be a triumph. Under the benign eye of the towering British Ambassador Ewen Fergusson, the program ran smoothly from one successful engagement to the next. Each was a classic set piece in which the Princess's striking beauty and crowd-pleasing style could be displayed to maximum advantage.

She glowed under the rapturous attention, responding as usual to the stimulus of public expectation by producing a flawless display of how to be a royal celebrity. Every gesture, every glance, every step of every walkabout revealed a professional at the peak of her form and no one, from the Pres-

ident of the Republic to the most cynical member of the
press circus, was immune to her charm.

The President was perhaps particularly susceptible. In
the ornate splendor of the Élysée Palace, he and his wife
hosted an intimate tea party. Differences of age, language,
and status were swept aside as the Princess's laughter and
the growing animation of her hosts overcame the formality
of our surroundings.

As she took leave of the Mitterands at the top of the
Palace steps, scores of flashbulbs erupted simultaneously,
bathing the Princess in an eerie blue light, freezing her
image starkly against the historic stonework. She somehow
dwarfed not only the head of state, who bathed in her reflected glory, but even the imposing imperial backdrop itself.

Perhaps it was the convergence of powerful symbols that
momentarily made me lose my professional detachment. I
was suddenly gripped by the realization that I was witness-
ing a defining moment, and even then I was poignantly
aware that it marked a peak that would never again be
scaled. Subconsciously I never forgot the marital clash that
awaited us back in London. Subconsciously I also knew
that, even if she won the battle for her independence, the
war would cost the Princess her crown. This was all still in
the future, however. In that instant, as the electronic day-
light threw the surrounding Parisian dusk into momentary
blackness, the Princess shone at her brightest.

Less than five years later, in the same city and under the
same remorseless flashbulbs, she lay broken and dying in the
wreckage of a car. This time there had been no police outriders, only paparazzi on motorbikes; there had been no benign Ambassador at her side, only a playboy lover; and there
had been no watchful protectors, under whose attention she
may sometimes have chafed but from whom she had fatally
cut herself off.

For me her Paris tour of November 1992 marked the
Princess's apogee. Many more great and uplifting achieve-

ments still lay ahead of her, but in my memory these were always tarnished to some extent by the shortcomings and doubts that her new independence all too readily exposed. Paris saw her, briefly, without that tarnish. To my eyes, knowing what she had already endured and what lay ahead in the immediate future, there was something heroic in her. Like much heroism, it was not without its flaws and may even have been the compensating flip side of some deep fear. Nonetheless, that night in Paris it sprang from a strength of spirit momentarily freed from accumulations of false sentiment in a simple bid for survival.

PART II

OUT

14

Horribilissimus

*T*he Princess returned to London on November 15, 1992, with the Parisian crowds' cheers ringing in her ears, a renewed confidence in her ability to outplay her in-laws—especially her husband—at their own game, and a large, pink, battery-powered vibrator. This had been obtained by one of our party with the aim of raising royal morale at critical moments. Although never used for its designed purpose, it performed this humorous role very well indeed—and God knows, we would find little enough to laugh about in the months to come, plagued by the harsh realities of the Waleses' marital crisis.

Under a long-standing arrangement, the Princess was due to play her usual role in support of the Prince at a private weekend at Sandringham on November 20 and 21. The prospect filled her with anger and dread. In many ways, that Sandringham weekend encapsulated the forces at work in the disintegration of the couple's marriage. The Prince seemed to resort to a reliance on the dignity and status of his title, if only to conceal exasperation with a wife now completely beyond his control or comprehension. For her part, the Princess felt a burning sense of injustice at her position, pilloried for Morton and Squidgygate, yet surely no more a sinner than her straying husband. The clash over that weekend—ironically planned originally as relaxation for them both—left the Prince's formidable strength undiminished and the Princess's equally formidable defiance in full blaze.

"They're all *his* friends," she complained to me. "I'm going to be completely outnumbered." Later her familiar mantra made an appearance: "It's all so *false!*"

I warned her that her absence would precipitate a crisis. In the discussion that followed she was undeterred, aware of her own strength after the success of Paris and perhaps recognizing a tactical opportunity to wrong-foot the Prince. I sensed that she was determined to force the issue, almost whatever the outcome. Anything would be better than this agonizing uncertainty.

I could see her point. The idea of playing happy families to an audience that would be at best cool toward her after the scandals of the summer seemed less than desirable, both for her and the children. Given the explosive tensions simmering below the surface, it also seemed plain folly.

Aware of the implications of what she was doing, therefore, this time she declined to play her allotted role. As so often in a real crisis, she was cool and utterly composed. She was also still able to find relief in black humor about her situation. "Just think, Patrick," she said. "Nicholas Soames Secretary of State for Defense can eat all the food they'd bought for me. I'd probably only have sicked it up anyway!" Perhaps because of her ability to make jokes like this, there was in fact no sign of the bulimia that sometimes returned to torment her at moments of tension.

Faced with what he saw as his wife's obduracy, the Prince's reaction was one of understandable but unwise frustration, expressed in blunt and peremptory tones. In response, to emphasize that her intentions were not simply to express some peevish fit of pique, the Princess took the children to see their grandmother the Queen. Her Majesty, one may imagine, did not welcome this turn of events but was not in a position to demur. She had already resigned herself to the idea of separation, at least on a temporary basis, but to the Princess's frustration she was still determined to remain above the squabble.

The Princess's refusal to take William and Harry to Sandringham that weekend has been cited as evidence of her readiness to manipulate the children as pawns in her maneuvering with the Prince. The allegation could not be rebutted convincingly, because in my opinion it was at least partly true. The children were too powerful an asset to be left out of the dispute completely. Given the Princess's highly stressed condition (undeniable despite her outward calm), and considering the strength of the opposition, such restraint would have been scarcely human and was certainly quite out of character.

Nevertheless, in order to assert her claim to the moral high ground, on her lawyer's advice she wrote the Prince a careful letter of explanation in which, among other things, she said that she felt the atmosphere at Sandringham would not be conducive to a happy weekend for the children. Nor could she be sure that he would not expose them to guests whose presence would be unwelcome to her—a scarcely veiled reference to Camilla Parker Bowles.

This was too much for the Prince. I was duly confronted by Richard Aylard, wearing his most important expression and asking to be told the name of the Princess's lawyers.

When I reported this escalation to the Princess, her reply added a plaintive echo of a time now far in the past; an echo more than tinged with apprehension. "But Patrick," she said, "I don't want to speak to his lawyers. I want to speak to *him*..." This was a touching sentiment, but even as she said it we both knew there had been ample opportunities to speak in the past, none of which had proved adequate. Except as a gesture, such a proposal was far too late.

The Sandringham weekend duly passed without the Princess or her sons. On November 25 she got her meeting with the Prince, but it was only to hear him say that he was determined on a separation. The lawyers went to work.

As if on another planet, elsewhere in the royal universe normal life maintained the even tenor of its ways—and very nice some of them were too. At the beginning of December, in a bizarre contrast to the separation negotiations painfully dominating life in St. James's Palace, I went to Windsor Great Park for a very sedate day's shooting with senior members of other households.

As always, the shooting was entertaining and we had the added interest on some drives of seeing in the distance the roofs of Windsor Castle, still all too plainly bearing the scars of the recent, disastrous fire. The occasion was also a useful opportunity to gauge attitudes in other households, not so much to me as to my mercurial boss.

This time my colleagues—all from secure posts in comfortably established households presided over by dull but reliable royal performers—regarded me with varying degrees of wariness. Some expressed a cautious sympathy, though whether because I had been put in an awkward position or simply because I worked for a madwoman was hard to tell. Others, even those I had known for years, appeared to fear contagion. To be fair, however, the speech and body language that conveyed their distaste had probably been bred into them.

I did my best to ensure that the Princess's reputation was upheld in the respectable tally of birds accounted for by our office. I also tried to adopt the neutral bonhomie that I judged the most appropriate mask to wear in the company of people who I did not think could even begin to understand the difficulties I faced and who did not care very much anyway.

Other routine aspects of royal life also carried on, regardless of the tortured state of relations between the Prince and

Princess. One fixture in particular was a far cry from the civilized predictability of the Windsor shoot. As the lawyers locked horns in earnest, the curtain was brought down on the final pretense of unity in coordinating the engagement calendars of the Prince and Princess. The biannual program meeting, scene in previous years of so much suppressed hilarity, was held at KP less than a week before the formal announcement of the separation. It was the merest fig leaf, the tail end of a process that had not worked harmoniously for many years, if indeed it ever had.

With a peremptoriness that seemed to be becoming a standard feature of the Prince's mouthpieces, I was informed that His Royal Highness would be holding his program meeting at such and such a time. Her Royal Highness very sensibly did not feel disposed to attend a meeting at which she would have been heavily outnumbered and the focus of hostile attention.

Less sensibly, I was determined to put in an appearance, not least because I knew that my presence was neither necessary nor welcome. I felt I needed no further justification and sat awkwardly through the usual interminable process of wheedling the Prince into agreeing his program for the next six months. I made some nervous, pre-scripted remarks where I thought the Princess's interests should be represented and stammered my replies to the Prince's pointed questions.

"*How* do you pronounce this disease?" he said, pointing to an entry on a list of his wife's charity engagements.

"DystrophicEpidermolysisBullosaSir!" A royal grimace produced the expected titter around the table. I wished I had stayed away. "Also known simply as 'EB,'" I added, remembering some defiance and the small, bandage-wrapped victims I had seen at Great Ormond Street.

At last it was over. We were dismissed and the Prince headed for his study. Not quite knowing what I was doing, I found myself following him and knocked on the door. "Sir, can I speak to you for a minute?"

The public face of the meeting had gone. He looked haggard and resentful of my intrusion. "What is it?" he asked, busily sorting through the piles of books that as usual had accumulated around the edges of the room.

That's a very good question, I thought, cursing the impulse that had brought me to this moment of acute shared embarrassment. Surely I was just salving my own conscience. "I joined this household to serve both Your Royal Highnesses," I eventually managed to say. It seemed a good start, but I was wondering what came next. Suddenly I had joined the ranks of those who thought that they alone held the key to resolving this poisonous marital impasse. As that thought entered my head, I also realized that any key had long since been mislaid. "I wish there was some way that this could still be the case," I finished lamely.

For a moment he looked even more resentful, but also more sad. "I don't know," he said. "Perhaps there's something..." He trailed off.

Perhaps there was, but neither of us could find it. After a few moments I excused myself, feeling very foolish. Letting myself out of the front door of KP, I trudged slowly across the gravel toward my car, lost in thought.

Suddenly a strong arm was clapped none too gently around my shoulders. It belonged to the Princess's duty policeman, a stalwart in every way. I had last seen him in Paris. "Cheer up, Pat," he said now. "Good God, man! I've never seen you looking so miserable!"

As in every separation, the involvement of the lawyers marked a significant deterioration in the atmosphere between the couple. Nevertheless, it also marked a further clarification for those of us who still sometimes woke up wondering if we were not just part of some horrible nightmare. This was no longer a nightmare: it was reality, albeit with nightmarish implications.

The Princess's lawyer Paul Butner had his priorities clearly marked out. First and foremost were the arrangements for her contact with the children as the parent with the closest involvement in their day-to-day care. Second— by a long way—came the negotiation of what initially seemed to me a colossal financial settlement that would enable her to pursue her career and style of living. (I did not think it was colossal for long. The costs of maintaining a working Princess in the manner to which she was entitled to be accustomed could quickly be rounded up into the tens of millions of pounds—as the Prince discovered when the divorce settlement was finally reached more than three years later.)

To my dismay, under Lord Goodman, Paul's opponents were the royal solicitors Farrer & Co. My view was that this choice was highly symbolic—and highly regrettable. It invited defiance. The watching world would clearly see from the involvement of the Queen's own solicitors that this was to be a fight between the royal establishment and the upstart Princess. To me this was a completely misleading message. The Princess's grievance was against the conduct of her marriage not against the monarchy, whatever her occasional frustrations with the people who served it. The choice of lawyers unnecessarily exacerbated the image of a house tearing itself apart, especially when the Queen herself was taking such trouble to remain neutral.

I was also dismayed because both Matthew Farrer and Henry Boyd-Carpenter—the lawyers initially most closely involved on behalf of the Prince—had been in turn my cotrustees of the Princess of Wales's Charities Trust. They had also, I hoped, become good friends and I think their dismay was little less than my own when they found themselves pitted against the Princess. As the pace of the divorce negotiations quickened over the next few years, their place was taken by Fiona Shackleton.

The dying weeks of 1992 were dominated by legal discussions, culminating in a separation document that was agreed in time for the Prime Minister's announcement to the House of Commons planned for December 9. This would be the first official acknowledgment that the Prince and Princess had legally separated.

Every part of our normal office routine and every engagement the Princess carried out took place against the continuous background accompaniment of these discussions. Some were just between the lawyers. Others involved Richard Aylard and myself, and sometimes also the Queen's private secretary Robert Fellowes and her deputy private secretary Robin (now Sir Robin) Janvrin.

Their subject matter, to borrow an expression from Lord McGregor, was genuinely "the stuff of people's souls," concerning contact with the children, financial arrangements, and the allocation of private possessions. This being no ordinary separation, however, the discussions were further expanded to include the question of the Princess's future role. This was where I became not only involved but also indignant.

Whatever other advice the Prince was receiving at this time, it seemed to include the suggestion that, having reached the difficult decision to separate from his wife, he might as well grasp the nettle now and thwart her obvious ambitions to become an independent royal operator—or what one of his advisers, with his lip only slightly curled, described as "a semidetached member of the royal family." It was at about this time that the phrase "loose cannon" also became popular.

They could perhaps see the danger (anticipated by both *Life* and the *Economist* in the articles I quoted earlier) in letting the Prince become a sitting target for a newly liberated Princess ready to wreak her revenge on him at every opportunity, and ready to continue eclipsing him in royal duties all over the world, wherever her fancy took her. Nevertheless, the Prince's advisers were mistaken in the tactics they chose to combat this. In trying to circumscribe the Princess's public activities—by, for example, restricting her use of the Queen's Flight and the royal train, or by down-grading in some way the protocol due to her when visiting destinations at home or abroad—the Prince's negotiators only succeeded in making themselves look petty and vindictive.

They also alerted some wavering minds at the heart of Buckingham Palace to the growing spite that had contributed to the present crisis. The negotiations were always outwardly polite, but I did not underestimate the forces arrayed against the Princess, or their capacity to act ruthlessly in defense of what *they* chose to interpret as the interests of the Crown. The problem for me was that, when they chose to make the Crown's interests synonymous with those of the heir, I seriously thought they were wrong.

In the end, since the Crown declined to come down on the Prince's side—particularly on the question of restricting the Princess's future activities—the way was open for the Princess to drive a hard bargain. Thanks to Paul's negotiating skills, she got practically everything she wanted in the separation agreement, including—against her husband's wishes—the continued presence of her office alongside his in St. James's Palace. Only the question of finance defied resolution and this was not achieved until the divorce was finalized in 1996. The Queen's one stipulation was that the Princess should not represent her abroad, though in practice it proved almost impossible to define exactly what "represent" meant in this context—a happy outcome that I like to think the Queen fully intended.

The refusal of Buckingham Palace to become involved in what was therefore solely a dispute between the Waleses was a great encouragement to me and, I think, to some of the Prince's advisers as well. In an attempt to promote bipartisanship among the occupants of all the Palaces, the Lord Chamberlain circulated a letter exhorting understanding for both sides.

Once the agreement had been settled, in legal terms the Princess was left in a very favorable position. Her role as mother had been reinforced as the parent with day-to-day care of the children. She would now have the apartment at KP entirely to herself and would be spared the weekly trek to Highgrove. Her finances, though not yet finally resolved, were at least ample. Her office remained where it should be, in the heart of London's royal compound.

In an unintentional side effect, her public profile—which could now add "gutsy independent fighter for the rights of scorned women" to its other laurels—had also been significantly enhanced. Furthermore, she held firmly in her own hands the opportunity to enhance it still further with an unfettered program of public engagements at home and at worst a legalistic quibble over the definition of her status abroad. The Queen's attitude seemed to be that no further injustice or demotion must be directed at the Princess, on the basis that she now had sufficient rein with which to do virtually as she pleased, and others should be left to judge whether her status and popularity were truly earned.

Exhilarating this might be, I thought as I contemplated the implications of Paul's success, but on the rein or not, it was going to be a very lonely field in which our thoroughbred could now kick up her heels. In the distance, of course, the gate out of the lush royal enclosure was open.

Such leisurely speculation was for the future, however. Right now the race was on to tidy up this mess as best we could so that it could be presented formally by the Prime Minister to Parliament. We were terrified that further leaks in the press would force a premature confirmation of news that was already being widely touted in the media.

The urgency gave Richard Aylard and myself a sudden and welcome sense of shared purpose. I had already sent him a short note telling him of my hope that, with good communication at our level, whatever the estrangement of our principals, we could minimize the damage that was bound to accompany our painful task. Although he did not feel inclined to reply on paper, we found that we worked well together.

This was fortunate, because there was no precedent to guide us. Nor was there much time, which was another blessing since we had little opportunity to reflect on the enormity of what we were doing—until later, that is, when there was also the chance to feel very, very sad.

We and a handful of like-minded others labored all weekend over draft statements and interminable lists of hypothetical questions and less hypothetical answers, to be used by the Palace press office when the expected deluge of inquiries hit them. Early drafts of possible statements and "Qs and As" had been circulated as much as three weeks before, but now the intervening lawyers' work had to be incorporated and our royal employers' own views reflected as accurately as we could manage. The results were very much a team effort and showed, I thought rather wistfully, what we could achieve when we all worked together. How ironic that our greatest moment of cooperation should also be our last.

Most of the Qs and As were remarkably honest. They dealt with practical details such as offices and staff with simple accuracy: "There will be few changes." Others attempted to be a little more philosophical. Lifting our eyes for a minute from immediate practicalities, we were dimly aware of the emotions that were being wrung by the crisis from the hearts of ordinary subjects. So, to the question "Why has all this happened?" we answered that the Prince and Princess had recognized with sadness that their relationship had broken down and that their marriage could not continue in its present form. They were, we said, still "fond and supportive" of each other and hoped that separation would help them and their children to live in greater harmony.

Going out on a limb, we denied that there was any other party involved. Going a little further, we also asserted that there was no reason why the Princess should not still be Queen. This last answer caused a lot of raised eyebrows and a few actual gasps of surprise. Nonetheless, until there was a divorce—and we had skirted *that* tricky question with the politician's "there are no plans" answer—it was the truth, at least as far as anyone could judge. The history cupboard was ransacked to find appropriate precedents, without much success. The British constitution being mostly unwritten, there was no helpful subclause to which we could refer for guidance. So we pressed on, in my case at least, aware that we were creating a piece of constitutional history as we did so.

By the evening of Tuesday, December 8 we were as ready as we could be and still, miraculously, the security held. In the end it was only when the teleprompt for Prime Minister's Questions was being loaded that the cat got out of the bag.

The Prime Minister was due to make his announcement to the Commons the following afternoon, but first he said he wanted a final private word with the Prince and Princess separately. John Major may have had his critics, but I could not fault the instincts that helped make him so sympathetic to the causes of the separation and do his best to soften the blow when it fell.

In one of several phone conversations, John Major's private secretary Alex Allan had said that the PM just wanted to see if there was anything he could do to help, even at this eleventh hour. In line with the PM's scrupulously observed neutrality in the dispute, Alex had taken care to consult me on several occasions about the Princess's concerns and intentions. Both then and throughout my remaining years with the Princess, I found him a regular source of encouragement and good advice (not to mention amusing lunches).

At 8:30 on the Wednesday morning I was at St. James's Palace ready to receive the Prime Minister and show him into the Prince's office, which, unusually, the Princess was borrowing for the occasion. By that stage, dog-tired and emotionally numbed as I was, the tall and energetic figure with its firm handshake and broad smile induced in me an almost uncontrollable urge to beg him tearfully to tell me the answer to the whole damn business. I did no such thing, of course. After my embarrassing encounter with the Prince, I had had enough of spontaneous gestures. They only caused trouble.

John Major and the Princess were alone together for about twenty minutes and when they emerged, I noted that they were subdued but friendly, as if consoling each other on the death of a mutual friend. I have no doubt that the Prime Minister's attitude was the same when he called on the Prince that day.

"He's terribly nice," the Princess said to me after he had gone. "And very supportive." Indeed he was, then and in all our subsequent dealings with his office, although he struck me as someone who would have been sympathetic to any young person in such dire straits. His impartiality was never in doubt, even if the Princess might have wished to see it as favoring her. That said, he always supported any proposal that would have cemented her position as an established public figure with an important role to play in national life.

Shortly before the Prime Minister was due to stand up in the House, Charles Anson, the Queen's press secretary, summoned a small party of senior royal reporters to his office in Buckingham Palace. Richard and I flanked him as he read out the prepared statements and took their questions, answering as agreed from our carefully written crib sheets.

The news cannot have been a surprise to them, yet from their expressions it was plain that several realized the gravity of what they were hearing. I watched with amusement as they were released from the Privy Purse Door and ran with what dignity they could muster across the great forecourt, toward the camera crews waiting outside the gates.

For us there was nothing more to do. A footman brought coffee and we drank it in virtual silence. I left the others and wandered through the warren of rooms in the Palace press office. They were almost deserted—the lull before the storm. I idly wondered if these same rooms had seen similar scenes as the minutes counted down to Edward VIII's immortal abdication broadcast. At least he had gone into exile straightaway, I thought, and had taken his immediate staff with him. A few weeks setting up a new life in France seemed like a welcome alternative to the future I was facing.

The Princess had rather gamely decided to carry on with the day's engagements on the Tyne. She had taken with her neither an equerry nor a private secretary, nor even a lady-in-waiting. Instead she had chosen one of the senior secretaries from the joint miscellaneous letters section of the office, a mature lady with a natural empathy that made her the ideal companion to a young woman in the very eye of the hurricane that raged about her.

That evening I called at KP to brief the Princess on the day's events back at base. She was buoyed up by the warm welcome she had received in Newcastle and invited me to help myself from the drinks tray. She sat down on the sofa and tucked up her feet. "Well, Patrick. We did it!"

"We did, Ma'am. Or rather, you did. Here's to your future." I raised my glass to her.

I was struck by how well my boss was weathering the storm. To go with her calmness and humor in the midst of the crisis, I also noticed an understandable relief. At long last the waiting was over. It was still unclear what was going to come next, but we were all still breathing and suddenly there seemed to be everything to play for.

In the weeks that followed this new mood deepened, particularly as it slowly dawned on the world that for both the Prince and Princess their new, separate status made little difference. "Business as usual" was the prevailing theme.

There were some changes, of course. The domestic staff underwent a fairly ruthless reorganization in the wake of the separation. A new, elite domestic team was ordained for Highgrove. The unchosen ones thus displaced were either paid off or, in a couple of cases, taken in as strays at KP by a sympathetic Princess (after some softhearted persuading by me).

In a series of raids, the Prince's staff made a thorough job of removing his effects from KP—so thorough, in fact, that they even ripped the lavatory out of his bathroom. Meanwhile, in the country, traces of the Princess's former occupancy were being systematically removed from Highgrove and designer Robert Kime moved in to complete a very thorough transformation.

This attitude reflected a residual bitterness in some sections of what was still nominally a joint household. The Prince and Princess themselves were able to begin rebuilding a more civilized relationship quite quickly (they were together again in public by the time of the Battle of the Atlantic commemorations in Liverpool in May). References to "the Rottweiler" disappeared entirely from the Princess's vocabulary. Some employees, however, particularly among the Prince's domestic staff, seemed somehow to nurse a resentment on his behalf. This reservoir of ill feeling grew into a constant reminder that neither side could really move on until the divorce was properly finalized—and that was years away.

The Princess's response was rather less divisive. At KP she tentatively began putting her own mark on the former family home that she would now have to herself, except when it was her turn to look after William and Harry. Family photographs and pictures of the Prince remained in several rooms, not least for the benefit of the children. Some of the self-mocking cartoons that I had admired in the cloakroom during my very first visit were replaced with others slightly less deferential. A couple of rooms received the expert attention of the interior designer Dudley Poplak.

After years of hushed voices and a perceptible tension, the atmosphere at KP lightened almost overnight. Happily, a great sense of team spirit developed, which brought relations between the house and office staff to a point closer than I had ever known it before.

A great party was held. The Princess played the piano. We all sang and many people danced as we glowed with the sudden feeling that the grown-ups had gone out for the evening and would not be back for hours and hours…if they were going to come back at all.

15

Payback

*T*he next year began well for the Princess. It was hard not to agree with the front-page judgment of *Vanity Fair* in February 1993. DI'S PALACE COUP it trumpeted, going on to list the Princess's extraordinary success in securing her own future at the expense of her enemies, who were seen to have been left leaden-footed and peevishly swatting at her elusive heels.

Disappointingly, however, the year ended with headlines of a different sort. HAS IT ALL GONE WRONG FOR PRINCESS DIANA? asked the *Daily Express* on November 3, 1993. Even more foreboding was the *Evening Standard*'s SENSATION AS DIANA CUTS ROYAL DUTIES on December 3. The story of how the year progressed is, I am afraid, a story of lost opportunities and old patterns of behavior that the Princess proved powerless to overcome. It is also a story of enemies unappeased, waiting patiently for the butterfly life to run its brief course.

Such an outcome certainly seemed remote at the beginning of the year. Although written by Anthony Holden, who was undeniably one of the Prince's more critical chroniclers, the February *Vanity Fair* article might claim to have been speaking for the public mood when it said:

> Since the announcement of the end of her marriage on December 9th, Diana, Princess of Wales, has been visibly reborn. There is a new bounce in her step, a cheekier smile on her face, a new gleam in those flirtatious blue eyes...At long last the sham was over. For Diana it was a moment of triumph. For Prince Charles it was a crushing defeat...

Looking into the future, he saw the Princess firmly in the ascendant, "a heavyweight on the world stage." It seemed reasonable enough, certainly to an outside observer. After all, she had just enjoyed a forty-minute meeting with President Mitterand. Holden went on to note an uncomfortable truth for the old guard:

> British historians were hard pressed to remember any previous Princess of Wales—let alone one with the looks of a Hollywood film star—conducting talks, in her own right, with a major foreign head of state...Diana's staff is discreetly orchestrating a rapid move to center stage, an upgrading from minor to major player in a drama whose plot gets thicker all the time.

The strength of the Princess's position received an unforeseen boost with the extraordinary emergence of the "Camillagate" tape in late January 1993. As with Squidgygate, excited rumors multiplied about the source of the recording. Rogue elements of the secret services were popular suspects with the tabloids and the Princess alike, but the truth was far more mundane. Analog phone technology in 1989, when the conversation had taken place, provided amateur eavesdroppers with hours of vicarious thrills as they listened in to mobile calls. Inevitably, some of these people were tempted to sell the results of their electronic garbage-can scavenging to unscrupulous newspapers.

A sinister GCHQ [Government Communications Headquarters] plot was therefore hardly necessary, at least to explain the initial interception. There were rumors of the intercepts being deliberately rebroadcast, which, so far as I am aware, never suggested anything more than casual malice. Fledgling digital phone technology—theoretically more resistant to eavesdropping—was probably the greatest beneficiary of the whole business. Certainly the Waleses' office was an enthusiastic early customer.

As further vindication of the truth of much of what Morton had revealed, the Camillagate tape was excruciating in content and devastating in timing. No one who read the transcript is likely to forget the intimate and affectionate telephone conversation it recorded between the Prince and Camilla Parker Bowles.

Rumors of its existence had appeared in the press as long ago as mid-November 1992. Even before then, I had been aware from remarks made by a Fleet Street editor that it existed and that—in the editor's opinion—it jeopardized the Prince's claim to the throne. Popular disgust and Church disapproval would be so strong as to make the Prince's accession an unacceptable option for a monarchy that reigns only by popular consent.

Such was the overinflamed atmosphere of those months that this seemed a credible outcome. Other, perhaps more worldly commentators—and they included many of the Prince's natural supporters—had views similar to Sebastian Faulks, who wrote a piece in the *Guardian* on January 14 dismissing the tape as just an "unguarded exchange of two people who are fond of each other."

Among the Prince's camp, faces that had reflected ill-concealed satisfaction at the timely appearance of the Squidgygate tapes now suddenly struggled to conceal less happy sentiments. A deep depression fell over the office. Our small staff perhaps shared it less than most.

The Princess took understandable comfort from finding that she was no longer the only victim of the Peeping Toms of the airwaves. She was, however, genuinely shocked by some of the cruder references in the transcription. "God, Patrick. A *Tampax*! That's *sick*!"

Needless to say, morale in the Princess's legal team also took a bit of a boost. Officially, there was no immediate prospect of divorce after the separation, but both sides knew that the chances of a reconciliation were remote in the extreme. We had instead an armistice of unknown duration, so the lawyers—if not actively rearming—remained on high alert. "We've got 'em cold with a cross-petition for adultery if we need it," said Paul, viewing his next encounter with "the Lord" (Goodman) and "the Knight" (Farrer) with more than usual relish.

If nothing else, it seemed to even the scores in our distasteful battle for public hearts and minds. In reality, of course, it was more of a victory for the Princess. Whereas the reporting of Squidgygate quickly directed public ire at the radio ham allegedly responsible for the tapes' publication, reporting of Camillagate was much less charitable toward the heir to the throne. It was perhaps understandable—and since his was the most recently exposed transgression, it remained uppermost in the public's mind.

Soon there were pictures to support the impression of an unequal race. A reduced traveling press pack relayed images of the Prince dolefully trying his hand at peasant farming in Mexico, while in March the Princess jetted to exotic Kathmandu to dine with the King and tour British aid projects accompanied by a Minister of the Crown, Lynda Chalker.

Even here, however, an underlying cautionary note was evident. Much press attention was devoted to establishing just why the band at the airport to greet the Princess's arrival in Nepal had not played the national anthem. The truth was that such a recital would not have been appropriate for what was, after all, simply a working visit. Its absence had passed without notice in Egypt, Pakistan, and Hungary, yet now it was front-page news. (I should know—I was pulled out of the delivery room during the birth of my eldest daughter to field calls on the subject over an agitated line from Kathmandu.)

The clear implication was that, whatever her success in front of the cameras, loyal supporters of the old royal status quo could have the satisfaction of knowing that the Princess did not enjoy unqualified royal status. Depending on your point of view, this either marked the Palace old guard as being determined to denigrate the beautiful, plucky Princess, or it marked the willful, manipulative Princess as being determined to flout the wishes of the established order. It did neither of them much good.

Leaving aside the pointless speculation about protocol, the Princess's trip to Nepal was a great success. Nevertheless, in the midst of her triumph there was one disturbing straw in the wind, though few realized its full significance. Emerging from a hut in a deprived rural village high in the Himalayas, the Princess—shocked by the poverty she had just encountered—was quoted as promising, "I will never complain again."

This called for a universal snort of amused incredulity. It certainly got one from her staff, albeit very discreetly. Surprisingly few public voices joined in, though, and our boss was thus left unhealthily ready to believe her own propaganda. Serving up such an appetizing soundbite was talent enough; getting so many people to take it at face value was verging on genius. The trouble was, the one person who should *never* have taken it at face value—herself—swallowed it hook, line, and sinker. The consequences for her sense of media self-preservation were disastrous and culminated in the infamous *Panorama* interview in 1995.

$\mathcal{T}$ he strategy for future work that I agreed with the Princess following the separation was conveniently vague.

She had not won her relative independence cheaply, so she was keen to enjoy being at least theoretically mistress of her own destiny. There was no doubt, however, that her taste for life in the public eye was undiminished.

Having seen those who would have curtailed her public duties forced to retreat, I was keen to get the Princess back on track, working what appeared to be an unchanged routine and answering her critics in the most effective way possible. The best thing she could do was to carry on with the work that was expected of her and that she did so well. The normal pattern of domestic engagements in support of her patronages therefore resumed.

A particularly heartening development for me—or so it seemed at the time—was the Princess's increasing willingness to consider doing more work with the International Red Cross. As patron of British Red Cross Youth, she had a perfect vehicle for involving herself in almost any of the organization's campaigns worldwide. This was precisely the area in which I felt her wish to carry out independent foreign tours could be exploited without raising the controversial issue of whether or not she was representing the Queen in the process.

The role of Lynda Chalker—then Overseas Development Minister—was increasingly valuable in our discussions on this subject. She perfectly combined an almost maternal concern for the Princess's welfare with a politician's dispassionate and pragmatic approach to media issues. In those first difficult months, I believe she made a major contribution to the Prince's and Princess's understanding both of each other and of the necessity for moderation in protecting the interests of the royal institution as a whole. Her concern extended to the Princess's office and, in a world which for me was also growing increasingly short of unpartisan council, she earned my lasting gratitude.

Her moderating role included keeping the Prime Minister informed of the reality of the Princess's situation and the caliber of her future ambitions, none of which was intended to conflict with her first duty of loyalty to the Crown. Like Lynda Chalker, the Prime Minster had established a trusted position in the Princess's eyes as an honest broker. In turn, he had the chance to judge for himself whether the anxious young woman he met on several occasions to discuss her future was the demonized inadequate portrayed by certain establishment sources.

In October 1992 the Princess had hosted a dinner for Dr. Sommaruga, president of the International Committee of the Red Cross. It was another expression of her determination to be taken seriously, a message to her husband and any others who were watching that she intended to involve herself with the work of world-class humanitarian organizations—and not just as a subject of heart-tugging photospreads. The dinner itself was a sparkling success, the newly opened Lanesborough Hotel making a stylish bid to establish itself as a royal watering hole to rank alongside London's other great hotels. The Princess, supported by Lynda Chalker and the British Red Cross Director General Mike Whitlam, played her part to perfection—every inch the beautiful but sophisticated angel of mercy.

In due course it became evident that the Princess had only to express an interest in any of the Red Cross's activities for them to be made available for her patronage. That dinner and other meetings like it were undoubtedly instrumental in achieving this aim.

Sadly, however, the seeds thus sewn did not take deep roots. Certainly, in the years that followed, the Princess carried out some spectacularly productive engagements on behalf of the Red Cross, who in turn frequently provided her with just the sort of headline-grabbing activity that helped her sustain her dream of becoming a true roving ambassador. Nevertheless, with instinctive caution the Princess maintained a maidenly elusiveness and never fully committed herself to the embrace of any single one of the many charity suitors who sought her favors.

Lynda Chalker and others, including me, tried to introduce her to the rewards and satisfaction of sustained commitment to a small number of reputable causes, but she lacked the inclination, if not the capacity. Thus she left a long legacy of raised expectations as she flitted her butterfly path through the garden of good causes that blossomed so invitingly for her.

With characteristically practical concern, the Prime Minister's office also became involved in promoting a national scheme of recognition for carers that would have borne the Princess's name. This too, despite all its attractions from my point of view, failed to attract genuine interest from the Princess. For this and other reasons that I could only guess at, but that probably had much to do with general uncertainty over her future status, the idea was quietly shelved.

My enthusiasm for all these suggestions was probably greater than the Princess's. This was not because she had a low opinion of an organization such as the Red Cross— quite the reverse. Rather, I believe her instinct was to protect her recent, hard-won independence, and that included a readiness to take up and then drop without much warning any of the attractive proposals that came her way.

Balancing this capricious reaction with the charities' reasonable expectation of an efficient and dependable booking system was one of the major challenges in my remaining three years as her private secretary. It was a challenge I knew I shared to some degree with many of my brother private secretaries, but in the Princess's case it was especially significant. She was setting out to reinvent herself, hopefully as somebody happier and more fulfilled. It was a worrying sign, therefore, that she could so easily fall back into patterns of shortsighted self-indulgence where work was concerned. Such indiscipline, I had hoped, belonged to the past, to a time when it had been a luxury that she had shared with those whose future status was unquestioned. Those days were gone. Now she really did have to work every day as if running for office.

Popularity issues were exercising other households too, especially in the aftermath of the so-called *annus horribilis*. Press preoccupation with royal matters moved from the Waleses' separation to the announcement that the Queen would henceforth pay tax. This did not greatly affect the Princess, whose income came from the Duchy of Cornwall via the Prince, but it heightened the already acute sense of turbulence that was the constant accompaniment to our daily lives. It also had the beneficial effect of shifting the spotlight—at least temporarily—away from the Princess as she marshaled her forces for the task of inventing for herself a historically unprecedented new role: a Princess of Wales with no constitutional position other than that of mother of a future King.

In doing this, her watchwords were an absence of obvious excess, a minimum of formality, a quick and flexible response to topical humanitarian issues, and an obvious—some would say *too* obvious—readiness to communicate with her public in ways that acknowledged and even encouraged the emotional dimension of her work. It was a formula that she created herself. Many of its elements were present in the working styles of other members of the royal family, but none, I believe, combined them all to such extraordinary effect as the Princess of Wales.

The prize would be to reinforce the link between this evolving and plainly popular style of royal work and the best of the historical, traditional roots from which it drew so much of its strength. It was desperately disappointing to discover that the Princess did not share this view of the ultimate prize, paying it lip service when it suited her and ignoring it entirely when it did not.

The opportunity so wisely created by the Queen for the Princess to symbolize the continuity of old and new was never properly taken up. It was smothered partly by the opposition of those who felt the best way of advancing the Prince's interests was to belittle his wife, and partly by her own inability to grow into the public image that she and fate had created. Too often, narrowness of vision or timidity of spirit denied her the prize that was hers for the taking and that so many observers still linked to the future health of the monarchy.

The future monarch, of course, was King William V and the Princess took none of her responsibilities more seriously than this—to prepare her children for life in the public eye. This determination only increased after the separation when, already in her heart believing that she would not be Queen, she concentrated instead on passing on to William the art of being royal, with the perspective that could only come from an outsider who had needed to learn so much so quickly and at such personal cost.

Her children learned from the outset to be considerate of the staff with whom they shared their homes and offices. They were taught not to fear the strong emotions aroused by the death and illness that would be their companions for as long as royalty involved itself with the care of the suffering. On the rare occasions when they accompanied her on public engagements, they also learned how to conduct a walkabout in streets lined with beseeching, expectant, and adoring faces—a daunting sight for a ten-year-old—with every sign of genuine delight. She once remarked to me about the irony of teaching her children to be friendly and outgoing to strangers at an age when most parents were warning their children to do the precise opposite.

Most important, the Princess taught them these things without ever surrendering her determination that her children should lead lives as similar as possible to those of their contemporaries. She therefore made sure that they also enjoyed trips to McDonald's, the cinema, shops, and parties with schoolfriends.

*T*he Princess set about preparing for her solo existence and independent role with several practical changes. The tabloids duly noted small but meaningful alterations to her hairstyle and wardrobe. Less obvious, but more significant in the long run, was her decision to continue work on her speech training, which reinforced her determination to be heard as well as merely seen. Another laughter-packed session with the photographer Patrick Demarchelier produced new images of a determined and confident-looking Princess.

This repackaging initiative was great fun, but it had to lead somewhere. I soon noticed that there was little sign of an intellectual makeover to accompany the new "executive Princess" look. The failure to follow up opportunities to expand her work with the Red Cross was a case in point.

I had my own ideas, of course, but part of my longevity was due to a recognition that my input would really only be heeded at each end of the decision-making process. I should make sure I was heard first—to start the ball rolling or in answer to a perceived need—and last—when all other options had been discarded. In between these start and end points lay a vast space, to be filled with ideas from other sources.

I saw it as a kind of laboratory of ideas in which the Princess could enjoy the freedom to take opinions from anyone she chose. I did not have to intervene—it would have been unwise to intrude on the freedom—but I still retained a degree of control. After all, I would usually have to implement whatever scheme the laboratory finally produced. That was when I could use my growing knowledge of her mind to add caution, direction, or encouragement to the other elements at work in the experiment.

There is no doubt about it: what we were doing *was* experimental. There had never been a Princess of Wales in this position before. This was constitutional research, aimed at reaching a formula that would keep the Princess happy and fulfilled while at the same time keeping her safe from the pressures that had destroyed her marriage.

It is a caricature of the despot of legend that he can control the news he hears. One thing is entirely certain: there will never be any shortage of it and increasingly it will be tailored to suit the perceived preference of the recipient's ear. In the months following the separation, the Princess was beset with advice good, bad, and indifferent. Although I was sure she had the capacity to distinguish between the three, it was something else again to ask her to exercise it, especially when her life was already riddled with so many doubts.

Some of the advice she sought and received was of the highest quality—wise, humane, patient, and delivered with a rare understanding of her isolated predicament. The opinions of independent-minded observers such as Lynda Chalker, Sir David Puttnam, Lord Mishcon, Margaret Jay, Jacob Rothschild, and the ubiquitous Sir Jimmy Savile did nothing but good as far as I could see. Rather less welcome from my point of view was my boss's equal determination to seek opinions indiscriminately. Some of those she sought out were highly professional and offered good advice; others wished only to ingratiate themselves, peddle their own quack theories, or in other ways exploit her vulnerability.

Her quest for personal growth took her into a whole range of areas, including astrology, reflexology, colonic irrigation, massage, fitness training, soothsaying, and psychoanalysis. Advice of wildly differing quality poured in. She was unrestrained in her appetite for it. Apart from her children and her public duties, I sometimes felt it took up the rest of her life. I am sure that in isolation many of the practitioners she consulted were sources of professional, honorable, and valid advice, but in combination they represented a bewildering cocktail of emotional stimuli that robbed her of equilibrium at times of stress and dissipated her powers of concentration. They fed the paranoia that never lurked far below the well-groomed surface, and they provided as many opportunities for mischief as for wholesome thoughts and actions.

Some constructive issues did emerge from this period of self-absorption. Perhaps most significant as new subjects of interest were domestic violence, particularly against women, and eating disorders, a highly personal subject for the Princess.

A visit to the Chiswick Family Refuge in March 1993 was followed by several more in the course of the next two years. The charity's director, the straight-talking Canadian Sandra Horley, seemed to have an instinctive understanding of the reasons behind the Princess's new interest in the subject. Although she was socially at her best in male company and impatient of any female presence that might constitute rivalry, when it came to the humanitarian side of her work, the Princess had a special sympathy for members of her own sex who had encountered types of unhappiness that she could recognize in herself.

She often betrayed a surprising lack of self-confidence, needing regular reassurance about her looks, importance, and lovability. She may therefore have felt some subconscious affirmation of her own value by being in a position to bring comfort, even if only in the form of glamorous distraction, to women in even greater emotional need than herself. Their gratitude and appreciation was for the most part entirely genuine.

In motherhood, unhappy childhood, and recent experience of marital strife, there was an enormous amount of common ground onto which the Princess briskly strode. She breezily joined discussion groups and toddler sessions with a range of contributions that was sometimes patronizing and sometimes expressive of her own neediness, but was always well intentioned and well received.

She would sit in a circle of women, all survivors of domestic abuse, her head cocked in the familiar attitude of sympathetic attention, prompting the assembled sisterhood with well-chosen bait: "Well, ladies! *We* all know what men can be like, don't we?" The PPO and I would try to fade into the wallpaper. Mind you, I learned a great deal not intended for male ears from the animated discussions that followed.

The Refuge benefited in many ways from the Princess's interest, which led also to her well-publicized attendance at a high-profile conference on the subject of domestic violence at the Queen Elizabeth II Conference Centre in 1994. By then, predictably, the Princess was beginning to believe that she was being exploited in some indefinable way. Unfortunately much of the early promise in the relationship eventually went unfulfilled.

Another long-term interest that developed at around this time was in the study and treatment of eating disorders, again particularly in young women. Dr. Brian Lask of Great Ormond Street proved to be an ideal guide and companion for the Princess as she learned more about the problem on a visit to the hospital. From her questions then and from my own very amateur observations, I was never sure she had fully overcome her battle with bulimia. For her there was never going to be the prolonged period of stress-free contentment and security that, as I understood it, was a precondition for a complete cure.

This visit to Great Ormond Street led in April 1993 to the Princess giving what became a famous speech in Kensington Town Hall. For a time this brought the subject of eating disorders to the top of the public medical agenda. Incidentally, it also produced a mailbag bulging with letters from young people affected by eating disorders or their anxious relatives.

As might be expected, a higher than usual proportion of that speech was contributed by the Princess herself, most memorably her description of the bulimic's wish "to dissolve like an aspirin." This, and the rather exaggerated style of delivery she adopted (the result of the unorthodox tuition methods of Peter Settelen), provided all the evidence the watching public needed that the Princess was ready to trade emotions with them whenever it was appropriate, and sometimes when it was not.

This endeared her to many who regretted the royal family's image of emotional constipation. Conversely, of course, it provided further proof of her emotional incontinence to those who thought that the rest of the royal family had a healthier outlook in appearing to believe that emotion was something best indulged in private, if at all.

In the car on the way back from the engagement, the Princess was elated. Not only did she feel that she had spoken well, but also, after years of spectating on other people's misfortunes, she had at last been able to speak about a subject of major medical importance from her own experience and thus from the heart. It made up for many of the occasions when she had been forced to invest her own emotions in other people's words, in speeches she dreaded on subjects she did not fully understand. On this subject at least, she felt she could deal with the experts on their own terms—a rare and intoxicating experience for a royal public speaker.

Her elation was only heightened by Peter Settelen's sudden appearance in front of the car, flagging down his pupil. "Not bad...for a whore!" he shouted. She was delighted. So were the driver and I once she had explained, between giggles, that her speech training included impersonating voices from dramatically varying walks of life.

After domestic violence and eating disorders, the Princess's interests in those first days of freedom also included a continuing fascination with alcohol, drugs, and mental health issues. As patron of Turning Point, she spoke at a conference in North London in June 1993 about the particular need for support for the plight of mentally ill women.

This was definitely not a lightweight Princess with time only for fashion, shopping, and Duran Duran. She did not deny herself such necessary pleasures, but a quotation from her speech—provided by me but willingly adopted by her—perhaps best describes the other side of her mental equation: "It can take enormous courage for women to admit that they cannot cope...as their world closes in on them their self-esteem evaporates into a haze of loneliness and desperation." She *could* cope, and she wanted the world to see that she could; but she also wanted the world to see that it was not easy.

The conference was chaired by Libby Purves, from time to time a commentator on the Princess's activities and one who did not shrink from criticism if she thought it warranted. From her opening remarks that day, however, it was plain that the Princess's message about her own struggle was getting through. "[The Princess] is one of us," she said. "A wife, a mother, a daughter who has known problems in her own life and who has courageously used these experiences to comfort other people."

*O*n a lighter note, that spring also saw the Princess making the first of many well-publicized visits with her sons to public amusement parks, in this case Thorpe Park. Significantly, she seemed unsurprised when the photographers turned up to capture the touching scenes as she put on a display of unstuffy modern motherhood. It only reinforced the esteem in which the amusement-park-going section of the public generally held her. On the other hand, it also reinforced the contempt in which she was held by many of those who would never have dreamed of setting foot in such a place.

I wondered sometimes how many of the latter group tut-tutted quite as vigorously on the many occasions when the Prince fielded his sons for the cameras for much the same purpose, albeit on the banks of a Scottish river rather than on a water-splash ride at a public funfair. The same thought occurred to me when I read glib descriptions of the Princess seeking out the empty-headed company of Hollywood film stars, or priggish questions about her decision to take her sons to Disneyland. What would have been the critics' response, I wondered, to the knowledge that King George VI and Queen Elizabeth, when they were Duke and Duchess of York (to say nothing of the then

Prince of Wales and the young Mountbatten), had spent rather longer in the company of movie people in bohemian, prewar Hollywood?

If, in the eyes of some, the Princess had a habit of choosing unsuitable forms of entertainment for her children, she also knew her obligations in the task of helping them establish strong relations with their own family. To this end, she regularly sought and received invitations to take them for tea with their grandmother the Queen.

After these meetings she would describe—with considerable affection but no little nervousness—her mother-in-law's evident pleasure at the uncomplicated time spent chatting with the boys. Between the two women, however, there seemed to be no substantial communication. It was as if both wanted to be of help to the other, but somehow the barriers erected by upbringing and recent painful events could not be overcome.

The Princess also used these opportunities to express loyalty and give assurances about her wish to do no harm either to the institution or to her husband who would inherit it. These assurances were not always entirely sincere. To judge from the lack of effective rejoinder, they had also probably been heard too often in the past. Such was the Queen's determination to remain above the Waleses' bickering, of course, that she could not be more forthcoming without her intervention being exploited by one side or the other.

For all that such restraint was statesmanlike, I think the Princess genuinely mourned the fact that her contact with the supreme family figure was confined to teatime small talk. "She seems so small," she said, "and sad." This view did not stop her—or anybody else, for that matter—living in dread of the Queen's disfavor. In the feuds that swirled continuously around the Palaces, I thought this ultimate threat was a sadly underused peacemaker.

The Princess made time occasionally for other people's families too. Giving little warning, one afternoon she called to make the acquaintance of my four-week-old daughter. Holding the gurgling and squirming cherub with all the experience conferred by years of hospital, crèche, and nursery visits, the Princess laughed. "I know I shouldn't say this," she said, "but she's really *squidgy*, isn't she?"

Such an ability to laugh at herself—and about a subject that still must have embarrassed her deeply—displayed a good-natured humility that I knew she carried within her, but which was too often obscured by self-doubt, anxiety, and the emotional brittleness they caused.

A constant backdrop to our lives as the year progressed, and a source of sneaking fascination to the Princess, was the biography of the Prince being written by Jonathan Dimbleby and the TV program that was to accompany it. Throughout the summer of 1993, the BBC film crew was a regular sight around St. James's Palace and wherever the Prince's travels took him.

I adopted an attitude of faintly amused cynicism, which may explain why the one scene they shot in which I was a contributor never made it beyond an early edit. This entertained the Princess hugely. "I know!" she said. "Next time they're filming, I'll make a grand entrance to the office for one of our meetings. Then I can poke my head round the Prince's door and say, 'Hope you're going to let *me* get a word in!'" Sadly this bit of fun never got beyond the planning stage. It would not have harmed the ratings.

I could understand the temptation of producing what in effect would be a counter to the Morton revelations of the year before. What was more, it would be a counter that had the authority of one of the most respected names in broadcasting. It also centered on a subject who embodied duty and traditional royal values in a way that could not have contrasted more sharply with the unstable, bulimic, suicidal Princess of *Diana: Her True Story*.

It was unfortunate that, particularly under the pressure it was then encountering, the Prince's organization took itself so extremely seriously. It probably still does. In palaces or parliaments, there is nothing like the presence of TV cameras to feed the desire to take oneself very seriously indeed. Like so many other people offered the poisoned chalice of fly-on-the-wall-style television documentary, the Prince's office seemed to think that all they had to do was let people in on the secret of what went on behind the Palace walls for the viewers to feel as enthused about it all as the people who worked there.

This delusion was not helped by the opportunities the program offered for some of the Prince's advisers to promote their own portfolios. In courts there is always competition for a prominent place in the latest pet project. Intoxicated with a wonderful sense of the importance conferred by their positions and by heady drafts of royal proximity, it seemed surprisingly hard for them to understand that, beyond vulgar curiosity, such sights held little appeal for anybody who was not naturally attracted to that sort of thing.

Given the situation in which we found ourselves, the atmosphere in our cramped office corridors was charged enough. The addition of camera crews with accompanying lights, soundmen, and important clipboards only exaggerated the sense of drama. The experience was made no more pleasant by the knowledge that, although it was never officially admitted, the main purpose was to create a favorable public impression of the Prince with all the resources that his staff, archives, and associated patronages could muster.

I realized that it would be unwise to lend the project any cooperation that could justify a subsequent claim to be the authoritative account of the previous two years' events. I was therefore dismayed to find that the Queen's office had agreed to review parts of the book, even if only unofficially. I spoke to Robert Fellowes of my fear that the project would acquire the status of the authorized record on some events—especially relating to the Waleses' separation—that were very much in dispute. I think he shared my concern. He was certainly at pains to reassure me that no such impression was intended. Regrettably, the distinction between informal fact-checking and official endorsement never made it to the book's acknowledgments list, where several of the Queen's top advisers, past and present, figure prominently.

It mattered a great deal to those who engineered Dimbleby's account that it should be seen as authoritative. On matters of architecture, the environment, the Prince's Trust, and his early life, I have no doubt that it turned out to be just that. Nonetheless, I resisted the Dimbleby team's attempts to acquire input on the Princess's behalf—even when they came in the form of a delightful lunch prepared for me by Jonathan himself at his home. No cooperation at all seemed to me to be the safest option.

When the great work was almost complete, however, through mutual friends I helped bring about a meeting between the Princess and Jonathan Dimbleby over lunch. My intention in arranging this encounter was to confront him with the reality of what she was like so that he could compare it dispassionately with what he had been told by sources close to the Prince. This, I mischievously hoped, might at least pull a brick from the foundations of the edifice created for his benefit. After months immersed in her husband's correspondence, organizations, supporters, and friends, he would, I reasoned, have formed a fairly clear picture of her. It was my intention to show him that large parts of it were demonstrably false, or at least incomplete.

I am pretty sure that this objective was achieved. The Princess put on a great performance in which regality and informality were mixed in proportions that would frustrate the most determined critic. She ate her lunch with obvious enthusiasm and laughingly sympathized with Dimbleby's Herculean task on the Prince's behalf. After she had departed in a cloud of fond farewells, I caught on Jonathan's face the dazed look familiar to me from so many others who had just received her dazzling best.

Having had a chance to judge her at first hand, he was asked, did it affect the impression he had gained from what he had been told? To me he seemed momentarily uncomfortable and I recall his reply was along these lines: "If I can't believe what I've been told about her...then I can't believe any of it." Amen, I thought. Although his research had probably already brought him to a conclusion he no longer felt able to change, the encounter with the Princess, if nothing else, must have caused some head scratching in the Prince's office.

"What about a biography of the Princess?" someone asked.

Dimbleby laughed. "That would require another lifetime!"

*I*n July we set off to Zimbabwe on another of the Princess's major set-piece tours. Following the established pattern, it was long on hard work and atmospheric photo opportunities and short on protocol.

As with all the Princess's overseas tours now, I took trouble to make sure that the Queen was acquainted with the proposed program in some detail. Most importantly, this helped to build a sense of confidence between the Princess and her mother-in-law and between their offices. It also helped me in my continuing battle to help the Princess see that she could enjoy practically all the independence she wanted and still keep what she referred to as "the system" informed of what she was doing. I hoped this would create the foundations for long-term healing of the wounds inflicted by the previous summer.

The move also neatly outflanked any predatory attempts by the Prince's supporters to claim that the Princess was acting irresponsibly, or to the detriment of the monarchy or national interests overseas. This was an ever-present risk, and one that was still being demonstrated two years later when several establishment figures went public to condemn the Princess's visit to Argentina as proof that she was "a loose cannon." The fact that the Queen had approved the program and the further fact that in my pocket I had a letter from the Secretary of State lending his support might have made them think twice. Then again, forcing them as it would to make a complete reappraisal of the Princess in their own minds, perhaps it would have been asking too much.

Previously the Princess had resisted attempts on my part to persuade her to visit Africa, scene of so much of the work carried out by her charities and much of it also with long, historical connections to the Crown. Her reason was simple. Africa was the Princess Royal's territory and she was not prepared to risk treading on anybody's toes. Before we went to Zimbabwe, therefore, as well as consulting the Queen, the Princess took the trouble to ensure that there was no objection from her sister-in-law.

By now the organization for transporting the Princess around the world on her tours was becoming quite slick. Certainly, I could never let my concentration slip when it came to domestic arrangements for my boss and her staff, but the overall spirit of teamwork, happy cooperation, and flexibility, mixed with fun at every opportunity (suitable and otherwise), was in stark contrast to my early, stressful experiences of trying to organize joint tours.

In large part, this improved morale was due to the Princess's own attitude. A royal boss who endured long flights, unfamiliar food, unconventional plumbing, and the exigencies of a concentrated program without complaining was a joy to work for. It was also the private secretary's ideal and therefore probably unrealistic. On the major solo tours that we did together, however, the Princess came very close to it—most of the time.

In return, what her ideal of a private secretary would have

been for such trips, I never discovered. I very evidently fell some way below it one night in Zimbabwe when there was a problem with her speech. Actually it was a problem with an antique fax machine, but this detail had no chance of being acknowledged by the Princess in her current mood. I could see she was brewing up into a state of self-pitying indignation, but I could not think of any obvious explanation.

This was worrying. I could not even begin to defuse the bomb until I discovered what had started it ticking. I consoled myself with the hope that her moodiness might just be a sign that everything else was going too smoothly for her liking.

The bomb kept ticking. It had been a long evening in a hot and overcrowded reception, during which old white Rhodesian society rubbed shoulders happily with the new black ascendancy in the scramble to shake the Princess's hand. In the good-natured melee, the Princess initially missed the fact that her sister Sarah—lady-in-waiting for the trip—was no longer hovering attentively in the vicinity as normal practice required.

Then suddenly the simmering mood came to a boil. "Patrick!" hissed the Princess, sandwiched between two burly Rhodesian farmers and a Land Rover salesman. "Will you get Sarah, please? I saw her talking to the rat pack. And *what* are they doing in here?" She had me on that one. I had also been surprised to discover that our media friends had got into what was supposed to be a carefully controlled gathering.

As directed, I found Sarah sharing a quick cigarette with the press party, some of whom had craftily acquired tickets. Dislodging her with some difficulty from conversation with Richard Kay of the *Daily Mail*, I steered her back to our besieged leader. It was too late. The impression of being abandoned had taken root and for the rest of the evening nothing could be right.

I was still wondering about it when we arrived back at the High Commissioner's residence. "Patrick, I'm very unhappy!" the Princess said reproachfully over her shoulder as she retired to bed. The High Commissioner and his wife and much of the surrounding wildlife pretended politely not to hear.

"Well, Ma'am," I said, thinking again of the scene at the crowded reception and managing to look slightly rebellious, "I'm not happy either." Her thanks and goodnight wishes came down to us in a snort.

In these circumstances it was usually possible to seek solace in a drink with the policemen and the lady-in-waiting. One glance at the elder Spencer persuaded me to make this an all-boys affair, for that evening at least. We retaliated the following night, however, by singing enthusiastically around the High Commission's grand piano until the Princess was forced to descend from her bedroom to complain about the noise. Then she allowed herself to be cajoled into joining us.

There were other minor hiccups too. As before on joint tours, the subject of official gifts still had the potential for trouble. After a long, hot day touring a refugee camp in the east of the country near the Mozambique border, we returned to Harare for a well-earned rest. The crew of the President's aircraft, which we had been lent for the trip, formed up at the foot of the steps to bid her farewell.

In the cabin I confronted a Princess who had packed up for the day. "Ma'am, the crew are lined up at the bottom of the ladder. Perhaps you'd like to give the Captain a set of your cuff links?"

I had them ready in a smart blue box. VIP pilots all over the world must have cupboards full of such trinkets, but in their own way these gestures were as important as the formal portrait photographs given to Ministers and Ambassadors. This pilot had done more than most, too, landing us smoothly on bush strips and with a punctuality that would have earned respect from the Queen's Flight itself.

I could see the complaint building in her eyes. When it came it was familiar. "Why does everybody want something from me? Why am I expected to give all the time?"

This required a fuller answer than the circumstances allowed. In a change of style, I did not wheedle her into making the presentation (which, incidentally, would have cost her nothing). Instead I just said, "OK, then," and slipped the box back into my pocket.

At once she was mollified. "All right, Patrick. I s'pose I'd better do what's expected of me." She did just that, giving our Captain an extra-long chat and an extra-white smile, just to show that she regretted her private professional lapse.

Such minor presentations were sometimes resented by the Princess because they were a reminder of the kind of formal protocol she disliked. The incident made me ponder on the purpose of such gestures, which I saw as harmless "thank-yous" but which my boss would occasionally see as a real irritant.

The general question of protocol was quite a simple one for me. Its origin, I imagined, lay in the mists of time when our cave-dwelling ancestors presumably went to some trouble to appease and flatter visiting chiefs of other tribes. Out of deference to the restraint that, though unstipulated, I deduced was the Queen's wish in such matters, I always played down suggestions from our hosts (many of whom loved the sight of a splendid guard and band at the airport) that there should be anything much in the way of overt ceremony laid on for the Princess.

In the same way, I did not seek meetings with heads of state or government as a matter of right. This would have been to test too far the deliberately ambivalent guidance about representing the Queen abroad. If the head of state himself proposed such a meeting, however—and few could resist the photo opportunity it provided for them—I did not fall over myself to turn it down because of quibbles over the Princess's precise status. It was far better and more courteous, I thought, to allow such invitations to be fulfilled.

It was certainly far more worthwhile. One photograph with a smiling leader more than made up for twenty minutes inspecting a guard of honor and if there was any doubt about this, a smiling Robert Mugabe (or Carlos Menem or Jacques Chirac) readily proved its truth. Especially Robert Mugabe: "She brings a little light into your life...naturally you feel elated, you feel good!" he beamed at the press pack. It put our protocol problems—wondering how much fuss the press would make about the presence or absence of the national anthem—into perspective.

In any case, protocol was not what the tour was about. In its content, the Zimbabwe tour covered familiar ground, with the Red Cross, Help the Aged, and the Leprosy Mission all providing high-quality projects for the Princess to visit and the world's cameras to admire. The subject of AIDS—both then and now a devastating blight on a whole generation of African children—was given particular prominence. Late one evening we visited a hospice for orphaned children with AIDS. None was over five. None was expected to reach the age of six. The Princess wept.

What was especially heartening was the new spirit of cooperation the tour had demonstrated between the Princess's major charities. Combined receptions were held in honor of all three and the shared experience produced a valuable crop of further cooperative ventures for the Princess to consider on future tours. The presence on such occasions of the charities' top management—faces familiar from a hundred small projects back home—added to the value the Princess gained from what would otherwise have been quite fleeting experiences in the townships and countryside of Zimbabwe. Since she rightly saw them as allies, such encounters also added to her confidence.

Another encouraging sign for me was the appearance among the press pack of correspondents from the serious broadsheets. Previously, if they came on what were characteristically tabloid outings, they would usually content themselves with essentially light-hearted accounts either of the press pack itself or the effect on the local social life of the appearance of such a glamorous figure from overseas.

This time there was a small but significant change. Robert Hardman, who was the *Daily Telegraph*'s respected court correspondent and generally thought to be more aligned with those who treated the Princess with suspicion, wrote a thoughtful and constructive account of her visit to Zimbabwe. In a report dated July 14, he compared it with the Princess Royal's contrasting style and found that both had merit.

> The latest tour has been a public relations triumph not just for her favorite charities but for the Princess herself. Africa, until now the undisputed realm of the Princess Royal, has a new champion. Were they ever to arrive at a refugee camp at the same time one could picture the Princess of Wales heading straight for the nearest cluster of ailing children and the Princess Royal marching over to the person in charge for an update on the sanitation.

Elsewhere in the article Hardman wrote, "Visits are vital if the Princess is to maintain her world profile and thus continue the work she sees as her mission. But she will need to use them sparingly and vary the diet. Too much of what cynics call the Mother Teresa routine could lead to compassion indigestion by the media, however well choreographed it all is."

I highlighted this paragraph and sent it to the Princess. She wrote beside it, "I totally agree—change of diet is very important!" We duly kept the diet as varied as possible, but the link with Mother Teresa proved irresistible to the press. To be fair, the Princess herself did very little to discourage it.

16

Solo

*I*n the summer of 1993 the Princess holidayed with her children at Disney World in Florida, undeterred by the barrage of criticism fired at her by the old guard. She jealously protected the time she spent with her boys and reacted with uncompromising hostility to anything that threatened it.

It was at about this time that Tiggy Legge-Bourke was introduced into the uncertain atmosphere of the Waleses' family life. Being the Prince's appointment—and very much involved with the children on his behalf—she and I had very few points of direct contact. Early in her time at St. James's, however, she did come to see me and probably rather unwisely I gave her a version of the briefing that I gave to all newcomers about the importance of not believing too much in the esteem of our employers.

She needed no lectures from me on the subject, having had a longer if less abrasive experience of royalty than I had. She probably thought I was completely paranoid. "Doesn't bother me," she said. "I'm just the nursery maid, guv." I knew, though, that her idealism and transparent good nature would be sorely tested. Whatever world of security and happiness she intended to build up around William and Harry, it was inevitably at risk of becoming an exposed position in the no-man's-land between two hostile front lines.

She immediately became an object of curiosity and suspicion to the Princess, of course, and an innocent target for much of her unhappiness about the rest of the world. In fact, it was ultimately the Princess's attitude toward Tiggy, especially when suspicion turned to vitriol, that was a conclusive factor in my decision to resign.

Meanwhile, a female figure from an earlier generation—from an earlier era, even—returned briefly to the Princess's preoccupations. Not long after our return from Zimbabwe, the death occurred of the Princess's grandmother, Ruth, Lady Fermoy. Much has been written about this redoubtable lady's role in the original plans for the Prince to marry Lady Diana Spencer, and about her estrangement from her granddaughter in later years. Much of it may well be true. My own observations were few, but they did bear out the widely held belief that Lady Fermoy personified an attitude that the Princess found anathema.

This attitude might be described as a stoic ability to suppress emotion in the interests of maintaining a certain outward appearance. The outward appearance was determined by reference to a code forged in the years of Empire, war, class-consciousness, and deference. The Princess refused—or was unable—to subscribe to it. It was a code that imbued the system into which she had married and against which, less from conviction than from instinct, she provided a national rallying point. In its place, however, she could put nothing but a haphazard expression of emotion and a rather calculated self-interest.

Not surprisingly, therefore, Lady Fermoy felt that she had nothing to learn from her granddaughter, but her granddaughter must be made to learn from Lady Fermoy. I was not present during the occasions when this "learning" was supposed to take place, but I did see the aftermath. Emerging from an encounter with her grandmother, the Princess was as flustered as I had ever seen her—shocked and upset, but defiant. The cause of her defiance was a simple sense of injustice that she should be made to pay the full price for errors that had largely been committed against her rather than by her. She later famously said of her marriage in the *Panorama* interview, "I'll accept 50 percent of the blame." Observers of the code would have had her shoulder far more of the guilt, as well as mend her ways to conform with the attitudes of a much older generation.

Despite this unhappy background, in a gesture of great symbolic importance, by the time of Lady Fermoy's death in 1993 grandmother and granddaughter had been at least partly reconciled. As further evidence of the contact that could be established across the generations if the will were there, the Princess was flown to and from her grandmother's funeral in the company of the woman who has come to symbolize all that was good about the values of that older era, Queen Elizabeth the Queen Mother.

*T*he summer drew to an end and in an abrupt return to the Palace politics of our less gracious times, the Princess seemed to be attracting growing interest from a new constituency that might traditionally have beaten a path to her husband's door. They approached her, I assumed, for reasons of curiosity or sympathy, or perhaps merely out of some form of disenchantment with mainstream royalty.

For some weeks that autumn I was in discussion with the BBC, who saw her as a strong candidate to deliver that year's Dimbleby Lecture. The irony of such an honor—bestowed only on speakers of undisputed national influence—had an irresistible appeal. The name alone saw to that. Such a prestigious platform would also have conferred on the Princess an unaccustomed intellectual credibility, a lethally powerful weapon in her battle to establish herself as an independent figure of international importance. I do not know whether it was for this or some other reason, but the project evaporated to the accompaniment of suitably scathing and suspiciously well-placed comment in establishment newspapers.

Another invitation that perhaps also owed its origin to the three reasons mentioned above, as well as to a desire to adorn an otherwise rather ponderous occasion with some youthful female company, came from Conrad Black, host of the Hollingsworth Dinner at Spencer House. The guest list read like a *Who's Who* of British and American media and political heavyweights. It was here that the Princess and Henry Kissinger first established what was to become something of a mutual admiration society, with tangible benefits for her in the form of guidance and assistance with later visits to the USA and for him in the shape of a lovingly presented pair of her trademark blue cuff links.

Also at the dinner were many representatives of the establishment press, some of whom appeared rather taken aback by her appearance among them. Criticism—witty and pompous by turns—that seemed so easy to dispense from the safety of the editor's desk suddenly seemed less relevant when confronted eye to eye with the elegant figure radiating a natural royalty that their equally natural sense of deference found hard to dismiss.

The Princess was well aware of both the opportunity and the effect she was having on the various dinner-jacketed commentators who were pulled out for her inspection. As was usually the case, through sheer force of personality she achieved more in an evening than a team of spin doctors might fail to achieve in a month.

"Ah, Mr. X," she might say, as a hostile editor made his embarrassed bow. "I always enjoy reading your paper."

"Ahem. You're very kind, Ma'am, but I'm afraid we're not often very kind to you."

"On the contrary," she would reply, with a precisely judged condescension. "We all need some criticism sometimes," and the black-tied miscreant would retreat, hopefully to brood on the encounter and think twice about how to present this loose cannon when next in front of his computer screen.

The aim of establishing the Princess's independent status received a further modest boost in September, when she fulfilled an official engagement to boost British interests in Luxembourg. Although small in area, Luxembourg carries a disproportionate importance in both royal and political terms. The principality's royal family is conspicuously Anglophile, the Grand Duke himself having participated in the liberation of Luxembourg while serving in the Irish Guards. We could expect their opinion of the Princess's performance to be passed down the most prestigious grapevine of all—that connecting the interrelated royal families of Europe.

The joint appearance at the British Trade Fair of the Princess with the Luxembourg Crown Prince made the point very clearly. Whatever tendencies there might be to ostracize the Princess from certain levels of the British royal family, so far as the European cousins were concerned, she was a welcome guest. Moreover, this welcome would not have been as warm—or might not even have been extended at all—without at least the acquiescence of the Queen.

In political terms, Luxembourg's role at the heart of the European Community made it a significant addition to the Princess's collection of high-profile European outings. This dimension was comprehensively covered with her attendance at a small dinner given by the Luxembourg Prime Minister, a certain Jacques Santer. For sharp-eyed watchers, his appointment soon afterward as President of the European Union was a reminder of the sort of circles in which the Princess was now accustomed to move. Even in territory so far removed from her traditional role as charity worker, it also drew from the Princess a letter of congratulation on his promotion which, from his reply, M. Santer obviously appreciated very much.

A couple of months later a similar set of objectives was

achieved with a visit to Brussels during which the Princess, as patron of Help the Aged, attended events intended to promote the work of the affiliated international charity HelpAge. Once again her well-shod heels were found treading corridors of distinctly unglamorous power in the EU headquarters. There she demonstrated that she could discuss provision for elderly people with the EU Commissioner for Social Affairs with the same self-assurance as she could quiz a refugee camp organizer in Zimbabwe, a drug addict in Huddersfield, or a society hostess in Washington.

She certainly did not possess a comprehensive understanding of EU provision for elderly people. Nor, however, did she claim any special expertise beyond an understanding based partly on instinct and partly on the accumulated experience of her years of concentrated exposure to great social issues and people's emotional needs.

She was quick-witted, flirtatious, a sharp observer, and a natural enemy of pomposity, yet she was royal to her fingertips—a fact you would be advised not to forget for long. In Brussels, no less than in any other of the places I have mentioned, this was a formidable combination of talents. It also had the potential to be a vehicle for far greater causes—the grand, global welfare crusades for which she seemed outwardly so suited. As events were to show, however, in the end she was tragically unable to prove herself a reliable standard-bearer for many of these.

Tea with Queen Fabiola at the Palace and a reception at the British Ambassador's residence rounded off a European day off that would have been fairly typical of any hardworking senior member of the royal family. For a semidetached member of that family, hanging on by her fingertips to her acquired status and questing about for a new role, it was significant to an extent that I do not think she fully realized.

Once again her regal performance owed more to an instinctive knowledge of her special status than to any rational understanding of its rather precarious foundations. Her deep curtsy to Queen Fabiola only emphasized her natural affinity with royalty—of any house—but I knew, even if she did not, that it would take more than such public self-assurance to repair the damage of the past year. I was left, perforce, to do much of the worrying for her on this account, all too conscious of the vital importance of notching up these cast-iron examples of her royal rank. By contrast, however, most of the time she just accepted it as her natural due. Ironically, it was probably the most royal thing about her—and a vital prop for her fragile self-confidence.

I did feel that we were making headway in some areas. All over "the system" that operated the interfaces between royalty and government, the simple reality was dawning that the Princess of Wales remained a major player, certainly in media terms. It also seemed that she could be entrusted with increasingly substantial responsibilities. Her status thus gained an important new element in many eyes. It had not been acquired or conferred; instead, through the ordeal of having to plough her own solo furrow, it had been *earned*. This was certainly a far cry from the dark days of the previous winter, when spite and bewilderment would have denied her the means to be as effective as she was now proving herself to be.

Back home, her standing on the diplomatic circuit showed itself equally resilient. In October she attended a reception at the Russian Ambassador's residence in support of the Moscow Children's Hospital, of which she had become patron. At various times, the Russian Ambassador and his Chinese, American, Hungarian, Pakistani, and Argentinian counterparts, among others, were all entertained personally by the Princess at Kensington Palace. If I was any judge, they took as seriously what was going on between her ears as almost anything else they encountered in the drawing rooms of London. What was going on London's front pages on an almost daily basis could hardly have escaped their attention either.

The same growing awareness of the Princess's potential had occurred to others. From time to time that autumn she had meetings with influential figures as diverse as Clive James, Lord Attenborough, Lady Thatcher, and Lord Gowry. As with the Ambassadors, these encounters produced high-grade discussions on subjects ranging from international events and world health problems to the possibilities now opening up for her own future occupation. The Princess contributed well when she could, listened attentively when she could not, and matched such signs of obvious intelligence with well-judged and disarming humor. (I had remembered an old French saying, that in England it is necessary only for a man to remain silent for everyone else to think he is wise. I relayed this to the Princess and I sometimes think she took it to heart.)

For some weeks, too, the prospectus for Birkbeck College lay on her desk. I was not alone in believing that the self-discipline one of its courses would have required—not to mention the external credentials it would have earned her—was just what she needed. Sadly, this prospectus was as close as she came to embarking on a brush with higher education. It has to be said, however, that I misspent three years at Cambridge in the company of people who could not have touched her for streetwise cleverness, however illustrious their academic record turned out to be.

Influences from the worlds of show business and the glossy media were rather less cerebral and therefore perhaps more warmly received. The Princess drew great comfort from the sympathetic affection she received from stars such as Elton John and George Michael—people whose lifestyles and experiences she felt more closely matched her own than a whole army of European royalty. Media figures such as Eduardo Sanchez Junco, proprietor of the society magazine *Hello!*'s Spanish parent, also supplied a surprising degree of understanding mixed with a generosity of spirit not normally associated with the notoriously superficial world of which they were the recording angels.

Also well received—at least for a week or two—were

suggestions from the dynamic American management guru Anthony Robbins that the Princess should take advantage of his techniques for maximizing untapped potential. His course of study appeared in the form of a set of enticingly wrapped videotapes, but I fear, despite its glossier packaging (in the shape of the proprietor as much as the tapes themselves), it ultimately received no more interest than Birkbeck College's more bashful charms.

More to her liking was the sort of university activity so courteously provided by Norman St. John Stevas, who, as Lord St. John of Fawsley and flamboyant Master of Emmanuel College, Cambridge, invited the Princess to lay the foundation stone for the college's new library. The engagement was a gem of its kind. The setting in one of Cambridge's more elegant colleges could not have been bettered. The host's sensitive and perceptive choreography of the proceedings was peerless. The choir sang love songs both courtly and vivacious. Even the November weather smiled. Only the building's questionable architectural merit might have added a note of controversy, but that was definitely her husband's province.

Perhaps best of all that day, by one of those unexpected, happy chances, the Princess found in the college chaplain Brendan Clover a man of God whose approachability and social conscience provided her over the next couple of years with occasional sips of spiritual nourishment as she visited him at his later work on behalf of London's homeless. At St. Pancras Church in North London she took a low-key but regular interest in Brendan's plans to convert the crypt into a shelter and advice center for the army of rough sleepers who congregate around the capital's railway termini.

This was religion at its most practical and Brendan's understated spirituality gave her, I believe, a valuable chance to see faith in action. It was not that she acquired an air of holiness as a result. Instead she gave support just by her presence and in turn, Brendan and his helpers lent her the peace

that comes from spending an hour or two in the company
of dedicated servants of those at the bottom of the heap.

Almost a year after the formal announcement of her separation from the Prince of Wales, the Princess reached a peak
in a year of remarkable survival against the odds. Despite
heavy discouragement from influential quarters in the establishment; despite a miasma of tacit disapproval that
seemed to hang over Buckingham Palace; despite a public
sympathy that was beginning to show signs of unraveling
(HAS IT ALL GONE WRONG FOR PRINCESS DIANA? asked the
Daily Express on November 3 above a well-briefed piece on
her "regret" at having "split with Charles," while *Tatler*
magazine quoted a survey that saw a small majority of participants define her as "a neurotic manipulator"); and despite God knows what internal trauma, she had successfully
built a foundation for herself.

She had become an independent voice on matters that
were unfamiliar to traditional royal thinking yet were uncan-
nily close to the unhappy daily experience of a huge
constituency of ordinary people. It was an impressive
achievement. Underpinning this success—and obviously an
effective antidote to the trauma she had suffered—was a daily
sense of relief that the worst was surely behind her. The sky
did not fall in after she separated from the Prince. Her public
life continued much as before, and so did her seemingly un-
stoppable popularity with the public at home and abroad.

There was a similar, if less sustained, improvement in her
temperament behind the scenes. Being a new and different
style of royal household appealed to her and for a while her
desire to be seen as modern, responsive, and unstuffy made
her a great deal easier to work for. She became noticeably
more flexible on matters such as when she was prepared to
start work—previously never before 10:00 A.M.—or how
much advance briefing she needed on straightforward en-

gagements. Although some of this flexibility persisted, as time went on it emerged that there was a limit to how seriously she was prepared to take this "working Princess" image, much as she liked the idea in principle. In reality she was a creature of royal habit and that meant reserving the right to turn very grand when the mood took her, and at short notice too.

On November 14, 1993, the Princess set the seal on her ability to combine her new, independent territory with more conventional royal domains by attending the Remembrance Day service at Enniskillen in Northern Ireland. In 1987 this picturesque country town had been devastated by a bomb that had killed eleven people at the same service on the same spot. Not least because of the groundwork she had put into developing working links with the province— helped by the discovery of a distant kinship with the Secretary of State Sir Patrick Mayhew and by sustained interest in initiatives undertaken by her patronages Relate and Barnardo's—she had been asked to attend what was probably the most emotive service of all those being held that day throughout the United Kingdom.

The Queen had given her approval, a decision unlikely to have been popular with those in the organization who still preferred to see the former Diana Spencer as a subregal figure. These more cynical observers might have rubbed their eyes in disbelief to see her become the focal point of commemorations that, for their simple sincerity and power to move, had few equals anywhere in the UK. After the service, the Princess reviewed a march past and joined officers of the local garrison and the Royal Ulster Constabulary at a reception. Once again on this bedrock on which loyalty to the Crown's traditions is built, she found she had a firm and secure footing.

In case it was all becoming too deadly serious, however, the Princess still managed to convince everybody on the plane that her only concern was which hat to wear. Before leaving KP we had disagreed on the choice, so the two favorites accompanied us to Northolt and onto the Queen's Flight 146. There, by a simple majority, hat A was discarded and hat B (her original choice) was worn instead—with a triumphant air, I might add, at least when looking in my direction.

The success of the day owed much to the genuine emotion and simple dignity of the people the Princess met. She played her part too, nonetheless. Slim, elegant, and very feminine, she stood surrounded by men in uniform at the head of the tribute to the dead of two world wars and the more recent bomb outrage. The scars of that dreadful day were still visible in damaged buildings around the memorial and in the faces of the large crowd that had gathered to share a common grief. Despite a massive security effort, there was still a threat of terrorist attack and it was greatest for the royal person standing conspicuously at the front.

During the two minutes' silence a pair of swans flew directly overhead, perfectly silhouetted against the crystal-clear winter sky. She talked about it afterward. "Did you see those birds?" she asked. "It was so moving. I couldn't help feeling they meant something."

I had felt it too. "You mean the spirit of the dead?"

"Yes. Something like that. Or peace."

I sometimes wondered what she really felt about the country she represented. How strong was her patriotism, and what form did it take? It was certainly not jingoistic—she was instinctively uneasy with flag-waving conservatives. Nor did she confuse, as some do, a blind loyalty to old institutions with love of country. Her knowledge of history, it has to be said—like much of her geography—was virtually nonexistent. Although, I reflected as we set off for beleaguered Ulster that day, that could be a positive advantage when trying to appear neutral in Northern Ireland.

She was also untroubled by any well-developed political awareness. Certainly she liked John Major, but that was as a man not as a politician. Her courtship by and of some Labour figures in the last years before the 1997 election only reflected a recognition of where power was likely to lie in the future. Her husband obviously came to the same conclusion.

In the end I concluded that she had a fairly healthy attachment to the status quo, at home and abroad, as one would expect of a woman of her birth and upbringing. Moreover, when the chips were down—as they memorably had been at the launching of HMS *Vanguard*—she had had the guts to do her duty against the weather, abusive heckling, chaotic organization, and her own ethical misgivings. She had shown the same determination in walkabouts on the streets of Ulster, as well as in flying the flag in factories, ministries, embassies, and export seminars in countries around the world. Whichever way you looked at it, it was an impressive record of service to Queen and country.

*A*fter the success of Enniskillen—in symbolic as much as in practical terms—I felt that the "new" Princess was consolidating very effectively her obvious claim to be a serious royal performer in her own right. I was soon to watch all my hopes being dashed to pieces. In quick succession, fate upset this carefully filled applecart with more than a helping hand from the Princess herself.

The first blow came a little later in November when, as the papers succinctly put it, she "lost her top cop." I have already written about the high regard I felt for all the PPOs. You might imagine how closely we had come to work together during the traumas of the previous two years, as the faultless presentation of the Princess's public duties became ever more important to her survival as a royal force to be reckoned with. After the death of the long-serving and devoted Graham Smith, the main responsibility—not just for her day-to-day safety but increasingly for freeing her from many extraneous and distracting worries—fell on Inspector Ken Wharfe.

I will not now do him the disservice of trying to describe the debt that the Princess and others, myself prominent among them, owed Ken for the work he did in those dark days. It would take another book and, given his taste for the theatrical, probably an opera as well. It is only necessary to say here that, during the five years he was with her, he understood better than anybody the professional risks he ran in working for such a high-profile, mercurial figure, ultimately as ready to swap dedicated staff as a funeral hat.

By the nature of Ken's duties and the personality of the woman he protected, for much of the time he had to act independently of his immediate superiors. If he was seen to be highly successful at his job, there was no shortage of envious eyes who would find opportunities to criticize him. If he established a close working relationship with the Princess, he would become the subject of unwelcome and utterly unfounded gossip and innuendo. If she felt he was too distant, then she would let him know that in some way he had failed in his loyalty toward her.

His good nature, conviviality, and complete professionalism would, he knew, be scant protection against the storm that would descend on him if—or rather when—the day dawned when the Princess woke up and decided it was time for a change. That day did dawn, inevitably, and the most painful of all her human sacrifices was offered up on the altar of the Princess's random axmanship. The man who had been through so much with her was abruptly posted to what were euphemistically termed "other duties."

In this case the pain was made even greater because, in her customary way, the Princess tried to find fault with him before the blow fell. She could find none. Ken was a professional to the tips of his elegantly shod toes. Instead, I watched her unhesitatingly exercise her influence over his superiors in the Royalty and Diplomatic Protection Group. These men were wise to the special hazards faced by bodyguards, as much from the people they were there to protect as from any outside threat. All administrative red tape was cut through and at least the transition was mercifully swift.

Perhaps in the end Ken had committed only one crime in her book, but it was as unforgivable as the condemnation was unjustified. He had seen and heard too many of her unroyal moments for the Princess ever to feel she could convincingly reinvent herself in his eyes. Rather than let herself be accepted for what she was—and Ken knew her warts better than most—she found it preferable to start with a clean sheet and so a replacement had to be found.

In some ways, I suppose it was not such an unreasonable wish. One of the least enviable aspects of being royal is the requirement to share so much time and space (to borrow a phrase) with these protective shadows, however good natured and convivial they may be. It saddened me, though, that once again personal loyalty, with all the vulnerability it inevitably exposes, had to be rewarded so harshly.

Again I had stood by while the execution took place, but this time there was even less that I could have done to change the Princess's mind. I knew she would miss him, but "Once gone, always gone" was still her motto and she turned instead to the new toy that the system obligingly offered.

Cuff links and photographs do not soften the blow and they are no substitute for a system that might better protect royal servants from the temperaments of their royal masters and mistresses. The police at least have their own administration to fall back on. A PPO past his sell-by date does not lose his job, he just gets reappointed. He carries out his duty with the reassurance that his mortgage is secure, if not always his path to the upper reaches of the service. Even on the grim day of his departure, I envied Ken that ultimate safety net and wondered when my turn would come.

I formed a theory then that may still be relevant. To get the best out of the kind of people who are attracted to royal service and who, for whatever combination of characteristics, royal people tend to want to employ, it would only be to the advantage of employer and employee alike for the consequences of their hiring and firing to be in the hands of an independent agency. If, for example, courtiers were classed as civil servants, with pay and conditions of service equivalent to the appropriate ranks in other government departments, their advice would be confident and impartial, their horizons wider, their futures secure, and the tender parts of their anatomy safe from royalty's sometimes ungentle grip.

For their part, the royal people would have to break the habit of growing their servants in the job and thus always being surrounded by reassuringly familiar faces. This habit is increasingly the mark of the older households anyway—the Waleses led the trend away from it—and breaking it would permit the introduction of fresh ideas and fresh blood throughout the institution, say every two or three years. The habit of simply dropping unwanted toys on the nursery floor is surely not the ideal way to introduce such freshness.

The new system would involve the regular reappraisal of working methods and philosophies that otherwise become accepted as unbreakable historical precedent. It would encourage the sort of nondeferential discussion that royalty quite naturally enjoys, but which at the moment it has to find by devious and divisive means. The game of favoritism, intrigue, and manipulation that makes people such irresistible toys to play with can now be seen to produce few winners. How much better to declare it over and give the modern monarchy the modern staffing system both it and its servants deserve.

A "Department of the Monarchy," augmented by secondments from private industry as at present and—why not?—from the voluntary sector as well, could become a jewel in the crown of public service. It could become a beacon of good practice, initiative, impartiality, and efficiency and demonstrate a healthy recognition of the part our rich heritage has to play in our modern national life.

Almost simultaneous with Ken's departure—and in some way linked with it in the Princess's mind—came the deeply unedifying saga of the "Peeping Tom" photographs taken of her as she exercised in a West London gym.

The Princess's growing addiction to physical culture posed a number of worries for those of us who tried to guard her interests. It has to be said that few of us shared her fascination with working out. Few of us, in truth, had the raw material with which she was so eminently blessed. Her life was sadly short of reliable sources of happiness and fulfillment, however, and I did not begrudge her the pheromone rush that I am told results from strenuous physical exercise.

The snapshots were originally splashed in the *Sunday Mirror*, but were later taken up by several other newspapers, alongside text of fairly blatant hypocrisy that justified their release either on the grounds of the proof it offered—as if any were needed—of the Princess's radiant physical health or, according to taste, of the slipshod security that had allowed such a daring subterfuge.

My initial reaction was probably unworthy. I had known of the dangers in publicity terms of her exercising in a public gym and had told her of my misgivings. At first, therefore, my reaction was one of petty vindication. Then a note in her voice as we discussed the outrage on the day of publication quickly informed me that this was not a minor, or even complimentary, prank to be laughed off. Instead this was the straw that might easily break the camel's back.

I found myself talking to an actress ready to deliver her best lines with all the considerable emotion she could muster. Just as she intended, the voice I heard belonged to an essentially modest woman whose privacy had been brutally invaded; who felt—in her own words—as if she had been "raped." The world must know of her hurt and outrage and armies must be mobilized to avenge her violated personal space.

I could understand that the Princess, so often accused of media manipulation herself, would seize on an opportunity publicly to demonstrate her abhorrence of the very type of tabloid tactic that had worked in her favor so often in the past. This is called having your cake and eating it, and not unsurprisingly the royal family, like many others in the public spotlight, would dearly love to believe that the spotlight can be turned on and off at will. I just thought the lady did protest too much.

The precise sequence of events that led Bryce Taylor, the owner of the L.A. Fitness Gym in Isleworth, covertly to photograph the Princess quickly became the focus of heated legal argument as soon as the big guns of Mishcon de Reya were brought to bear on the Princess's behalf. So too did the implications for standards in the media as a lively discussion ensued about who was manipulating whom.

Against the *Sunday Mirror* Lord Mishcon fielded a rising star in the legal firmament, Anthony Julius. Although Anthony and I were contemporaries at Cambridge, we had not met. I quickly developed a keen respect for his professional ability, while also finding him stimulating company. His owlish urbanity concealed a rapierlike intellect, unhampered by so many of the doubts and sensitivities that had crept like ivy across what passed for my own. During the two years that we worked together on this and subsequent legal business for the Princess, I benefited from his many acts of friendship and from his Jewish, leftish, republicanish perspective, so refreshingly different from my own. The Princess took an even greater shine to him, probably for many of the same reasons.

The eventual victory over the *Sunday Mirror* was as emphatic as all Anthony's skill could make it. Nonetheless, in a way that I doubt deprived him of much sleep, I continued to feel uneasy about this and other attempts—not just by the Princess—to censor what the tabloids published and then censure them when an ill-defined privacy line was thought to have been crossed.

It was not uncommon in the red-carpeted corridors I then trod to hear "the comics" being mocked. "There are lies, damned lies, and *Sun* exclusives" was just one of many witty ways of dismissing tabloid talk as unworthy of serious consideration. I would always maintain, however, that the tabloids got most of their facts right most of the time. It just took a while for our denials to be blown away.

It might be a crude test, but if a visiting extraterrestrial wanted to take back to his spaceship a broadly accurate picture of the Princess of Wales's public life, he could do worse than take a complete set of tabloid front pages. As they set off on their next intergalactic journey, the watchers from outer space would have a pretty accurate picture not just of the main events in the Princess's later life, but also of the extraordinary fascination they held for other dwellers on our planet.

Of course there were times when the popular prints got their stories spectacularly wrong, and they often paid a spectacular price as a result. After the gym photos scandal, the *Mirror* was buried under a blizzard of high-minded criticism from its fellow newspapers, few of whom could have claimed a completely clear conscience on matters of press intrusion. A list of the media's gross errors would not be a long one, however. Time and again I saw stories printed that I knew to be fundamentally true but for the sake of some inaccurate detail could be dismissed as invention.

What galled me more were the commentators, especially in the broadsheets, who were happy to ride with the hunters by joining in with the chorus of disapproval when tabloid excess offended establishment taste, but who were also happy to run with the fox when enough of that excess was known to be true, using it as the basis of a partisan rant in favor of their readers' perceived prejudices.

*T*he saga of the sneaky snapshots took another year to resolve. Its significance in the winter of 1993 was the part it played in contributing to the Princess's most melodramatic decision of the year—her very public "withdrawal" from public life, which she announced on December 3 at a charity lunch in aid of Headway, the head injuries organization of which she was patron.

There was a large part of the Princess that sincerely believed that she was the victim of unrestrained media harassment. It was the same part of her that was always able to provide ample evidence of her absolute right to feel victimized. Her famous "Time and Space" speech at that Headway lunch only just avoided blaming the media directly for her dramatic decision. I believe she knew very well that a decision not to open a new hospital wing in Newcastle—which was what her withdrawal amounted to—would not protect her from the attentions of the paparazzi. In the climate then prevailing, however, especially in the wake of the gym photos, the press found that their ability to respond to her criticism was severely restricted.

For some months the Princess had been musing aloud about her wish to find a quieter life. I found it hard, though, to reconcile this wistfully expressed dream with the new, independent Princess single-mindedly applying her considerable talent to the task of plotting her own course in national life.

I should have spotted the danger signs. Of course this was a contradiction. She said she wanted peace and quiet, but in fact the day-to-day routine of her charity patronage, as much as the grand, set-piece occasions of the overseas tours, provided her with vital self-belief and job satisfaction. I also knew that her increasing confidence in speechmaking had put in her mind the idea of making a truly grand oration. This, not peace and quiet, was her real dream.

As she knew very well, peace and quiet were not beyond her reach. For political as well as therapeutic reasons, I had often urged her to buy a seaside house in Wales. There she could have had all the peace she wanted, interrupted only by heartfelt expressions of Welsh devotion inspired by the fact that someone carrying the name of their principality should actually want to live there. "And anyway, Ma'am, a week in Pembrokeshire would buy you a month of hassle-free sunshine in Necker Island."

The grand oration, however, grew into an obsession. It was not a means to an end. It was an end in itself. With mounting anxiety, I resorted to humor. We joked about it as a Churchillian event, but I always added the rider that when she decided to put this fantasy into practice it should only be for the sake of an exceptionally important statement. "You'll only get one chance at this," I said to her. "So you need to be quite sure that what you're saying is what you want to be remembered for."

"Yes, Patrick," she said with a suspicious meekness. Really she meant, "No, Patrick."

Our thoughts were on divergent courses. I had a growing conviction that the one great speech she should make—one that would secure her future from every threat—was publicly to offer a reconciliation with her husband and his family. This would be on her own terms, of course, and that was its principal attraction. If she could bring herself to do it, her moral victory would be complete. Forgiveness, after all, is divine and what more powerful credential could she claim for herself, especially since such a large proportion of world opinion seemed prepared to deify her anyway?

It was a suggestion I came back to several times before my resignation. Each time she listened attentively. Once, impatiently, she retorted, "But *they* have to do it *first!*"

"Ma'am, don't you see? Who does it first is the winner!"

She could not do it. Certainly, the bitter invective of pre-separation days was by then a thing of the past, otherwise I would not have dreamed of making such a suggestion, but the resentment ran too deep and was now so familiar that she was unable to let it go. Or perhaps she was just more honest than I, even if—as I believed—forgiveness in her heart could follow forgiveness publicly expressed.

Instead she had other plans—a tearful and very public withdrawal from public life, implying as it would her victimization at the hands of the press. It also invited sympathy for her (questionable) inability any longer to carry the great burden of public expectation that had been placed upon her. This, rather than a statesmanlike offer of reconciliation, irresistibly appealed to the martyr, the emotionally deprived child, and the showgirl within her. It also gave her a wonderful platform from which to launch yet another assault on her husband. As if the point needed emphasizing, on the day after the speech the *Daily Mail*—well briefed by its royal subject as always—spelled it out: CHARLES DROVE HER TO IT announced the headline confidently.

I saw it rather differently—at least privately. "Just you wait: you'll be sorry!" was my private synopsis of her speech, which she had kept out of my hands until only a few days before it was due to be delivered.

Its early drafts owed much to the influence of her speech trainer Peter Settelen, who bombarded her with faxes sent to a new machine set up on her desk for the purpose. He assumed a familiarity that nettled me, but only because of its irresistible novelty value to the Princess. Under its influence she swallowed ideas that sounded daringly honest in the privacy of a training session, but on the world stage and in the mouth of a serious contender for international influence I thought them disastrously banal and peevish.

Especially in view of my own understanding of her motives, the expression "Give me time and space" made my toes curl. I also knew it to be fundamentally dishonest. Whatever else she had planned, a quiet private life was never going to be the Princess's style.

My cynicism was fueled by virtuous thoughts of the thousands of charity workers and their clients in all her patronages whom she now wished to deprive of a glamorous figurehead and unsurpassed fund-raiser. I thought of the hours her staff had spent and the promises they had made on her behalf in drawing up her engagement calendar for the six-month period that was about to begin. I thought of the assurances I had given in good faith and the promises I felt she would appear to have broken. I thought also of the outpouring of genuine sympathy that would undoubtedly be forthcoming, which I knew was deserved for a hundred wrongs she had suffered—but not for this.

Needless to say, I shouted all these fine, brave sentiments from the rooftops, but only in a whisper. Instead, in the usual way, I ran myself and the rest of the Princess's staff ragged trying to minimize the consternation that her decision would inevitably cause.

One tangible benefit of the preceding traumatic months had been the close relationship it had once again forced me into with Buckingham Palace. More than ever, for my own sake as much as hers, I recognized how essential it was that the Queen's office should be spared any more unwelcome surprises about what the Princess was going to do next.

The task of rebuilding trust—which had never been entirely broken so far, only severely strained—was one that suited my instincts and inclinations. It helped buy the Princess the "time and space" that she was preparing to request so publicly, enabling her to experiment with whatever form of occupation she finally decided she could really sustain. I therefore spent uncomfortable hours at 10 Downing Street and in the inner recesses of BP, trying to convince skeptical ears of the Princess's sincerity. I tried also to keep open the door back to some form of fulfilling public life—a door on which I confidently predicted she would wish to knock almost as soon as the speechmaker's exultation had evaporated.

Using my most charitable analysis of what was happening, I explained that the Princess put so much of her own emotion into her work for those in need that, especially after the trauma of the previous year, she was now exhausted and near to breaking point. While she did want to take a pause to recharge her batteries, she would in all likelihood wish to return to the public stage once she had worked out her own priorities.

Unknown to my boss, I had written a briefing note for the Queen herself, which referred to the fact that in my view, despite all her protestations of strain and exploitation, the Princess retained a desire to serve. I also expressed the opinion that such ongoing service would be essential to her mental equilibrium. I doubt if Her Majesty needed this observation. By her intervention—with the significant support of Prince Philip—she limited the Princess's lemminglike urge to abandon the exposed public position she now needed like a drug, while still allowing her the space she required for this melodramatic rite of passage.

In the later drafts of her speech—in which I managed to excise the more histrionic references to a self-imposed and irreversible exile—my main concern was that, having stamped her foot and called for everyone to stop what they were doing and listen to *her*, she should actually have something to say that was worthy of their attention. Hopefully it would also not appear to have been planned with that attention as its only objective. Given the brevity of her "withdrawal"—which was just as I and a few others such as Lynda Chalker had anticipated—I later felt some justification for the belief that, despite all the other reasons that may have accumulated inside her to make such a high-profile announcement, the desire for that moment of attention was overriding and irresistible.

In the days before the speech I worked hard, with the help of others, to wind the Princess back from what I thought risked being a dive into the void. "Don't just jump off the cliff," I told her anxiously. "You don't know where you're going to land."

Arms crossed, she was pacing up and down in her sitting room. I sensed her annoyance: here she was, preparing for the greatest role of her life, and I was trying to rewrite her script at the eleventh hour. She had nerved herself for the ordeal and now her craven private secretary was clucking about the boring consequences. Why could he not see that the gesture, not the detail, was what mattered?

I had an idea. "Ma'am, why not look on it as a retreat, rather than a final withdrawal? Time to review what *you* want to do and set new priorities. And don't ditch all your patronages. The good ones will stick with you as long as you tell 'em what you're doing..."

This appealed to her on different levels. The semireligious overtones of a "retreat" acknowledged the hard-pressed spirit's need for space in which to heal. The concept of setting her own priorities appealed to the executive, dynamic, working Princess. Offering herself up to the mercy of her patronages—and a more generous-hearted panel of judges it would be hard to find—appealed to the martyr.

She continued pacing, but at least she was no longer looking at me as if I were trying to take away her latest toy. Of course, the need to make a big statement would not be denied. When it finally appeared, however, her speech was ambivalent enough to leave her some open doors through which she could reemerge when the fuss died down. I even got her to agree to retain her military affiliations.

Two years later, however, when in *Panorama* she found another irresistibly tempting attention-grabbing opportunity, she did not repeat her mistake. No interfering private secretary was going to try and talk her out of *that* one, let alone get his hands on the draft script.

At long last, in another echo of the previous year's crisis, all our preparations were complete and there was nothing more to be done. The statements were ready, the draft Qs and As had been rehearsed, and the press had been briefed. The patronages had been laboriously faxed. The other households had been informed—"Oh God, here she goes again!" came clearly through their noncommittal and personally sympathetic responses. The die was well and truly cast.

It was agreed that I would stay at mission control in the Palace press office with the Princess's press secretary Geoff Crawford, while she went with the equerry to her lunchtime engagement with destiny. The MC of the Headway lunch was to be Jeffrey Archer, for whom the Princess had a soft spot, not least for his preeminence as a charity auctioneer. He was the ideal man for the job and called at KP that morning to be let in on the big secret. Her faith in him was fully justified by the sympathetic but reassuring way in which he conducted the dramatic departure from the scheduled program, as a stunned audience—including Headway's top management—heard rather less than they had expected about head injuries.

Despite my last-ditch success in getting her to tone down the rhetoric, I had an overwhelming feeling that the Princess was cutting herself off from the very opportunities that would be her lifeline in the future. If she was to retain her status not just as a royal person but also as a credible and honest symbol of hope, she would need *more* of the links we had painstakingly built up, not fewer. As I saw her planning methodically to hack away at these lifelines, I prayed that what we had salvaged would be enough to let her start again, as I knew sooner or later she would realize she had to do anyway.

In a melodramatic moment of my own, I was tempted to throw away the keys to her car. I restrained myself with the thought that there were probably enough pointless gestures arranged for the day without me adding to them.

Geoff and I waited at BP for the dramatic lunchtime news headlines and exchanged unconvincing jokes. Every now and then I would walk to the window and peer through the net curtains at the crowds outside the Palace railings. Did they have any idea, I wondered, how lucky they were to be on the outside looking in?

At the appointed hour, as the Princess stood up to speak, we briefed a small handful of selected journalists. The Princess's words were hurriedly scanned by expert eyes.

I hope you can find it in your hearts to understand and to give me the time and space that has been lack-ing in recent years... When I started my public life 12 years ago I understood that the media might be inter-ested in what I did. I realized then that their attention would inevitably focus on...our private lives...But I was not aware of how overwhelming that attention would become; nor the extent to which it would affect both my public duties and my personal life in a manner that's been hard to bear...

The man from the Press Association spoke for many of his colleagues. "Have we killed the goose that lays the golden eggs?" he asked.

Geoff and I reassured him that it was not the intention to paint the media as the villains of the piece. It was, nonetheless, a telling example of the harsh reality of the Princess's relationship with the media. She supported a whole industry of investigators, reporters, photographers, commentators, editors, publishers, and proprietors. In return, she occasionally made use of their services to communicate over the heads of the conventional court organization to reach her public in the country and world at large. The famous "withdrawal" speech was a classic example of the process at work.

Forgetting my own lunch—for once—I drove to KP to greet the returning, uncaged Princess. After one look at her excited face, flushed with the rapt attention she had received, I gave in to a grudging optimism. Early reports were of uncritical understanding and sympathy. Perhaps everything would be all right after all and I had simply allowed my curmudgeonly caution to get the better of me.

As I followed her upstairs, she was still chattering about the looks of shock that had greeted her opening words. I followed her into her sitting room and she threw down her handbag, kicking off her high heels with the usual gasp of relief. "What have you got for me?" she asked brightly, spotting the sheaf of papers under my arm.

I handed them to her with a smile. They were our calendar planning sheets for 1994. "What's this?" she asked, flicking through them. They were completely blank.

"It's your program for next year, Ma'am."

Her smile faded and she looked rather thoughtfully at

the empty pages. "You know, Patrick," she said, suddenly serious. "I wouldn't blame you if you wanted to run away screaming from this."

I said no, I was sticking with her and so were all her other staff, for as long as she needed us. I reminded her of what I had said the previous year about being prepared to find a note on my desk saying that she had run away and would I sort everything out. Rather self-consciously and almost completely sincerely I said, "What matters to us, Ma'am, is that you should be happy."

She looked touched by this thought, but before it required any serious consideration from her I added, "I mean, it's no fun for us if you're not!" Then we could both laugh away our embarrassment.

"You realize I'm going to have to start being less formal with you," I said. "Our relationship is going to have to change."

"Well, that's good," she replied. "I'm all for that. I'd much rather you told me what you really think." It was too late to say that so often I *had* been telling her what I really thought, but she had not wished to listen—especially on the many occasions when her mind was already made up on a particular course with which I disagreed.

*F*or me the fallout from that speech was considerable. There was the small practical matter of disentangling six months' worth of lovingly prepared engagements, accompanied by the understandable and painful disappointment of some who had stood to gain large amounts of money from the Princess's involvement in fundraising activities. The restraint showed by most was further evidence for me of their semi-angelic status.

The rump of the 1993 program, only a couple of engagements, passed off relatively peacefully, despite Richard Branson's valiant efforts to turn the Princess's christening of his new Airbus A340 into a day of fun to raise her morale. On her seventh and final visit to Northern Ireland, the Princess visited a children's hospital where, amidst the kind of welcome only the people of Ulster can provide, she was briefly once again in her element.

As I had anticipated, I was also already hard at work preparing alternative occupations for the Princess, now that her calendar was so invitingly clear. Among other things, the possibility of a Birkbeck course arose again and was dismissed again.

Worse was to follow. Relieved of the discipline of the six-month program planning system, she leapt at the chance "to set her own priorities"—a euphemism that soon became an excuse to reenter the limelight with so-called private visits that then mysteriously got reported in the *Daily Mail* or other tabloids, and even descended to cherry-picking from the old, friendly patronages who knew their Princess and the score. I sometimes wanted to attach to my office door an agent's sign saying, ANYTHING OVERSEAS OR PHOTOGENIC CONSIDERED.

So this was the "time and space" she had asked us to find it in our hearts to give her, I thought to myself. It was agreeable enough for us workers—for a while—but I could not see it leading anywhere except into a slow spiral of decline and ennui.

Following her sincere but not very well-thought-out wish to be involved in a smaller number of subjects more deeply, I canvassed suggestions from some of her more senior patronages. They duly responded with enlightened programs for the further education and development of their beloved patron. Their attitude was unsentimental but totally positive: for many years they had benefited from her patronage and now there was an opportunity for them to return the favor. They were ready to help in whatever way she needed them to.

Many of these suggestions—involving as they did a real commitment to some of her favorite forms of humanitarian work, along with the chance to acquire new skills, to sharpen her existing talents, and to immerse herself in therapeutic activity—held up the exciting prospect of the Princess leaving behind the wreckage of her marriage and her formal royal position and replacing it with a fresh start. There would be interesting new work, of a type for which she had already demonstrated her aptitude and with people who supported her without judging her. Also on offer was the gratifying prospect of growing older, wiser, and more substantially the icon that much of the world already thought her to be.

One by one the Princess rejected all these suggestions, leaving just one—a remnant of the Red Cross proposal. This offered a minor but still potentially significant part in a group of experts charged with guiding the worldwide organization toward its main future areas of operation. Even this was to fall victim in the end to the Princess's reluctance to commit herself in any one direction. Less kindly, it could be said that she lacked the necessary discipline, application, motivation, and intellectual ability to be anything more than just a figurehead for other people's good work.

Good works surely need good figureheads, and none came better than the Princess of Wales. Her campaign on landmines (itself, incidentally, salvaged from the Red Cross proposals of the winter of 1993, when she had rejected it out of hand) demonstrated once again her extraordinary power to draw world attention to urgent humanitarian issues. It dawned on me during the aftermath of her speech, however, that in my country at least, the place for such a figurehead was still *within* the royal family, not in competition with it, as inevitably she would be portrayed and moreover as she would sometimes like to see herself.

In the long run she would either damage the monarchy or, more likely, run out of the necessary higher motivation, leaving herself driven only by self-pity and a desire for vengeance. Meanwhile, the organizations and institutions that had contributed to building her up would transform themselves into a widening circle of disillusioned former friends. It was not a happy prospect.

Still, I thought, I *am* on the side of the greater good, even now. I have not yet compromised my loyalty to the monarchy either. Properly managed, the Princess could still be a reliable source of fascinating occupation for me, not to mention high-quality travel and lunches to match. I should stick around, I concluded, and see what happened.

In the meantime, semiretired or not, in presiding over her own household the Princess surrendered not one jot of her innate hauteur. The idea of a more open and honest relationship between us—which had seemed so possible in the cozy afterglow of her big speech—remained just an idea. What little self-discipline she had possessed was also slowly unraveling. She was demobilization happy and the devil found work for her underused talents.

The influence of junior members of staff, whose opinions she covertly solicited, fed her desire for plots. The continuing ascendancy of "therapists"—including ever-more-influential astrologers—fed her self-obsession. Finally, the exposure of her furtive meetings with Richard Kay of the *Daily Mail* revealed a continuing need for dangerous male company that fed, I supposed, a continuing need to feel wanted.

I was not particularly proud or possessive, however much she might have tried to provoke such reactions. It was just that life was already hard enough as I attempted to be on her side, without the sense that she was drawing a bead on my back while I was doing it. I was under no illusions. The reinvented Princess had as few scruples as the old one when it came to swapping friends and staff who had passed their sell-by date. I was permanently on the alert for the softening-up process that would—hopefully—precede my own demise.

I did not have to wait long. One morning the *Daily Mail* told me that the Princess did not trust in the loyalty of even those closest to her. I knew my employer well enough to recognize a career prospects review when I saw it. For the first time I began to make serious but very secret plans to leave her.

17

Topple

*T*he public verdict at the end of 1993 was still far more favorable to the Princess of Wales than to her husband. On a funereal front cover showing a top-hatted Prince in a carriage at Ascot, the *Mail on Sunday* dubbed it "*annus horribilis* II" for the royal family.

There was broad agreement that although 1993 had seen a bruising publicity war between the Princess and her husband, she appeared to have won it hands down. The *Daily Express* headline for December 2, 1992, WHY DIANA CAN DO NO WRONG, effectively summed up her public image at the beginning of 1993 and, despite occasional near misses (the gym photos and the sacking of Ken Wharfe spring to mind), her first twelve months of "going solo" ended with the *Guardian* concluding that she was "more squidged against than squidging."

Her coup in December 1993 with the dramatic announcement of an ill-defined "withdrawal" from public life was sufficiently ambivalent for it to be interpreted as either the gracious decision of a champion quitting at the top of her career, or the tragic outcome of a campaign of vilification unsuccessfully directed against her by those we all thought should know better. Generally speaking, the reaction to her announcement was uncritical. Even those who only a month before had been ready to write her off as "Sad Di" (in the words of the *Express*) full of regret about her separation, were silenced by the enormity of her gesture. She seemed to share a politician's gut instinct that huge amounts of even moderately sympathetic publicity could be a worthwhile end in themselves.

The early months of 1994 were spent gingerly tiptoeing back onto the familiar stage of public good works from which she had tearfully swept only a few weeks before. Just over a month after so publicly bowing out of public life, the Princess had resumed a scaled-down but recognizably similar pattern of engagements, receiving the commanding officers of her regiments, visiting the dying at Mildmay Hospice, and spending time in that favorite retreat, Great Ormond Street Hospital for Sick Children.

She did not blush at this glaring contradiction. She had an unmatched ability to disregard her own inconsistencies, of which this was only the most obvious. I did the blushing for her, not least when those who had been disappointed with the cancellation of engagements originally scheduled for 1994 observed others receiving the benefit of their patron's involvement without apparently having waited patiently in line, or indeed having much obvious merit other than their convenience to KP and their unblinking readiness to be used as part of the Princess's rehabilitation program.

Something of this disillusioned mood communicated itself to me through a visit from Keith Hellawell, then Chief Constable of West Yorkshire and later to be created head of the Government's antidrugs task force. He spoke movingly to me of the sense of abandonment that was felt in certain deprived parts of his constabulary. In such poverty-stricken areas, the Princess represented a figure from another, better world who nevertheless took the trouble to come and meet ordinary people on their own terms.

Mr. Hellawell was particularly concerned by the demor-
alization of unemployed young men and the numbers in
which they were resorting to drugs. The Princess, he said,
offered a symbol of hope to such people. Her loss would be
grievously felt, and not just in the salons of London or the
smart shops of Bond Street. A return to the good times was
not to be, however. While the Princess did maintain a vestigial interest in her drugs charity Turning Point, her days
treading the backstreets of industrial cities in the service of
her patronages' good works were sadly now largely behind
her.

With her calendar now being less demanding, the
Princess expanded her list of lunch guests at KP. To existing
regulars such as Margaret Jay, Lynda Chalker, Clive James,
and David Puttnam were added new figures such as Barbara
Walters and Oprah Winfrey. The inclusion of these last two
reflected a shrewd recognition of the importance of maintaining a strong popularity base in the US—a country to
which she would always want to return and which at times
even seemed a possible permanent refuge. These older,
wiser women already knew all there was to know about life
in the media spotlight and were ready to trade experiences
with sympathy and good advice. The friendships she
formed with them were, I believe, of long-term benefit.

In another significant development, the Princess even
began to lunch with her stepmother Raine. This delighted
Hello! readers, but dismayed other diary scribblers who preferred the feud to carry on in the traditional way. Her rapprochement with her father's widow was a source of real
comfort to the Princess. Sadly, her new talent for reconciliation only ever made limited progress in her husband's direction, despite some apparently positive gestures.

Meanwhile, the saga of the L.A. Fitness Gym photographs rumbled on, as it would all year. Lord Mishcon, An-

thony Julius, and others became regular callers at KP and in due course the firm's family section took responsibility for the Princess's marital negotiations with her husband.

A matter of passing interest was whether or not she should pay rent. Her use of apartments 8 and 9 at KP included their status not only as her family home but also as her place of work. If her rate of public duties dropped below a significant level, then the question of their advantageous financial position would be reexamined. If nothing else, it gives an indication of the thoroughness with which Sir Michael Peat—the eagle-eyed new Keeper of the Privy Purse—was conducting his rigorous review of royal expenditure.

The administration of each parent's contact with William and Harry was also becoming a regular aspect of office life. The Princess relied on me to work out how many days she could expect to have her sons with her and to check that a fair allocation was being maintained. Negotiations over changed dates and substitutions took up an increasing amount of my time. Encouragingly, these negotiations were conducted without any animosity and, perhaps because they had been devolved to functionaries such as myself and Richard Aylard, they freed the boys' parents to re-establish some sort of direct relationship.

This they duly did, no doubt at some personal cost, and a pattern of quite formal visits became established, during which they could talk alone. On alternate dates the Princess would go to the Prince's new apartments in St. James's Palace and the Prince would visit his old home at KP. This pattern of civility between the estranged parents had begun soon after the separation and gradually grew to what I thought was a fairly warm mutual regard. It never stopped the public competition between them for popularity or moral superiority, however—much of it conducted by proxy and all of it regularly resuscitated by a media that would not let such a good story die of natural causes.

Before her meetings with the Prince, the Princess would

usually visit her office in St. James's and build up her courage for the coming encounter with much laughter amongst the women. She was nervous but composed, and was invariably calm and thoughtful when she set off for the short walk to Color Court, where the Prince had set up his new base after an abortive attempt to move into Clarence House, the Queen Mother's residence. Afterward she would usually call on us again, less nervous and less in need of laughter, but always positive in her remarks about the Prince's growing role as father.

Her greatest frustration was her inability to influence the day-to-day direction of Tiggy Legge-Bourke's contact with the boys. Although this caused her genuine distress, my sympathy was tinged with the thought that the Prince's role as father would have been very hard to discharge *without* Tiggy's assistance, given his other commitments. On her instructions, I drafted letters from the Princess to her husband pointedly asking for clarification of Tiggy's duties and asking to be involved in decisions concerning her contact with the boys. I do not think she ever got an entirely satisfactory answer, but I doubt if one was possible. It was hard for her to be content with the reality of her reduced influence over her children's activities.

My sympathy became even more conditional as the Princess developed an increasingly lurid fantasy picture of Tiggy's private life. No man in the Prince's entourage was safe from her suspicions, including the Prince himself. The inevitable outcome followed at Christmas 1995, when the Princess delivered a poisoned remark that drove even easy-going Tiggy to retaliate.

When it suited her purpose, the Princess was just as ready to employ the velvet glove as an alternative to the knuckle-duster in dealings with her husband's staff. Given the speed with which she could change one for the other, however, any perceived warmth had to be treated with caution. Her motives were rarely straightforward.

In the midst of her galloping suspicions about Tiggy, the

Princess found time to send her congratulations to her husband's private secretary Richard Aylard, who was appointed CVO (Commander of the Royal Victorian Order) in the Queen's 1994 Birthday Honors List. "Many congratulations on your award. I know what hard work the last few years must have been. Few CVOs can have been so thoroughly deserved!" I wrote, and she happily autographed it. Generosity from a position of perceived weakness is usually the sign of the greatest strength. It did not come naturally to her, but whenever she could be persuaded to display it, the results were always disproportionately gratifying. She felt strong, and those on the receiving end knew it. It was that simple.

One very disturbing spin-off from the Princess's newfound freedom—and a sign of her increasingly erratic judgment—was her decision to dispense with her police bodyguards except at public engagements. This was a bold, even reckless move, the result in varying parts of a desire to secure some privacy, a wish to appear different from her in-laws (some of whom could claim rather less personal risk than herself but who nevertheless clung on to their PPOs as powerful status symbols), and a willingness to demonstrate her popularity in the most practical way possible.

To me, as I morbidly recalled a little Freud, she also seemed to be indulging her developing death wish. I could think of no other explanation for the whole series of decisions that marked her descent into self-destruction. I had only to think of the Morton book, the "Time and Space" speech, and the self-harm so apparent in many of her personal relationships to find plenty of evidence for this. All this was well before the suicidal gesture of *Panorama*, too.

This apparent appetite for self-destruction was inextricably linked with a craving to be noticed. When—as was inevitable in the absence of a PPO—photographers got too close, crowds too insistent, or even parking wardens too zealous, the inconvenience and occasional alarm she suffered could be borne as something akin to the wounds of martyrdom. The experience was painful but somehow holy, and suffered in the cause of reminding the world not only that she was there but also that she was defenseless and occasionally at least potentially in danger.

Being dimly aware of this unspoken desire for vulnerability, I found it difficult to do more than express my genuine concern for her safety. "I don't need any of that stuff, Patrick," she responded briskly. "Nobody's going to hurt me." It was true enough. I knew that, with rare exceptions, the police assessment of risk to the Princess's life was fairly reassuring. (As someone who spent a great deal of time sitting or standing very close to her, I took a rather personal interest in these intelligence reports.)

This unorthodox approach to her own security nonetheless caused headaches among the professionals at the Royalty and Diplomatic Protection Group. What was the best course of action? They were under tight budgetary constraints, so the lifting of the requirement to field a four-man team for the Princess of Wales was certainly an attractive economy. Indeed, in the name of economy her hitherto automatic assignment of a motorcycle escort on official engagements had been withdrawn on several occasions in the previous year, sometimes at short notice and with undesirable consequences for the punctual running of her program.

Despite the innocent reasons I was given, whenever I was feeling unusually suspicious I thought I saw in such moves a subtle attempt to downgrade the Princess's engagements. My suspicions had been strengthened by my discovery at the traditional police pre-Christmas cocktail party in 1993 that the Princess's portrait was missing from its usual place among the other members of the royal family in the headquarters building. It was away for cleaning, explained a senior officer guilelessly, but its absence still made me un-happy.

The question of the Princess's security remained a bone of contention for a while. A desire to accede to her wish to dispense with her bodyguards was quite naturally at odds with the fear that heads would roll if anything should happen to her. Eventually the Home Secretary's views were sought and it was decided that the Princess should receive protection as before, but only when she asked for it.

Regardless of the mixture of signals they received from her, her erstwhile team of PPOs and their backups retained a deep loyalty for their wayward charge. I was later moved by the distress some of them expressed to me that she should eventually have died in circumstances that they would never have allowed to develop.

Unprotected by such professionals, the Princess soon found herself being pursued by unwelcome photographers on many occasions. Images of her panic-stricken dodging around parked cars outside the house of her therapist Susie Orbach, or her televised hounding in the concourse of a Spanish airport that summer, must have brought feelings of concern and disgust to the mind of any reasonable observer. In some cases her altercations with cameramen even prompted acts of robust gallantry from members of the public.

All the same, the concern I felt when I saw these pictures was mixed with a nagging doubt. Every one of these incidents could have been avoided, either with greater foresight on her part, or with the help of the PPO to whom she was entitled but chose to disdain. I also knew—and the cameramen all knew—that this was the same woman who would think nothing of tipping off photographers if there was a message she wanted to convey by means of an apparently random picture taken in a public place.

It was the clearest and most distressing example of her apparent inability to understand that public attention could

not be courted and spurned with impunity. Nor could its
sometimes heavy-footed servants in the media be trusted to
direct their attention only toward the subjects and at the
times that she ordained.

*D*espite the paradox of her relationship with the media,
there were still a few of us who tried to portray the Princess
as the victim of greater injustice than she herself was attempting to commit. Even her duplicity retained for me a
kind of admirable gutsiness. In early June 1994, when I was
questioned about her latest bout of media incontinence—
most notably the notorious photographs of her clandestine
rendezvous with Richard Kay in his parked car—I still felt
able to point out, "Well, at least she does her own dirty
work." For me this was still the key difference between her
and those who sought to reduce her public standing
through cynical manipulation of the media, an unwholesome task for which her opponents never seemed to be
short of willing volunteers.

I had been aware for some time of the Princess's close
lines of communication with the reporter Richard Kay.
Since her death, Richard Kay has spoken openly of the
close friendship he believed he enjoyed with the Princess.
He was often surprisingly close at hand, even during private
holidays, and her messages on his mobile phone provided
some of his tabloid competitors with considerable amusement. Articles bearing his name, usually on the front page of
the *Daily Mail*, were sometimes so obviously briefed by the
Princess that I recognized whole sentences from things she
had said to me only the day before. Now, with the evidence
of her complicity spread all over the front pages, the polite
charade by which I turned a blind eye to such private initiatives could no longer be maintained.

On the morning the story broke, the Princess was sitting
for the portrait painter Nelson Shanks in his airy studios in

Tite Street. Of all the artists who painted her, Shanks developed the happiest relationship with his subject and, far from being a chore, his sittings became occasions that she looked forward to. When I arrived, artist and subject were engrossed in lighthearted banter as usual, while Nelson's wife and daughter created a soothing background of happy domesticity—a background I sometimes found hard to enjoy with true equanimity, given the startlingly detailed nude portraits of his wife that even the most hastily averted eyes could not fail to spot among earlier work so proudly displayed.

My private secretary's expression of worldly imperturbability, which I had carefully arranged on my face while climbing the stairs, must have failed in its task that morning. After just one glance at me, the Princess laughed and said, "Oh Patrick, I am sorry."

I immediately put on a more normal expression—something between panic and pained tolerance. "Don't worry about me, Ma'am," I said. "But some people are going to make this very awkward for you."

Her denial reflexes were in good shape, however, and she seemed to have put the entire episode out of her mind already. Far from being deterred by her embarrassing exposure, she went on to exploit it to the point where Richard Kay acquired the status of an illicit, de facto spokesman. (As if life were not complicated enough already—as he and I joked over lunch several years later.)

Media troubles were never far away. In May the Princess had spent a not very restful weekend with friends near Malaga. Having dispensed with all the assistance she was accustomed to when traveling, she tried to pass through the airport incognito and attracted much uncomfortable attention. She then discovered that her destination was home to a particularly virulent strain of paparazzo. Her holiday on that stretch of coast duly produced a crop of fuzzy but otherwise unremarkable long-range photographs of the Princess sunbathing.

Then word reached me through Eduardo Junco, the proprietor of *Hola!* (sister magazine to *Hello!*), that an especially enterprising photographer had secured snaps of the Princess momentarily topless as she adjusted her swimsuit. "And you know, Señor Jephson, Her Highness is not as young as she was..." No further description was necessary. Now that *was* an emergency!

The swimsuit's owner was adamant that she had not allowed any such opportunity to occur. Knowing her to be extremely deliberate in matters of dress and appearance, I was inclined to believe her. The trouble was that, in the unlikely event that she really had let something slip at a critical moment, she did not relish the thought of such photographs appearing for public consumption.

The choice was between calling the photographer's bluff or allowing the considerate Señor Junco to make good his offer to enter the market, buy the photographs, and destroy them. Such an act of generosity was in line with the opinion I had formed of him during an earlier visit he had made to KP, but the Princess took a more worldly view and feared that to accept such an offer would lay her open to exploitation at a later date. In the end my view prevailed. We really had little choice, although sadly Señor Junco's staff were unable to send me the negatives so that the Princess could destroy them herself. To my relief, the Princess's Spanish benefactor never pressed the opportunity to exact a quid pro quo.

Another example of the media pitfalls that surrounded the Princess appeared at around the same time but in a very different disguise. In late May the hidden opposition to her that lurked among the darkened thickets of the old royal establishment made an appearance in the shape of Lord Charteris, former private secretary to the Queen, speaking to the *Daily Express* on May 27, 1994. His Lordship plainly found it impossible to maintain his reticence on the subject of the Duchess of York and the Princess of Wales. Without much dissent, he described the Duchess of York as "vulgar vulgar vulgar."

The Duchess's regal response to this outburst—"We're all entitled to our own point of view"—struck me as a supreme form of reticence in itself. A slighting remark about the Princess in the same article, however, could not be allowed to pass unanswered.

I duly telephoned Lord Charteris to convey Her Royal Highness's disappointment. "She knows how these things can be exaggerated," I said, "and she hopes they were taken out of context. But as they stand she really finds them rather hurtful."

My Lord would not accept a scold from a pup such as I. He also seemed to have developed great difficulty in hearing me. I suppose I would have done exactly the same, had our roles been reversed.

*T*he Princess's engagement calendar for the summer of 1994 was a pale shadow of the packed program of previous years. No longer able to justify such a considerable public investment, the post of equerry to the Princess lapsed when its final occupant, Captain Ed Musto, returned to a promising career in the Royal Marines.

Having divested herself of much of her earlier activities but not, it seemed, of her desire for publicity, the Princess soon found that the rather more self-indulgent lifestyle that she had adopted had its shortcomings. Her preoccupation with mysticism turned temporarily sour as her former astrologer went public with a book claiming to have been sanctioned by the Princess herself. An extensive legal digression resulted that was costly both in time and money.

A series of uncoordinated and impulse-driven visits to hospitals, hospices, and night shelters for the homeless produced little long-term benefit for visitor or visited. Only the hungry media pack, deprived for the moment of its normal rich diet, was happy to gobble up such scraps, especially if mysteriously tipped off in advance.

As I had so frequently observed, the Princess was happiest when she was working, preferably quite hard. The sort of work she had been doing since her great "withdrawal" speech was desultory and lacked any sort of theme, other than that it was vaguely humanitarian with just enough social conscience to make her feel she was doing some good. It was not enough. I knew the emotional self-indulgence that only work could keep at bay was waiting to claim her underfilled time and underused talents. My own waistline—both physical and mental—was also beginning to suffer. Nevertheless, trying to organize a satisfying program without her active interest, let alone commitment, was like trying to make bricks with straw.

Any new program of sustained, rewarding activity would, I reasoned, probably best be shared with an organization already familiar with its royal visitor's mixed motives. I therefore put more effort than usual into persuading the Princess to take up the Red Cross's offer of a place on a special planning commission, which was all that remained from the discarded package of proposals presented the previous winter.

My recent knowledge of the Red Cross had been largely confined to organizing the Princess's regular contacts with its national and overseas activities connected to her position as patron of British Red Cross Youth. In Zimbabwe and Nepal, as well as in many centers around Britain, the link had proved a highly profitable one for both the charity and the Princess. The British Director General Mike Whitlam had established a good working relationship with the Princess, who enjoyed his frank conversation and buccaneering approach. This was intended to flatter her as a patron who was not just a figurehead, but one who actually got involved with the charity's work in some of its most harrowing missions at home and abroad.

The tactic succeeded. Mike's concern for the Princess as an individual was genuine and appreciated. So, too, was his desire to maximize the relationship with the Princess to the benefit of his organization. With a few rare exceptions, he managed to achieve a remarkable balance between two such potentially opposing objectives.

With the Princess's cautious agreement, Mike helped to arrange for her to be nominated as the British member of a special commission set up to advise the International Red Cross Federation and the International Committee of the Red Cross on how better coordination between these two sometimes discordant organizations might be achieved in the future. A knowledge of the labyrinthine politics of the Red Cross was not required. Where the Princess was thought to be able to make a valuable contribution was in her ability to speak from a position of some firsthand knowledge and to ask the sort of objective questions that the process required and that it was felt only a well-briefed layperson might provide.

The commission, about twenty strong, was made up of similarly influential Red Cross "outsiders" from several different countries and came under the benign chairmanship of Darrell Jones, a retired Canadian judge. It was well funded, had a brilliant secretary in the redoubtable British former diplomat David Wyatt, and would be at liberty to poke its nose into almost any aspect of the Red Cross's worldwide work with the not very onerous task of providing a report on its findings, at least in interim form, by the end of 1995. As an opportunity for the Princess to develop her own knowledge and confidence, to establish herself as a truly independent, working Princess and make good, visible use of her abundant talents in highlighting the plight of people in need, it seemed practically ideal.

The first few meetings were held in Geneva in the summer of 1994. The plan was to hold a series of two or three preliminary meetings there before the commission set off on its travels to world trouble spots. To begin with all went well. The image of the business-suited Princess, briefcase in hand, striding with the other commuting executives onto the morning Swissair flight at Heathrow appealed to her.

From my viewpoint it also seemed appropriate for her current status and a promising model of things to come.

It was not to be. As the serious meetings got fully under way, I watched my boss's eyes glaze over as the proceedings failed to grab her attention. By September she had had enough. Saying that she felt unwell, she cut short our involvement and headed back to the hotel to pack for an early flight home. Her formal resignation from the commission followed some months later. Her departure was greeted with understanding and sympathy from all sides, but I was not alone in regretting such a squandered opportunity.

On the day of her departure, however, I had other things on my mind. The Princess having excused herself early on the grounds of an unspecified indisposition, by a supreme irony I was the one who was feeling unwell. Something in the delicious Swiss lunch laid on for the commission, on which I had hoggishly indulged myself, suddenly began seriously to disagree with me.

It was the nightmare waiting to befall every courtier and suddenly it was coming true for me. Sitting next to the Princess during our interminable drive back to the hotel, I suddenly knew without any doubt that I was going to be sick. I had been unusually silent since our departure from the meeting as I debated whether or not to admit to the rebellion that was breaking out in my stomach. Foolishly, I had calculated that I could make it back to the sanctuary of my hotel bathroom before succumbing.

Interpreting my silence as tacit disapproval of her failure to stay the course with the commission, the Princess tried to cheer me up with irreverent impressions of her fellow commissioners. When this produced only a deeper silence from me, together with a faraway look in my eyes, she asked if there was anything the matter.

Without shifting my fixed gaze from the back of the driver's head, I mimed being violently ill. She burst into giggles. "Well, for God's sake don't throw up over me!" she said. "Do you want to stop the car?"

Having come this far, however, I was grimly determined to hang on. Breathing deeply, I gestured that we should carry on to the hotel as quickly as possible. As soon as we had stopped, for once in my life I jumped out of the car and ran through the hotel doors ahead of the Princess. Without turning round, I managed what was intended as a wave of farewell combined with apology and then dived into the *Messieurs*, where, in marble luxury and before an offended audience of UN delegates, I was flamboyantly sick.

Later, feeling much better and having apologized for my frailty, I flew back to London with the Princess. Nothing more was said of the incident. The next morning I received a little note from her.

> *Patrick.*
> *Thank you so much for braving Geneva out when you'd been that sick . . . you are always a wonderful source of strength and support. That means an enormous amount to me!*
>
> *D.*

At least for the moment, then, I was riding high in the Princess's favor. Now outnumbered some thirty-five to four by her husband's staff, she seemed to appreciate more than ever how much she depended on her small team at St. James's and, for what it was worth, their unswerving loyalty.

Regardless of her negative experience with the Red Cross commission—and in retrospect I blamed myself for having inadequately warned her of its more turgid aspects—it had done her a service, jolting her at least temporarily out of the directionless muddle that had threatened to become her working life. A world of possibilities for future projects still lay at her feet.

New ideas landed on my desk almost every day. After due research and discussion all were rejected, most for very good reason. There had to be another way. The idea was growing in me that there was an alternative option that would enable the Princess to choose her own rate of progress and select her own areas of involvement, while at the same time developing her reputation as an international and independent force for good. After exploratory discussions with some of her senior patronages as well as with the ever-helpful Lynda Chalker, Margaret Jay, and others, I drew up an outline plan for a charity to be headed by the Princess that would be an adaptable but substantial vehicle for all her humanitarian ambitions.

Precisely how humanitarian her own motives were, I did not need to contemplate. In anybody, including the Princess, the answer to such a question is found only in the privacy of one's own conscience. From what I could see, my boss's capacity to care about others' suffering was as great as it ever had been. It had just been joined by a growing and generally healthy wish to find her own fulfillment within it as well.

My job was simple. The Princess's concern needed the right context, at least if it was to be noticed. If it was not 100 percent genuine all the time, then whose was? It was certainly not in parts of the aid industry we had encountered in some grand Geneva headquarters. Nonetheless, they were on the side of good against the world's countless evils and that was an adequate starting point according to *my* moral references. My priority was to lead the Princess to the right sort of work and from there her natural gifts as a caring communicator would work their own magic.

The core of her new charity would be the Princess of Wales's Charities Trust, set up on her marriage in 1981. In the light of the much grander charitable organization set up after the Princess's death, this earlier Trust looks modest by comparison. One reporter, stumbling upon it by chance, has even referred to it as "Diana's secret charity." Its income derived largely from investments made at the time of the Princess's marriage. From time to time it was supplemented by donations, perhaps from a large company the Princess may have supported with an engagement, which then wished to mark the event by making a donation to an unspecified charity of her choice. I was one of two trustees, the other being Sir Matthew Farrer. It was a sign of the good sense and goodwill that still permeated much of the Wales organization that the Princess opted to keep Matthew as trustee of her fund, even though she had switched to Mishcon's for all other legal requirements.

The main purpose of this fund was to enable the Princess to make small donations to individuals and organizations who wrote to her asking for money. It was a quick, efficient, and responsive system, albeit quite small in scale. The average donation cannot have been more than a couple of hundred pounds. Nonetheless, over the years during which I was responsible for it, we probably made several hundred donations, each of which was intended to make a crucial difference to a small but deserving project. (In a sublime piece of irony, one of the Trust's small donations was to an organizer of trips for disabled youngsters who also happened to be a radio ham. He later used his hobby to record the notorious Squidgygate conversation and sent it to a newspaper.)

Since mid-1993 I had been considering ways in which the Princess of Wales's Charities Trust could become a more useful tool in her evolving style of work. An early and successful example of such development came with the West End premiere of the Harrison Ford film *The Fugitive*.

Traditionally, royal film premieres are staged to benefit one or two charities, whose formidable ladies would assemble committees to sell tickets, arrange any accompanying reception, and generally organize the event to their satisfaction, while the film company provided the film and the cinema. I had observed, however, that even with the best run premieres, and particularly when charities were being called upon to act in unison, there was considerable scope for duplication, inefficiency, and even bickering—not least over the film company's own wishes concerning seat allocation.

As an experiment, I negotiated with Warner Brothers and we agreed on an innovative arrangement. They would organize the entire event without the interference of any well-meaning charity committee, in exchange for a preagreed donation to the Princess of Wales's Charities Trust.

The evening was a great success, not least because Clint Eastwood (present as a Warners' "elder statesman") gave a private supper party for the Princess afterward at the Savoy. Eastwood himself spent most of the film in a Leicester Square pub, mingling apparently unnoticed with the evening's revelers. At the beginning of the film I had suggested that he might like to go and take his seat, but he told me he had some urgent business to attend to and disappeared. It was the sharp-eyed police who later told me that he had apparently preferred the surroundings of one of England's less atmospheric public houses to watching a film he had seen too often before. After the premiere, a large check—probably the largest in its history—was deposited with the Princess of Wales's Charities Trust and, as agreed with Warner Brothers, a large slice of it went to one of the Princess's patronages, the Tushinskaya Children's Hospital in Moscow.

Around the core of the existing Trust, I proposed to assemble a board of advisers drawn from the upper echelons of the Princess's patronages and a board of trustees drawn from her formidable list of contacts in industry and finance. Thus provided with funds and expertise, through an appointed chief executive the Princess could dispense largesse in the form of grants, practical aid, education, or publicity. She would have a completely legitimate reason to involve herself in whatever branch of humanitarian activity caught her attention, traveling the world to oversee the work of projects she had helped to fund.

The funds would be substantial, there was no doubt about that. They would not just be raised through film premieres (all of which would follow the pattern set by Warner

Brothers) but also through special events. In this context I was thinking of the Concert of Hope formula, which the Rod Gunner Organization had developed with the Princess's cooperation and which had already successfully raised funds for the Red Cross, for AIDS charities, and for children's hospices.

These concerts—masterminded by the buccaneering impresario Rod Gunner, who had also organized the Prince's "Symphony for the Spire" concert in aid of Salisbury Cathedral—had already added to the Princess's tally of celebrity admirers. She had invited Take That to tea at KP (a qualified success due to the distracting presence of one of her typists) and Pavarotti remained a passionate admirer for the rest of her life. There was no doubt about the caliber of big names she could pull in and no limit to the earning power of an organization bearing her name.

I sketched the organizational diagram on the back of a menu in the Princess's suite in Geneva one evening. Outside it was growing dark, but through the plate-glass windows we admired a spectacular electrical storm that flickered and flashed eerily across the Alpine skyline. Her initial enthusiasm was practically unbounded. Ideas for projects and fund-raising events sprang to her mind in the course of the next few weeks, accompanied by great excitement and genuine eagerness. This really could be her ticket to the world. And mine, I thought irrelevantly.

Sadly, this project followed the fate of all the others. The same blow fell. When the Princess realized that the project's success depended on a genuine and sustained commitment on her part, her enthusiasm ebbed away. She had no appetite or aptitude for undertakings beyond her immediate horizon, and that was often no further away than next week's staff lunch.

Eventually we reached the point where I felt that the risk of starting such a potentially huge ball rolling without the unequivocal and clear-eyed participation of its propelling force was too great. The files were put away. I have since idly wondered if today's heirs to the Princess's name ever found them, or if they even looked.

*H*aving only six months previously announced that she no longer intended to take part in royal events at a national level, the Princess reacted with some enthusiasm to the suggestion that she should participate in that summer's celebrations for the fiftieth anniversary of D-day. Her continued participation in national events had been agreed in our pre-separation negotiations in late 1992 but they had proved to be few and far between, and then she had made her "withdrawal" speech. The D-day invitation was an enlightened sign from the Queen's office that they had not forgotten their side of the bargain, even if she was no longer seen as central to the royal machine. She had, after all, been excluded from the "Way Ahead" group of core royal figures.

She did not seem to mind very much, at least outwardly. "We've left all that behind, Patrick," she told me. "We've got new things to do that *they* couldn't understand."

I resisted the temptation to say, "In that case I'd like to know who can," and paused to reflect on what this eagerness to be part of the D-day celebrations might mean. Her enthusiasm seemed to offer further evidence that she secretly craved direction from above. Something I had read while studying Political Science came back to me, with disturbing implications. The nineteenth-century philosopher Émile Durkheim had a theory that, far from wishing to cast off their chains, the workers of the world would be lost without them. In certain cases it could lead to anomic suicide.

It could be just as true for Princesses as for humble workers, I thought, as I watched my boss nervously prepare for a big day of Commonwealth ceremony straight out of an elementary guide to being royal. She was due to attend the unveiling of the Canadian Memorial in Green Park (two of her affiliated regiments were Canadian) and later to appear at the main celebrations in Portsmouth.

She was visibly anxious and appeared to feel very much out of place. "God, Patrick!" she gulped, adjusting her hat. "This is terribly grown up. What shall I say to them all?"

This seemed a bit extreme, coming from a woman who thought nothing of hobnobbing with Presidents and un-flinchingly spoke on live TV. I knew what she meant, though. She was terrified of the hostility she expected from her in-laws. After all, in their view she had put herself out-side their charmed circle and was now relegated to the role of an invited outsider.

"Relax, Ma'am," I replied. "Don't try so hard. They'll be more nervous of you." It cheered her up, even if neither of us quite believed it.

For part of the commemorations, the Princess was in the royal yacht *Britannia*, mingling with other notables from all the Allied nations. There she encountered Bill Clinton. She was impressed, and not only by his grasp of the historical significance of the occasion. "He's terribly *sexy*," she con-fided to me rather breathily. I judged this placed him in close contention with President Mubarak of Egypt for the top spot on my private league table of heads of state.

She and the Prince behaved in public toward each other with the civility they had shown at their first joint outing since the separation, at the Battle of the Atlantic service in Liverpool the previous year. It was a strain nevertheless, and I think the whole experience reminded the Princess of what she had given up.

While perhaps feeling scant regret, the uncertainty of her own immediate future can only have been heightened by such confident displays of relentless establishment continu-ity. She had always been sensitive to the Hanoverian impla-cability of her in-laws. That day it had radiated from them unmistakably and she had felt it, however outwardly civil they may have appeared. Ironically, that very continuity was about to come under scrutiny again.

*F*or anybody watching royal events, 1994 was the year of Dimbleby. It was the year in which by default the Princess achieved her moment of clearest ascendancy over her husband and the future he represented.

Jonathan Dimbleby's much-trailed television documentary about the Prince of Wales was screened on June 29, and the book was due to follow in the autumn. It represented the fruition of some two and a half years of painstaking research by Dimbleby and his team, during which they had been given access to all the Prince's archives and had conducted nearly a hundred interviews with people well acquainted with him and his work. It achieved an enormous impact mainly because of the Prince's televised admission of adultery, but also because of the debate it stirred up about his role as future Defender of the Faith, and even his suitability to succeed to the throne.

Some months earlier I had held a valuable meeting with the Archbishop of Canterbury's private secretary Andrew Purkis, a move I thought important given the high profile the Archbishop was then receiving as a key player in constitutional matters. Andrew received me kindly as a distant comrade in the private secretaries' trade union and I spent an instructive hour or two at Lambeth Palace, learning much about Church and State that would later prove relevant as controversy raged over the Prince's publicly questioned suitability to become head of the Church of England. It was no secret that the question of Camilla Parker Bowles was going to need some kind of pretty miraculous answer.

Predictably, the tabloid papers scoured the Dimbleby extracts for the juiciest tittle-tattle, which they then luridly reproduced. The more thoughtful commentators dwelled at long and damaging length on the poor advice the Prince must have accepted to undertake what was seen to be little more than a glorified PR stunt.

NOT FIT TO REIGN screamed the *Daily Mirror* on June 30, the day after the TV film was shown. "This will only make it worse," intoned W. F. Deedes magisterially in the *Daily Telegraph* on October 17 after the book had been published. Even *The Economist* took time away from its normal areas of interest to pronounce authoritatively on October 22 that the Crown was "an idea whose time has passed. No wonder the Princess felt that the occupants of St. James's and Buckingham Palaces had no business criticizing her." The story dominated the royal scene all summer and autumn, except when the press could be persuaded temporarily to shift their attention back to the Princess.

Debate also raged about whether the film should ever have been made, with most commentators believing that, however brave an attempt it had been at telling the truth, the questions it had answered had only begged more. In any case, whose truth was it? Even though Dimbleby's project had begun long before the publication of Andrew Morton's book—let alone the separation—it was inevitably seen as the Prince's riposte to the earlier work. In addition, by allowing such privileged access to one individual and with the subsequent serialization rights going to just one Sunday newspaper, the reaction of the vast, excluded portion of the media was always likely to be resentful.

In the midst of so much negative coverage, the Prince's advisers must have wondered whether honesty had been the best policy after all. I wonder if even now, years later, anybody truly believes that something so complex could be accurately reported by just one account, however well sourced. Moreover, where Dimbleby dealt with matters relating to the Princess, he did so without any direct cooperation and his coverage of this aspect of the story was inevitably incomplete and nonauthoritative. Since this was the only part of his account that attracted a universal interest, such an omission was bound to devalue to some extent the exhaustively researched remainder of his work.

The day of the program turned out to be another example of the Princess winning the publicity war largely through happy accident. By an extraordinary twist of bad luck, the Prince was at the controls of a Queen's Flight BAe 146 that day when it overran the runway while landing on Islay, substantially damaging the aircraft. ANOTHER ERROR OF JUDGEMENT? howled the papers.

Long before the date of the transmission had been announced, the Princess had accepted an invitation to attend a dinner that evening at the Serpentine Gallery in Hyde Park, having recently become the gallery's patron. The dinner provided a perfect opportunity for her to demonstrate that, although an estimated fifteen million people might be watching her husband's program, she was at work—and, what's more, looking as glamorous as only she knew how.

It was generally thought that the Princess had deliberately intended to upstage her husband's program by appearing at the Serpentine Gallery dressed in a not very demure frock and inviting the press to come and admire her. In fact, the dress was a last-minute substitute because details of the outfit she had originally planned to wear had been leaked to the media. The huge press presence probably owed more to the fact that it was well known that the Prince was about to admit his adultery to the watching world, and nothing could make a better accompaniment to that story than pictures of his wife.

Her response to the dire publicity attracted by Dimbleby was surprisingly not to crow. She had been on the receiving end of enough media feeding frenzies to know that the release of such elemental forces created waves in the public mood whose direction was impossible to forecast. Also something about the sheer volume of coverage, regardless of its tone, perhaps reminded her that others could steal headlines too—intentionally or otherwise.

Nonetheless, the moral boost it gave her in the public's

eyes and in her own was incalculable. "There, Patrick! Now everybody can see what we've been up against," she said on our way to the next day's routine engagement. That was fair comment, I thought—but she had also denied watching the program, even though Richard Aylard had distributed videotapes generously in advance. Behind the outward display of insouciance, there lay a tangible anger.

The Prince's "definitive" account of what had constituted the irretrievable breakdown of their marriage offended her to the extent that she asked me to draft a letter to her husband's solicitors, asking if they had known in advance of what was to be revealed and recording her disappointment about not being informed beforehand herself. She cited her genuine concern about the effect of the program and book on William and Harry, both then and in the future. (Smart remarks about pots and kettles sprang to my lips, but I suppressed them.)

Meanwhile, the Princess was to be found at a hospital in Roehampton, quietly making the point that whatever media storm was blowing, she was getting on with the work she did best. Even in this moment of potential triumph, her own form of loyalty to her husband remained unbroken and she hardly ever criticized him directly. Instead she reserved her harshest criticism of the project for the Prince's advisers, who, she felt, had taken advantage of his naiveté. Naturally, she also relayed accounts of her concern for the boys through the usual media contacts.

Most important of all, the Princess now felt that the error she may have committed over authorizing Andrew Morton's book and the regret it stirred in her had been paid off. While it had never been the Prince's intention that his project should contribute to the War of the Waleses, it was inevitable that the press would portray it as just that. Here for everyone's entertainment was a public brawl and every media initiative thereafter was going to be seen as a punch aimed by one side or the other, in a contest that appears to continue even after the Princess's death.

It was her good fortune that, while this brawl may have appeared to bring them both pretty close to the gutter, it was the Princess who was still looking at the stars. Even when, suspiciously soon afterward, her public image came under fire once more, from the Oliver Hoare phone calls story and the publication of *Princess in Love*, neither attack reversed this widely held impression.

It was not just a lucky escape. The Dimbleby exercise had done nothing to shift the general perception that the Princess was more sinned against than sinning. She capitalized on this almost immediately, when in mid-August several papers were tipped off that the Princess had been making up to twenty phone calls a day to Oliver Hoare, a married London art dealer. The circumstances were quite enough to stir up a welter of suggestive press speculation.

As it happened, I had known for some time that the Princess was in touch with Oliver Hoare, although nobody except the two of them can really know the truth of their relationship. I was aware that he frequently visited KP— once, I was gleefully told, going so far as to arrive hidden in the trunk of the Princess's car. Later they seemed not to notice (or care) what people saw. He eventually parked his Volvo openly at the Palace.

For me, there was a more serious aspect to the friendship. The papers spoke of a police investigation that had traced what were thought to be nuisance calls all the way back to the Princess's private line at KP. On the morning that the story was published, I asked a contact in the Royalty and Diplomatic Protection Group if there had been such an investigation and if there was a printout of the calls made. The answer was "yes" to both questions. Could I have a copy next morning, please? (This was a Sunday.) "Yes" again. Next morning, however, the printout was unfortunately missing. There was never any explanation as to where the newspapers had obtained their information on the police investigation.

It soon emerged that at least some of the calls had been made by a disgruntled schoolboy, and this contributed to the speed with which the incident was forgotten. I had my own uneasy feelings about the absence of any hard evidence, scrutiny of which might have enabled the Princess to cast further doubt on the likelihood of her complicity.

Commentators preferred instead to dwell on the plight of a healthy and attractive young woman deprived of male company. They wondered sympathetically at the state of mind she must have been in to make even one obsessive phone call to a married man. Verdict: unhappy Princess, possibly depressed enough to make the calls, but who could blame her?

Similarly, *Princess in Love,* published in September 1994, did her little real harm. It was an account of her love affair with James Hewitt, obviously written with the assistance of James himself. Hostile invective was heaped on the "kiss-and-tell love rat," but in truth the book revealed little that was not already widely suspected. The public verdict seemed to be: the Prince and Princess were now separated, would presumably soon be divorced, and, anyway, he had Camilla, so what was the poor girl to do?

For form's sake I asked the Princess if she wanted to sue and drew my own conclusions when she decided she did not. In media terms she had nothing to gain by it. While debate continued to rage over her husband's public admission of adultery, further indignity was heaped on the beloved Princess by the kiss-and-tell memoirs of a man she was later publicly to say she adored. We let sleeping dogs lie, and now the book reads with a certain innocent charm. Nobody was going to begrudge the Princess any happiness she may have found with the handsome cavalry officer. In any case, I knew enough of her emotional complexity to suspect that any guilt attaching to the affair could not be laid entirely at one door or the other.

*T*hat autumn the influence of good friends encouraged the Princess to make another trip to the USA's East Coast.

Having spent part of the summer at Martha's Vineyard, her natural affinity with much of American life was at a high pitch. There were several reasons for going to America this time, each of them a soothing antidote to the simmering acrimony of her daily life in London.

One of these was a dinner given by the portrait painter Nelson Shanks, now back in his native land and with his reputation enhanced by his completion of a work that many thought was the finest portrait ever painted of the Princess. The event given in her honor was held at the National Arts Club. To her amusement, the Princess found that she had arrived before her host, but so had one of the other guests and she was happy to be swept up in a bear-like embrace by Luciano Pavarotti. So, slightly to my consternation, was I.

The evening was as relaxed, convivial, and flattering as she could have wished. As she returned to her suite at the Carlyle Hotel—which, under the direction of James Sherwin, quickly assumed the status almost of a second home for her—the Princess's contentment was all the better to see after the ordeals of the previous year.

It was heightened the next day when we flew from Teterboro to Washington in a G IV private jet belonging to the Forstmann Little Corporation. The Princess's sunny mood was at odds with the weather. Our typically overstated convoy inched its way noisily through the Manhattan traffic in a steady drizzle before ducking under the Hudson River in the Lincoln Tunnel.

The head of her security detail, a worthy successor to the legendary Doug of earlier visits but rather more forthcoming, made an inconsequential remark that on emerging from the tunnel the Princess would be in the State of New Jersey.

Equally inconsequentially, the Princess politely expressed her pleasure at the prospect. "I've never been to New Jersey before," she said.

Our other special agent, at the wheel of the borrowed Range Rover, was prompted to speak the first words we had heard him say. "Don't worry, Ma'am, it's just a state of mind," he said before lapsing back into silence.

At Teterboro, a sophisticated little airport at which executive jets parked like taxis at a cab rank, the G IV was awaiting our arrival. The tasteful eye that had overseen the cabin decorations had even extended to the cockpit, where leather and chrome had transformed the utilitarian workspace into something like a flying Bentley.

The aircraft had been lent to the Princess by Teddy Forstmann, partner of Forstmann Little and chairman, among other things, of Gulfstream. An occasional visitor to KP, he had also entertained the Princess at English restaurants such as the Manoir aux Quat' Saisons in Oxfordshire. He was a bachelor—generous, warmhearted, discreet, and in many ways an ideal companion for a Princess in need of dependable male company. Apart from his unselfish concern for my employer's well-being, the dapper tycoon endeared himself to me by referring to me as "Boss" and, both then and later, proved to be a welcome source of typically candid American advice.

I think it was his common sense, delivered straight and with the worldly wisdom that only experience and pots of self-made money can bring, that was his greatest service to the Princess. It may also have been why the relationship never developed beyond friendship and mutual respect. That it might have developed into something more—after all, Teddy was one of the most eligible men in America— was an unusually agreeable subject to ponder. They looked good together, I thought, especially if you discounted a slight disparity in height. What's more, he was kind to her. Sadly, Teddy's commonsense advice would probably have proved no more welcome in the long run than anybody else's. The friendship and mutual respect endured, however, albeit at long distance. It never failed to raise her spirits.

In Washington we stayed with the Brazilian Ambassador and his wife, Paulo Tarso and Lucia Flecha de Lima. It seemed to me that the Flecha de Limas, in the course of a friendship that lasted until her death, were a source of true companionship to the Princess. In good times and bad they gave her the kind of support that never questioned her actions without offering wise alternatives. They did not judge her without also understanding the reasons behind her misjudgments, and they did not demand anything of her other than that she should be free to be herself.

From a natural generosity of spirit, they gave her the kind of encouraging words and openhanded, practical support that might characterize the best type of family relationship. Indeed, their home in Washington, as in London, became a refuge for the Princess and a place of comfort and tranquillity where she could rediscover and tentatively exercise those parts of her personality that had not been taken over by her celebrity and responsibilities.

We stayed at the Brazilian residence for three nights. On the morning after her arrival the Princess called on Elizabeth Dole, wife of the Senator then preparing to run for President and a formidable figure in her own right in the worlds of politics and charity work, notably with the American Red Cross. She seemed to find an affinity with the Princess, having succeeded (as my boss sadly never would) in putting good intentions and original ideas into practice in a way that brought her personal fulfillment as well as public recognition and respect.

That evening the Princess was guest of honor at a dinner given by the redoubtable Katherine Graham, owner of the *Washington Post*. She was able to rub shoulders with many of the leading political figures in Washington, particularly from the Democratic Party, which was preparing itself for office.

The Princess's glamour, coupled with Kay Graham's polished but informal hospitality, created an atmosphere in which anything seemed possible. The presence of so much power and wealth in a form so refreshingly devoid of the undercurrents of equivalent gatherings in London gave the Princess's confidence wings. When she rose to thank her hostess in a few well-chosen words, she could, as she later told me, feel the enormous energy gathered in that old Virginia mansion.

In her own speech Kay Graham had spoken with some tenderness about the public dissection suffered by the younger woman, toward whom it seemed she felt an almost maternal concern. If the guests had expected self-pity from the Princess, then they were in for a surprise. When it was her turn to speak, she joked about the newsprint that had been devoted to speculation about a person she said she could hardly recognize as herself. Then she ended on a high note that seemed to strike the right response from her hard-bitten fellow guests. "So I will always remember tonight," she said. "This is a warm and welcoming city in a great country. It symbolizes hope and the promise of better things to come."

The next day we attended a lunch given for the Princess by Sir Robin and Lady Renwick at the British Embassy. Prior to that lunch, the Princess had a private meeting with Hillary Clinton at the Ambassador's residence. I lurked outside the door, through which came indistinct sounds of animated discussion and occasional bursts of laughter. After about twenty minutes the door flew open and the two most photographed women in the world emerged, radiating mutual admiration like an electrical charge. "She's very intuitive," confided the Princess later. "A very strong lady!" This was high praise from someone who so longed to be thought the same.

The guest list for lunch was of a similar caliber. The eminent figures assembled on the terrace in the autumn sunshine included General Colin Powell, only recently retired as Chairman of the Joint Chiefs of Staff. He and the Princess hit it off immediately.

"Do you miss wearing all the uniforms then, General?" she asked him brightly. "I expect they've all been put away in wardrobes."

"Well, almost, Ma'am," the victor of the Gulf War

replied with a wink. "But I did keep a pair of overalls handy. Alma likes me to use them when I'm working on the car."

We returned to London the following day. The day after that, with typical speed and courtesy, the Princess wrote me a letter of thanks. The positive tone of the note was a clear indication of the exuberant confidence that she appeared to have discovered on her trip. For once, her own requirement for happiness had been satisfied to the point where she felt there was enough spare to pass around. "What an incredible experience we have just been through during our 5 days in America!" she wrote. She thanked me for my "strength and support" and ended by saying that she was exhausted, but "thrilled by the new path we are treading."

As I once heard the eminent psychologist Dr. Brian Roet remark, "If you're going to have delusions they might as well be positive ones." There was little doubt that the Princess's "new path" was a delusion. She had no idea where it was leading, it originated by chance from a happy trip to America, and, looking ahead, it seemed distinctly rocky to me. It was at least a positive delusion, however, and I did not begrudge her any of it.

The upturn in her morale may also have been connected with the drubbing the Prince was still receiving in the press after the autumn's serialization and publication of Jonathan Dimbleby's book. Even establishment voices such as Charles Moore, writing in the *Spectator* on October 22, 1994, was able to say,

When the Royal couple separated I wrote a column in this space which criticized the Princess for indulging her "craving for private happiness" and ended "how do you know some will object that the Prince does not suffer from this same debilitating craving? I do not know but since he is the next King I do not think we should discuss the matter." Now he is forcing us all to discuss it, wrenching the conversation back, just when we hoped it might stop, to him and his woes.

On the heels of this, the Princess was sent an 1845 quotation by Henry David Thoreau by an admirer who had proved just as ready to send messages of reproof when he thought them necessary:

> Do a little more of that work which you have sometime confessed to be good which you feel that society and your judge rightly demands of you. Do what you reprove yourself for not doing. Know that you are neither satisfied nor dissatisfied with yourself without reason. Let me say to you and to myself in one breath, cultivate the tree which you have found to bear fruit in your soil. Regard not your past failures or successes—all in the past is equally a failure and a success. It is a success in as much as it offers you the present opportunity...if you can drive a nail and have any nails to drive, drive them.

Inspired by the sentiment if not by the detail of such an exhortation, the Princess embarked on two further projects that ended her year on a note higher than we had ever had reason to believe could have been achieved during the weeks of aimlessness that followed her precipitate "withdrawal" from public life in December 1993.

Once again, it was possible to question her motives. She was always uneasy knowing that the latest photograph on the picture editor's desk was of some glamorous foreign jaunt, however distinguished the company. She was therefore anxious to be seen to be back at work after her American trip, preferably delving into something pretty gritty. A focus on mental illness seemed appropriate, so I quickly went to work.

During visits in rapid succession to the special hospitals at Broadmoor and at Carstairs in central Scotland, it was her concern for the welfare of the patients—even these ones—that once again left the strongest impression on me. I was less charitably inclined to check the height of the perimeter fence and the proximity of the nearest member of what I still found hard to think of as the nursing staff.

The management of both establishments were enlightened and confident enough to welcome the Princess's visit with its attendant publicity as a constructive contribution to a vocation that few might have envied. In the case of Carstairs, the publicity was further heightened by the Princess's traveling companion for the day, Jayne Zito, who was already a prominent campaigner for improvements in the care of the mentally ill.

At Broadmoor the Princess attended a meeting of the patients' council, an internal representative body whose activities sometimes drew the ill-informed criticism of certain sections of the press. I watched her take her seat in what was to be a private session of the council, surrounded by men who were thought to be a serious threat to the public. As the door closed, I heard her voice and whatever she said raised an immediate warm laugh of greeting. No wonder rarefied gatherings of politicians in Washington failed to intimidate her.

As her finale for the year, the Princess returned to Paris. In a short program of engagements in support of her presidency of the children's charity Barnardo's, she visited community projects in some of the poorer districts of the city, followed by an emphatically less austere experience at a grand banquet in the Hall of Mirrors at the Palace of Versailles.

There, over a microscopic portion of what looked like raw pigeon, the Princess traded *doucements* with the incorrigible Valéry Giscard d'Estaing. Finally, she drew a thunderous standing ovation from 900 diners as she made a majestic exit in a style that might have won approving nods from the ghosts of the Bourbons, who (on that night at least) you could believe still inhabited the home of the Sun King.

18

❧

Plummet

*T*he final year of my life with the Princess of Wales opened auspiciously enough. She still rode the crest of a wave of confidence typified by the reception she had received in Versailles. Aided and abetted by a private secretary never happier than when climbing onto an airplane, she then set her rather vague sights on a program of international stardom, drawing on whatever charity links were conveniently to hand.

In many respects it was a parallel of the path trodden by the Duchess of York, at least on the surface. As long as I was going to be involved, however, I was determined that it should be a path that protected the Princess's unique status. She was still at that time the wife of the future King; she was still technically the future Queen herself; and she was indubitably the mother of a future King.

Despite my fine ideas, her continuing lack of a coherent personal strategy, plus her readiness to be easily swayed by a fashionable opinion one minute and obdurately stubborn for no logical reason the next, made it difficult for me to plan a strategy for her public life. To be taken seriously, I suggested to her on several occasions, she should limit herself to a few well-defined objectives. These could be flexibly contrived so that almost any of her favorite activities could be related in the public mind with a couple of central themes.

The amount of self-discipline and application required would have to be kept to a minimum, I realized. This was just as well. As I also suggested, she had been through enough purgatory in recent years and was now in a position to be able to start enjoying herself. If she was happy in her work, I believed she would be more resistant to temptations—never far from her shoulder—to indulge her pathological craving for victimhood and self-justification.

Man, as they say, but proposes. In reply, woman in the form of the Princess of Wales listened politely, made numerous flattering references to my foresight, wisdom, loyalty, etc.—and then proceeded a few months later to draw up very secret plans for what turned out to be her calamitous *Panorama* broadcast.

Panorama has often been cited as the reason that I, among others, resigned from the Princess's service. In my case, however, it was only one (albeit a heavy one) of several straws that ultimately broke the camel's back of my loyalty. With several years' close-hand experience of my boss's capricious and occasionally cruel approach to personnel management, I was more than ever aware of my professional mortality. However much I might appear to be in favor, I knew my shelf life was akin to that of the organic yogurt with which the KP fridge was so well stocked.

The subject was never discussed between us and on the surface we remained, I hope, the picture of benign Princess and devoted servant. Meanwhile, on a subliminal level my working life had become a complicated game of chess in which, with increasing certainty, I was waiting only for the right opening to present itself in order to make my escape.

With ears everywhere, the Princess was constantly updating her mental intelligence file on a huge cast of characters, including me. This gave her a sense of control that was,

I observed, a kind of substitute for self-confidence. She felt able to move people like pieces round a board.

She would, for example, make a casual remark to a secretary such as, "I know it's an unfair question to ask . . . but has Patrick had lunch with X recently?" The result was the same as if she had asked me directly, but the desire to manipulate was sometimes overwhelming. The bond of complicity thus established with the secretary could be more deeply exploited next time. By just such means, the Princess discovered and attempted to thwart my tentative plans to find another job during my last days in office.

In order to deter this game of divide and rule, I made it a policy that everybody should share information with everybody else. It was not much of a safeguard. Also, the habit of trying to guess an ulterior motive behind every innocent remark—however necessary for survival—was a hard one to break.

Perhaps because of this increasingly convoluted existence, I had a growing sense of the opportunities and obligations that lay just outside my work-centered field of view. The chance of a proper holiday would be welcome, for a start. More important, I was pressingly aware of obligations to friends and family, too long postponed due to the job's constant number-one spot in my disordered list of priorities.

A life spent teetering on the high wire of royal approval, however thrilling the view and however tempting the prospects for personal involvement in historic events, seemed less and less defensible. The glow of self-importance that I distantly remembered from my early days as an equerry had long ago been replaced by a dogged belief in the Princess as a force for good, whatever her human shortcomings. This in turn was being replaced by an undeniable cynicism as I wearily contemplated the task of shoring up her public credibility in the face of her self-destructive instincts. Our outing on the night-time streets of King's Cross with which I opened these reminiscences dates from this uneasy period.

The cumulative effect was to reinforce my desire to resign. Knowing how and when to do this was going to be difficult in the extreme. An open approach might seem the obvious answer, but I knew that in the Princess's current state of mind it would be interpreted as disloyalty. Worse, it would put me beyond her reach. Making a smooth transition to a new career while salvaging some credit from the old one was not going to be easy at the best of times. A boss bent on being the victim of betrayal and avenging what she saw as the worst of all crimes would make it impossible.

I sometimes pictured myself as a man locked in a cage with a tigress. In the roof of the cage was an escape hatch, but to have any chance of reaching it the man had to distract and pacify the tigress for long enough to enable him to get under the hatch and make his leap to safety. Otherwise he was lunch. I should add that this rather melodramatic image was largely subconscious, but I did discover a greater motivation than ever for keeping my boss happily occupied.

*P*artly in response to my urgings and partly in response to comparable advice I think she was getting from other sources, in early 1995 the Princess drew up an attempt at her own, very private manifesto. It was a positive, forward-looking document containing a longer list of things she wanted to do than of things she wanted to avoid.

It also betrayed her own muddled thinking. She expressed a wish to avoid "endless bureaucrats," but her own staff could not have been smaller, while an involvement in the sort of mind-numbing occupation usually associated with bureaucracy was never something she was likely to have to encounter for herself.

She said she wished to avoid being "treated as a puppet"—neglecting the fact that, if she had ever been anybody's puppet, she had comprehensively cut any strings that might have been trying to control her movements.

Tellingly, she also wanted to avoid "being used by others

who then take praise." As I wryly reflected on the amount
of praise she received for things that perhaps in the strictest
truth were not of her own doing, I recognized her continuing, avid requirement for reassurance, popularity, and recognition, which nothing was going to satisfy.

She bemoaned the "inflexibility" of her engagement calendar too. Having only just over a year earlier presented her
with a completely blank calendar for her to fill in pretty
much as she chose, I interpreted this as a request for license
to change her mind without being made to feel bad about it
afterward.

Her ambitions were similarly revealing and easier for me
to sympathize with. She wanted her "true worth to be recognized," the chance to use her "healing interests and abilities," and the chance to "address increasing world
problems." With this went a desire to make "a contribution
on a world platform...and to deal with many countries."
Nowhere, to my regret, could I find any reference to a desire to acknowledge the requirements of the rather less
glamorous causes and charities in her own country, from
which the bedrock of her support was drawn.

Quite reasonably perhaps, given all she had gone
through, this appeared to be a plan to enable her to write
her own ticket to wherever she wanted to go, in support of
whatever cause she currently favored, in a continuing quest
for her most elusive ambition. This ambition had been repeated to me on so many occasions, but was conspicuously
and strangely absent from her own list: "peace of mind" was
what she always said she craved.

I had my own doubts as to whether this manifesto would
help her achieve that ambition. I kept them to myself, however, only referring to it when there was a good opportunity to make a connection or nudge her in a particular
direction that might prove rewarding.

As the year progressed, despite all the minor battles we
won against the reactionary forces that would have restricted her chances to exploit her extraordinary world

celebrity, she was ultimately unable to win the war. At its most elevated, her war was fought to establish herself as an independent, globe-trotting channel for good works. I think I coined the word "ambassador" to describe what she wanted to do and she seized on it with enthusiasm. At its least elevated, it was a struggle within herself for control of everyone and everything she could possibly reach. The more danger she detected, the more plots she saw, the more disloyalty she imagined, the more injustice she felt, the greater grew her sense of victimhood. Control of all these threats—by aggression if need be—seemed to be her only way of feeling safe.

The victory that seemed close enough to grasp at the beginning of 1995 had been snatched out of reach by the year's end. This was not the result of some dark conspiracy by faceless men in gray suits plotting in the corridors of Buckingham Palace or St. James's. Such people existed and so, in a fairly benign form, did their plots, but she had out-maneuvered them before with ease and was developing a capability to do so with even greater ease in the future. Her worst enemy, as so often in the past, was herself. Her single-handed and devastating assault on any prospect of progress through consensus—with her husband, with Buckingham Palace, with the still considerable establishment forces in-clined to her side—by making her *Panorama* broadcast fi-nally condemned her to life as an unsupported solo act.

Thereafter, any assistance she required—and she would always be a high-maintenance proposition—would be in-spired by the giver's self-interest or sympathy, rather than by the respect and duty that were her real due. I wondered how she would ever find the peace of mind she sought if the means of achieving it were controlled by people who would always want something back from her in return for their support, be it jet, yacht, holiday, pet project, or even love. Their agendas, however well intended, would always be far removed from that of the only real source of her own status, the British royal family.

The irony was that, with perfect clarity, she saw her priority as being survival against the forces that had so nearly suffocated her. In choosing a path of high-profile indulgence, however, she only accelerated the result that her enemies had been trying so vainly to bring about.

A better private secretary might have succeeded in the painstaking task of stitching together a rapprochement with our ruling family. Ultimately it was my failure to succeed in this as I had hoped to do that brought about my decision to resign. A better private secretary might also have persuaded the Princess to revisit the scenes and origins of her own popularity, and perhaps find the elusive peace of mind she wanted in a restrained program of hard work and real involvement with some of the causes close to people's daily lives.

How I longed for the legions of good people who made up the forgotten armies of her charities to feel that their patron had turned her back on at least some of the glamour that now tempted her in order to strengthen them—and herself—through a systematic, disciplined involvement in what they were doing. Then, from a restored and virtuous position on the moral high ground, she could attempt the task of publicly forgiving her husband and building on the reconciliation already begun with him in private. Such a strategy would have won her something more like the admiration and respect she felt she deserved. It would certainly have won her something more substantial than a self-appointed role as "Queen of Hearts."

From early 1995 onward, I knew this was expecting too much. The long-term publicity benefits of a disciplined return to a systematic, UK-based program—back to the grass roots of her support—were no longer attractive enough to wean her off the exotic new diet of globe-trotting photo calls. Nor was the idea of a public expression of forgiveness for her husband more attractive than the expression of hurt victimhood that she still saw as her due. *Panorama* proved it.

As always, such philosophizing was only an afterthought, a luxury I allowed myself when the increasing tempo of the daily alarums and excursions permitted. Nonetheless, with varying degrees of intrusiveness, these thoughts were always with me, like a dull, repeated bass note underlying the day-to-day cacophony of almost single-handedly running the public life of the world's most famous woman.

Work time merged indistinguishably with family time. I was never beyond the reach of my boss, thanks to the pager that I carried everywhere. The newspapers were a constant source of anxiety, and it usually reached a crescendo at weekends. At least they provided a distraction from the boxes of correspondence that were my regular baggage as I headed out of town on Friday afternoons. There was little time to think, and I became increasingly desperate to stop the roller coaster and get off.

Ultimately, I suppose, Princesses—and Princes too, for that matter—get the private secretaries they deserve. For a number of reasons, I felt I was no longer the private secretary she deserved, and I thought I should make room for somebody who might be. I no longer felt the degree of commitment for her that I needed if I was to sustain this deformed version of royal life. I therefore formed a one-man escape committee and began to dig my way out, putting out tentative feelers to prospective new employers, taking all the advice I could get from people who were successful in the world beyond our Palace walls. Meanwhile, I kept the tigress appeased as best I could.

The pace was hectic. In 1995 I counted no fewer than ten overseas trips made by the Princess of Wales. Each had to be planned, organized, and executed with the same precision that had characterized the set-piece expeditions I recalled from my early days in the Wales office. Whatever lip service the Princess paid to the new regime she had brought about—a regime of accessibility, flexibility, and increased enjoyment—like so much else in her life the dream was not accompanied by the fundamental change of attitudes necessary to make it a reality. Some of my most uncomfortable moments with her could still be sparked off by a minor failure of organization, however far out of my control it may have been.

The best response when the Princess was in a foul mood was to do what you could to ignore it and carry on with business as usual, feigning (with difficulty) a complete lack of concern. Very late one night in 1995, we were waiting to go in to a dinner of unsurpassed grandeur in an Italian military academy. The dinner was the crowning event in a program of music organized by Luciano Pavarotti to raise money for child victims of war in the Balkans. The great tenor had been not uncharacteristically delayed *en route* from dressing room to banqueting hall and the Princess, used to being the only star of the show, was chafing at the delay.

Unable in these surroundings to betray a fraction of the frustration she was feeling, she had to content herself with turning to me with angry eyes and a vicious whisper. "Patrick! It's *midnight!*"

"Gosh, Ma'am," I replied, eyeing an approaching drinks tray. "Is it really?" What on earth, I wondered, did she expect *me* to do about it?

No significant relaxation was permissible in the high standards she legitimately demanded of her staff, but no recruitment was possible either. It was a matter of pride and also part of her new image to be not only more glamorous, responsive, and efficient than the rest of the royal family, but thriftier too. There was certainly no slackening in public demand for her, so the task of keeping her show on the road was becoming an ever more demanding one.

There was hardly a night that year when she did not appear in my dreams—but not for me the happier visions I am told some people experienced of her. As often as not, my dream Princess had a telephone in her hand, a desk thick with unanswered mail, revenge in her heart, and danger in her eyes.

*T*he first major set-piece tour of the year was to Japan. The published purpose of the visit and the focus of the program was to enable the Princess to acquaint herself with the work of various charitable centers for the old, the young, and the disabled. There was also to be a formalizing of the link between Great Ormond Street Hospital for Sick Children, of which she was president, and Tokyo's National Children's Hospital.

Such innocent objectives nevertheless attracted scrutiny from those now convinced that the Princess of Wales was a dangerous unguided missile, ready at a moment's notice to explode with devastating effects for British diplomacy and the prestige abroad of the British royal family. It did not matter to such people that the Princess's solo foreign trips had so far attracted nothing but praise from the countries she visited. I had a fat file of telegrams from Embassies and appreciative letters from Foreign Secretaries to back up this important but awkward fact.

As part of a "hearts and minds" policy toward those who could influence her future role, I had encouraged the Princess to cultivate a personal relationship with whoever was occupying the post of Foreign Secretary. With Douglas Hurd in particular, I felt she struck up a rapport that may have reassured him about her competence and good intentions. In return, I know it represented a kind of paternally concerned interest that she badly missed when he left the post.

Knowing the mistrust with which we were viewed, as well as just knocking out another royal program with all its attendant nuances and permutations, I also had to wage a subtle campaign of persuasion to reassure suspicious minds in Buckingham Palace and the Foreign Office that they had nothing to fear from such an expedition other than further laurels for the Princess of Wales. I wished to make it clear that if anybody had any objection to such laurels being earned, then they should kindly say so clearly, preferably with accompanying reasons, because otherwise we were going to press on regardless.

Unsurprisingly, since nobody could raise any legitimate complaint about the Princess's conduct of her foreign tours, no overt objection was made. There was, however, still a strong enough undercurrent of disapproval for me to encourage the Princess to hold a personal meeting with the Foreign Secretary before her trip.

Our former leader on the Indonesia/Hong Kong tour, David Wright, was now back from Korea and installed in some splendor at the Foreign Office. Japan was his area of special responsibility (he later went on to be our Ambassador in Tokyo). David's view of our intentions was, I suspect, as immune as any to the charms of a laurel-hunting Princess. He had been the Prince's man and this type of royal visit, which did not really conform with any of the established categories, must have offended his sense of propriety. Nevertheless, any reservations he may have harbored he magnanimously kept to himself, and I hope he was not disappointed with the results we achieved.

As in the past, the view from the Embassy was rather different from the vistas of doubt we faced at home. Properly handled, the prospect of a visit from the Princess of Wales was enough to arouse enthusiasm in most countries. Ambassadors, insulated from the shifting currents of the Whitehall–Buckingham Palace axis, were able to report what was only the evidence of their eyes. People wanted to see the Princess of Wales. They approved of the causes she supported. They admired her beauty. In her life, touched as it was by tragedy, they could see something of themselves. These were potent, if unconventional, national symbols.

She might at times be described as a mere clotheshorse, a loose cannon, or a glitzy Mother Teresa, but she attracted headlines from New York to Tokyo and was thus a powerful

magnet for politicians, businessmen, and cultural figures—
the very people upon whose doors British diplomats might
politely knock for months without achieving the success
made possible by a three-day visit from the Princess of
Wales. The same held true at the highest levels of the countries she visited. While I fenced tensely with officials in
Buckingham Palace and the Foreign Office about the precise definition of the Queen's stricture that the Princess
should not represent her abroad, Presidents, Kings, and
even—in the case of Japan—an Emperor let it be known
that they expected the Princess of Wales to come to tea
when she was in town.

Even in Japan, however, she was not free from the effects
of her other, less statesmanlike public image. At long last a
resolution, in the Princess's favor, had been found with the
Sunday Mirror on the illicit gym photos. I blearily received
the news over the telephone in the small hours of a Tokyo
morning. Tiptoeing across the Embassy landing, I pushed a
note under the Princess's bedroom door, inscribed with the
agreed code: "The man from Delmonte, he say yes."

Together with an invitation to tea at the Imperial Palace,
this news represented a sweet victory for the Princess. It
was not that she thought particularly ill of the *Sunday Mirror*, or even of the sneaky photographer. He had been pilloried enough. What I believe gave her the greatest pleasure
was the recognition the legal ruling represented that her
outrage had been genuine.

The next morning I found her trying on several different
pairs of shoes. Finally the dresser had had enough. In the
forthright tones that made her such a refreshing, if ultimately
short-lived addition to the Princess's entourage, she pronounced, "They'll just have to do. They're quite high
enough."

The Princess appeared to accept this ruling meekly.
Catching my quizzical look, she laughed. "It's very important," she said, "to wear really high heels. I'm already taller

than the Emperor, but it won't do any harm to look just that bit taller!"

The Emperor and his family seemed duly impressed, if not by the Princess's height then at least by the entourage of international pressmen who were lying in wait for her at the Palace. The most exciting moment, however, came right at the beginning. "I had to curtsy below the Emperor's eye line," she explained to me later. "But with those heels and that skirt..." She did not finish the sentence, but simply waved a copy of an English newspaper at me. An eye-catching photograph showed her curtsying deeply before the diminutive head of state, the perfect picture of respectful modesty, but for the generous expanse of athletic royal thigh it tastefully revealed.

None of this deterred the Ambassador from reporting the outcome of the Princess's visit in eulogistic terms. Despite thus further adding to her impressive tally of overseas successes both for herself and for the country, if not—technically—for the Queen, the suspicion about her motives and her trustworthiness remained at home. I found myself playing the same ponderous game of grandmother's footsteps before every high-profile foreign visit made by the Princess.

Never was this more true than in the preparations for her visit to Argentina, due to take place at the end of 1995. For a start, I felt it was necessary to arrange with the excellent Argentine Ambassador for an appropriately "charitable" invitation to be sent from Buenos Aires to the Princess as a trigger for the tour. It was always going to be a sensitive trip, given the recent unhappy history of relations between Britain and Argentina, and it was not until I had a letter of support from the Foreign Secretary safely in my pocket that I allowed myself to feel with relief that once again we had pulled it off.

Nothing inspired a greater feeling of sedition than having to go to such convoluted lengths to carry out a visit that would bring pleasure to all but those who wished the Princess ill. In the end, the trip to Argentina turned out to be another outstandingly successful tour, capped predictably with an invitation to lunch with President Menem. Nonetheless, each time we went through this rigmarole, the sense of a battle won in a war we would ultimately lose became stronger.

It was not just the whispering suspicion in Palace corridors that I found so demoralizing. In the early days of my royal service, all aircraft—even the long-range VC-10—were provided as a matter of course for such essentially diplomatic missions. Now I was reduced to negotiating on the Princess's behalf with rich men for the use of their executive jets, or with British Airways for suitable seating on scheduled flights. I sometimes felt I was a conspirator even though I was trying to bring about perfectly respectable ends. It did not feel like a job with a future.

Perhaps I was just good at talking myself into a pessimistic frame of mind. The present still offered plenty of distractions if I wished to enjoy them. It might not turn out to be a job with a future, but right now I had unprecedented latitude in proposing ideas for the Princess's program. Thus it was that, not long after returning from Japan, I found myself on a plane to Hong Kong with the irrepressible David Tang.

Entrepreneur, bon viveur, socialite, and unsung hero of many a charity, David Tang was not famous for shunning the limelight. Like many who choose a high-profile existence, he had attracted detractors as well as supporters in the course of a life that seemed to have been led according to the principle that not a minute should go by that had not been filled with some worthwhile and preferably entertaining activity.

Sitting in his study in Government House, Chris Patten, then Governor of Hong Kong, banished any lingering doubts I might have had about associating the Princess with such a figure. "You can rely on David Tang one hundred ten per cent," he said. I later came to the conclusion that, where the Princess was concerned, the Governor's figure was if anything an underestimate.

Resisting a temptation to which some others in his position might have succumbed, David took care to look after the underlings as well. During my four-day recce for the forthcoming Hong Kong tour I learned so much, and enjoyed myself so much, that my gathering cloud of gloomy thoughts about the future scarcely got a look-in.

On my last night in Hong Kong, David included me with characteristic generosity in a small dinner he had arranged for Lady Thatcher, who was passing through on her return from China. He had also invited several representatives of the mainland government and a lively ideological conversation ensued in the fabulously retro surroundings of the China Club. Lady T's politics may not have been to everybody's taste, but for a lapsed political scientist such as myself it was an evening of rare fascination. It was also evidence of the conciliator and philanthropist lying behind David's cigar-chomping, ebullient exterior.

The Princess's visit to Hong Kong was perhaps a model of how her working life might have evolved. In one evening she raised a quarter of a million pounds at a dinner attended by the colony's socially competitive benefactors. The funds, channeled through her Charities Trust, went to medical and youth charities in Hong Kong and China—most notably to the work of the Leprosy Mission. They in turn provided the working focus of the visit, giving ample opportunities for the press to report on the good causes that were the Princess's offering to our consciences that week.

A sponsor whose motives were spotless—exemplified on this occasion by David Tang—relieved the taxpayer of any nagging doubt that the public purse was footing a significant part of the bill. The local administration—in this case the Queen's own representative—lent the visit a well-founded legitimacy and attracted valuable luster to itself. What was more, the Princess, with all requirements for security, recognition, glamour, and job satisfaction expertly provided, was able to feel justifiably good about herself.

*B*ack home, life was not so smooth and the distractions were not all so positive. The Princess's brother's disclosure of an extramarital affair, and the subsequent painful and public end of the Spencers' marriage, resulted in an outpouring of public acrimony. The end of her brother's marriage drew uncomfortable parallels with the Princess's own recent past, while her continuing tendency to lobby journalists and court celebrities filled me with a growing sense of unease.

It was not that I disapproved of her entertaining Jenny Bond (BBC Royal correspondent), Max Hastings (editor of the London *Evening Standard* naturally aligned with the establishment), or Barbara Walters to lunch at KP, but I was concerned that these encounters represented a significant expenditure from her limited reserves of intellectual capital. One lunch with the Princess of Wales was, at the very least, a change in the normal routine for people who lunch as part of their daily business. Almost invariably, it created a favorable firsthand impression as the captivatingly pretty, modest, articulate, and transparently well-intentioned hostess revealed her hopes and fears with disarming frankness. However, much of the positive outcome that she hoped for from such encounters depended on their exclusivity. Perhaps wrongly, I felt that such access should only be given in pursuit of a specific strategy. The investment in credibility that these meetings represented should be directed toward a particular, measurable purpose. They should not just be seen as an end in themselves.

On a larger scale, it was this short-term desire for media gratification that was my main disappointment with the *Panorama* interview. As had happened with her "withdrawal" speech, it was as if a small child had stamped her foot and demanded that the adults pay attention to what she was about to say. Then, having successfully attracted the attention of all the adults in the room, into the expectant hush that followed she could only venture the evidence of her own unfinished and frequently banal thoughts.

Her ever-growing taste for the company of celebrities was in some ways a safer bet than her wooing of journalists. I thought such encounters played very much to her strengths. In a room filled with the world's most beautiful women, heads still turned when the Princess of Wales entered.

Her experiences in the public eye, the traumas of her private life, and her struggles with her own form of addiction all attracted recognition—if not sympathy—from most celebrities, and even a tinge of envy in some. When she beckoned, whether it was to Take That! to top the bill at her latest Concert of Hope, or to Luciano Pavarotti to raise funds for her children's hospice in Wales, they came with alacrity.

As I watched the more established members of the royal family recruit pop stars to their causes without apparent demur, I swallowed any scruples I had about the Princess following suit. Since she was so often tarnished with the accusation of being an uncultured devotee of cheap music, her charities might at least feel the benefit of it. It might have come as a surprise to some people to know that her husband actually attended more pop concerts than she did. His taste for being photographed in the company of the icons of youth culture seems undiminished today, without affecting his reputation as something of a cultural highbrow.

It was actually surprisingly dangerous territory. Just as individual members of the royal family had identified themselves with particular spheres of interest in the charitable world—and even in some cases with particular geographical areas as well—so they recruited loyal bands of celebrity followers on behalf of their patronages. Some organizations, such as the Prince's Trust, operated a well-oiled machine to capitalize on their patron's ability to attract performers to his famously successful fund-raising concerts.

Such established interests watched with no great pleasure as the Princess tentatively began to flex her muscles as a magnet for performing talent in her own right. As Pavarotti had shown by accepting at short notice the Princess's invitation to perform for her Welsh children's hospice—despite his long-standing support for the Prince's Trust—the lady's wishes were not to be lightly denied.

One rather surprising lunch guest during this period was Auberon Waugh, scourge of the trendy, the commonplace, and the banal. I had been an admirer of his writing for as long as I could remember, but had him mentally pigeon-holed as an instinctive opponent of my employer and the muddled, emotionally indulgent thinking she was thought to represent.

I had occasionally encountered him on the train up to London from the West Country, but had lacked the courage to interrupt his methodical dissection of the morning newspapers with a comment such as, "You should meet my boss, you know. You might be surprised by what she's like in real life." One day, however, in the spirit of experiment that her unstructured life sometimes encouraged, I suggested that he might make an entertaining companion at lunch and a potentially influential convert. Contact was made and the great man of letters duly appeared at KP.

He and the Princess got on well from the start, perhaps attracted as opposites are by recognizing in each other qualities or experiences that could only ever be enjoyed vicariously. I was touched and pleased that a mind that I had respected and admired from afar should meet the Princess and immediately see in her perhaps some of the same things that made her worth working for. Auberon Waugh described her later as "a free spirit," a compliment that from him I thought carried more weight than most.

Perhaps in the same spirit of adventure, and certainly with great generosity, he invited the Princess to present the prize at the *Literary Review* annual Poetry Competition Lunch. This produced some scornful comment in the press: what was the famously thick Princess doing at such a cerebral gathering? Deep in the cellars of the Café Royal, surrounded by wine racks and a bohemian mixture of literati, she undoubtedly found herself in an unusual milieu. Perhaps because of the novelty, however, or the curiosity of her fellow guests, she sparkled with a rare and genuine happiness.

The Princess and I had thought it might be amusing if she replied to Bronwaugh's speech of welcome at least partly in rhyme. Her few words ended, So I've made time between therapy sessions and secret trysts to attempt a reply:

> *"A Princess was heard to declare*
> *Let gossips poke fun if they dare.*
> *My real inspiration was Bron's invitation.*
> *Stick that in your tabloids, so there!"*

The assembled guests guffawed uproariously and banged the table in approval. Here was the Princess displaying that special brand of strength not often found in the ruling classes, the best evidence of which is the ability to poke fun at oneself.

I guffawed too. I had enjoyed a very good lunch and I suppose even limerick writers like to hear their stuff being warmly received. Nonetheless, I already felt that making up jokes for my boss to read out about her reported mental fragility and well-publicized weakness for English rugby captains was an occupation whose attractions would pretty soon start to wear rather thin.

Along with poetry writing, a visit with the Princess to the Cézanne exhibition in Paris, and a thrilling evening at the premiere of *Apollo 13*, I was uncomfortably distracted by recurrent tabloid interest in my boss's friendship with Will Carling, captain of the England rugby team. Here was

further proof if I needed it that I had been right in harbor-
ing misgivings about the Princess's regrettable habit of
hanging around public gyms. At the fashionable Harbour
Club in Southwest London, the Princess and Carling had
recognized in each other a mutual interest in keeping fit. As
has already been too well documented, the acquaintance
thus born developed into a relationship that ultimately took
the blame for the collapse of Carling's marriage.

I was happy to remain at least ostensibly unconcerned
about who the Princess met in gyms, or, for that matter,
who brought her sons rugby shirts. But his tendency to visit
my office—invariably in my absence—tended to disrupt
the secretaries' work, however amusing it was for them.
(One secretary subsequently left to work for his company.)
I became more concerned later in the year when, already
fretting over our belated departure for the airport on the
way to Argentina, the Princess caused a further delay while
she scrabbled to find the right phone card to go with the
special mobile phone she had acquired to take Carling's
calls.

When eventually the Princess discovered that in Julia
Carling she had met a younger, blonder, and in many ways
feistier female opponent, the reverberations for her public
image proved disproportionately damaging. The Princess
had always been blessed with more than her fair share of
forgivability, but the Carling affair moved her noticeably
farther away from the fairy-tale image that had for so long
been her greatest asset. Patience, even among her supporters, was growing thin.

*T*he publicity surrounding the Princess's relationship
with Will Carling injected further tension into her already
tightly sprung emotional framework. It was at about this
time that she became involved in covert negotiations with
the BBC regarding the filming and broadcast of her

Panorama interview. Given her state of mind at that time, an exciting subterfuge like *Panorama* was undoubtedly most attractive.

The Princess had an obsessive concern that others should think well of her. Her misdemeanors, which she lacked the self-discipline to prevent, must therefore remain undiscovered. If by bad luck they *were* discovered, then the consequences must be preempted or other distraction offered to draw attention away from them. On a deeper level, it also seemed to be necessary for her that whatever she might be accused of, others must be accused of as well, or preferably of something more heinous. This maintained the established order inside her mind. If she was going to be cast into the gutter, let others be found there too, if only to demonstrate the fact that she had not mussed her hair as she fell.

Bearing this in mind, what I believe mattered most to her in the *Panorama* interview was the attack it included on her husband's suitability to be King. The confession of her love for Hewitt she accurately predicted would bring her more sympathy than condemnation, especially since her husband had never been heard to express such a feeling. (She could overlook the fact that his reticence might have been a recognition of the indefinable nature of the whole subject.)

Yet even as she spoke of both men, I doubted if she knew what she really meant—either about the succession or about love. As for her ambitions to be an ambassador or "Queen of Hearts," there was nothing new in this for me, or for any of those who had heard similar saccharine protestations in the preceding months.

This small but decisive saga had begun exactly a week before the broadcast. We were sitting on the sofa in her sitting room, preparing to drive to Broadmoor for what would turn out to be her last visit to the scene of so many instructive and satisfying engagements. "Patrick," she said, eyeing me nervously, "I've done an interview for TV."

My first thought was that she must have been persuaded to contribute some moist-eyed snippet for a charity promotional video. We had been planning quite seriously over the previous two months for a possible documentary about the work of the Special Hospital Authority, using her own involvement to focus public attention on mental health issues. I wondered if this might be an innocent piece of freelance work to boost her confidence for the main project. Later, I realized that the main project had probably been a feint all along.

"Really, Ma'am?" I said in my most neutral voice. "For which program?"

"*Panorama*," she replied.

That started the alarm bells ringing. This was no moist-eyed insert. This was the BBC's flagship current affairs program, vehicle for the nation's most momentous and significant issues. This was a major undertaking. Premeditated. A *fait accompli*. This was a *conspiracy*.

"Good," I said with as much sincerity as I could muster, knowing that this was the only way in which she could be persuaded to reveal more details. Perhaps it was not due to be broadcast for weeks yet, I said to myself. There was lots I could do to stop it in that time, or at least dilute its more dangerous aspects. Something in her eyes told me it was lethally packed with dangerous aspects.

"It's going out next week." She looked at me steadily. I looked back. Oh *shit*, I thought.

"That's good, Ma'am." I took a deep breath and added calmly, "Perhaps we can talk about it in the car."

In the time it took us to drive to Broadmoor, I conducted a tentative interrogation, as if probing a wound or unmasking an affair. When had this happened? Who knew about it? What legal controls did she have over its broadcast and rebroadcast? Had there been a fee? Could the enormous sums of money it could command be somehow diverted into her Charities Trust? Were there constitutional implications in anything she had said? Did she realize we would have to tell the Queen? Were we all going to be out of a job?

Her replies were patient, then evasive, then flustered, and finally nonexistent. She returned again and again to what became her central theme—a mantra: "It's terribly moving. Some of the men who watched were moved to tears. Don't worry, everything will be all right..."

"I'm sure it will be." I tried to sound soothing. "But can't I at least get Lord Mishcon to look at a tape of it so that you're protected from a legal point of view? We can prepare answers for your critics..."

As I had done two years before when confronted with her "withdrawal" decision, I searched for an angle that might divert her. "We can use it as a springboard into a follow-up, structured campaign to highlight the importance of your new work." That sounded good. The Jaguar purred on. Other cars full of happy people leading uncomplicated lives drifted silently by. She sat back in her seat, fiddling with the door catch. My God, was she going to jump out? How much did I mind if she did?

"No, Patrick. Everything will be all right..." We were back to the mantra.

The M4 sped past as the implications sank in. Her inner child was going to grab the attention of every grown-up in the room and move them to tears with the poignancy of her tale of injustice. But there would be nothing to justify that demand for attention. Every expectation would be heightened, only to crash down farther than before. It would be an epitaph for everything I had tried to do.

Then training took over. I could not just dissolve into a puddle of despair. Two days after the broadcast we were due to go to Argentina and two weeks after that we had another trip planned to New York City. There were speeches to prepare, letters to write, staff to hire and fire, and right now I was about to usher the Princess once more into the company of the criminally insane.

There and then I rang Buckingham Palace on the car

phone and, in Robert Fellowes's absence, gave the bare bones of the situation to the Queen's press secretary Charles Anson. His carefully modulated response would have been just right for Broadmoor, I thought. He would have been great at talking suicidal maniacs down from high ledges. I wished I had his talent.

In the days leading up to the broadcast on November 20, the Princess remained obdurate in her refusal to reveal any of the program's contents. Once again the Queen and her office were involved in attempting to wheedle, reason, plead, or otherwise persuade the Princess into reconsidering her planned course of action. I drew on all my years of experience of her in trying to get her to reveal more. Her lawyer Lord Mishcon applied every form of persuasion, from avuncular sympathy to dire legal warning. Even her husband weighed in to express concern.

Whether it was a reaction against the combination of all these or whether she took exception to some of the individual efforts, the Princess was having none of it. Robbed of at least some of her thunder at the time of her "withdrawal" speech in 1993, this time she was not going to repeat the mistake. She would not confide anything to anybody who might try to stop her.

In the end, sensing that she was beginning to enjoy the game, I gave up and went along quietly with her decision. "Don't worry, Patrick," she said. "You'll see. Everything will be all right. I *promise*." I was unconvinced, but as so often in the past, I saw my job now as doing what I could to stop the traffic during her latest bid to run naked down Piccadilly.

It was some satisfaction, therefore, to make the final arrangements for her attendance on the night of the broadcast at a glittering dinner at Bridgewater House in aid of the European Organization for Research and Treatment of Cancer. This enabled the Princess to present herself to the world, as so often before, as the very image of what she and others wanted her to be, while her other image simultaneously went through the motions of baring its soul on prime-time TV.

As always in moments of great tension, she raised her game and gave Sir Ronald Grierson—the distinguished former banker and chairman of the charity's fund-raising foundation—and his distinguished guests full value in return for their unusually generous efforts on behalf of the charity. Then they and I and the lady-in-waiting could escape to watch our videotapes and learn the awful truth.

Anne Beckwith-Smith and I returned to her flat with a sense of foreboding. But, we joked, it was the kind of foreboding that parents experience when returning home after a dinner party in the knowledge that the nursery will have been left in a bit of a shambles. We sat on Anne's sofa drinking her whiskey and let the tape roll.

The program was filmed secretly at KP; the chosen interviewer a relatively unknown reporter called Martin Bashir. The final product showed signs of heavy editing, and in a disjointed collage of revelations we learned that she had "adored" James Hewitt, that she doubted her husband's suitability for the crown, and that she herself had no real expectation of being Queen, preferring instead to be "Queen of people's hearts."

Groans and exasperated laughter rose like nausea to our lips. Then we uttered terse exclamations of horror. Finally we watched in silence until we could stand it no more. Anne switched off the TV and the ghostly face with the smudged, dark eyes faded from the screen.

I emerged wearily from behind the sofa where I had taken refuge. "That's it," I said.

Anne, of course, had taken her own decision to leave the Princess five years earlier. Now, as a part-time lady-in-waiting with a new and prestigious life of her own, she was in the relatively comfortable position of spectator. Yet she gave no hint of *schadenfreude* at my distress, despite the fact that I had been at least partly instrumental in her own departure.

As she let me out into a wintry street, she wished me

luck for the trip to Argentina. "Think of the air miles," she said. "You must have enough for your gold card by now."

"Actually," I replied, "you're right. This trip should qualify me for it." That was a cheerful thought.

"Oh well, then," said Anne. "It *must* be time for you to resign."

I spent a restless night, rose late, and so found myself standing fretting at a bus stop in the Wandsworth Bridge Road, hoping for either a bus or a taxi to take me to work, where I knew every phone in the office would be ringing as the Princess sought my reaction to what I had seen. An icy wind blew. The leaden sky, shivering trees, and huddled, hunched commuters formed a perfect backdrop to my mood. As if handling a lump of pure plutonium, I reluctantly dragged my mobile phone out of my pocket and switched it on.

It immediately emitted a nerve-jangling electronic bleat. Feeling dead inside, with chattering teeth and slush round my ankles, I told the Princess that it had been a remarkable performance and the papers were full of it. I had not even looked at a newspaper yet. I had not dared.

"What are they saying?" she asked excitedly. She *knew* what they were saying. I was probably the fifth person she had asked and she would have read them all by now anyway.

"It's a bit mixed," I said, feeling fairly confident of my ground. "Can I call you when I get onto a better phone?"

"All right," she said, now sounding very flat.

We did not speak again all day. By then we both silently acknowledged that the program had been a public relations triumph, but only with the people who already supported her. For the rest, and that included the forces with whom I had been trying to reconcile her, it was all the evidence they needed to cut her loose to twist on the end of the rope she had so eagerly grabbed. There was no windfall for her Trust;

no follow-up ideas and objectives; no new guiding philosophy. There were very few tears from strong men too, unless you counted me, and I was not feeling very strong.

On the other hand, I had a tour to run. My thoughts of resignation remained secret from her. She later thanked me with persuasive warmth for my loyalty for not resigning in the immediate aftermath of the program. With greater integrity, her press secretary Geoff Crawford had already had the courage to do so, even though he was typically generoushearted enough to come to Argentina with us.

Argentina provided a wonderful, highly colored, and highly successful respite from the crisis that *Panorama* had provoked. For a while in the South American sunshine, as the Princess once again delighted the crowds, I actually thought it could be all right.

Back in a gray London, grim reality waited. In the week leading up to *Panorama* I had made a point of keeping in close contact with the Queen's office and had not hidden the fact from the Princess. In a way, the situation was easier now. Having also been kept in the dark, I was exonerated from complicity in the plot. From the Queen's office, the sympathy for my position that I had always sensed during the previous tumultuous couple of years was now expressed more openly.

Somehow, however, my instinct to protect the Princess and encourage others to see the situation from her point of view remained intact. She had kept me in the dark, I stoutly maintained so that I could convincingly deny that I had been part of any conniving by her and thus remain a relatively honest broker between what was now an outraged Palace and an increasingly penitent Princess.

She had lived for weeks and even months with the knowledge of what she was doing in preparing the program. She had built up with delicious anticipation to the moment of emotional release in front of the cameras. Yet she had made no plans for what to do with the deluge she had released—least of all, it seemed, in herself. The aftermath, as I had sensed on the phone at the bus stop, was an anticlimax followed by bewilderment. She had taken the biggest possible injection of her favorite drug, and now she felt even worse.

I therefore felt able to tell the Queen's private secretary that the Princess had shot her bolt and was as ready as she would ever be to respond to the firm but compassionate intervention of the senior household to keep her out of further harm's way. But this, it seemed, presented insurmountable problems. After *Panorama* there was no way back.

19

⚘

Under the Wire

*T*he day after we returned from Buenos Aires, I hurriedly drew up a blueprint for the reconciliation with Buckingham Palace that I still hoped was possible. Its central theme was to bring the Princess more directly under the benign control of the Queen's household.

I went through the document point by point with the Princess and she agreed with everything—rather too meekly, I thought, but I was pretty sure she was not just humoring me. Probably she was still shell-shocked from the enormity of what she had done. Gray reality after the sunlit glamour of the tour had a distinctly sobering effect. I felt it too. Well, what the heck, I said to myself. There really was no alternative now. It was a time for radical measures if we were to save anything at all from the wreck.

I suggested that I and her secretaries should move to offices in Buckingham Palace. That the Queen's press office should cover her press relations. That she should be removed from dependence on her husband's financial support and placed on the civil list. That Buckingham Palace's own infrastructure should provide domestic support for her apartments at KP. That her areas of work, geographical as well as charitable and public, should be clearly defined and agreed.

These points, with the Princess present, were all discussed at a meeting held at Buckingham Palace on November 29. All received a sympathetic but guarded hearing. Sir Robert Fellowes, like me, had learned the hard way that the Princess's apparent agreement to a course of action on Monday did not rule out the possibility that she would turn against it on Tuesday, with heartrending details of her impossible predicament being eloquently disclosed to the newspapers on Wednesday.

Sadly, the senior household's misgivings—and mine—were proved justified. With my blueprint, I believed I had finally acquired the sugarcubes necessary to coax the troublesome thoroughbred back into the safety of the ring. It was too late, though. The sugarcubes did not look that attractive after the rich tidbits to be had from the crowd. Moreover, a relentless instinct to find an impossible freedom still drove her on. Even the influence of the Prime Minister, who in a characteristic gesture of concern called on her shortly before Christmas to renew his wish to be of help, could not halt the Princess's seemingly irreversible descent into a chaotic form of liberation.

Robert's guarded response to the blueprint was evidence, I sensed, that patience with the errant Princess was at breaking point. Whatever goodwill there might have been in Buckingham Palace toward her as a person—and I had no doubt there was plenty, not least from Robert himself—the offense she had caused was too great. It was a classic case of "love the sinner, hate the sin."

There was also another factor that the Queen's office had to take into account. With their moral ascendancy restored by *Panorama* after the Dimbleby debacle, the Prince's team were watching his wife's maneuverings with interest. How much love there was in St. James's Palace for the sinner was a moot point. It was no secret that they wanted to shift our office out of St. James's, but their preferred destination was KP. A move under the wing of the senior house-hold, and hence to the center of royal power, was hardly going to have the marginalizing effect they undoubtedly hoped for.

Whatever support my proposal might have had in some quarters at Buckingham Palace, it received only a holding reply. Soon I realized why. Events were taking their own course and the Princess's days of springing big surprises on major issues were numbered.

It's impossible to exaggerate the shock caused by the Princess's decision to make such a public display of her emotions. It was unprecedented. It was also a huge gamble. The shock was part of the intended effect, but that alone was not enough to justify her actions. There were many—myself among them—who doubted the sincerity of her motives.

The receipt shortly afterward of a letter from the Queen urging her and the Prince to put the country out of its state of uncertainty and seek an early divorce seemed to confirm in the Princess a sense that she was jettisoned. She decided, characteristically, to take the initiative herself. She elected not to stay at Sandringham for Christmas, but instead to be with her own family in Northamptonshire. She took steps to recruit her own press secretary and instructed her lawyers to take the offensive in the divorce proceedings that were now to be resumed in all seriousness.

Two months later, having agreed to an uncontested divorce, she even issued her own press statement, preempting an agreed joint Palace line. In it she announced that she would henceforth be known as "Diana, Princess of Wales." I had left her by then and was intrigued by the possibility that her omission of the rank "Her Royal Highness" had been a clerical error as much as a calculated act of defiance. Either way, the Palace took no steps to correct her and the perceived demotion passed into accepted use.

Set against such defiance, however, I could not forget the catch in her voice when she read the Queen's letter to me over the phone shortly before Christmas. "D'you know, Patrick, that's the first letter she's written to me." She tried to laugh, and for once she failed.

With a pang, I thought back to the few days since our last trip together. We had gone by Concorde to New York, where the Princess was to receive a humanitarian award from her old admirer Henry Kissinger. Everything about the trip had encouraged a wistful sense of happier times. There were motorcades, Secret Service agents, adoring crowds, and rooms full of rich, powerful, and beautiful people to be charmed.

During her acceptance speech at the awards ceremony in the New York Hilton, the Princess had even dealt with a heckler. "Where are your kids, Di?" someone shouted. "In bed!" she shot back, with a coolness that would have surprised anyone who remembered the tongue-tied novice public speaker of only a few years before. It also earned her the biggest ovation of the evening.

As a sign of special affection, the Princess had appointed the courageous Liz Tilberis as honorary lady-in-waiting for the visit. Liz was by then the New York editor of *Harper's Bazaar*, but had been a friend and staunch ally of the young Princess when she was still at *Vogue* in London in the 1980s. (At the time of our New York visit she was fighting an inspiring battle against cancer, for which she won the deep admiration of the Princess and many others besides. She died in 1999.)

In a direct echo of her former triumph, I had also arranged for the Princess to revisit the Harlem Children's Hospital, where, six years earlier, she had made headlines around the world with her visit to the AIDS unit. A gratifyingly large number of pressmen turned out to see her, and she was surrounded by smiling and appreciative patients, nurses, and families.

Momentarily I had been optimistic. Here was another example of the kind of low-key, officially sanctioned good work that could be a model for a future, divorced Princess.

Maybe even for her private secretary as well, I mused. As sometimes happens at the end of a long and occasionally acrimonious acquaintance, recent disagreements were forgotten and the Princess and I shared an almost conspiratorial conviviality during our brief stay in New York. Over a late-night glass of champagne, her review of the day's events and characters had never been more acute or amusing, and her recognition of her own position and potential had never been more modest or realistic. She was a different person from my temperamental London employer.

For a few days, it had been fun to be royal again. Now this. The Queen's letter, urging divorce, had snuffed out the illusion.

As always when forced onto the defensive, the Princess protected herself by lashing out. It mattered very little who was in the firing line. First of all, she felt she had to rid herself of people close to her whose minds must now surely be filled with unspoken accusation and reproof. Her suddenly baleful eye fell on her own office.

To paraphrase that haunting poem about the consequences of looking the other way, I had stayed silent when they came for the cook, the butler, the secretary, and the housemaid. Now they were coming for me. I thought of the Princess as "they" because it now seemed that I was dealing with several people in one person—in fact, I felt as if a legion were coming after me.

Such was the pressure she herself was under, the Princess's moods could swing from small-voiced vulnerability to icy hostility in the space of a single phone call. So many voices seemed to be lining up inside her to have their say that it was becoming very hard to guess what she was really thinking.

On top of this, her paranoia had reached new heights. She saw plots everywhere, was obsessed with the thought that she was being bugged, and honestly told me that her car's brake lines had been cut. Looking me straight in the eye, she even said that somebody had tried to "take a pot-shot" at her with a gun in Hyde Park. Needless to say, I had all these accusations checked out, but the truth was as I had known all along: such threats were all in her imagination.

On one occasion, after yet another bugging story, I expressed my polite mystification—exasperation would have been nearer the mark—that none of these hidden microphones had actually been discovered. "Come with me," she said, looking grave.

In one of the rooms upstairs, she knelt and pulled up a stretch of carpet. Putting a finger to her lips, she motioned me to look at the floorboards. They had been recently disturbed. She pointed silently at the sawdust and nodded significantly.

I said nothing until we were back downstairs. "Ma'am, you know that's just where they've been rewiring?" It was true. In a colossal undertaking after the Windsor fire, huge amounts were being spent on upgrading all the Palaces' electrics. She did not seem to hear me. Her look was enough. By then I knew when to make my exit from such conversations.

It is probably fair to say that I was not in a very good state of mind myself by this stage. Apart from the occasional snatched week, I had not had a proper holiday with my family for more than three years, and even then I had spent most of it writing a speech and answering letters.

In addition, while I had watched the infrastructure of the Prince's office expand, our own had been whittled away in a spirit of virtuous self-denial. The things from which courtiers traditionally drew strength when their royal employers made life difficult—such as the conviviality of household social events—had largely been denied to me. Or, I admit, I had denied them to myself out of sensitivity to the increasing isolation of the Princess and the thickening climate of whispering directed against her. I had no appetite for even kindly remarks over household lunch about the old guard's mystification with my boss's thought processes.

Now, it seemed, Nicholas Soames's view of her mental state was widely shared in Palace circles. As he had unwisely announced, to many she seemed to be suffering from galloping paranoia. "She really has gone too far!" confided one senior figure, as if brilliantly identifying the cause of all our misery, his exasperation inadequately disguised as sympathy. Tell me about it, I could have replied—or rather, please don't. Instead I just nodded. We were planets apart. I felt as if I were the only occupant of mine.

The qualities that probably made me a loyal and obedient servant were the very ones that I now felt had been exploited. At the same time, my ingrained instinct of duty to the Crown made me feel that the entire weight of the Princess's perceived transgressions lay on my shoulders. I was very, very tired.

In my reduced state, I found myself musing on her hypocrisy with uncharacteristic hostility. She was charming and foul by turns, but recently it always seemed to be the foul that came out on top.

As I had long ago realized, working with royal people does not suit everyone, not least because there are times when you just have to accept that you are there specifically to absorb without complaint the occasional personality lapses that are to be expected in a family dedicated—or condemned—to an eternity of public service and ever more public scrutiny. Everybody, from private secretaries to butlers, dressers, and PPOs, knew this. They either accepted it as part of the conditions of service, or they left.

More vulnerable, I felt, were those not on the payroll whose loyalty was given out of personal generosity of spirit. Foremost were the ladies-in-waiting, whose gentle stoicism in the face of some of the Princess's most icy and undeserved disfavor seemed all the greater because of their perceptive tolerance of her spitefulness.

From what I could see, her friends were in a similar category. One by one she picked them up and dropped them, but not before they too had first been smothered with attention, impulsive affection, gifts, and secrets, all of which were then suddenly withdrawn. Some, such as Lucia Flecha de Lima, Rosa Monckton, and Kate Menzies, had the stamina and inclination to go back for more. Others, such as Angela de Serota, Cosima Somerset, and Prue Waterhouse, retired hurt. She played the same tactics with the camera—and always adopted victim mode as soon as she started to lose the game.

Finally, the patron of Birthright, Barnardo's, and dozens of children's charities, the icon of maternal devotion and embodiment of feminine virtues, crept up behind her children's nanny at the combined office Christmas lunch party in 1995 and whispered, "*So sorry about the baby.*"

The Princess herself told me the story as I accompanied her out of the lunch. She was exultant. I immediately knew what she had done. Such was her suspicion of Tiggy that she was even prepared to spread the false suggestion that the nanny had had an unwanted pregnancy terminated. The identity of the "father" was left tantalizingly inexplicit.

"Jesus Christ!" I said to her, holding my head and thinking of my own two daughters.

The Princess was blind to my horror and consternation. As she strode happily to her room, she added, "I *knew* I was right. After I'd told her, [the butler] said she practically fainted and had to be held upright!" I bet she did, I thought.

"Ma'am, have you any evidence?"

"I've just told you. Anyway, I don't need evidence. I *know*..."

Once again the Princess's "intuition"—which was now replacing practically everything else as her lodestar—proved inadequate for the task she set it. Evidence was exactly what she needed and certainly did not have. Tiggy's legal rebuttal was swift and conclusive, and must have caused consternation in Anthony Julius's legal team, even if it left the

Princess's own denial mechanisms undisturbed. By then I was long gone.

My boss's treatment of Tiggy was all that my wavering resolve needed. Later rather than sooner, I discovered that loyalty to the Princess *did* now conflict with a higher loyalty—namely to elementary decency. In the face of the Queen's letter urging divorce I also concluded that, if I was to stand up for the Princess as I should, I would inevitably be in conflict with the head of state. I had never felt this was the case before.

On their own, these considerations would have been enough to activate my long-planned resignation. Conscientious chap that I was, however, I realized that it would take time to recruit a successor, train him or her, and generally smooth what would be, in all modesty, quite a shake-up for our small organization. This put me in a dilemma. The Tiggy incident and my growing sense of estrangement from the powers at Buckingham Palace urged a quick departure. On the other hand, minimizing disruption in the office and for my boss—to whom I still felt an instinctive loyalty, despite everything—dictated a slower, more carefully paced withdrawal.

Then I remembered my image of the man trapped in a cage with a tigress. Maybe this was my moment to reach for the escape hatch. The tigress seemed sufficiently distracted—or subdued—to let me get out unscathed. How wrong could I be.

Wrestling with the problem of how to go about resigning was made no easier by the fact that I was feeling so physically and mentally wrecked. In this condition I was particularly vulnerable to attack from unexpected quarters. The assault, when it came, consequently caught me with my guard down. I too fell prey to the Princess's particular style of aggression, which with sinuous dexterity combined a radiant smile with a knife between the shoulder blades.

The omens were all there, had I only seen them. The exaggerated thanks for my loyalty after *Panorama*, the conviviality of New York, and the devastating confession about Tiggy were only the prelude to a violent reversal of attitude. Once again, I realized later, she felt she had revealed too much, allowed someone too close; she had made it impossible to reinvent herself in my eyes. It was my turn for execution.

The chosen instrument, as so often before, was the pager. As others had before me, I now got the poisonous message treatment. I was sitting in a deserted railway carriage, staring out at a pitch-black Wiltshire, when with an immediate stab of dread I felt the familiar summons of my pager.

I fumbled for the button to stop that awful, reptilian vibration. Then I stared uncomprehendingly at the stark letters.

The Boss knows about your disloyalty and your affair.

It was anonymous.

I had to read it several times before the enormity of it sank in. The message was timed so that, but for a delay on the train, I would have received it as I walked through my front door. Then I knew it was from the Princess. She was always so punctual.

There had been a spate of such messages addressed to members of her husband's staff and nobody doubted where they came from. It spoke volumes for the atmosphere in which we were working by that time. Recently her own chauffeur—long an object of unfounded suspicion—had told me practically in tears of his own barbed message.

I was practically in tears myself now, though whether from rage, self-pity, or impotence I was not sure. I knew that an attack on my professional or personal reputation was exactly the form of retribution that the Princess would choose once she had recognized that I was slipping beyond her control. I also knew with a frightening conviction that she could do untold damage to my future reemployment chances if she chose to use her media muscle. As for my private life... My horror deepened. I knew I had not had an affair with anyone, but that was an insignificant detail to someone who could accuse her children's nanny as the Princess had done.

I told nobody of my agonized thoughts except God— over and over in the course of a sleepless night. He had heard most of it before.

The next day I found a chance to confront the Princess. This was definitely not the victim's proper response, but having only recently counseled the chauffeur, my blood, belatedly, was up.

"Ma'am," I began, "I've been getting nasty little messages on my pager and so have others." I named them. "I have to ask. Did you send them?"

Her eyes widened with the practiced innocence I had seen so often before. As I expected, she answered a question with a question. "Why would I do a thing like that? You should ignore it. I get them all the time."

Suspicion turned to certainty in my mind and I heard myself saying, "Ma'am, I think it may be time for me to move on. You'll be divorced soon and you'll be starting a new life full of new opportunities. I belong to your old life. I think you should have someone new to help you with what comes next."

She was staring at me intently. I could tell that I was doing myself irreparable damage in her eyes. *Nobody* dumped the Princess of Wales.

I felt giddy. I had never spoken so directly to her before and the urge to pour out several years' accumulated frustration was almost irresistible. It might even have done us both some good. That missed opportunity belonged to the distant past, however. Right now I had to concentrate on getting out of the room alive.

Having started, I had no option but to carry on burning

bridges. "If you want, I'll stay until the legal stuff is over, but we could start looking around for my replacement right away. Then there'll be less disruption for you. Anyway, I wouldn't want to leave until you were happy with whoever came next. But I thought I should tell you now what I have in mind, so we all know where we stand."

"But what about the program?" she asked, in a voice familiar to deserting rats caught balancing on the ship's rail and measuring the distance to the jetty.

"The calendar is very quiet at the moment. Chicago [our next planned tour, not due for several months] is all set up. There's time for my replacement to read himself in and Anne and the police will show him the ropes."

"But who will I find?"

"Ma'am, they'll be lining up round the block." I was not quite sure about this, so I carried on quickly, "But, I repeat, I won't leave till you're happy with my replacement."

I sat back in my chair, feeling exhausted. By contrast, the Princess looked ominously calm and behind her eyes I saw that a shutter had descended. I remembered her reaction to Richard Aylard's offer of help six years earlier and her words came back to me: "Once gone, always gone." I was now back on the nursery floor and destined for a very painful end.

Whatever I said about staying to ensure a smooth transition, I no longer had control over the speed of events. The twin torches of victimhood and revenge, now ignited in my employer's mind, would see to that. This was going to be quick. I already sensed that she would be drawing a deadly bead on the only thing I could hope to take with me from the wreck. It was worth rather more to me than cuff links or a signed photograph. It was my reputation.

Later that afternoon I called on Robert Fellowes. I told him of the messages that I and others had received and of my reasons for believing who was responsible for them. I explained that I felt I was now in an impossible position. His sympathy and later that of the Queen, when I was unexpectedly received by her, touched me more deeply than perhaps either of them knew.

The next morning some routine memos I had sent up in the Bag came back unopened. I turned with something like relief to drafting my own resignation statement and Q and A list, just as I had drafted so many for the Princess in the past.

In an attempt to impose some honesty and goodwill on the situation, I then sent the Princess a carefully worded memo in which I repeated what I had said at our meeting: that I felt it was time for me to move on, but that I would not do so until I had had a chance to recruit a successor and see him or her safely into the job, if that was her wish. I also repeated my offer to stay until her current legal actions were resolved.

I handed it to my secretary and asked her to drive it at once to KP. Then, as if to take leave of it, I looked round the office that had suddenly become a prison, having been a palace to me for so long. It seemed impossible that something so familiar would now become part of my past. The thought triggered a jolt of fear and I almost ran after my secretary to stop her. Out of the window I glimpsed the taillights of her car disappearing in the direction of Lancaster House. There was no going back.

The expected phone call came less than an hour later. Perhaps she had blanked what I had told her yesterday about resigning. That was why I had sent my memo. Given the conciliatory way I had tried to write it, and the sensible offer of continuing service and a smooth transition to a new pair of hands, the response was far worse than anything I had feared.

She was hysterical. Her voice lost all semblance of control and expressed instead the raw emotion of a soul in torment. The theme was repeated over and over, in tones varying from the plaintive to the vicious. *What had she done to deserve this?* I struggled to repeat what I had said in the memo, but she did not or would not hear me.

Eventually her voice became clipped, flat, cold. "I have to decide what to do about you." There was a click. She was gone, hugging her power for comfort.

I should have left then, but some masochistic urge drove me into the office again the next morning. On my desk I found a letter on the Princess's notepaper, plainly drafted with legal help, illogically forbidding me from sending her such a memo again. It seemed that somebody had failed to copy-check the typing. It did not make sense. Who had done the typing anyway? My mind briefly considered the unhappy implications for my staff's loyalty—to me if not to her.

As I was digesting these implications, I simultaneously learned that the Princess had put in phone calls to several friends and acquaintances of mine who she might reasonably expect would help me find another job. In each case the calls were calculated to give the impression that I was not fit to be entrusted with so much as a dustpan and brush. Again by special messenger, I sent a further and probably foolish letter, protesting that such a transition would be more efficiently accomplished in a constructive and preferably amicable spirit. It was returned unopened.

I departed soon afterward for the weekend, resolving to clear my desk on Monday morning and so free myself properly to look for some new way of earning a living. Before reaching Paddington, I had also taken the precaution of asking some discreet media contacts to be alert for any sudden interest in my direction.

On Saturday afternoon this early warning system tipped me off that the *Daily Mail* was planning to run a major story on Tuesday morning in which it would be reported that the Princess had sacked her private secretary for professional incompetence. This was no longer a resignation. It was a race.

I spent Saturday redrafting my curriculum vitae and avoiding questions from anyone. I had caught a bad dose of

the Princess's paranoia. Plots and imminent ruination
chased each other through my jumbled thoughts, along
with a dull sense of loss. I would have to look at that later.
For the moment I had a great deal to do and very little
time in which to do it if I was to beat my boss to the media
draw.

I returned to London to empty my in-tray as conscien-
tiously as possible—a Herculean task—and to write as many
farewell letters as I could manage, then finally to clear my
desk. There was a Sunday calm about the deserted offices as
I read the last rites to my royal career. Down in Ambassador's Court the usual genteel congregation was emerging
from the Chapel Royal. I experienced a sudden pang, wishing that I too could be comfortably thinking of a warm fire,
sherry, Sunday lunch, and a secure future in the royal household. My future, whatever it was, now lay in a different
world.

How sad, I thought, as I looked out on the cozy ritual
and listened to the loud, confident voices. For nearly eight
years I had worked in the same organization as a small army
of eminent clerics, from the Archbishop himself to the
household chaplains, all of us called to serve the head of our
Church. Yet in all the trials and crises we had survived together, neither the Princess nor I had thought to call on
them for the spiritual guidance they were presumably employed to provide.

Not that they had seemed particularly eager to offer it, I
reflected. Beyond the routine conduct of the court's religious business and their own silent intercessions, I never felt
the benefit of my pastoral colleagues' spiritual support.
Here were more missed opportunities, missed connections,
to regret. Surely we should all have been pulling in the
same direction, working together to uphold the same principles and values. To me, what was happening to our foremost national institution had the greatest symbolic
importance. Without its symbolic value, I seriously ques-

tioned the purpose of our royal system. "It's all about principle," I murmured to myself, adding pompously, "or it's nothing at all." On that gloomy note, I turned back to the loose ends on my desk.

At 2:30 A.M. on Monday January 22, 1996, I fell into a bed kindly lent to me by a friend in St. James's Palace. He and a couple of others had come to my rescue and I will never adequately express my thanks to them. We drank a bottle of champagne to toast my escape and, if not for very long, I at least slept more peacefully than I had managed for weeks.

Later that morning, feeling curiously calm, I wrote my formal letter of resignation and obtained an audience with the Princess for 10:00 A.M. Then, feeling distinctly less calm, I realized that in the hurry of returning to London I had forgotten to bring my suit. I rushed out to spend an expensive but therapeutic half hour in Jermyn Street, buying myself something suitable to wear when resigning from royal service.

I left my resignation statement with the Queen's press secretary, ready to be released on receipt of my telephone signal. Then I jumped into a taxi to make the familiar journey for the last time.

At KP I was received by a stony-faced butler who bade me wait in the Equerries' Room. I waited and waited. This was another room full of potent memories. Here was the rug I must practically have worn out with anxious pacing. There, the desk on which I had laid out the day's programs and briefed myself Navy-style on their objectives. Over there was the musty drinks cabinet from which I had occasionally fortified myself before an evening at the opera. And here at last was the familiar sound of the Princess's approaching footsteps.

Then she was in the room. She was wearing a pale blue suit, in honor, I realized, of the lunch she was due to have with the Argentinian Ambassador—a lunch she would shortly cancel. She looked pale and oppressed. Suddenly I saw that she was nervous too.

She carried an unopened envelope in her hand and as we sat down on opposite sides of the table she held it up. To my relief there was no sign of her phone hysterics. "What's this about?" she asked. Her voice was carefully controlled, but in her eyes I could see apprehension as well as sadness.

"I'm afraid it's my resignation, Ma'am."

"Why?"

This was not a conversation I wanted to protract. She knew very well why. "Because I feel our working relationship has broken down. It's probably my fault, but in any case I don't think it would get better. I think it will only get worse."

"I see."

She stood up and headed for the door. I stood up also and half made to follow her. Suddenly she turned, color rushing back into her cheeks. "Well. We can at least shake hands," she said, and so we did.

Then she was hurrying back up the stairs. I heard a door slam. I waited for a minute, feeling the sudden silence. So that was it.

I felt numb. As if in a dream, I let myself out of the Palace. Then I walked with quickening steps to the police lodge, where I phoned the press office at Buckingham Palace. I had foiled tomorrow's lethal story and now I would give the papers my script instead. My resignation statement was brief and respectful. It could now be released, and so could I.

For the last time, I stepped out through the Palace gates. I felt the January sunshine on my face and looked up into a clear blue sky.

*T*hat was not the end, of course. You cannot just walk away from the Princess of Wales. I must have sensed that my royal experiences were not over yet, that more painful twists lay in store. They have no part in this book, however. At that moment, as I strolled away from Kensington Palace, all I knew was that on the inside I was running.

Epilogue

❦

D'you want to see where Di's buried?" The words sank in slowly. "It's just over there. Five minutes."

I waited for the surprise to settle in my chest before I spoke. It was a coincidence. He could have no idea I had any connection with the dead Princess. It was impossible to say no, or even to ask why.

"OK," I said eventually.

"Make your heading 290. And go down to 3,000..."

The airplane was unfamiliar. I was just getting the feel of the thing and was going nowhere in particular, least of all down memory lane. The man sitting next to me was here to see that I did not make any expensive mistakes. Idle gossip was not his style. And now he had mentioned the Princess. It only goes to show, I thought. That name still means so much to the most unlikely people.

The fields of Northamptonshire rose to meet us as we descended. Soon I recognized the shape of Althorp in the distance. Beyond the house I could see the lake. Suddenly I was back 10 years, seeing the same view from the window of the royal helicopter as we clattered in to land on the

broad lawn in front of the house. At my shoulder, my boss
was making a joke about her stepmother as we dropped in
on her family home on our way to some charity event in
the neighborhood. I was wearing a dinner jacket. My bow
tie was too tight. Above the engines I could hear her laugh.
You never forgot it.

"Her grave's on the island. You can see it."

Gently, I lowered the wing. A pale dot appeared amongst
the green undergrowth on the little island. That must be it.
That must be her.

Even from this height, seeing her grave gave me a jolt. I
remembered that awful morning when, from my place in a
discreet corner of Westminster Abbey, I had strained to
catch a glimpse of her coffin. Instantly, this seemed more
private—a chance for a personal farewell.

Silence lay over the cockpit. I set the plane into a slow,
descending spiral round the island, my wing tip pivoting on
the pale stone. Sun streamed through the windscreen.

She had often joked about my fascination with planes.
"Just going up to the cockpit, Ma'am," was a regular excuse
to escape a royal compartment grown suddenly tense. On
more relaxed occasions, if she was invited onto Concorde's
flight deck she might say, "*I* won't—but you'll enjoy it,
Patrick. Go on, I'll be OK."

I smiled at the memory. It was enough. As if dismissed, I
lifted the wing. The island disappeared. For a moment our
shadow flew ahead of us over the face of the lake. Then we
gathered speed and began to climb again.

The Best in Biographies

HAVE A NICE DAY!
A Tale of Blood and Sweatsocks
by Mankind
0-06-103101-1/$7.99 US/$10.99 Can

THE ROCK SAYS
by The Rock
0-06-103116-X/$7.99 US/$10.99 Can

JACK AND JACKIE:
Portrait of an American Marriage
by Christopher Andersen
0-380-73031-6/$6.99 US/$8.99 Can

CYBILL DISOBEDIENCE
by Cybill Shepherd and Aimee Lee Ball
0-06-103014-7/ $7.50 US/ $9.99 Can

WALK THIS WAY:
The Autobiography of Aerosmith
by Aerosmith, with Stephen Davis
0-380-79531-0/ $7.99 US/ $9.99 Can

EINSTEIN: THE LIVES AND TIMES
by Ronald W. Clark
0-380-01159-X/$7.99 US/$10.99 Can

IT'S ALWAYS SOMETHING
by Gilda Radner
0-380-81322-X/ $13.00 US/ $19.95 Can

I, TINA *by Tina Turner and Kurt Loder*
0-380-70097-2/ $6.99 US/ $9.99 Can

....